THE STRUGGLE FOR THE
AMERICAN
CURRICULUM

THE STRUGGLE FOR THE
AMERICAN CURRICULUM
1893–1958
THIRD EDITION

HERBERT M. KLIEBARD

Routledge
Taylor & Francis Group

NEW YORK AND LONDON

Published in 2004 by

Routledge
711 Third Avenue
New York, NY 10017

Published in Great Britain by

Routledge
2 Park Square
Milton Park
Abingdon
Oxfordshire, OX14 4RN

Routledge is an imprint of the Taylor & Francis Group, an informa business

Copyright © 2004 by Taylor & Francis Books, Inc.

Library of Congress Cataloging-in-Publication Data
Kliebard, Herbert M.
   The struggle for the American curriculum, 1893–1958 / Herbert M. Kliebard.–
3rd ed.
      p. cm.
   Includes bibliographical references and index.
   ISBN 0-415-94890-8 (hardback: alk. paper) – ISBN 0-415-94891-6 (pbk. : alk.
paper)
   1. Education–United States–History–20th century. 2. Curriculum planning–
United States–History–20th century. 3. Education–United States–Curricula–
History–19th century. 4. Curriculum planning–United States–History–19th
century. I. Title.
   LB1570.K585 2004
   370.11'3'0973–dc22
                              2004004891

ISBN 13 : 978-0-415-94891-3 (pbk)

To Bernice,
of Blessed Memory

TABLE OF CONTENTS

PREFACE
TO THE THIRD EDITION

UNDER THE BEST OF CIRCUMSTANCES, THE PUBLICATION OF A NEW EDITION of a book offers the author an opportunity not only to make a few modifications and editorial changes but to address issues of some consequence. The first edition of *The Struggle for the American Curriculum* appeared in 1986, and, although I have been gratified by the reception the book received, I have had lots of time to reflect on what improvements could be made.

Writing history, of course, is never simply a matter of setting down facts and events in some kind of chronological order. It inevitably entails interpretation. For the second edition, then, I tried to make explicit the theoretical framework behind *Struggle* that led to my interpretations. When the second edition was published in 1995, I decided to address certain concerns in an Afterword. It took the form of a historiographic essay dealing with issues that lay behind my undertaking to write the book in the first place, alluding to where my interpretations were derived from other sources and how my depiction of this era differs from that of other historians who cover roughly the same ground chronologically. That Afterword is reprinted in this volume.

Every now and then, someone urges me to bring this book up to date, that is, to go beyond 1958 when the book ends. That would be a massive undertaking, however, and I never really considered it for a third edition. Such a project would require another volume. There was also a particular reason I decided to end my account in 1958. The interest group framework I used to shape my interpretations in the period from 1893 to 1958 underwent something of a sea change with the passage of the National Defense Education Act of 1958. Not only was the whole discourse about the curriculum radically altered, but the entry of the federal government onto the scene of battle on such a massive scale changed the dynamics of how the curriculum was shaped and instituted. Any interpretation of the post-1958 era in education would require a serious consideration of how the curriculum in general and the interest groups in particular responded to the new influx of federal dollars along with the accompanying controls that such funding entails. Fortunately, some historians are beginning to deal with the issues that arose from those federal interventions. I am particularly impressed with John L. Rudolph's (2002) *Scientists in the Classroom: The Cold War Reconstruction of American Science Education*. William J. Reese's (in press) *America's Public Schools: Continuity and Change Since the Early Nineteenth Century* in the latter chapters also deals with the post-1958 period in a particularly informed and perceptive way.

In the end, therefore, I decided to address issues of another sort for the third edition of *Struggle*. As indicated in the original edition, I have come to believe that the reform efforts of three of the four interest groups were directed largely at unseating (or greatly modifying) the subject organization of the curriculum, and much remained to be said about both the efforts to dethrone school subjects and the way in which the school subjects themselves responded to such pressures. This was particularly true following the publication of the five volumes of the Eight-Year Study in 1942. The Eight-Year Study, after all, was initiated by leaders of the Progressive Education Association largely because they fervently believed that the secondary school curriculum continued to be dominated by college-entrance requirements, and they designed that massive experiment to demonstrate that alternatives to the traditional academic curriculum could be developed without fear that it would result in inadequate preparation for the rigors of college study.

Accordingly, I decided to write two new chapters for the third edition. In the new Chapter 9, I deal with the renewed drive in the 1940s to redirect the organization of the curriculum away from the traditional subjects of study and particularly with the concerted efforts by many curriculum reformers to organize the curriculum around needs. These endeavors eventually acquired the label "core curriculum," but a variety of different practices, which I tried my best to untangle, were subsumed under that name.

In the second of the new chapters, Chapter 10, I review the ways in which the traditional subjects were actually affected by this drive into the late 1950s. This entails a subject-by-subject review of the ways in which individual subjects responded not only to the deliberate efforts to unseat them but to the massive influx of new students over the course of the twentieth century.

These two chapters, both centering on the role and function of school subjects, necessarily deal to a much greater extent with the secondary-school curriculum than with the elementary-school curriculum. While reformers of various stripes were able to implement some of their ideas in elementary schools, their efforts met with much less success at the secondary-school level, as the leaders of the Eight-Year Study fully recognized. It is for this reason that the period of the 1940s and 1950s was an era when the main arena of contestation in terms of curriculum reform became the suitability and effectiveness of traditional schools subjects in the secondary-school curriculum.

In writing these two new chapters, I was also trying to redress in this edition what was an inadvertent imbalance in the book. Although the period covered is still from 1893 to 1958, the first and second editions are tilted to the earlier part of that period. By devoting the two new chapters principally to the 1940s and 1950s, I was hoping not only to address a formidable challenge to the venerable subject curriculum, but to achieve a better chronological symmetry.

I have been at the University of Wisconsin-Madison for a long time and have been blessed with friends and colleagues who have been of inestimable help to me in concrete terms, such as reading a chapter or two, but also in the course of informal office visits and even hallway chit-chat. In past editions of *Struggle*, I have sought to enumerate at least some of the people who have offered such support, but I am reluctant to add new names because I will almost inevitably omit some who have been of special help. Although my gratitude to the people I mentioned in the earlier acknowledgments has, if anything, been reinforced, I cannot resist letting this opportunity go by without special mention of the students I have taught over the years and how their eagerness and intellectual curiosity have never failed to inspire me. Thanks to you all.

My debt to my family is profound. My children, Diane and Ken, and their spouses, Mark and Judy, as well as my grandchildren, Marissa, David, and Brianna have been a continual source of solace and joy.

There is one specific and immediate debt I need to acknowledge. The editor I have worked with on this project, Catherine Bernard of Routledge, has been a delight to communicate with, not only knowledgeable and supremely competent, but unfailingly cooperative and understanding as well.

Herbert M. Kliebard
University of Wisconsin-Madison
January 2004

PREFACE
TO THE SECOND EDITION

I WAS REALLY UNPREPARED FOR THE WARM RECEPTION THAT GREETED THE first edition of this book from students, colleagues, and even critics. If nothing else, then, I can take this occasion to express my appreciation to those people who took the trouble to express their support.

In considering the question of a second edition, I gave serious thought to what might merit such an undertaking. For one thing, the publication of a second edition could afford me an opportunity to address implied or explicit criticisms that have been directed toward the book, but I felt that merely replying to the criticisms that have been voiced hardly warranted a new edition. Another option that was proposed to me from more than one source was to add a chapter or so that would go beyond the 1958 ending point of the first edition. I seriously considered this option but concluded ultimately that accomplishing that would really require a sequel rather than a second edition.

In the end, I decided that the most reasonable and perhaps most appropriate option would be to set forth an explicit theoretical framework for the book, and this now appears as the Afterword to this second edition. I assumed when I was first writing *Struggle* that the theoretical framework I had in mind would somehow emerge from the narrative, and it was therefore not really necessary to lay it out in very explicit terms. It is difficult for me to reconstruct entirely what my thinking was at the time, but that choice may have been influenced by some uneasiness or perhaps lack of confidence as to how that theoretical framework would stand up. In any case, since the publication of the first edition in 1986, I think I was able to sharpen my theoretical focus particularly through exposure to a rich literature in symbolic action and status politics.

My decision now to plunge into that theoretical jungle was influenced, for example, by my reading of the epilogue that Joseph R. Gusfield (1986) wrote for the second edition of his widely acclaimed, *Symbolic Crusade: Status Politics and the American Temperance Movement*. Written 22 years after the publication of the first edition, that epilogue is to me a model of its kind, reflecting not only on the substance of the book but casting new light on the way a symbolic politics framework enriches his interpretations— not rejecting the earlier interpretations but imbuing them with new insights. I cannot hope to duplicate Gusfield's feat, but, in more ways than one, it served as a model for what I aspired to accomplish.

My own afterword pursues two lines of inquiry: First, it traces a series of interpretations of what is commonly called the progressive era in education in an attempt to sort out which aspects of those interpretations influenced the writing of *Struggle* and which were rejected on the way to arriving at my own framework. Most conspicuously, I draw on the work of historians such as Peter Filene and Daniel Rodgers in order to cast doubt on the very existence of a progressive education movement. This, I hope, serves to explain why the focus in *Struggle* is not on anything even vaguely resembling a unified progressive education but on the four interest groups that constitute the structure of the book. These interest groups, it should be emphasized, do not add up to one movement. They exist side by side, each with its own agenda. While it is true that two or more of these interest groups will occasionally form a temporary coalition around a particular reform, their platforms in the struggle for the American curriculum are not simply dissimilar or even contradictory; they are, more often than not, antagonistic.

Second, I tried to cast my interpretation of those interest groups in the context of status politics much as Gusfield did with the temperance movement. In that way, I sought to address a nagging question that I am sure arose in many readers' minds. In an era when social history rules the day, it is perfectly natural to wonder whether the reforms that leaders of the various interest groups advanced actually made their way into schools and classrooms. Although I tried to address that question here and there in *Struggle*, that issue admittedly does not form the centerpiece of the book. Without that emphasis, there is always the danger that a particular account will degenerate into (gasp!) intellectual history or so some people believe. As I try to indicate in the Afterword, much useful historical research in recent years has addressed that very question of implementation, but although I readily acknowledge that such research is valuable, it is not exactly the way I chose to address the issue. Instead, I sought to show that, apart from the instrumental question of what actually gets taught in schools as a result of the efforts of educational leaders, there is another equally important way in which those actions may be framed, and it is here that Gusfield's (as well as, for example, Murray Edelman's) theoretical formulations were particularly useful. In the context of status politics, conflicts revolve around the question of whose cherished beliefs shall be sanctioned, officially or otherwise. The struggle I tried to depict, in other words, is primarily a symbolic one over whose most fundamental beliefs shall occupy center stage in a continuing drama. In that drama, protagonists representing competing values and beliefs vie for public validation and approbation on the national stage. To say that the struggle is symbolic or dramaturgical in nature is not to detract from its significance. For one thing, it should never be assumed that given acts are either strictly symbolic or practical. For the most part, they are both, but it is the symbolic significance of those acts that is the more easily overlooked. This is particularly unfortunate since it is the symbolic side of these actions that has most to do with cultural and social dominance and all that that entails.

Finally, I must express once again my gratitude to the many people who directly or indirectly influenced my interpretations of the events depicted in this book. Echoing Gusfield's concern in his acknowledgments, I am acutely conscious of the fact that "no author can recall everyone from whom he has borrowed unfootnoted thoughts" (p. viii). I did the best I could in my acknowledgments to the first edition. For this second edition, I particularly wish to acknowledge the assistance of Jack Dougherty and David Levine in helping me to create a greatly expanded index. If I left anyone out then or now, I am truly sorry.

November 1993

PREFACE
TO THE FIRST EDITION

IN A RECENT REVIEW OF TWO HISTORICAL STUDIES IN EDUCATION, CARL
Kaestle (1984), commenting on one of them, remarked that it
"moves beyond the two competing models of interpretation that
have shaped debates for the past fifteen years." He went on to
describe these two competing schools of thought as to the course
of education in the United States:

> School systems exemplify democratic evolution, said the tra-
> ditionalists. No, responded the radical revisionists, school
> systems illustrate the bureaucratic imposition of social con-
> trol on the working class. Recently, some historians have
> emphasized that public school systems are the result of con-
> tests between conflicting class and interest groups.

Although I did not chance on the review until I had substantially
completed this book, I realized that Kaestle expressed in that last
school of thought almost precisely what I had been attempting.
I had been actively following the development of the competing
schools of thought in the twentieth century and invariably came
away with the feeling that they were both faulty. They were both
right as well, but simply saying that the main thrust of American
education in the twentieth century lay between the two was hardly
persuasive. What I sought was a way of expressing the nature of
the forces that eventually determined the result of the conflict.

Actually, I had seriously entertained the idea of writing a history of the modern curriculum in the United States for several
years and had published perhaps a couple of dozen articles on
the subject. I think I can reconstruct pretty accurately what
prompted my initial interest in this subject. First, I was bothered by the imbalance in historical studies in education. A great
deal of attention has been lavished on the question of who went

to school but relatively little on the question of what happened once all those children and youth walked inside the schoolhouse doors. In a sense, reluctance to tackle that kind of question is understandable; it would be a formidable task to try to answer it in the contemporary context. Trying to address that question, even in the recent past, means drawing interpretations from grossly incomplete evidence. Regrettably, it often means making inferences from the statements of leading figures in the education world rather than from classroom documents and reports of participants.

On the other hand, it is not inconceivable, to say the least, that certain major statements on key subjects reflected what was actually going on. Throughout my writing of this volume, I tried to treat those documents, usually issued by major leaders in education or by national committees, not as influencing the course of events, but as artifacts of a period from which one might be able to reconstruct what was actually happening in the teaching of school subjects. Apart from the question of whether any of the ideas presented were worthwhile (and in a few cases I think they were), those statements represented for me a kind of weather vane by which one could gauge which way the curriculum winds were blowing. One important rule of thumb I tried to follow in this matter, however, was to assume from the outset that statements were invariably far more ambitious and grandiose than one could possibly expect in practice. For example, most statements issuing from the leaders of the activity movement argued for their version of the curriculum as the major part or even the whole of what children would study in school. We all know that that did not happen except in the case of isolated experimental schools. But this does not mean that the impact of the activity movement was not felt in school practice. To the extent that those ideas were incorporated in the public schools generally, they tended to appear within the existing framework of the curriculum. Something like the activity curriculum, in other words, became visible within the context, say, of social studies or English. The subject organization of the curriculum, by and large, persisted, but within that framework there were internal changes reflecting the influence of the major reform movements. In some cases, this may have led certain historians to underestimate the impact of curriculum reform in the twentieth century. The labels that we give to the school subjects do not tell the whole story since those labels do not nearly reflect the diversity that actually exists in terms of curriculum practice.

Second, I was frankly puzzled by what was meant by the innumerable references I had seen to progressive education. The more I studied this the more it seemed to me that the term encompassed such a broad range, not just of different, but of contradictory, ideas on education as to be meaningless. In the end, I came to believe that the term was not only vacuous but mischievous. It was not just the word "progressive" that I thought was inappropriate but the implication that something deserving a single name existed and that something could be identified and defined if we only tried. My initial puzzlement turned to skepticism, my skepticism to indignation and finally to bemusement. As I hope readers of this book will discover, I came to the conclusion that there was not one but several reform movements in education during the twentieth century each with a distinct agenda for action. Delineating the main ideological positions of the various interest groups and the way they balanced as well as contradicted one another became my main task. In other words, I felt that the evolution of the modern American curriculum could be interpreted in terms of the interplay among the predominant interest groups that saw in the course of study the vehicle for the expression of their ideas and the accomplishment of their purposes.

The main actors in this story, then, are the leaders of the various interest groups, but their ideas must be seen against the backdrop of the hard realities, not only of school practice and the bureaucratic structure of schooling in this country, but the political and social conditions of the time. All of this cannot be given equal weight, of course, and center stage is given over to the battle among competing ideas about the curriculum of American schools. In making this decision, I was hoping that, if nothing else, the book would serve to clarify those ideas and their implications and thereby help identify and explicate the curricular options that we have inherited from our professional forebears.

One issue that presented itself almost immediately was how to treat the towering figure of John Dewey. Although I had been a student of Dewey's work for almost all my professional life I found myself puzzled as to where he belonged in the context of the interest groups I had identified. I decide in the end that he did not belong in any of them and that he should appear in the book as somehow hovering over the struggle rather than as belonging to any particular side. I suppose I should also confess to using Dewey's voice in some of the chapters as a way of commenting myself on how the battle was proceeding.

Before undertaking a major work, my dear friend and colleague, the late Edward A. Krug, liked to write an essay covering the major themes just to see if it would all hang together. I decided to try that this time. Once it was completed, however, it occurred to me that the essay might serve both as a first chapter and as a way of foreshadowing later developments in the story.

Therefore, Chapter 1 of the present volume is both a beginning chapter and an introduction (or at least I intended it as such). It begins at the beginning (for my purposes the 1890s), but it also touches on themes and developments that are treated much more elaborately in subsequent chapters. All four of the central interest groups along with some of their major leaders and certain of their key ideas, for example, are introduced in Chapter 1, but a fuller treatment of the ways in which their ideas functioned to affect the evolution of the curriculum in American schools is presented in later chapters.

Another problem that continually presented itself in the organization of this volume was that so many things were happening at once. In my attempt to deal with that, I decided against attempting a strict chronological rendering of the story. Thus, in the 1920s, scientific curriculum-making was at its zenith, but the movement that supported the activity curriculum was also rising to the fore. Rather than trying to tell both stories at once, I thought it best first to tell one story and then the other, hoping thereby to be reasonably coherent in telling each of them. That approach, however, was not without its cost, since I found it necessary to backtrack constantly into time periods that had already been treated in order to pick up another thread.

The 65-year span that is covered in the book encompasses a period of intense activity in curriculum matters—actually when curriculum reform emerged from somewhat tentative beginnings to become a national preoccupation. The seed-bed for the period of intense interest in the curriculum was the 1890s with the Report of the Committee of Ten, published in 1893, being the single most significant event. But it was also the decade when the main lines of curriculum change were being drawn up and recognizable features of the various interest groups that were to do battle over the curriculum were becoming visible. Over the course of that period, each of the interest groups won its victories, but there were no unconditional surrenders or overwhelming triumphs. It is this ambiguous outcome of the struggle that accounts for much of the diversity in interpretation that has surrounded the course of American education in the twentieth century. The book ends with the passage of the National Defense Education Act of 1958, a massive entry by the federal government into curriculum matters that dramatically changed the political balance and the nature of the interplay among the protagonists in the struggle. The way in which the curriculum of American schools was determined was never quite the same after that.

1986

ACKNOWLEDGMENTS

OF THE CONSCIOUS AND CONSPICUOUS DEBTS THAT I OWE IN THE WRITING of this book, I should start with one that is over twenty years old. When I was a graduate student, very few people identified with the curriculum field exhibited any interest in history. The mood was one of "sweeping away the cobwebs of the past" as the basis for a total reconstruction of the course of study. Arno Bellack, my graduate advisor, was very much an exception. He not only encouraged my historical interests but possessed an astonishing knowledge of the roots of the American curriculum. His incredible insights into a wide variety of areas, even snatches of actual conversation, recur to me to this day. Over the years, Arno has continued to be not only my friend but also my most important sounding board.

When I arrived at the University of Wisconsin, it was my great good fortune that there was a space shortage. (The School of Education was undergoing growing pains.) As a result, I was plunked into Edward Krug's basement office. I was, therefore, in daily interaction with a man whose sheer brilliance was, at that time, evident only to a happy few. Out of the corner of my eye, I was privileged to watch his monumental *Shaping of the American High School* in the making. It isn't often these days that one has the opportunity to learn a craft while sitting, literally, at the elbow of a master. Beyond the brilliance of his mind, Ed Krug's kindness is legendary, and I shall always be thankful to him for his readiness to provide gentle but astute criticism of my youthful endeavors and, of course, for his encouragement.

I am also deeply grateful to a great number of people for their assistance in the preparation of this manuscript. For their invaluable help in locating source documents, I would like to express my thanks to Dianne Bowcock, JoAnn Brown, Hsiao Chin-Hsieh, Sharon Keller, and George Stanic. Maria Dalupan deserves special commendation for her skill and dedication in accomplishing the tedious task of checking the accuracy of the numerous references, tracking down gaps that appeared in my original manuscript, and reviewing the final draft for errors.

Actual preparation of the final draft required assistance from more people than I can possibly acknowledge here. I owe special thanks to Joanne Foss and Sally Lanz for faithfully correcting the many errors that appeared in my original drafts. Other members of the office staff in both the Department of Curriculum and Instruction and the Department of Educational Policy Studies stood ready at short notice to provide whatever assistance I needed. Donna Schleicher supervised the preparation of the manuscript with her usual aplomb and good humor, thereby helping to preserve what sanity I had left. Colleagues such as Michael Apple, Carl Kaestle, and Gary Wehlage stood by in times of trial and offered support and encouragement.

I am grateful to the Graduate School of the University of Wisconsin, Madison for granting me a semester's research leave, which permitted me to do the bulk of the research required to undertake the writing of this book. Research support from the John Dewey Society is also warmly appreciated.

The task of including a set of photographic plates turned out to be a much more formidable one than I ever imagined. For their assistance in obtaining some of the photographs that appear here, I would like to express my appreciation to Louisa Brown, Morris Library, Southern Illinois University; Stuart Campbell, Robert Hutchins Goddard Library, Clark University; Kenneth C. Cramer, Dartmouth College Library; Ruth Jones, University Archives, The Ohio State University Library; Robin McElheny, University Archives, Harvard University Library; David M. Ment, Special Collections, Milbank Memorial Library, Teachers College, Columbia University; Warren E. Phillips, President, Dunwoodie Industrial Institute; Richard L. Popp, University of Chicago Library; and Myrna Williamson, State Historical Library of Wisconsin. Professor Craig Kridel of the University of South Carolina was especially helpful in providing me with leads in locating certain of the photographs that were included.

An abridged version of the first chapter was published earlier in *Education Researcher*. Short segments of the manuscript were incorporated in articles I wrote for the 1984 and 1985 Yearbooks of the National Society for the Study of Education and the *Journal of Early Adolescence*.

1 | CURRICULUM FERMENT IN THE 1890s

i

AT THE HEART OF AMERICA'S EDUCATIONAL SYSTEM IN THE NINETEENTH century was the teacher. It was the teacher, ill trained, harassed, and underpaid, often immature, who was expected to embody the standard virtues and community values and, at the same time, to mete out stern discipline to the unruly and dull-witted. But, by the 1890s, nineteenth-century society, with its reliance on the face-to-face community, was clearly in decline, and with the recognition of social change, came a radically altered vision of the role of schooling. As cities grew, the schools were no longer the direct instruments of a visible and unified community. Rather, they became an ever more critical mediating institution between the family and a puzzling and impersonal social order, an institution through which the norms and ways of surviving in the new industrial society would be conveyed. Traditional family life was not only in decline, but even when it remained stable, it was no longer deemed sufficient to initiate the young into a complex and technological world.

With the change in the social role of the school came a change in the educational center of gravity; it shifted from the tangible presence of the teacher to the remote knowledge and values incarnate in the curriculum. By the 1890s, the forces that were to struggle for control of the American curriculum were in place, and the early part of the twentieth century became the battleground for that struggle.

Preoccupation with the curriculum did not, of course, appear suddenly full-blown. There had been signs earlier in the nineteenth century of a growing attention to what had become the course of study in American schools. From about 1800 to 1830, the monitorial method, an English export, had enjoyed a short-lived favor in cities like New York and Philadelphia, and the Lancastrian system, as it was sometimes called, required a careful breakdown of the course of study into standard units of work (Kaestle, 1973). Perhaps the most profound standardizing influence on the curriculum of nineteenth-century schools was the widespread use of popular textbooks such as the McGuffy reading series and the famous blueback spellers. Insofar as poorly educated teachers had to rely on such textbooks as the standard for what to teach, these books contributed to a growing nationalization of the curriculum. In Chicago, between 1856 and 1864, the superintendent of schools, William Harvey Wells, divided all students in the city into grades and established a distinct course of study for each subject at each grade level (Tyack, 1974, pp. 45–46). This early attention to curriculum was a portent of what, in the twentieth century, became a national preoccupation.

Although changes in American society were being wrought throughout most of the nineteenth century, public perception of those changes seemed to reach crisis proportions in the 1890s. An acute public awareness of the social changes that had been taking place for some time was tied to such developments as a tremendous growth in popular journalism in the late nineteenth century, including both magazines and newspapers, as well as the powerful influence created by the rapid advance of railroads as a means of relatively cheap and reliable transportation. Both these developments, in addition to the continued growth of cities, were significant factors in the transformation of American society from one characterized by relatively isolated self-contained communities into an urban, industrial nation. The decade of the 1870s, for example, was a period in which the sheer number of newspapers in America doubled, and by 1880, *The New York Graphic* published the first photographic reproduction in a newspaper, portending a dramatic rise in readership. Between 1882 and 1886 alone, the price of daily newspapers dropped from four cents per copy to one cent, due largely to the success enjoyed by Joseph Pulitzer's *New York World* (Mott, 1941, p. 508), and the introduction in 1890 of the first successful linotype machine promised even further growth. In 1872, only two American daily newspapers could claim a circulation of over 100,000, but, by 1892, seven more newspapers exceeded that figure (p. 507). A world beyond the immediate community was rapidly becoming visible.

But it was not newspapers alone that were bringing this new consciousness to Americans in the late nineteenth century. Magazines as we know them today began publication around 1882, and, in fact, the circulation of weekly magazines in America exceeded that of newspapers in the period that followed. By 1892, for example, the circulation of *Ladies Home Journal* had reached an astounding 700,000 (p. 507).

Nor should book readership be ignored. Edward Bellamy's utopian and socialist-leaning novel, *Looking Backward*, sold over a million copies in 1888, giving rise to the growth of organizations dedicated to the realization of Bellamy's ideas. The printed word, unquestionably, was intruding on the insulation that had characterized American society in an earlier period.

Of at least equal importance to mass circulation journalism was the effect on American social life of the growth of railroads in the late nineteenth century. By 1880, the East and the Midwest had adopted four feet, eight inches as the standard track gauge, but the overwhelming majority of the Southern track lines were five feet, and the Western states had laid very narrow track lines in the early 1880s. By 1883, however, leaders of the railroad industry had created the system of standardized time zones that are in use today, and, by the end of that decade, most railroad track in the United States had become standardized.

In 1889, the United States already had 125,000 miles of railroad in operation, whereas Great Britain had only about 20,000 miles and Russia 19,000. As Robert Wiebe (1967) has pointed out, "The primary significance of America's new railroad complex lay not in the dramatic connections between New York and San Francisco but in the access a Kewanee, Illinois, or an Aberdeen, South Dakota, enjoyed to the rest of the nation, and the nation to it" (p. 47). Like mass journalism, railroads were penetrating the towns and villages across the United States creating not only new industries and new markets but changing social attitudes and remaking Americans' sense of what kind of world they were living in.

For a time, that social transformation seemed almost unacknowledged, or, in some cases, attributable to radical influences or other external forces. By the 1890s, however, the signs of change were unmistakable, although these signs were sometimes viewed with alarm and sometimes with approval. The population of the United States doubled in the last four decades of the nineteenth century due in large measure to the arrival of 14 million immigrants. Cities like Chicago grew enormously over that period, with that city reaching a million in population by 1900, a growth of about tenfold in forty years. Psychologically, the impending arrival of the twentieth century must itself have been one source of reflection and national soul-searching. Underneath the gaiety that, in popular terms, is supposed to have permeated the 1890s, there lay a profound psychic tension that made people wonder what kind of America was in the making. Surely, the panic of 1893 and the severe economic depression that followed was also the occasion for deep concern and reflection. With the society in such a rapid state of flux, it should not be surprising that the matter of what to teach America's children in school should also come under scrutiny.

The curriculum status quo in the 1890s was represented by the doctrine of mental discipline and its adherents. Although the roots of mental discipline as a curriculum theory go back at least as far as Plato's notion that the study of geometry was a way to improve general intelligence, its nineteenth-century version was derived most directly from the eighteenth-century German psychologist, Christian Wolff (1740), who laid out a carefully detailed array of faculties that were presumed to comprise the human mind. Mental disciplinarians built on that psychological theory by alleging that certain subjects of study had the power to strengthen faculties such as memory, reasoning, will, and imagination. Moreover, mental disciplinarians argued, certain ways of teaching these subjects could further invigorate the mind and develop these powers. Just as the muscles of the body could be strengthened through vigorous exercise, so the mental muscles, the faculties, could be trained through properly conceived mental gymnastics. Thus, they were able to elaborate a rather coherent and seemingly plausible way of addressing the persistent problems that had perplexed educators and philosophers for centuries. Such puzzling questions as what we should teach, what rules we should apply to the teaching of subjects, and even questions of balance and integration in the curriculum could be addressed simply, but effectively, through the analogy of mind and body. There was even assumed to be a natural order for the emergence of faculties, and if this order were followed, a defensible sequence in the curriculum could be enunciated. Moreover, the range of faculties presented a basis for defining the scope of the curriculum. Since neglect of any faculty meant atrophy of that mental muscle, it became incumbent on educators to see to it that no imbalances were created in the curriculum by emphasizing subjects that developed certain faculties and not others. An ideal education meant all-around mental fitness, not just the development of one or two mental muscles.

The most famous document of nineteenth-century mental disciplinarianism was the report of the Yale faculty in 1828, essentially an impassioned defense of traditional education and humanistic values in the face of possible intrusions by the natural sciences and practical subjects. The report recognized two main functions of education, "the *discipline* and the *furniture* of the mind" (Original papers, 1829, p. 300), that is, strengthening the powers of the mind (what would be called today developing the ability to think) and filling the mind with content (what would be called today the learning of knowledge and skills). The chief authors of the report, Yale President Jeremiah Day and Professor James K. Kingsley, a leading classical scholar, had no doubt that the former was by far the more significant function of education (as we would probably assert today), and, to them, this meant a reaffirmation of the curriculum they had been teaching all along. Greek, Latin, and mathematics as well as *belles lettres* had, after all, in their experience, established their value, whereas some of the newer subjects, such as modern foreign languages, were unproven quantities. Thus, there was firm resistance to any tinkering with what appeared to be a sound and proven program of studies. By the end of the nineteenth century, the textbooks being written for the growing number of normal schools in the United States overwhelmingly adopted the mind-as-a-muscle metaphor as the basis for explaining to future teachers what they ought to teach and how they ought to go about it. As that metaphor became firmly established, the implicit injunction to think of the mind *as if* it were a muscle began to lose its "as if" quality, and, to many teachers, the mind became quite literally a muscle (Turbayne, 1962).

To a large extent, the belief that the mind was in fact, or at least like, a muscle provided the backdrop for a regime in school of monotonous drill, harsh discipline, and mindless verbatim recitation. This may very well have gone on anyway, since the poorly trained and often very young teachers undoubtedly were at a loss to do anything else, but mental discipline provided them with an authoritative justification for continuing to do it. Anecdotal accounts of school life in the nineteenth and early twentieth centuries attest to the fact that, with few exceptions, schools were joyless and dreary places. In 1913, for example, a factory inspector, Helen M. Todd, decided to find out from the child laborers themselves whether they would prefer to go back to school rather than remain in the squalor of the factories. Todd systematically asked 500 children in these factories whether they would choose to work or go to school if their families were reasonably well off and they did not have to work. Of the 500, 412 told her, sometimes in graphic terms, that they preferred the often-grueling factory labor to the monotony, humiliation, and even sheer cruelty that they experienced in school. These children, it would seem, did not choose the sweatshops of Chicago strictly out of economic necessity. To some extent, the schools around the turn of the century drove them there. With a reevaluation of America's social institutions in the air, it was no wonder that the doctrine that had become identified with existing conditions in the public schools should come under critical scrutiny.

By the 1890s visible cracks were becoming apparent in the walls of mental discipline. As a theory of curriculum, after all, it represented a curious and not very stable compromise. If, indeed, the mind were really like a muscle and could be strengthened by exercise, why could not we exercise it on a wide variety of different subjects rather than the restricted set that was customarily prescribed? Why, even, could not a faculty like memory be developed through exercise with nonsense syllables? The psychological theory of faculty psychology had merged with the nineteenth-century version of the liberal arts, forming a shaky coalition that served to perpetuate a time-honored literary curriculum. The question emerging in many people's minds was whether a curriculum that could trace some its origins to the courtly life of Renaissance Europe was appropriate to the demands of the new industrial society. Although the demise of mental discipline has often been associated with its failure to survive the test of empirical verification, first by William James (1890, pp. 666–667) and later by several experiments conducted by Edward L. Thorndike (Thorndike & Woodward, 1901; Thorndike, 1924), the collapse of mental discipline and the effort to restructure the schooling that was associated with it was most directly a consequence of a changing social order, which brought with it a different conception of what knowledge was of most worth.

Although lags between what knowledge a society values and what knowledge gets embodied in the curriculum of its schools are not uncommon, it is hard to imagine a culture in which the knowledge deemed to be valuable for whatever reason does not find its way into what is taught deliberately to the young of that society. This holds true whether it be knowledge of how to hunt in a society sustained by hunting animals, or the study of Latin as a rite of initiation into a special class, or sex education in a society where unwanted pregnancies have become a source of national concern. The route between the knowledge a society values and its incorporation into the curriculum becomes infinitely more tortuous, however, when we take into account the fact that different segments in any society will emphasize different forms of knowledge as most valuable for that society. Rarely is there universal agreement as to which resources of a culture are the most worthwhile. The practical knowledge of how to hunt animals must somehow be reconciled with a knowledge of the myths of the tribe; a knowledge of Latin declensions must be weighed against linguistic competence and literary traditions indigenous to the culture; and sex education must be seen against a backdrop of conflicting moral and religious values. Hence, at any given time, we do not find a monolithic supremacy exercised by one interest group; rather, we find different interest groups competing for dominance over the curriculum and, at different times, achieving some measure of control, depending on local as well as general social conditions. Each of these interest groups, then, represents a force for a different selection of knowledge and values drawn from the culture and hence a kind of lobby for a different curriculum.

In the 1890s, not only do we see the theory of mental discipline starting to unravel as a consequence of increased awareness of a social transformation, but we see beginning to gel the interest groups that were to become the controlling factors in the struggle for the American curriculum in the twentieth century. One immediate impetus for change came as a consequence of a massive new influx of students into secondary schools beginning around 1890. In that year, only between 6 and 7 percent of the population of youth fourteen to seventeen years old was attending secondary school. By 1900, it was already over 11 percent, and in 1920, about a third of that age group was enrolled in secondary schools. By 1930, the number had reached almost four and one-half million, over 51 percent of that population. It is difficult to establish precisely what created this sudden interest in secondary education on the part of American youth. To some extent, it may have been related to the growth of the American common school in the three or four decades preceding 1890, which created a new population whose children were now ready to enter upon a secondary education. In addition, technological changes such as the use of the telephone affected the ability of early adolescents to find employment. (A ready source of jobs, for example, had been delivering messages.) A technological unemployment among teenagers, in a sense, left them with nothing better to do than to go to high school (Troen, 1976). To a large extent, also, clerical jobs requiring higher levels of training were consistently better paying than manual labor in this period, making attendance in high school a worthwhile investment. In addition, the clustering of a larger segment of the American population into cities made attendance in high schools simply more convenient. Evidently, the social changes that were becoming increasingly visible in the 1890s were serving to focus new attention on the institution of schooling. Certainly, the dramatic rise in secondary school enrollments could not long go unnoticed. In particular, it raised the question as to whether the curriculum that had been so ardently defended in the Yale report and had remained essentially intact ever since could continue to serve a new population of students and, for all intents and purposes, a new society.

ii

Although the National Education Association's Committee of Ten was originally appointed in 1892 to deal with another issue, the rather mundane problem of uniform college entrance requirements, their work and their recommendations inevitably were affected by the curricular implications of the growing demand by adolescents and their parents for a secondary school education. The immediate impetus for creating the committee in the first place was that high school principals had been long bewailing the fact that different colleges were prescribing different entrance requirements, and this made it exceedingly difficult to prepare students differently, depending on their choice of college. While this in itself was a problem of considerable practical importance, almost inevitably, it became imbedded in broader matters of principle, such as the extent to which a single curriculum, or type of curriculum, would be feasible or desirable in the face, not only of larger numbers of students, but, more importantly, of what was often perceived to be a different type of student.

When Charles W. Eliot, the patrician president of Harvard University, was appointed chairman of the Committee of Ten, it was in recognition of the great influence he had exercised not only in higher education but in elementary and secondary schools as well. Eliot had been active in the National Education Association and was in demand as a speaker for local and regional teacher associations. His appointment also symbolically indicates his leadership, at least for this period, of one of four major interest groups that were to vie for control of the American curriculum in the twentieth century. Eliot, for a time at least, was in the forefront of the *humanist* interest group, which, though largely unseen by professional educators in later periods, continued to exercise a strong measure of control over the American curriculum.

Eliot, a humanist in his general orientation, was also a mental disciplinarian, but, although this commitment affected his thinking on curriculum matters to a large extent, he was not exactly a defender of the status quo in curriculum matters. His reputation as an educational reformer extended beyond his espousal of the elective system at Harvard to his recommendations for reform at the elementary and secondary levels. In an article written in the same year that he was appointed to head the Committee of Ten, for example, Eliot (1892b) argued that "there has been too much reliance on the principle of authority, too little on the progressive and persistent appeal to reason" (pp. 425–426) and that "no amount of *memoriter* study of languages or of the natural sciences and no attainments in arithmetic will protect a man or woman . . . from succumbing to the first plausible delusion or sophism he or she may encounter" (p. 423). Eliot, essentially, was the champion of the systematic development of reasoning power as the central function of the schools, and he recognized that much of what transpired in schools was simply unrelated to that function. Undoubtedly drawing on his own background as a scientist, Eliot saw reasoning power as a process of observing accurately, making correct records of the observations, classification and categorization, and, finally, making correct inferences from these mental operations. It was with respect to these mental habits that Eliot thought the curriculum should be directed, adding, however, that the power to express one's thoughts "clearly, concisely, and cogently" (p. 4) was also a critical task of schooling.

Eliot differed from most mental disciplinarians in that he thought that any subject, as long as it were capable of being studied over a sustained period, was potentially a disciplinary subject. This meant that he was not nearly as restrictive as other mental disciplinarians in curriculum matters and it was consistent, of course, with his strong commitment to the elective principle at Harvard. That commitment represented a sharp break with a tradition in higher education of rigidly prescribed curricula as exemplified in the Yale faculty report. Eliot's support for electivism in curriculum matters extended as far down as the later elementary grades. In a sense, although Eliot did not emphasize education for the purpose of direct social reform, he remained an optimist with respect to human capabilities. The right selection of subjects, along with the right way of teaching them, could develop citizens of all classes endowed in accordance with the humanist ideal—with the power of reason, sensitivity to beauty, and high moral character. To those skeptics who pointed to great individual variation in native endowment, Eliot's (1892a) response, essentially, was that "we Americans habitually underestimate the capacity of pupils at almost every stage of education from the primary school through the university" and that, for example, "the proportion of grammar school children incapable of pursuing geometry, algebra and a foreign language would turn out to be much smaller than we now imagine" (pp. 620–621).

When the Committee of Ten published its report early in 1893, it bore Eliot's unmistakable stamp although, here and there, some compromise was evident. Eliot, for example, had to settle for a choice of four different courses of study in the high school rather than the system of electives that he would have undoubtedly preferred. Here was the measure of uniformity in the high school curriculum that the school administrators had been seeking. Colleges were expected to accept any of these four as a basis of admission. But on the question of dividing the school population according to the criterion of who was going to college and who was not, the committee was firm and unanimous. There would be no curricular distinction between those students who were preparing for college and those who were preparing for "life," a position entirely consistent with the doctrine of mental discipline, as was the stand taken by the committee that the subjects should not be taught differently to different population groups. All students, the committee reasoned, regardless of destination, were entitled to the best ways of teaching the various subjects. What is more, education for life, they maintained, *is* education for college, and the colleges should accept a good education for life as the proper preparation for the rigors of college studies (National Education Association, 1893).

iii

Eliot's report was greeted with much approbation, but also some sharp criticism, mainly on the ground that the committee had not attuned itself sufficiently to the changing nature of the school population. Undoubtedly, the most powerful of the critics—and surely one of the most vocal—was the person who had, early on, assumed unquestioned leadership of the child study movement in the United States, G. Stanley Hall. Hall was the pivotal figure in the second of the four interest groups seeking to influence the curriculum at the turn of the century, the *developmentalists*, who proceeded basically from the assumption that the natural order of development in the child was the most significant and scientifically defensible basis for determining what should be taught. The child study movement, with whom the developmentalists were associated, was one outgrowth of the new status accorded science in the latter part of the nineteenth century and consisted, to a large extent, of research that involved the careful observation and recording of children's behavior at various stages of development.

Coincidentally, it was Eliot who had invited Hall to deliver lectures on pedagogy at Harvard in 1880, and that appointment led eventually to Hall's (1893) first major research in child study, an article entitled "The Contents of Children's Minds." As the title indicates, Hall's study consisted, essentially, of an inventory of the contents of children's minds. Presumably, if we knew what was already in those minds, we could proceed much more systematically in determining what ought to be taught in school. Reflecting his distinctly mystical reverence for rural life (he once claimed that he liked to take off his clothes and roll naked in the fields of his native Massachusetts), Hall tried to discover what children really knew about animals and plants. Did they know what a plough was? Or a spade? Or a hoe? Did a city child really have any notion of what a pond was or the distinction between a river and a brook? Did they know the parts and organs of their own bodies? Could they identify a square or a circle? Hall concluded on the basis of his investigation that teachers assumed too much about the contents of children's minds, and that a lot of Boston's schoolchildren did not know what a cow was or a hill or an island. Although Hall himself often enlivened these cold data with his distinctive penchant for myth and mysticism, his criticism of the position of the Committee of Ten was perceived by many as the voice of science and progress directed against an entrenched establishment, barely courageous enough to put forward moderate reforms in the face of a monumental challenge to the efficacy of the existing curriculum.

Hall (1904b) attributed to various National Education Association committees the growing tendency to count and measure everything educational. "Everything must count and so much for herein lies its educational value," he complained. "There is no more wild, free, vigorous growth of the forest, but everything is in pots or rows like a rococo garden." Such uniformity, according to Hall, was at variance with the natural spontaneity that adolescents presumably exude: "The pupil is in the age of spontaneous variation which at no period of life is so great. He does not want a standardized, overpeptonized mental diet. It palls on his appetite" (p. 509).

When Hall focused specifically on the recommendations of the Committee of Ten, he asserted what he referred to as their "three extraordinary fallacies." The first was that all pupils should be taught in the same way and to the same extent regardless of "probable destination." His charge that this was a "masterpiece of college policy" became the conventional wisdom about the Committee of Ten in the twentieth century. It was here that Hall referred to the "great army of incapables, shading down to those who should be in schools for the dullards or subnormal children" (p. 510). The school population, presumably, was now so variable as to native endowment that a common curriculum was simply unworkable. Hall's second objection was to the assertion that all subjects were of equal educational value if taught equally well. He could "recall no fallacy that so completely evicts content and enthrones form" (p. 512). For mental disciplinarians, such as those who comprised the committee, the form of the subject was what conveyed its disciplinary value; the content was, after all, only the "furniture." Here, Hall was rejecting that fundamental assumption. Finally, Hall saw "only mischief" in the doctrine that "fitting for college is essentially the same as fitting for life" (p. 512). In this last charge, Hall was turning the committee's recommendation on its head. They had argued that fitting for life was the same as fitting for college. They felt they had designed an appropriate curriculum for life and were asking colleges to accept that curriculum as the basis for admission. To Hall, however, this was just part of the strategy that the committee had used to impose college domination on the high school curriculum.

In responding to these charges, Eliot reiterated his optimism in the power of human intelligence and reason. He rejected, for example, the notion that there was a "great army of incapables" invading the schools of the 1890s, contending instead that the actual number of "incapables" was "but an insignificant proportion" of the school population. Also, in a statement that has a peculiarly modern ring, Eliot (1905) foresaw the possibility that a differentiated curriculum could have the effect of determining the social and occupational destinies of students, rather than reflecting their native propensities and capacities: "Thoughtful students of . . . [Hall's] *Psychology of Adolescence* will refuse to believe that the American public intends to have its children sorted before their teens into clerks, watchmakers, lithographers, telegraph operators, masons, teamsters, farm laborers, and so forth, and treated differently in their schools according to these prophecies of their appropriate life careers. Who are to make these prophecies?" (pp. 330–331). Here again, however, Hall proved to be more prescient in terms of emerging educational policy than was Eliot. Predicting future destination as the basis for adapting the curriculum to different segments of the school population became a major feature of curriculum planning in the decades ahead.

As the twentieth century progressed, the Committee of Ten became a kind of symbol of the failure of the schools to react sufficiently to social change, the changing school population, and to the crass domination exercised by the college over the high school. The academic subjects the committee saw as appropriate for the general education of all students were seen by many later reformers as appropriate only for that segment of the high school population that was destined to go on to college. In fact, subjects like French and algebra came to be called college-entrance subjects, a term practically unknown in the nineteenth century. Even subjects like English became differentiated with standard literary works prescribed for those destined for college, while popular works and "practical" English were provided for the majority. Many of these curriculum changes reflected Hall's perception that the new population of high school students simply was incapable of pursuing the kind of curriculum that the Committee of Ten advocated.

Actually, however, the recommendations of the Committee of Ten represented a moderate departure from the traditional curriculum of the nineteenth century. The study of Greek was restricted to the Classical course and, even there, the amount of Greek was reduced from the traditional three years to two, and two of the four courses of study, the Modern Languages and the English, had no Latin requirement at all. While the committee expressed the view that the Classical and the Latin-Scientific curricula were in some sense superior to the Modern Languages and the English, this was because the two former programs were better developed and had more experienced teachers, not because they were intrinsically better. The committee hoped that the effect of their doctrine of the equivalence of school studies would eventually put modern academic subjects on a par with classical ones, at least in principle if not in actual practice. Where the committee refused to compromise was in terms of the humanist ideal of a liberal education for all.

iv

In its time the Report of the Committee of Ten engendered so much lively controversy that, by 1895, another committee, unimaginatively called the Committee of Fifteen, was ready to report on the elementary school curriculum. Wearing the mantle of the humanist position this time was America's leading Hegelian, the powerful and articulate United States Commissioner of Education, William Torrey Harris. (Superintendent of Schools William H. Maxwell of Brooklyn, New York, the chairman of the committee, divided the fifteen members into three subcommittees of five, each dealing with a different aspect of elementary education. As head of the subcommittee that was to deal with the correlation of studies, Harris was responsible for the curriculum portion of the report.) As a highly regarded superintendent of schools in St. Louis between 1869 and 1880, Harris had the practical experience that lent one sort of credence to his pronouncements, but he also was the editor of the *Journal of Speculative Philosophy*, the leading organ of American Hegelianism, and his scholarly reputation was considerable as well. Although he had been a member of the Committee of Ten, Harris took pains in his subcommittee report to disassociate himself from the mental discipline position, then beginning to decline (National Education Association, 1895). Instead, Harris tried to articulate a new rationale for a humanistic curriculum, not only in the report itself, but in his many articles and speeches at National Education Association conferences. Harris, perhaps more than Eliot, was sensitive to the social changes that were occurring all around him, but he maintained that a curriculum constructed around the finest resources of Western civilization was still the most appropriate and desirable for America's schools. Whatever may have been the magnitude of the transformation in America's social institutions or the alleged changes in character of the school population, his five "windows of the soul," as he liked to call them—grammar, literature and art, mathematics, geography, and history—would remain the means by which the culture of the race would be transmitted to the vast majority of Americans. Somewhat suspicious of the rise of the natural sciences, Harris emerged as the great defender of humanistic studies in the curriculum. Although he embraced certain reform causes such as women's access to higher education and the introduction of the kindergarten, Harris earned a reputation as a conservative in educational policy through his lukewarm reaction to manual training (a cause that was then meeting with almost universal approbation among leaders in education), his deep reservations about the virtues of child study as a basis for determining what to teach (once referring to it as "so much froth"), and as an outright opponent of specialized vocational training. In his view, the intrusion of new values by industrial society made it even more imperative that the school become a haven for the tried and true virtues he so deeply cherished. The common school for Harris was a specialized institution with a very distinct function to perform: the passing on of the great Western cultural heritage, leaving other institutions—the family, church, and industry—to perform theirs.

But by 1895, the forces of opposition to the traditional humanist curriculum had grown in numbers and organization. At the same National Education Association meeting in Saratoga Springs, New York, in 1892 where the Committee of Ten was appointed, a group of American educational leaders, many of whom had studied in Germany and who thought of themselves as scientific in outlook, formed the National Herbart Society. Among them was a shy, thirty-three-year-old University of Michigan faculty member, John Dewey. Despite the fact that, like Hall, Dewey disagreed with the American Herbartian position on a number of fundamental matters (although for different reasons), he probably saw the group as the most promising in terms of effecting change in what had become a stagnant, often repressive, American school system. Three years after its formation, at the 1895 meeting of the National Education Association in Cleveland, Ohio, the Herbartians felt ready for direct confrontation with the person they saw as the embodiment of conservatism and reaction, the United States Commissioner of Education. Although Herbartianism, as a movement with a specific identification in American education, had a rather short-lived heyday, beginning to decline as early as 1905, Herbartian ideas and reactions to these ideas continued to exercise a profound influence on the American curriculum long after the movement itself faded from existence as a distinct entity.

Leading the attack on Harris was the president of the National Herbart Society, Charles DeGarmo. The details of the rather convoluted criticism of the Committee of Fifteen Report are not as important as the daring and the symbolism of the confrontation. Actually, much of the controversy revolved around the fact that Harris, in making his subcommittee Report on the Correlation of Studies in Elementary Education, had used key Herbartian terms, such as correlation and concentration, but not in the prescribed Herbartian manner. When reporting on the five major branches of study, for example, Harris, although avoiding his own standard term for these branches, "the windows of the soul," clearly was making the case for each separately as an important study and not in their interrelationship to one another, a pivotal point in Herbartian curriculum theory. Harris used the term "correlation" to mean "correlating the pupil with his spiritual and natural environment" (National Education Association, 1895, pp. 40–41), but not to mean the interrelationship among the subjects themselves. When he used the Herbartian concept "concentration," he used it only in the everyday sense that the work of the elementary school should be "concentrated" around the five coordinate groups of study that Harris had been advocating for years. Although there were some differences among themselves in their own use of the term, Herbartians usually used "concentration" to refer to the practice of using a particular subject, such as history or literature, as a focal point for all subjects, thereby achieving the unity in the curriculum they sought. Here and there, Harris seemed to go out of his way to attack Herbartian practice, such as the frequent use of *Robinson Crusoe* as a way of unifying all the studies in the third grade, Harris referring to it as "a shallow and uninteresting kind of correlation" (p. 84).

The reaction to Harris's report on the part of his battle-ready opponents was fierce. The first to plunge into the fray was Frank McMurry who, along with his brother Charles, were central figures in the Herbartian movement. McMurry used the example of "Egypt" as a way of showing how the various branches of the elementary school curriculum could be correlated around such a concept. Colonel Francis Parker, who had by this time earned a national reputation as an educational reformer, was only a fringe member of the Herbartian group, but he unequivocally made his sympathies clear, comparing Harris's report to "the play of Hamlet with Hamlet left out" ("Discussion," 1895, p. 165). When DeGarmo took the floor, his criticism was also sweeping. He suggested that, contrary to the charge of the committee, the committee had not actually dealt with the correlation of studies. Harris, a skillful platform performer, defended himself vigorously, and, in the months that followed the confrontation, the debate continued with almost the same intensity in professional journals. The meeting in Cleveland became, in a sense, the Fort Sumter of a war that was to rage for most of the twentieth century. Whatever may have been the merits of the Herbartian criticism, the clash between Harris and the Herbartians marked the beginning of a realignment of the forces that were to battle for control of the American curriculum. The atmosphere at that 1895 meeting was so tense and the sense of drama so great that, thirty-eight years later, DeGarmo, at the age of eighty-five, was moved to write his friend Nicholas Murray Butler, "No scene recurs to me more vividly than on that immortal day in Cleveland, which marked the death of the old order and the birth of the new" (Drost, 1967, p. 178).

V

Another witness to that "immortal day" and critic of Harris's report was a young pediatrician who, by 1892, had essentially given up medicine to undertake a career as an educational reformer. Joseph Mayer Rice, like Hall, Parker, and Dewey, was loosely affiliated with the American Herbartians, having left the country in 1888 to study at the great university centers of pedagogy in Germany. Having observed several school systems in Europe, Rice returned to the United States with a similar purpose in mind. In a tour sponsored by an influential journal, *The Forum*, Rice undertook a survey of American elementary education that lasted from January 7 to June 26, 1892. A tireless worker, he traveled through thirty-six cities in that period making careful observations of the schools and classrooms he visited. The result was a series of nine articles published in *The Forum*, from October 1892 to June 1893. Those articles created an immediate sensation, and, in 1893, they were collected in book form and published under the title, *The Public School System of the United States*, thereby reaching an even wider audience.

Rice's (1893a) sense of outrage is present on almost every page. One passage from his observation of the lowest primary grade in a New York City school conveys his tone as well as his general findings:

> Before the lesson began there was passed to each child a little flag, on which had been pasted various forms and colors, such as a square piece of green paper, a triangular piece of red paper, etc. When each child had been supplied, a signal was given by the teacher. Upon receiving the signal, the first child sprang up, gave the name of the geometrical form upon his flag, loudly and rapidly defined the form, mentioned the name of the color, and fell back into his seat to make way for the second child, thus: "A square; a square has four equal sides and four corners; green" (down). Second child (up): "A triangle; a triangle has three sides and three corners; red" (down). Third child (up): "A trapezium; a trapezium has four sides, none of which are parallel, and four corners; yellow" (down). Fourth child (up): "A rhomb; a rhomb has four sides, two sharp corners and two blunt corners; blue." This process was continued until each child in the class had recited. The rate of speed maintained during the recitation was so great that seventy children passed through the process of defining in a very few minutes. (p. 34)

If nothing else, Rice's survey conveys the sense of urgency that many reformers felt about what had become a largely lifeless system of schooling. But beyond that, Rice found some school systems, such as the one in Indianapolis, to be better than some others, and he was determined to find the secrets of their success. Rice initially shared with the developmentalists the idea that in scientific data on the child lay the key to the relatively successful classroom techniques as well as to a rational curriculum. But he also attacked superintendents of schools for their lack of knowledge of pedagogy and for the superficial attention they gave to what was really going on in classrooms. School boards, he thought, were also composed of unqualified people, usually political appointees. The public also was the subject of Rice's wrath. But, at least in terms of emphasis, it was the quality of teaching that seemed to Rice to be most responsible for the catastrophic state of American education. Many teachers whose incompetence had been generally recognized, he contended, continued to teach year after year in the public schools.

Rice's first series of *Forum* articles met with almost violent public reaction. These articles began to appear, after all, a year before the generally acknowledged beginning of muckraking journalism (Curti, 1951). Teachers and school administrators rushed to their own defense, attacking Rice with almost hysterical intensity. Some criticism focused on his own lack of classroom experience (Schneider, 1893), some on his alleged misuse of English ("Critic at sea, VII," 1895, p. 295), and there was even a hint of anti-Semitism here and there in their replies ("Critic at sea," V, 1894, p. 149). Professional educators appeared to be simply unused to such open and unrelenting attack. Theirs had been a life of relative invulnerability within the walls of their schools and classrooms.

Unrepentant, Rice undertook a second survey of American schools in the spring of 1893. Although he expressed interest in those school systems that were in the process of experimenting with new curricula, in fact, he focused almost entirely on gathering data on the achievement of third-graders in reading and arithmetic. Rice was seeking comparative data that would indicate why some schools and teachers were more successful than others in these subjects. In this respect, he is the acknowledged father of comparative methodology in educational research, a fact recognized by Leonard Ayres as early as 1918 (Engelhart & Thomas, p. 141). In particular, Rice's work in the teaching of spelling, which he began in 1895, was a monumental effort, involving initially some 16,000 pupils and designed to discover superior techniques of teaching spelling. When that test failed to accomplish its goal, apparently because some teachers in administering the test virtually gave away answers through their careful enunciation, Rice, indefatigably, undertook another comparative study involving 13,000 more pupils, this time supervising the administration of each test himself. After all that work, he could only conclude that the amount of time spent in drill on spelling appeared unrelated to achievement on the part of the students, but the secret of how spelling should be taught remained a mystery.

When Rice's new series of *Forum* articles was collected into one volume in 1912, that book was entitled, significantly, *Scientific Management in Education*. Although there were still vestiges of his concern for the well-being of the child in the school environs, the major thrust of Rice's work had shifted from the monotony and mindlessness of school life to the themes of standardization and efficiency in the curriculum. Rice's genuine dismay and disgust at what was going on in American schools in the 1890s had evolved into a grim determination that teachers and administrators must be *made* to do the right thing. Supervision, for example, would take the form of seeing to it that the achievement of students reached a clearly defined standard (p. xvi). School administration, generally, ought to be governed, Rice (1912) claimed, by "a scientific system of pedagogical management [that] would demand fundamentally the measurement of results in the light of fixed standards" (p. xiv). Such an interpretation of science, applied to education and curriculum, represented a fundamental departure from science in the interest of discovering the developmental stages through which a child passes. "The child's capital," Rice declared, "is represented by time; and whether certain results are to be lauded or condemned depends upon the amount of time expended in obtaining them" (p. 9). It is the job of the teacher to see to it that "this capital . . . be expended on sound economical principles, i.e., without waste" (p. 9). Educational reform, Rice argued, revolved around a clear articulation of definite goals (pp. 24–25) and on finding the techniques of measurement that would reveal whether those results have been realized.

In slow but perceptible stages, Rice's position had evolved from outraged humanitarian to a zealot for the elimination of waste in the curriculum through the application of the kind of scientific management techniques that, presumably, had been so successful in industry. Almost against his will, Rice became the principal forerunner of the third of the major curriculum interest groups that was to appear just before the turn of the century, *social efficiency educators.* The social ideas that were to characterize that group in the twentieth century are sometimes difficult to detect in Rice, but he unquestionably reflected the version of science and the techniques of curriculum-making that were to become the trademark of that movement. Although the social efficiency interest group represented a reform movement in most senses of that term, it proceeded from fundamentally different assumptions and pointed in different directions from those of the developmentalists. With Hall and the developmentalists, Rice and his ideological heirs found common cause against the humanistic position that Eliot and Harris, for example, tried to articulate, but the social efficiency educators and the developmentalists, ultimately, were as far apart from one another as they were from their common enemy. Their bitter battles would be reflected in their professional writings, in their open debates at professional meetings, and in colleges and universities as curriculum issues and problems gained academic respectability and were formalized into courses and degree programs.

vi

Far from the center of National Education Association proceedings and the hallowed halls of academe where the battle lines for the American curriculum were being drawn, there labored a relatively obscure, largely self-taught, government botanist and geologist whose ideas were to emerge as the major challenge to what was rapidly becoming the established dogma in social theory. By 1883, Lester Frank Ward had somehow found the time in the midst of his paleobotanical work for the United States Geological Survey to produce a two-volume tome, *Dynamic Sociology*. Although himself strongly influenced by Darwinian theory, Ward took almost the opposite position on its application to society from the doyen of the new sociology, Herbert Spencer. Spencer's enormously successful lecture tour in the United States in 1882 and his widely read works in such journals as *Popular Science Monthly* had spread the message of Social Darwinism, and his disciples, such as William Graham Sumner at Yale, were promoting his ideas in American universities. Basically, they argued that the laws that Darwin had enunciated in terms of natural selection had their parallel in the social realm. Survival of the fittest, in other words, was a law, not only of the jungle, but of society, and the unequal distribution of wealth and power was simply the evidence of that law's validity.

By contrast, Ward's (1883) position was that, in the social realm, "there is no alternative but to renounce all effort and trust to the slow laws of cosmical evolution" (p. 153). The laissez-faire position that the Social Darwinists had advocated was, in Ward's view, a corruption of Darwinian theory because, in the course of their evolution, human beings had developed the power to intervene intelligently in whatever were the blind forces of nature, and in that power lay the course of social progress. Civilization, he argued, was not achieved by letting cosmic natural forces take their course, but by the power of intelligent action to change things for the better. For Ward, "if any moral progress is ever too [sic] be made other than that which would naturally be brought about by the secular influence of cosmical laws, it must be the result of *intellectual* direction of the forces of human nature into channels of human advantage" (p. 216). In these respects, at least, Ward foreshadowed in his 1883 work significant elements of John Dewey's educational philosophy.

Critical to social progress, in Ward's mind, was a properly constructed and fairly distributed system of education. Ward liked to use the metaphor of legacy in connection with education, and he argued in *Dynamic Sociology* that social inequality was fundamentally a product of a maldistribution of the social inheritance. Like Eliot, Ward expressed great optimism about the power of human intelligence, asserting without equivocation that native endowment was equally distributed across social class lines as well as gender, and whatever the differences that could be observed in the human condition, they were directly attributable to that maldistribution. Unlike Eliot and the other humanists generally, however, Ward saw education as a direct and potent instrument of social progress.

Dynamic Sociology did not go unnoticed. Albion Small, for example, Dewey's respected colleague at the University of Chicago, declared several years after its publication that, "All things considered, I would rather have written *Dynamic Sociology* than any other book ever published in America (Commager, 1967, pp. xxvii). Nevertheless, on the first of January 1892, Ward resolved to embark on another ambitious project, and within about three months, *The Psychic Factors of Civilization* was nearly complete. Published in 1893, *Psychic Factors* became recognized as the most significant among Ward's voluminous writings. In it, Ward reiterated his attacks on "survival of the fittest" as a doctrine that had any application to the social world and welcomed intervention, particularly by government, in human affairs. The trouble with governmental intervention as it now existed, declared Ward, was that it was controlled by the wrong groups. The right sort of intervention would be accomplished once the influence of partisan pressure groups were eliminated, and practical and humanitarian approaches to social problems were substituted.

Ward's (1893) commitment to egalitarianism was unequivocal. "The denizens of the slums," he said in *Psychic Factors*, "are not inferior in talent to the graduates of Harvard College. . . . Criminals are the geniuses of the slums. Society has forced them into this field, and they are making the best use they can of their native abilities" (p. 290). The key to progress and the great undertaking that lay before us was the proper distribution of cultural capital through a vitalized system of education.

In his *Psychic Factors,* as well as in his other works, Ward reveals himself, not only as the prophet of the welfare state in the twentieth century, but as the principal forerunner of the fourth and last of the major interest groups that were to battle for control of the curriculum in the decades ahead, the *social meliorists.* By the 1890s, Ward had already laid down the main outlines of the arguments that were to put education at the center of any movement toward a just society. To be sure, Ward's position on education was often taken to be a particularly American obsession. Spencer, for example, when asked to comment on America's future, declared, "It is a frequent delusion that education is a universal remedy for political evils" (Commager, 1967, p. xxxvii). Whether a practical faith or a popular delusion, it was a belief that Dewey and many American educators came to share in the twentieth century. Ward himself noted that the most perceptive review of *Psychic Factors* was Dewey's (1894), and Dewey certainly believed that in education lay the key to social progress. While the possibility exists, of course, that Americans share an inordinate faith in the power of education to correct social evils and promote social justice, inordinate or not, it became a powerful force in the shaping of curriculum policy in the years ahead.

vii

By the time the twentieth century arrived, the four major forces that were to determine the course of the new American curriculum had already emerged. First, there were the humanists, the guardians of an ancient tradition tied to the power of reason and the finest elements of the Western cultural heritage. Although, in later years, the leaders of this interest group remained, for the most part, outside the professional education community, they exerted a powerful influence through their standing in the academic world and among intellectuals generally. To them fell the task of reinterpreting, and thereby preserving as best as they could, their revered traditions and values in the face of rapid social change and a burgeoning school system.

Arrayed against this group were three different kinds of reformers, each representing a different conception of what knowledge should be embodied in the curriculum and to what ends the curriculum should be directed.

Hall and the others in the child study movement led the drive for a curriculum reformed along the lines of a natural order of development in the child. Although frequently infused with romantic ideas about childhood, the developmentalists pursued with great dedication their sense that the curriculum riddle could be solved with ever more accurate scientific data, not only with respect to the different stages of child and adolescent development but on the nature of learning. From such knowledge, a curriculum in harmony with the child's real interests, needs, and learning patterns could be derived. The curriculum could then become the means by which the natural power within the child could be unharnessed.

The second group of reformers, the social efficiency educators, were also imbued with the power of science, but their priorities lay in creating a coolly efficient, smoothly running society. The Rice exposés, begun in 1892 and impelled by genuine humanitarian motives, turned out to be a portent of a veritable orgy of efficiency that was to dominate American thinking generally in the decades ahead. In fact, efficiency, in later years, became the predominant criterion of success in curriculum matters. By applying standardized techniques of industry to the business of schooling, waste could be eliminated, and the curriculum, as seen by such later exponents of social efficiency as David Snedden and Ross Finney, could be made more directly functional to the adult life-roles that America's future citizens would occupy. People had to be controlled for their own good, but especially for the good of society as a whole. Theirs was an apocalyptic vision. Society, as we know it, was flying apart, and the school with a scientifically constructed curriculum at its core could forestall and even prevent that calamity. That vision included a sense that the new technological society needed a far greater specialization of skills and, therefore, a far greater differentiation in the curriculum than had heretofore prevailed.

Finally, there were the social meliorists as represented by one of their great early figures, Lester Frank Ward. Ward was the forerunner of the interest group that saw the schools as a major, perhaps the principal, force for social change and social justice. The corruption and vice in the cities, the inequalities of race and gender, and the abuse of privilege and power could all be addressed by a curriculum that focused directly on those very issues, thereby raising a new generation equipped to deal effectively with those abuses. Change was not, as the Social Darwinists proclaimed, the inevitable consequence of forces beyond our control; the power to change things for the better lay in our hands and in the social institutions that we created. Times indeed had changed, but, according to the social meliorists, the new social conditions did not demand an obsessional fixation on the child and on child psychology; nor did the solution lie in simply ironing out inefficiencies in the existing social order. The answer lay in the power of the schools to create a new social vision.

The twentieth century became the arena where these four versions of what knowledge is worth teaching and of the central functions of schooling were presented and argued. No single interest group ever gained absolute supremacy, although general social and economic trends, periodic and fragile alliances between groups, the national mood, and local conditions and personalities affected the ability of these groups to influence school practice as the twentieth century progressed. In the end, what became the American curriculum was not the result of any decisive victory by any of the contending parties, but a loose, largely unarticulated, and not very tidy compromise.

2 | THE CURRICULUM VERSUS THE CHILD
HARRIS, HALL, AND THE
APPEARANCE OF JOHN DEWEY
ON THE EDUCATIONAL SCENE

i

AS THE IDEOLOGICAL BATTLE LINES IN THE STRUGGLE FOR THE AMERICAN curriculum were being drawn, there hovered above the fray the man who at the same time personified and transcended what was to become American education in the twentieth century. John Dewey was not a man who chose sides easily. The positions advanced by the major curriculum interest groups emerging in the 1890s did not so much present options from which he would choose as they represented the raw material from which he would forge his own theory of curriculum. It is, in all likelihood, this feature of Dewey's approach to educational issues that most accounts for the curious role that he was to play in twentieth-century American education. He found himself using the same language as his contemporaries, but he generally meant something quite different and, while competing interest groups eagerly looked to him for support and leadership, Dewey's own position in critical matters of theory and doctrine actually represented a considerable departure from the main line of any of the established movements. As such, he was not so much a central figure in one or another of these groups as someone who reinterpreted and reconstructed certain of their ideas, and, consequently, became identified in a way with all of them. In the long run, Dewey's position in curriculum matters is best seen, not as directly allied to any of the competing interest groups, but as something of an integration and, especially, a transformation of the ideas they were advocating.

Given the subtlety and complexity of that reconstruction it is not surprising that his ideas were frequently perverted when attempts were made to translate them into practice and that only during the period between 1896 and 1904, when Dewey himself undertook to test his theory by establishing the Laboratory School at the University of Chicago, do we get a reasonably accurate picture of how his curriculum would work in practice. The Dewey School, as it is frequently called, is without doubt a significant chapter in the annals of pedagogical history, but it is mainly because of the integrity of the theory that guided it and because the school became a symbol of pedagogical reform in general. It cannot be said that the particular curriculum ideas Dewey tested there actually became translated, as is commonly believed, into widespread practice. As his reputation grew, Dewey was invoked in connection with curriculum and general school reforms of all sorts whether they reflected his ideas or not. At the same time, the educational theory Dewey so painstakingly developed during his Chicago period was either converted into a pitiful caricature, such as "learning by doing," or neglected altogether. The paradox of John Dewey's reputation is that, although he gained worldwide recognition during his own lifetime and has unquestionably earned a place in the panoply of the world's great educators, his actual influence on the schools of the nation has been both seriously overestimated and grossly distorted. It was his fate to become identified with a vague, essentially undefinable, entity called progressive education, either an inchoate mixture of diverse and often contradictory reform or simply a historical fiction.

There was little in Dewey's career prior to his arrival in Chicago that would indicate that he was to become the towering figure in American educational thought in the twentieth century. When, for example, Assistant Professor James H. Tufts, in late 1893 or early 1894, wrote to President William Rainey Harper of the University of Chicago urging consideration of Dewey as Head Professor of Philosophy, he failed to mention any qualifications that would pertain to pedagogy. Tufts cited the fact that Dewey's *Psychology* had been widely adopted as a textbook in prestigious Eastern colleges and that his *Leibnitz's New Essays* had been very favorably received in philosophical circles (Brickman & Lehrer, 1961, p. 167). Tufts also reported that Dewey was "utterly devoid of any affectation or self-consciousness, and makes many friends and no enemies" (p. 168) as well as the fact that Dewey was a popular and successful teacher at the University of Michigan. Also mentioned was the fact that he was a church member and a friend of Jane Addams's Hull House (p. 168).

There had been a few signs in his earlier career, however, of Dewey's growing interest in philosophy of education. He had, after all, some teaching experience below the university level. He had served for two years as a high school teacher in Oil City, Pennsylvania, and subsequently, as a teacher in a village school in Charlotte, Vermont, but this teaching was probably more reflective of a young man unsure of his direction than of a conscious intent to follow a career in professional education. Early on, Dewey undertook to pursue philosophy as his vocation. His decision to make philosophy as his life's work was an outgrowth of a number of early influences, including that of H. A. P. Torrey, a professor of his in his undergraduate days at the University of Vermont. But perhaps the most immediate spur to his interest in philosophy as a career came from the editor of the *Journal of Speculative Philosophy*, William Torrey Harris, who not only accepted an article that Dewey had written while a high school teacher, but urged him to continue his philosophical pursuits.

The letter apparently helped him overcome his disappointment at being denied a fellowship by Johns Hopkins University, and with borrowed money from his aunt, he left for Baltimore in 1882. In his first year of graduate study, Dewey came under the influence of George Sylvester Morris who instilled in him a commitment toward German idealism and an antipathy toward British empiricism. When Morris returned to his regular position at the University of Michigan, Dewey continued his graduate work, working to some extent in G. Stanley Hall's psychology laboratory. He received his Ph. D in 1884 after presenting a dissertation on the "Psychology of Kant," a work that has not been preserved.

It was undoubtedly through Morris's intervention that Dewey was offered his first academic appointment at the University of Michigan as instructor in philosophy. There had been some student agitation among Michigan students to recruit a philosophy instructor who represented a modern scientific viewpoint (Martin, 2002, pp. 86–88). As was common in the late nineteenth century, philosophy and psychology were joined together. Dewey's teaching was almost exclusively in the area of psychology, while Morris taught most of the philosophy courses himself. Dewey's reputation grew rapidly both as a philosopher and psychologist of great promise and as a popular instructor with students. When he was offered the chair in philosophy at the University of Minnesota in 1888, he reluctantly accepted, but he returned to Michigan a year later when the chair in philosophy there became vacant upon the death of Morris.

It was during his Michigan period that Dewey took his first tentative steps in the direction of a serious involvement in educational matters. First, his marriage to Alice Chipman and the subsequent births of their children seemed to arouse in him a natural curiosity about children's mental growth and how they gain increasing intellectual command of their world. Second, Dewey's work in psychology led him to direct some attention to its practical applications in the classroom. He is listed in later editions as the co-author of *Applied Psychology* with James A. McClellan, a book directed to normal schools, and, although there is some suggestion that it is principally the work of McClellan (Boydston, 1969), it does indicate something of Dewey's growing interest in educational matters at least as they relate to psychology. Third, the period of Dewey's appointment at the University of Michigan coincided with the development of the Michigan Plan, a college admission plan based on admitting students who had completed a high school program approved by the University of Michigan faculty. This brought Dewey out into schools and into contact with teachers and curricula below the collegiate level. While inspecting the high school in Ypsilanti, for example, he observed that while the instructor in Greek may have given too much attention to minutiae, his work was "more than ordinarily effective" (Williams, 1998, p. 18). Finally, and probably most important to the development of Dewey's theory of education, he became associated with the American Herbartians.

Many of the prominent educators who were members of the National Herbart Society had studied at the great German centers of pedagogy in Jena and Leipzig, and ostensibly at least, they were committed to promoting the educational theories of their master, Johann Friedrich Herbart, although their interpretations of his work are open to some question (Dunkel, 1970). More importantly, however, they served for a relatively brief but intense period as a focal point for a challenge to the old order in education, as represented largely by mental discipline and by traditional humanists such as Harris. When in 1900, the Society changed its name to the National Society for the Scientific Study of Education, their specific identification with Herbartian concepts diminished sharply, and the challenge to the humanist curriculum was carried forward by reformers representing platforms that bore little or no resemblance to readily identifiable Herbartian concepts, such as correlation, concentration, apperception, and culture-epochs. Although certain Herbartian ideas were not necessarily congenial to the burgeoning child study movement, such as the original Herbartian emphasis on model citizenship, Herbartianism was for the most part absorbed into the developmentalist interest group. In general, the Herbartian emphasis on child growth and development and children's interests blended nicely with the main thrust of the child study movement.

ii

When Dewey arrived at the University of Chicago in 1894 to head the Department of Philosophy and Psychology (pedagogy was added a short time later), the educational world was dominated by the antagonism of two major interest groups representing widely divergent positions as to the future course of American education. Each was led by a dynamic and influential spokesman, and Dewey had had some previous contact with both of them. William Torrey Harris, as editor of the *Journal of Speculative Philosophy*, had provided the encouragement that the young Dewey needed at a critical point in his life. Granville Stanley Hall had been one of Dewey's professors in his latter year at Johns Hopkins, and Dewey had conducted some psychological experiments in Hall's laboratory there. By this time, Harris had, more or less, succeeded Eliot as the central figure among those forces that sought to preserve the humanist ideal by incorporating into the curriculum the finest elements of Western civilization even in the face of the rapidly increasing population of students then enrolling in American schools. Hall, whose personal goal was to become known as the "Darwin of the mind," (Hall, 1923, p. 360), was the epitome of the new breed of psychologists who saw the schools as in need of drastic reform if they were to bring their program of studies in line with scientific findings about the nature of child life.

The preeminent figure in the world of education during the last quarter of the nineteenth century was undoubtedly Harris. The fact that he never produced a magnum opus like Hall's *Adolescence* may lead to an underestimation of the pivotal role he played in the educational affairs of his time. During his long career, he addressed National Education Association national meetings no less than 145 times (Wesley, 1957, p. 48), and one attempt to compile his bibliography listed 479 publications (Evans, 1908).

The force of his intellect and his incredible energy were undoubtedly vital ingredients in Harris's national stature, but beyond his personal influence, he gave voice to that large constituency of school teachers and administrators who were made uneasy by the threat of massive reform then looming on the horizon. In particular, Harris helped build a plausible platform for the segment of the educational world that resisted the idea of a major change in the nation's schools, presumably reflecting the great social transformation that had taken place in American society or, for that matter, the intellectual transformation represented by the rise of science. He was able to strike a tone of moderation in the midst of cries for a revolution in education. Harris, in a sense, was perhaps the last great spokesperson for a humanistic curriculum that education was to produce from within its midst.

Educational leaders in the twentieth century were essentially advocates of change of various sorts, while the banner of humanism in educational policy, usually identified with the school's role in the development of the intellect, was carried by academicians and intellectuals drawn from outside the professional educational establishment. Although Harris's position steadily lost ground among the leaders who regularly assembled at educational conferences and wrote for pedagogical journals, it is likely that his basic position in curriculum matters continued to hold sway with the majority of teachers and administrators across the country for years to come.

Born in 1835, when America was still an agrarian country, Harris was keenly aware of the changes that had been wrought in American society in his own lifetime, but he did not regard these changes as dictating a major reordering of the school's curriculum. Although certain modest adaptations to modern society could be incorporated, the basic function of the school, the development of reason, remained the same. In fact, the restructuring of American society made it even more imperative that the schools perform their distinctive function effectively. Harris's interpretation of Hegelian philosophy permitted him to see industrialization, with its profound effect on America's social institutions, not in any apocalyptic sense, but as part of the unfolding of the Divine Will. Harris could, at one and the same time, be an advocate of rugged individualism and believe that the individual achieves realization only by subordinating himself or herself to social institutions, institutions that embody the fruits of civilization.

It was through these institutions that the wisdom of the race would be transmitted. A consistent advocate of what he liked to call "self-activity," Harris (1898a) identified that activity with the rational through the exercise of will, and his persistent emphasis on rationality in children put him in direct conflict with the advocates of "education according to nature," like Hall. The school, according to Harris, must train children to gain control over their natural impulses, not to submit to them. "Rousseau's doctrine of a return to nature," Harris said, "must . . . seem to me the greatest heresy in educational doctrine" (p. 37).

As early as 1880, Harris was proclaiming the centrality of the curriculum in educational matters. "The question of the course of study," he said, "is the most important question which the educator has before him" (p. 174), and the curriculum, in Harris's mind, should take its cue, not from the vagaries of children's interests or their spontaneous impulses, but from the great resources of civilization. For Harris (1886), psychological inquiry into child growth and development had its place, but it could never, in itself, direct the course of a proper education. "Self-activity," he said, "is in every newborn soul as a spontaneity—a possibility of unlimited action good or bad" (p. 92). Essentially, he wrote, it was the function of the curriculum to direct the development of self-activity in the interest of "a knowledge of truth, a love of the beautiful, a habit of doing the good" (p. 92). Considering the self-styled "New Education" maxim—"Learn to do by doing" (a saying he attributed to the prominent German pedagogue Friedrich Adolph Wilhelm Diesterweg)—Harris was careful to point out that it was incomplete without some "guiding direction" (p. 92). That direction would be provided by a properly constructed course of study. Each branch of study in the curriculum (or, as he liked to call them, "coordinate groups of study") he felt could open the way for an ever more adequate appreciation of the Western social and intellectual tradition. His familiar "five windows of the soul," represented by arithmetic and mathematics, geography, history, grammar, literature and art, were chosen because to him they represented the best ways of initiating the child into the kind of self-activity that would lead to a command of the resources of that civilization.

Harris (1888) claimed that the school should first provide the command of language in reading and writing that goes beyond the "colloquial vocabulary" the child acquires in the home (p. 574). That increased command of language would open up the wisdom of the race contained on the printed page, thus emancipating the child from "the thraldom of dependence on the spoken word" (p. 575). Once that was achieved, the child could reach beyond the world of personal experience and oral language, and the first of the "windows,'" arithmetic, could be opened. Arithmetic permitted entry into the abstract relationships that govern the physical world. Arithmetic, especially exact measurement, represented for Harris (1898b) a first step in the conquest of nature, and he favored proceeding expeditiously from basic arithmetic to those mathematical operations that were useful in the natural sciences, opposing extensive drill in arithmetic operations (pp. 325–326). Geography, the second of the windows, served to relate the inorganic world to the human world. Harris (1888) opposed what he called "sailor geography," the memorization of the names of rivers, islands, and cities, in favor of the "dynamics of geography," the interrelationship between natural forces and human beings that led to various forms of commerce and industry in different parts of the world. History focused directly on the unfolding of the will "realized in institutions rather than in mere deeds of the individual" (p. 575). In historical studies, the State and how collectivities made civilization possible should be emphasized. A particular enthusiast for the study of grammar, Harris, waxing poetic, claimed that the window of grammar "lets in a flood of light for the explanation of all problems which human experience can enunciate" (p. 576). For Harris, the logical structure of language was a kind of model for the nature of thinking itself. And, finally, literature opened up that window that permitted us to see life as a totality and to appreciate what is essential in human character. That understanding of human experience, according to Harris, could best be instilled through careful study of standard literary works. These works, not only led to an understanding of the roots of human action but provided the principal form of aesthetic appreciation available in the curriculum.

These basic components of the curriculum, Harris (1888) claimed, were "the five great lines of study that radiate from the center and relate to the five great departments of human learning" (p. 579). Other subjects were not exactly excluded; they were simply subordinate. "Industrial drawing, for example, should have its place in the common school side by side with penmanship" (p. 579). While his position permitted him to support certain proposed changes in the curriculum of the late nineteenth and early twentieth centuries, such as systematic instruction in art, he was probably the leading champion of the continued study of classical literature and never wavered in his support of Greek and Latin, then becoming a lost cause. Harris's defense of the study of classical languages, however, differed in its rationale from that of the typical mental disciplinarian. While Harris seems to have given qualified support to the proposition that mental power could be developed through use, he was skeptical of the mental disciplinarians' belief that mental power developed in one field could be transferred to another. Harris (1898b) was more interested in what the subjects had to offer directly than in their alleged value as vehicles for strengthening innate powers of the mind. Thus, memorizing dates may have some positive effect on "the health of the nervous system," but that activity derives its most immediate justification "on account of the intrinsic usefulness of the data themselves" (p. 178). Although, almost inevitably, Harris found himself using the vocabulary of formal discipline on occasion, his fundamental justification for retaining Greek and Latin in the curriculum lay in the fact that Greece and Rome were seminal to Western civilization, and no understanding of modern society, Harris believed, would be complete without an appreciation of that heritage. For Harris, it was the content of the subjects rather than their form that was crucial in determining their value. Thus, unlike the reform-minded mental disciplinarian, Charles W. Eliot, Harris opposed the substitution of French and German for the classical languages. While Eliot could argue that French, properly taught, could discipline the mind as well as Latin, Harris would hold that a knowledge of French simply was not as valuable as a resource of our culture as was Latin.

Unlike Eliot, too, Harris was deeply suspicious of electives, advocating substitutions only within each of his five coordinate groups of studies, where content was sufficiently similar. By emphasizing the virtues of the content of what was learned instead of disciplinary value, Harris was reconstructing the justification for a curriculum that would preserve the humanist ideal.

The distance that Harris was able to create between his version of a humanist curriculum and the doctrine of mental discipline was particularly important in an era when the psychological underpinning of that doctrine, faculty psychology, was under serious attack by respected psychologists.

The rise of experimental psychology was seriously undermining the rationale that faculty psychology had successfully provided during most of the nineteenth century for the continuance of not only Greek and Latin but other traditional subjects in the curriculum. Undoubtedly, part of the appeal of Harris's rationale was that it did not require a fundamental change in the basic organizational structure of the school, since, essentially, the same things were to be taught, but for different reasons. Moreover, the central role of the school, the development of the intellect, remained substantially unchanged. What remains of humanistic studies in the modern American curriculum follows, at least in broad outline, the program that Harris enunciated.

Although the development of the intellect was always paramount in Harris's educational theory, that development could not proceed without the parallel development of the will. Only in the lowest form of self-activity, sense perception, was the will absent. Here the mind was only the passive receptor of the senses. The true development of intellect began when the will produced attention and with it the ability to select some sense impressions and to neglect others. "Attention," Harris (1896a) argued, "may be regarded as the name of the first union of the will with the intellect" (p. 442). As we proceeded to higher orders of knowing—analysis, synthesis, reflection (analysis and synthesis), and finally to insight or philosophical knowing—the will continued to play a vital role. The training of the will, therefore, especially through correct habit formation, became an essential element in the principal function that education performed, the broadening and deepening of the intellect. Harris's persistent emphasis on the schools' function in the transmission of the Western cultural heritage through a proper choice of subjects reinforced his reputation as "the great conservator" in the educational world of his time and his identification with the training of the will made him a special target for those reformers in education who saw the existing curriculum as antithetical to the natural impulses and interests of the child, and, therefore, hopelessly out-of-date and unscientific. In his advocacy of a humanistic curriculum in an era when mental discipline was being seriously undermined, Harris actually was not the stereotypic advocate of mindless drill and stern authoritarianism in American schools; but moderate reform at the turn of the century was easily equated with defense of the status quo, and this put

Harris in the position of swimming against the strong tide of radical change that the new leadership was advocating.

iii

With Herbartianism losing its early potency as a reform movement, it was the child study movement that soon posed the most direct threat to Harris's position. Although the leaders of the movement liked to trace their ancestry, with some justification, to Comenius, Froebel, Pestalozzi, and Rousseau, the idea that the key to the curriculum lay in child study did not really achieve national prominence until the latter part of the nineteenth century. In the 1870s, the cause of child study gained impetus through the criticism of American education advanced by Charles Francis Adams (1879), especially by his efforts to draw attention to children's' mental habits as a way of bringing the light of science to a benighted pedagogy. Adams's high praise for the work of Colonel Francis Parker in the Quincy, Massachusetts school system not only brought Parker national prominence but seemed to indicate that drudgery and repression were not, after all, necessary concomitants of schooling. Parker had not simply introduced a much greater measure of freedom for the child than was typical of the regimented schools of that time; he had, essentially, discarded the old course of study in favor of one that was congenial to the child's penchant for play and activity. Parker introduced what he called the "word method" of teaching reading, replacing drill in phonics, because it was the "natural" way by which a child learned language. Problems in arithmetic were favored over the mere manipulation of numbers, and rules and generalizations were reserved for later periods of schooling. Formal grammar in the early grades was also discontinued, and natural language activities, such as letter writing, were introduced. The Quincy schools were held up by Adams as a model of schooling, not only because the natural predilections of the child could be used to enrich the spirit of the school, but because effective learning was taking place.

But it was not until Hall returned from Germany in 1880 that the developmentalists found the champion that would make them a potent force in American education. Such was the power of Hall's personality that William James, after a conversation with him, wrote to the president of Johns Hopkins University recommending him for a temporary lectureship for which James himself had been invited, adding, "He is a more learned man than I can ever hope to become" (Ross, 1972, p. 104). Although Hall did not get that appointment, it was then that President Eliot came to the rescue (according to Hall, actually appearing to him mounted on a horse) and offered him a chance to lecture at Harvard on pedagogy and history of philosophy. Hall's lectures on pedagogy were held on Saturdays so that Boston teachers could attend, and they were an immediate and resounding success. The appeal of a pedagogical system based on sound scientific principles must have been enormous at that time. Moreover, Parker's work at nearby Quincy had made Hall's arrival on the scene particularly propitious, and after a period of drift and uncertainty in his life, Hall, at the age of thirty-seven, was suddenly thrust into prominence. He brought to the cause of education according to nature a quality that Parker lacked. Parker's pedagogical reforms were largely instinctive and, although he could be an inspiring speaker, he was not terribly effective in articulating a coherent rationale for his work.

Hall, on the other hand, could bring to bear the authority of science to the growing belief that the child's own natural impulses could be used as a way of addressing the question of what to teach. When Hall (1893) published "The Contents of Children's Minds," it quickly became a kind of model for scientific pedagogy, and the following year, Hall accepted the prestigious appointment of full professor of pedagogy and psychology at Johns Hopkins. Hall's success at Johns Hopkins in his appointment as lecturer, beginning in 1882, as well as his soaring reputation as a scientist had apparently put him in a position to win the appointment over Morris, Dewey's friend and mentor, who had desperately wanted the position. By 1887, Hall helped found *The American Journal of Psychology* and, a year later, he left Johns Hopkins to become the first president of Clark University. When, in 1891, he founded *Pedagogical Seminary*, with himself as editor, he was in a position to assume unquestioned leadership of the developmentalist strain in American educational reform. With Hall at the helm, the cause of child study became identified with scientific, and hence valid, ways of addressing the great educational issues of the day, while the efforts of the humanists to preserve in the curriculum the great accomplishments of Western culture were increasingly being regarded as speculative and old-fashioned.

Child study flourished in the 1890s. In 1894, Hall (1895) was able to announce at the annual meeting of the NEA that "unto you is born this day a new Department of Child Study" (p. 173), and in the same year, the Illinois Society for the Study of Children was also founded. Over the next two years, the Illinois Society's child study congresses attracted audiences of as many as three thousand persons and, by the end of the decade, at least twenty other state child study organizations had been founded. To be sure, there were some differences within the burgeoning movement. Some leaders, for example, favored the study of the child under laboratory conditions; others urged an "anthropological" form of data collection in the child's natural setting, a form of observation perhaps best illustrated by Hall's (1888) own, "The Story of a Sand-Pile." Whatever the form, however, there was common agreement that ever more data on the child needed to be gathered. The leaders of the movement were also convinced that, from that mountain of data, direct inferences could be drawn (through what they sometimes called the Baconian method) as to how a child should be educated. Beyond the general proposition that education would proceed according to the child's own nature, however, most leaders of the movement were rather vague. It remained for Hall himself to take the lead in actually spelling out the implications of child study for school programs.

There was general agreement, of course, among the developmentalists that schools thwarted the child's basic need for activity by treating children as passive receptacles and presenting them with a program of studies that ran contrary to their natural tendencies and predilections. To some reformers, this meant simply the introduction of more active pursuits such as manual training or industrial education and more considered attention to recreation and play activities. But Hall had a much grander scheme in mind, and, although he had covered himself in the armor of science, it is significant that his curriculum ideas were drawn, not so much from the scientific data so diligently collected by him and his fellow psychologists, as from his metaphysical, even mystical, assumptions about the alleged relationship between the stages in individual development and the history of the human race.

From his early period of study with the German disciples of Herbart, Hall returned to the United States convinced of the validity of the doctrine of culture-epochs applied to pedagogy. Culture-epochs theory posited the notion that the child recapitulates in his or her individual development the stages that the whole human race traversed throughout the course of history. In Hall's (1904c) mind, that recapitulation had strong mythic overtones:

> The principle that the child and the early history of the human race are
> each keys to unlock the nature of the other applies to almost everything
> in feeling, will, and intellect. To understand either the child or the race
> we must constantly refer to the other. This same principle applies also to
> all spontaneous activities. Thus in seeking the true principle of motor
> education we must not only study the plays, games and interests of the
> child today, but also try to compare these with the characteristic activi-
> ties of early man. . . . The child relives the history of the race in his acts,
> just as the scores of rudimentary organs in his body tell the story of its
> evolution from the lower forms of animal life. . . . The all-dominant, but
> of course mainly unconscious, will of the child is to relive this past, as if
> his early ancestors were struggling in his should and body to make their
> influences felt and their voice heard. (pp. 443–444)

The general proposition that "ontogeny recapitulates phylogeny" (the
development of the individual—a person—follows the order of the historical development of the species—the human race) had been widely
assumed as a valid scientific principle from at least the seventeenth century,
but its application to pedagogy—its enunciation as a curriculum theory—
was closely identified with both the German and the American disciples of
Herbart during the late nineteenth century. The widespread acceptance of
culture epochs as a general principle was associated with Darwinian theory. Just as "gill-slits" in the human embryo were a tie to the beginnings
of life in the sea, so were the present behavior and impulses of the child
considered clues to our ancestral heritage ("Discussion [on work]," 1901,
p. 521). Children's behavior had roots in historical periods or epochs, and
this connection allegedly provided clues as to what to teach. A child undergoing a particular stage of development, in other words, would have a
natural and therefore scientifically valid affinity for studying matters associated with the analogous historical period.

Much of culture-epochs theory's wide appeal in education lay in its
association with a scientific order of studies and with the promise it held
out for an integration of the curriculum instead of what Hall once referred
to as a "mob of subjects." A curriculum comprising interrelated parts
rather than isolated entities remained an ideal of curriculum reformers
throughout the twentieth century. In the case of culture-epochs, the
sequence of epochs in human history and the actual materials for study
were concentrated around the cultural content of those epochs. Thus,
while children were in their "savage" stage of development, they would

study materials in all their subjects derived from that historical epoch, such as ancient mythology and fables. What was especially attractive to Hall and others in the child study movement was that a curriculum organized in this way had a guaranteed appeal to children's interests. Not only Hall, but virtually all the child-centered and Herbartian reformers—Parker, Charles and Frank McMurry, Charles DeGarmo—lent culture-epochs theory their firm endorsement. It was widely discussed at national education conferences and figured prominently in textbooks designed for normal schools, such as Charles McMurry's (1893) *Elements of General Method*, a work that went through ten editions in the eight years following its publication.

Although the theory of culture-epochs provided the general configuration for Hall's curriculum, it needed to be supplemented by other principles of child development. He remained deeply suspicious of intellectual training for the young largely because, in his view, reasoning power was not yet part of the child's repertoire. In one of his most influential addresses, Hall (1901b) pointed out that the etymology of the word "school" derives from leisure, and hence the function of the school was not to impose civilization upon the child, a course of action not only futile, but harmful; rather, the school should, as far as possible, stay out of the child's way, seeking, if anything, to prolong the stages of childhood and adolescence. "The guardians of the young," he proclaimed, "should strive first of all to keep out of nature's way, and to prevent harm, and merit the proud title of defenders of the happiness and rights of children." Every invasion of the child's leisure "has a certain presumption against it," and, therefore every curricular intrusion must be conclusively justified (p. 475). One of Hall's most persistent, if not overriding, concerns in this regard was the injury to the child's health that would follow the unwise curtailment of the child's playful tendencies. "Sooner or later," Hall (1892) once argued, "everything pertaining to education, from the site of the buildings to the contents of every text book, and the methods of each branch of study must be . . . judged from the standpoint of health" (pp. 7–8). Hall's persistent advocacy of health as the school's principal purpose put him, of course, squarely in opposition to Harris, the champion of the development of the intellect as the school's distinctive and central function.

As Hall's criticism of the Committee of Ten's Report indicated, another of his preoccupations was with what he called "individualization," leading him to prescribe wide variation in what was taught, not only in terms of the great range of intellectual abilities within the school population, but in terms of other genetically determined characteristics such as those related to gender. Nature not only fixed the stages through which all human beings passed but determined the limits of human educability and, hence, the nature of the social hierarchy. A strong believer in hereditary determinism, Hall (1911) advocated differentiated instruction based on native endowment and even urged separate schools for "dullards" in the elementary grades (p. 605). Segregation by sex, according to Hall (1903), should begin at the outset of adolescence since marked divergence among the sexes begins suddenly "in the pubescent period—in the early teens" (p. 446). Hall noted with some alarm that, although girls until about the age of ten adopt ideals associated with their own sex, statistical studies had shown that, thereafter, girls began to adopt the ideals of males, citing the concern of one writer that "we shall soon have a female sex without a female character" (p. 448), Hall, while not opposing coeducation per se, advocated some segregation within the high school in order to insure "the full and complete development" of both sexes (p. 449). Boys' development, he felt, was endangered by "the progressive feminization of our schools" in a period of their lives that should be dominated by "strong men" and where the curriculum should be geared to the adolescent boy's natural propensities, such as his penchant for studies that maximize content and minimize form (p. 448). Girls predominate in English and history, according to Hall, out of "inner inclination," whereas their preponderance in Latin and algebra was a function merely of "custom and tradition" or, perhaps, "advice" (p. 448). Hall advocated special versions of botany, biology, and chemistry designed for girls and toyed with the idea of creating two kinds of high schools for girls, one with a curriculum that emphasized "motherhood and home life" for "the vast majority of women" and another for those who wished to pursue a career (p. 450).

In general, the elementary school curriculum would be dominated, at least until the age of eight, by play, with special care taken not to overtax the child with needless and potentially harmful intellectual tasks. Reading and writing, Hall (1901b) recommended, "should be neglected in our system before eight, and previous school work should focus on stories, the study of nature, and education by play and other activities" (p. 478). Emphasis after the age of eight should be on drill and memorization since "the age of reason is only dawning" (p. 478). The teaching of arithmetic, for example, should be "mechanized" with little emphasis on rules and explanations (p. 479). Since it is still too early to expect good grammar, written work should be sharply reduced, and, instead, the "child should live in a world of sonorous speech" (p. 479), which would lay the foundation for correct English once the age of reason was attained. Hall regarded the emphasis on geography in elementary school to be a "relic of mediaevalism" and urged that it be sharply curtailed (p. 481). What remained of this study should respect the stages of growth reflecting culture-epochs. A child's interest in primitive peoples, for example, reached its highest point from nine to ten, while interest in "trade and governmental parts of geography" emerged in the period between sixteen and twenty (p. 480). Latin and Greek, "if they are to be taught" (p. 480), should be introduced not later than ten or eleven when verbal memory is at its highest point. The child should not be presented with unfamiliar passages, but lessons should be based instead on repetition of what the teacher has already done.

When Hall (1902) turned his attention back to the secondary school curriculum, he was, curiously, even less tolerant of Latin as a subject. He was particularly distressed by the fact that between 1890 and 1900, a period in which high school enrollment had more than doubled, the percentage of students in secondary schools taking Latin had actually increased from 34 percent to 50 percent, all this in a decade when, according to his figures, the number of students preparing for college had declined from 14 percent to 11 percent (p. 261). Why was that "great army of incapables" that Hall referred to in connection with his criticism of the Committee of Ten's recommendations perversely gravitating to such a useless and probably harmful subject? Apart from the fact that Latin is, compared to science, for example, a cheap subject to teach and that "Latin teaching is more open to women then [sic] science" (Hall, 1901a, p. 655), Hall attributed the disturbing (albeit short-lived) trend toward greater Latin enrollments to "superstitious reverence" (p. 655). On at least two occasions, he compared it to a reference in Booker T. Washington's autobiography alleging that "colored people" had an almost supernatural belief in the power of a knowledge of Latin, however small, to confer superior status (p. 655), a superstition that Washington strove to eradicate.

If the high school were successful in eliminating the superstitious reverence for Latin, Hall would replace it with an emphasis on English, but upon its content rather than its form. Since high school boys would have passed the Homeric stage in their development, Hall would concentrate literary studies around such heroic legends as King Arthur, Parsifal, Siegfried, and Lohengrin, the noblest feature of the feudal period being its emphasis on chivalry and honor. The purpose of literature in the high school, Hall (1902) argued, was not so much its aesthetic value as its positive influence on morals (p. 265). Second only to English in the high school curriculum would be science with special emphasis on astronomy, since "natural curiosity about the heavens is now almost at its strongest and best" (p. 265), as well as geology and biology. Such content subjects, in general, should be given greater emphasis than form subjects such as language study and mathematics. The third area of emphasis Hall advocated was motor training, which would prepare boys for the "strenuous life of achievement [so that] every man-Jack of them will want to bring his whole self to bear where he can compete and meet the verdict of his peers" (p. 266). In this connection, Hall boasted that he could do virtually every kind of farm work and that, based on his training in German schools, he could "bind, gild, and cover a book; make a shoe and a broom complete, do a little glass-blowing, plumbing and gold-beating" (p. 267). Such activities served the purpose of training the muscles and training the will at the same time, he believed. It was around the triumvirate of English, science, and motor activities that Hall would build the secondary school curriculum, with other subjects added, as he put it, *ad libitum*.

Hall never tired of extolling the virtues of science. To him, science represented the culmination of the process of evolution, and it was on his own status as a scientist that his enormous reputation was built. But of the great intellectual traditions that had survived in the world of Hall's time, it was ultimately romanticism rather than Darwinism that dominated his thinking. His proposals for reform of the curriculum amounted almost to a denigration of intellect in favor of a sentimentalization of childhood, and especially adolescence. Throughout Hall's writings, intellect was subordinated to the virtues of robust health and racial vitality. The development of reason as the chief goal of education, to Hall, was a product of a prescientific era, and to attempt to realize that goal in elementary and secondary schools would serve only to sap energy and impair health. In the concept of adolescence, Hall (1904a) expressed not simply an idealization of a stage in individual development, but an idealization of a stage in the human race. It was the period when "the floodgates of heredity seem opened and we hear from our remoter forebears, and receive our life dower of energy. . . . Passions and desires spring into vigorous life" (p. 308). But just as Hall's (1901b) pedagogical theory reached back eons in time, so it looked ahead ultimately to a race of supermen, a vision that, for him, represented "the highest and final test of art, science, religion, home, state, literature, and every human institution" (p. 488). Hall's "ideal school" held out no promise of social reform except in the mythic sense of "removing the handicaps from those most able . . . in ushering in the kingdom of the superman" (Saunders & Hall, 1900, p. 591). Developmentalism, as represented by Hall's vision, not only found a natural enemy in traditional humanism but represented a radically different reform thrust from that of the social meliorists.

iv

Dewey's reaction to the rapidly growing child study movement was at least mixed. As one who was clearly dissatisfied with the state of education in the late nineteenth century, he was naturally drawn to the prospect of reform that the leaders of that movement held out. Moreover, as one who was born in the same year as the publication of the *Origin of Species*, and who, like most intellectuals of his generation, had become imbued with the promise of science in general, Dewey welcomed the scientific study of the child. He was very cautious, however, about applying such study to the practical exigencies of the classroom. Scientific findings, he felt, could not be converted readily into prescriptions for action, as much of Hall's work implied. He was critical of the insistent demand that science be put to work immediately and directly in transforming school life. "There is no more sense in attacking the scientific investigator . . . because he doesn't provide on demand usable recipes, ticketed and labeled for all pedagogical emergencies," he said, "than there would have been in attacking the early pioneers in electricity because they worked quietly in the laboratory upon seemingly remote and abstruse subjects instead of providing us off-hand with the telegraph, telephone, electric light, and transportation" (Dewey, 1897a, pp. 867–868). The clear implication was that the leaders of the child study movement were promising that their scientific inquiries would bring about the pedagogical equivalents of those ingredients of modern life virtually in the absence of a basic understanding of what childhood and adolescence were all about. Dewey was also uneasy about the fact that child study had become isolated from the parent discipline of psychology, resulting in an indiscriminate, almost atheoretical, pursuit of data. He cited William James as arguing that there seemed to exist in the child study movement "a fear of theory, of speculation, of hypothesis, which is as absurd as pure speculation divorced from fact. The mere collection of facts, uncontrolled by working hypothesis, unenlightened by generalization, never made a science and never will" (p. 868). It was almost as if Dewey were saying that there was more evangelism than science in the movement.

But Dewey reserved his strongest criticism for those within the movement who, behind the mask of science, merely used child study as an expression of their own sentimentality and, therefore, as a vehicle for supporting questionable practices. He formulated this criticism by first tracing the development of interest in the child through three major historical stages, each coinciding with a period of social disorganization. To Plato and Aristotle, he attributed the political interest in the child, that is, the proper training of the child in the interest of a desirable social order. "The first source of conscious interest in the child," Dewey (1897b) said, was the position of the child as a factor in social organization" (p. 18). The proper training of children became an important factor in the reconstruction of society, but primarily from the point of view of fitting the child into "the social life-structure they are best adapted to fit into" (p. 20). In its best sense, the political interest in the child represented a recognition that the social order was capable of intelligent direction and that the proper education of children was an important step in that direction. The pedagogical expression of that ideal "takes shape in the statement that the supreme consideration controlling the whole curriculum of the school lies in the demands of the civilization into which the child is born" (p. 21). The chief weakness of that ideal is that the child is not considered as an individual but is seen exclusively from the perspective of the social order into which he or she is to be fitted. By fixing such an end in advance, according to Dewey, we see only those things that are related to that end, and this impairs both our view of the child and our social vision. "If we have in view a fixed end to which the child is to be adapted," he said, "the things in the child which relate to that end are the only things which we are capable of seeing" (p. 21).

The second great period of interest in the child that Dewey identified was the Renaissance, where the principal perspective from which the child was viewed was aesthetic rather than political. The child, in this period, began to appear prominently in works of art as representing a kind of ideal of lost innocence. In children people saw the spontaneity and the freedom to which they had once aspired. In the main, such a view of the child served to soothe emotional stirrings within the adult, rather than as an actual spur to action. "The child," Dewey (1897b) argued, "is taken as affording consolation, as a relief from the ideal, for the adult, and there is no easier or cheaper way of deceiving ourselves than by setting up something as an ideal in order to free ourselves from the responsibility of realizing it" (p. 23). At its best, he claimed, such a view of the child helps humanity formulate its ideal, but, at its worst, the child becomes a mere plaything of the adult in an effort to make life more bearable or pleasurable.

The third and current source of interest in the child Dewey called the scientific, and, like the others, it was associated with a time when older habits and traditions were breaking down, but it was also related to the two earlier periods. Given the fact that this interest in the child was an outgrowth of German romanticism, part of its heritage involved the belief that childhood was somehow tied to the "childhood of humanity," that it was associated with "a lost Garden of Eden," and a return to childhood was somehow connected with idyllic, primitive conditions. It was this sentimental primitivism, Dewey (1897b) contended, that prevented a fruitful blending of the aesthetic and the scientific interest in the child. While the aesthetic interest in the child provided "the crowning motive for scientific study . . . the return to nature . . . must be literal and not sentimental" (p. 26). It was when Dewey turned his attention to the relationship between the political and the scientific that he became critical of one of Hall's favorite themes, the notion of a different kind of education for a special role in society, based on alleged natural tendencies already present in the child:

> We cannot, whether we approve the fact or regret it, educate the child for special membership on the basis of habit, routine, or tradition. The society for which the child, to-day, is to be educated, is too complex, makes too many demands upon personality to be capable of being based upon custom and routine without the utmost disaster. We must educate him by giving him the widest powers and most complete tools of civilization. Only a study, only the knowledge, of what those powers are and how to master them, and what would instrumentally aid or hinder in their development, and how, is in any way adequate to this task. (pp. 26–27)

Dewey thus set himself against the growing tendency in educational policy not only to educate the child based on predictions of what the society would be like, but to differentiate the curriculum based on the particular role an individual would be expected to occupy in that society.

V

Within a year after assuming his appointment at the University of Chicago, Dewey (1896a) made his first major contribution to the literature in philosophy of education, "Interest in Relation to Training of the Will," a work that, not surprisingly, dealt with the raging controversy between humanism and developmentalism. Published as a supplement to the first National Herbart Society Yearbook (1895), it provides a significant indication of the direction Dewey was taking in his thinking on the conflict, and, in many respects, is typical of his approach to educational, and even general, philosophical issues. As the title of his essay indicates, Dewey was trying to shed light on the burning controversy between the advocates of interest, the Herbartians and the child study advocates on the one hand, and the advocates of the training of the will, the mental disciplinarians and the humanist position represented by Harris on the other.

Characteristically, Dewey (1896a) took neither side. His approach was first to restate both positions in the "educational lawsuit of interest *versus* effort" (p. 6), and then, in effect, to find them both guilty of the same fallacy. The advocates of interest, according to Dewey's account, seemed primarily concerned with adding a layer of sugarcoating to what was taught to the child, a practice from which the child learned not even the object that had been superficially sweetened: "He soon learns to turn from everything which is not artificially surrounded with diverting circumstances. The spoiled child who does only what he likes is the inevitable outcome of the theory of interest in education" (p. 8).

Dewey's criticism of the doctrine of will was equally sweeping. "The theory of effort," he claimed, "simply says that unwilling attention (doing something which is disagreeable and because it is disagreeable) should take precedence over spontaneous attention" (p. 6). What the child really learns under these circumstances is to appear "to be occupied with an uninteresting subject, while the real heart and core of his energies are otherwise engaged" (pp. 6–7). In the case of both doctrines, Dewey was obviously trying to draw attention not merely to the ostensible purpose of the activity, but its unintentional and probably more significant consequences. Ultimately, however, he argued that the choice did not lie between engaging the child in mere amusement on the one hand, and forcing the child to pursue disagreeable tasks as part of the training of the will and thereby building moral character on the other. Both sides in the lawsuit, plaintiff and defendant, proceeded, according to Dewey, from the identical assumption: "the externality of the object or idea to be mastered, the end to be reached, the act to be performed, to the self" (p. 9). For the advocates of interest, things that were in fact uninteresting had to be made interesting because they fell outside the scope of the child's real interests; for the advocates of will, strenuous effort had to be expended in order to overcome the distance between the self and the object. Dewey portrayed the self here not as subject to a natural and inevitable unfolding, as the developmentalists seemed to feel, nor as consisting of innate powers such as the will that could be strengthened by the external application of mental effort, usually of an unpleasant kind. Dewey seemed to be making the case for a child as a striving, active being capable of intelligent self-direction under the proper circumstances. He concluded his essay by pointing out that, like happiness, interest can best be achieved "when it is least consciously aimed at" (p. 33). Instead of mere sugarcoating or relying on a spurious self-unfolding process, one should first discover the child's own "urgent impulses and habits" and then, by supplying the proper environment, direct them "in a fruitful and orderly way" (p. 33). Interest, under those circumstances, will take care of itself.

Dewey's 1896 monograph thrust him into the forefront of the most important educational controversy of the time. Interest and effort as fundamental concepts in education, after all, were reflective of the historic battle between the Herbartians and Harris that had taken place earlier that year over Harris's report of the Committee of Fifteen. It must have been evident that Dewey was reconstructing the terms of that debate. Harris, for example, felt impelled to comment on Dewey's criticism. Considering Harris's senior status, his reputation for defiance in the face of attack, and the fact that he was in the middle of his reign as America's most powerful commissioner of education, he treated the thirty-six-year-old Dewey with unusual deference.

Harris (1896b) began his reply with effusive praise for Dewey's work, and then, in effect, tried to turn Dewey's analysis into at least a partial defense of his own position. By defining interest essentially as "a form of self-expressive activity" (p. 487), Dewey, Harris claimed, had actually subordinated the Herbartian concept of interest to a higher principle. Interest, in the Herbartian sense covered all sorts of interest "good, bad, and indifferent" (p. 489), but Dewey's term, self-expression, actually introduced a higher defining principle to which mere interest was subordinate: "Interest that lies along the line of self-expression is the desirable interest. The interest should be such that it appertains to this fundamental act of revealing the Divine will in the world—self-expression of all that is highest. Here interest is subordinated to a higher category, the Divine will or the self-expression of reason" (p. 489). Harris was thus enlisting Dewey as a fellow Hegelian and ally against the Herbartians. "Interest," Harris concluded, "must be acknowledged as subordinate to the higher question of the choice of a course of study that will correlate the child with the civilization into which he is born" (p. 493). Child study, for Harris, was merely one instrument by which the great aim of making the pupil acquainted with the rational order of the universe was accomplished.

Harris's claim of Dewey as an ally was clearly an exaggeration. Had Hall bothered to make a similar claim on behalf of child study, however, it would have been equally far-fetched. Nor would it be quite fair to say that Dewey stood somewhere in between these two antagonists. Dewey was struggling with the possibility that the apparent opposition between the curriculum and the child could be, not so much reconciled, as vitiated.

Dewey's guarded optimism about child study aligned him in a general way with the forces of reform in the educational world, but his reservations about the direction that child study was actually taking placed him far indeed from the mainstream of that movement as represented by Hall. In fact, his criticisms of an idealized primitivism and a differentiated course of study that amounted to determinism put him squarely in opposition to some of Hall's most cherished ideals. Dewey saw in the child and the adolescent, not the possibility of a mystical union with a primitive paradise or the eventual realization of a super race, but the potential for intellectual mastery of the modern world. In this respect, Dewey was not as far removed from the humanists' emphasis on the development of the intellect as is sometimes imagined. Although he surely differed from someone like Harris as to what the "most complete tools of civilization" were, he shared with both Eliot and Harris a basic optimism about the power of human intellectual capacities that ran contrary to Hall's hereditary determinism and mistrust of intellectual activity in children and adolescents. Dewey was not exactly a bystander during the heated battle between the humanists and the developmentalists around the turn of the century, but neither was he a staunch ally of either side. Clearly, however, the dispute between Harris and the humanists on one side and Hall and the developmentalists on the other was providing Dewey with the context for formulating his curriculum ideas. It was in the throes of that effort that the Dewey School was born.

3 | THE CURRICULUM OF THE DEWEY SCHOOL

i

WITHIN TWO YEARS AFTER JOHN DEWEY ASSUMED HIS APPOINTMENT AS head of the Department of Philosophy, Psychology, and Pedagogy at the University of Chicago in 1894, the Laboratory School opened its doors. It is unlikely that Dewey's two years as a graduate student in the city of Baltimore had prepared him for the turmoil and excitement that was Chicago in the 1890s. It was a metropolis of striking contrasts, ranging from the Gold Coast to the squalid slums of the newly arrived immigrants from southern and eastern Europe. It was the Chicago rampant with political corruption and a breeding ground of agencies of municipal and social reform, such as the Civic Federation, the Municipal Voters' League, the Chicago Women's Club, and, of course, Jane Addams's Hull House. It was the Chicago where "Hog Butcher to the World," Philip Armour, built a huge industrial empire and where Marshall Field and George Pullman amassed vast fortunes; and it was the Chicago where factory inspector Helen Todd (1913) could describe the children of the working class as a "human-rubbish pile" (p. 70). It was also the Chicago school system that Joseph Mayer Rice (1893b), in his celebrated series of exposés, had called "the least progressive" (p. 200), but it was the same Chicago school system where Ella Flagg Young, the woman Dewey (1939) regarded as the "the wisest person in school matters" with whom he had ever come into contact (p. 29), had served as District Superintendent for twelve years.

The atmosphere at the University of Chicago must have been heady as well. Although the university was barely four years old at the time of Dewey's arrival, President William Rainey Harper had already assembled a formidable array of scholars in a variety of fields, but particularly in the social arena. Albion Small, a brilliant disciple of Lester Frank Ward's, had been recruited as head professor of social studies, and the subsequent appointment of scholars of such eminence as Thorsten Veblen, W. I. Thomas, George Herbert Mead, and Charles Horton Cooley were to make the University of Chicago the nation's citadel in the area of social inquiry. Harper, who had been a renowned teacher of Hebrew at Yale University, had a particular interest in pedagogy and, undoubtedly, some of his appointments reflected his desire to make the University of Chicago a center, not only of scholarship in that area, but a resource for practicing teachers. Harper assiduously sought to build relationships with elementary and secondary schools, a practice quite common in state universities at that time, but unusual in private universities (McCaul, 1959, p. 261).

An early address of Small's (1896), "Demands of Sociology upon Pedagogy," delivered to a meeting of the National Education Association (NEA), illustrates both the interest in pedagogy that pervaded much of the atmosphere in the early years at the University of Chicago and the general intellectual climate that surrounded Dewey in his new position. Three years after the Report of the Committee of Ten was issued, Small began his address by apologizing for reopening "a closed incident of ancient history" in using that committees recommendations as a vehicle for proposing a different conception of a proper course of study (p. 174). Small was particularly disturbed by the report of the Conference on History, Civil Government, and Political Economy. He interpreted that subcommittee to be assuming that the purpose of education was, first of all, "completion of the individual," and second, "adaptation of the individual to such co-operation with the society in which his lot is cast that he works at his best with the society in perfecting its own type" (p. 174). Small felt that, lacking any social philosophy, what we had left and what the report presented was a "classified catalogue of subjects good for study" and no real sense of what it meant as a whole. If there were any conception of education as a whole, it was dominated by "a naively mediaeval psychology . . . which would be humorous if it were not tragical" (p. 175). Such a dependence on faculty psychology led the committee to believe, according to Small, that history could train the faculty called judgment, mathematics the faculty called reasoning, and so on, as if powers of the mind existed as isolated entities and as if intelligence itself were somehow separated from the rest of existence. "Education," he claimed, "connotes the evolution of the whole personality, not merely of intelligence" (p. 175).

Throughout his address, Small emphasized that subjects as the report treated them were presented as "an unorganized procession of pedantic abstractions" unrelated to the real world and that such a conception served only to make us think of subjects as independent bodies instead of parts of one reality. "The proper educator," he said, "is reality, not conventionalized abstractions from reality" (p. 176). Turning to the question of whether one subject can serve as a center for the concentration of studies, a position closely associated with the Herbartians, Small simply denied that any such subject exists. Rather, "the rational center is the student himself . . . [and] pedagogy should be the science of assisting youth to organize their contacts with reality," not in thought alone, but "for both thought and action" (p. 178). Students must be led to see the whole if they are to make any sense or derive any meaning from the abstractions from the whole that these subjects presumably represent. Knowledge so far as it is gained at all, Small emphasized, must be seen in its relations, "not as self-sufficient knowledges" (p. 180). Not simply the study of sociology, but all branches of knowledge, should begin at the heart of "concentric circles of social activity," starting with the household and gradually extending outward until the "social *desideratum*" is finally reached, whereby "the developing member of society shall become analytically and synthetically intelligent about the society to which he belongs" (p. 182). Small concluded his address with a strong endorsement of the social meliorism of his master, Ward. Educators, he insisted, "shall not rate themselves as leaders of children, but as makers of society. Sociology knows no means for the amelioration or reform of society more radical than those of which teachers hold the leverage" (p. 184). When teachers begin to recognize and accept their social function, rather than thinking of themselves merely as providing "tonics for various kinds of mental impotence" (p. 180), he concluded, they will begin to fulfill their vital role "in making a better future" (p. 184).

In general, Small's ideas on education reflected the growing impatience with the traditional course of study, but, more particularly, his ideas foreshadowed the growing tendency to see education not simply in terms of individual development of intellectual powers but in broad social terms. More often than not that tendency emerged from a concern for social stability in the face of a rapidly changing society. In Small's case, and later in Dewey's, the social significance of the curriculum lay in its promise of social progress. Intellectual development, the great purpose of schooling according to the mental disciplinarians, was of course vital, but it had to be reconciled with the school as a social institution and its place in the larger social order.

ii

Ideas do not arise *ab initio*, and it was from the educational and social conceptions of people like Small as well as from his reconstructions of the concepts of Harris, Hall, and the Herbartians that Dewey began to forge the basis of what ultimately became the theory of the Laboratory School. Dewey seems to have begun his deliberations for an experimental school associated with the University of Chicago very shortly after his arrival there, and, within a year, he circulated a privately printed "plan of organization" for what he was then calling the University Primary School. Dewey (1895) began this statement by declaring that, "the ultimate problem of all education is to co-ordinate the psychological and the social factors" (p. 224), a problem that Dewey wrestled with all his life. On the one hand, we had the individual, and education aimed at the fullest possible development of that individual's powers. On the other hand, there was the social environment in which the individual lived, and social environment implied that the expression of the individual's powers would somehow be coordinated with "social end." One way of achieving such a coordination, Dewey believed, was to make the school a miniature community where the child lived, participated, and contributed—where, in effect, the child's emerging individuality was at one and the same time used to enrich the social community and tested against the dictates of social reality. Particularly important in such a conception of a school was that the work of the school was directed toward what was of value to the child in the present and not "simply as a preparation for something else, or for future life" (p. 224). Such a conception of education rejected both the notion that the function of education was to prepare the next generation to operate efficiently in the existing social order and the idea that the present interests of the child must be subordinated to future rewards whether they were represented by vocational competence or by a command of the cultural heritage. The process of leading the child from present interests to an intellectual command of the modern world, however, remained for Dewey a controlling purpose, and the critical problem was to construct a curriculum that best facilitated that process. It was with this in mind that Dewey conceived of the proposed school as a laboratory by which theoretical designs for how this could be accomplished would be tested in a world of real teachers and real children.

At various times, both before and during the operation of the Laboratory School, Dewey considered the extant theories of curriculum in the light of what he had set forth as the controlling purposes for his school. Dewey was vitally interested in "the theories which have attempted to give some principle or philosophy for the various subjects of the curriculum," and Harris's position was certainly one of them (Dewey, 1899a/1966 p. 187). Harris was generally sympathetic to the idea of representing in the course of study the whole of human experience and, through his five groups of studies, was attempting to do just that. It was important in the curriculum, Dewey thought, "to represent and present, with a certain degree of symmetry, all the intrinsic factors in human experience" (p. 189). The problem was that Harris's five subject areas just did not do that in any sort of cohesive way. Each of the groups of studies was taken, more or less, "ready made," Dewey felt, and each taught as isolated from the next with "no real principle of unity given us" (p. 189), thus reflecting the criticism the Herbartians had made of Harris's subcommittee report on that "immortal day in Cleveland" a few years before. As a result of this isolation of subject areas, the study of any given subject suffered: "geography loses much of its meaning when separated from history, and history loses a good deal of its content, if you isolate it entirely from geography" (p. 191). The distinctions among the various groups of studies, therefore, were formal and artificial, particularly in the way a child would see them. While such a system of organization and classification of subjects may make sense to the mature mind "to introduce them to the child as distinct from the start, is to disorganize and disintegrate, instead of coordinate and connect" (p. 193). Even at the highest levels of scholarship, neat demarcation among the various branches of knowledge may not be a good thing. Dewey recognized, for example, even at the turn of the century, that some of the most exciting experimental work being done in biology was the result of the introduction of concepts and methods from physics and chemistry (p. 194).

A related problem arose when subjects were presented in a more or less finished form. Dewey was convinced that it just made it all the more difficult under those circumstances to see organized knowledge as related to human needs and human aspirations. Organized bodies of knowledge, Dewey was fond of pointing out, were, after all, the outcomes of a long period of historical development. Rather than springing up full-blown as rarefied abstractions, they were outgrowths of the human condition and the attempts of people to do the things that had to be done. "Even mathematics," Dewey (1899a) claimed, the most abstract of the subjects commonly taught in schools, "originally sprang up, not out of the ground, not out of nature, but out of human life and human needs" (p. 191). To present school studies as finished abstractions not only distorted their origins, but widened the gulf between knowledge and human affairs. Dewey's basic objection to Harris's position, then, was not with its attempt to bring to the child the intellectual fruits of Western civilization, but with the fact that this was being attempted without respecting the way children see their world and with a view of knowledge that exaggerated and distorted distinctions among the branches of study and obfuscated, rather than enhanced, their relationship to human purposes. Moreover, the promise of unity among the major subjects in the curriculum was not fulfilled as long as each of Harris's five areas of study was treated independently from one another. In bringing these criticisms to bear on Harris's basic position on curriculum, Dewey was aware that he was also criticizing the standard curriculum of his day, since what Harris advocated bore a striking resemblance to what the curriculum already looked like.

One curriculum that held out some promise for change in the right direction was, of course, culture-epochs; but Dewey had mixed feelings about its efficacy. Part of its appeal lay in its attempt to take children's interests directly into account in constructing a course of study. If children at a given stage in their development had a natural interest in the heroes of Norse mythology, why not take that as the starting point for leading on to something else? Furthermore, a culture-epochs curriculum proposed to move progressively from the early stages of human evolution to more or less contemporary civilization, and it was with the ability to deal effectively with the modern world that Dewey felt the school curriculum should ultimately lead.

As an active member of the National Herbart Society, it was almost inevitable that Dewey should have to come to grips with the theory that, by common agreement, was the foundation of the Herbartian's approach to the course of study. The immediate occasion for Dewey's considered reaction to culture-epochs was a lengthy article on the subject by C. C. Van Liew (1895), a leading Herbartian, and prominent figure in the child-study movement. Dewey (1896b) saw the theory in general as addressing the critical problem of finding a principle "that will give correspondence between child and subject-matter" (p. 233), and culture-epochs theory posited a sympathetic correspondence between what was contained in an historical epoch and what appealed to the child. While Dewey was careful to say that he did not question the fact of correspondence in a general way, its application to education was not really a fact but an analogy to biological recapitulation, and to draw implications from that analogy was a rather tricky business. "No one proposes," he said, "that the mother shall modify her diet when the human embryo has reached the 'fish' phase, or take any practical note of it" (p. 234). There were, then, two problems to be considered: one was that the parallelism between the child and the race was not as literal as was sometimes supposed and, therefore, one could not merely make inferences from race development to individual development without some sort of independent verification as to whether a corresponding stage actually existed in the child. If one were to recapitulate the historical epochs too literally insofar as the curriculum were concerned, one would certainly run the risk of "arresting development" (p. 234) by unduly prolonging some aspect of study simply because the human race had experienced a prolonged historical period in its development. At best, the existence of an historical epoch could suggest the possibility of a corresponding developmental stage in the child, and, even then, it was not clear that we should single out that interest as supreme, making the corresponding epoch the chief basis for what the child studied. In Dewey's view, it would have to be further recognized, even if these corresponding interests were identified in the child, that they existed among other interests. "There was never a mind," Dewey (1899a) said, "simply mythical or simply heroic" (p. 207). In an apparent reference to the sort of reasoning so often employed by Hall and others in the child-study movement, Dewey argued that "any one can set out and collect lots of instances of the spontaneous myth-forming by children," but this does not warrant "the inference that the child at this stage of his being is essentially a myth-forming person and therefore is in the same kind of emotional atmosphere that the primitive people were when they formed myths" (p. 207).

The second major aspect of the culture-epochs curriculum to which Dewey objected was the practice, in both Germany and the United States, of using the cultural products of the historical period as the basis of what was taught. In practice, the culture-epochs curriculum sometimes used such products of historical periods as the legends produced by the people of that era, but, often, Dewey pointed out, it was not so much a true artifact of that period as it was a kind of literary representation of an historical epoch, such as the common practice in the United States of using Longfellow's *Hiawatha* to represent to children undergoing the "savage" stage in their development the corresponding stage in human history. This made Dewey's criticism all the more cogent. If there were such a thing as an agricultural stage in a child's development, Dewey (1896b) argued, it "requires, according to the true analogy, to be fed in just the same way in the child in which it was fed in the race by contact with earth and seed and air and sun and all the mighty flux and ebb of life in nature" (p. 235). Dewey was here not so much objecting to the idea of a basic analogy of recapitulation guiding the curriculum as he was rejecting the common assumption in culture-epochs theory that history and literature had to be made the basis of study when such a parallelism was assumed. Myths, for example, so far as children were concerned, "are a very excellent thing" when regarded simply as stories, but, in another reference to the way Hall would interpret their pedagogical value, Dewey took the position that "it is self-deception to suppose that they have a value other than that of a story—that by some inner affinity to the child's nature, he is being morally introduced into the civilization from which the myth sprung, and is receiving a sort of spiritual baptism through 'literature'" (p. 236). Dewey concluded his analysis by alluding to the ability of children to engage in serious intellectual endeavor, a position almost directly opposite to that of Hall's: "Let us treat the intellectual resources, capacities, and needs of our children with the full dignity and respect they deserve, and not sentimentalize nor symbolize the realities of life, nor present them in the shape of mental toys" (p. 236). While Dewey was intrigued by the Herbartian concept of culture-epochs, he was obviously a long way from giving it his complete endorsement.

In developing the curriculum theory that was to guide the Dewey School, Dewey thus rejected the two alternatives that presented themselves most forcefully around the turn of the century. While each had its own appeal to him, neither was able to deliver, in his view, on the claims made for it. The humanist curriculum, as exemplified by Harris, sought merely to impose a collection of subjects on the child, and, although the ultimate aim of intellectual development through the study of these subjects was a noble one, that curriculum had neither the coherence nor the appeal to the child's interests that Dewey sought. It was that appeal that attracted him to culture-epochs as a curriculum theory, but, upon examination, the promise of a sympathetic relationship between the child and an historical epoch in human history appeared more symbolic than real. The implications drawn from the metaphor of recapitulation were just too farfetched. The promise of a curriculum sympathetically attuned to children's interests was simply unrealized. It remained for Dewey to construct out of those rejected theories something that could stand as the curriculum theory for the Dewey School.

iii

Early one Monday morning in January 1896, Dewey's school, with a complement of two teachers and sixteen pupils, held its first session. So far as has been recorded, that morning's activities consisted of a song, a tour of the premises at 389 57th Street, including the garden in back, the construction by the children of a paper container for their school materials, a story told by one of the children, and, finally, some physical exercise ("The model school," 1896, p. 707). The curriculum that was to guide that school's activity in the years to come had not as yet been fully worked out in Dewey's mind, and, in the first couple of years of its existence, a casual observer could have construed it as a culture-epochs course of study. "Superficially," Dewey (1936) admitted later, "there was a similarity to the 'recapitulation' theory in this method of enlarging the intrinsic experience of the children by means of subject-matter drawn from the development of the culture of mankind" (p. 472). The skeleton of Dewey's curriculum did, in fact, bear a marked resemblance to that of culture-epochs, especially in its progression from early stages in human history to later ones, but the flesh, muscles, and tissue were of a quite different order. In those early years, the youngest groups concentrated on the "building of the homes of the primitive peoples" (Mayhew & Edwards, 1936, p. 43), and "reinvented Ab's trap for the sabre-toothed tiger" (p. 44), while older groups dealt with the ancient Greeks and progressively later historical periods. But beyond those superficial resemblances, there lay a fundamental transformation that Dewey had wrought in what was to be the unifying center of the course of study. Like Small, Dewey felt the Herbartians to be misguided in assuming that any of the existing subjects, such as history or literature, could serve to provide the unity in the curriculum that he sought.

Instead, Dewey found that unifying concept in what he called *occupations*. The term, perhaps, was an unfortunate choice because it could easily be identified with vocational education or with an overriding emphasis on overt activity, but Dewey, at various times, took pains to explain the special meaning he attributed to that concept. Perhaps the fullest explication of the importance that he attached to the notion of occupations is found in one of his most brilliant essays, "Interpretation of the Savage Mind," a work written during the period of the Dewey school, but not on any pedagogical topic. In that essay, Dewey (1902b), usually a gentle critic, was uncharacteristically harsh in attacking the anthropological interpretations of Herbert Spencer. He was disturbed by the fact that Spencer, in his interpretations of so-called primitive peoples, seemed to take his own civilization as the standard for which to measure others, as if the savage mind could be gauged on some kind of "fixed scale" (p. 218). Primitive people were always seen as lacking this or that quality that the civilized mind possessed. But, as Dewey asserted, "the physical attitudes and traits of the savage are more than stages through which mind has passed, leaving them behind. They are outgrowths which have entered decisively into further evolution, and as such form an integral part of the framework of present mental organization" (p. 217). Curiously, he pointed out, such a positive view was commonly accepted in the case of the evolution of animals, but was lacking in the work of Spencer and some anthropologists in their interpretations of human evolution. Rather than seeing the human mind on some kind of hierarchical scale, Dewey urged that we see human intellectual activity, and indeed the culture as a whole, in relation to the characteristic activities in which the individual or society engages and the ability of that individual to achieve command of his or her environment. "The biological point of view," he argued, "commits us to the conviction that mind, whatever else it may be, is at least an organ of service for the control of environment in relation to the ends of the life process" (p. 219). Hunting peoples, agricultural peoples, and so on cannot be judged by the extent to which they have mastered or adopted the trappings of what we call civilization, but only in relation to the dominant activities required by the kind of world in which they live. "The occupations," Dewey said, "determine the chief modes of satisfaction, the standards of success and failure. Hence they furnish the working classifications and definitions of value.... So fundamental and pervasive is the group of occupational activities that it affords the scheme or pattern of the structural organization of mental traits" (pp. 219–220). Not only did an understanding of fundamental occupations give us insight into present mental operations, but it provided a way of understanding other features of a culture—art, religion, marriage, laws.

In a manner similar to the way Hall applied "ontogeny recapitulates phylogeny" to the construction of a course of study, Dewey took his own interpretation of the evolution of the human species and tried to reconstruct it in the curriculum of the Laboratory School. In an important sense, like that of Hall and the Herbartians, Dewey's curriculum was also an historical recapitulation, but what it recapitulated was not the historical stages through which the human race had presumably passed; instead, it traced the evolution of the basic social activities he called occupations. "This simplified social life," Dewey (1896c) hoped, "should reproduce, in miniature, the activities fundamental to life as a whole, and thus enable the child, on one side, to become gradually acquainted with the structure, materials, and modes of operation of the larger community; while, up on the other, it enables him individually to express himself through these lines of conduct, and thus attain control of his own powers" (p. 418). For Dewey, then, a curriculum built around fundamental social occupations would provide the bridge that would harmonize individual and social ends—what for him was the central problem to be resolved in any educational theory. It would also serve to tie together the various component parts of the curriculum and give it the kind of unity that Dewey saw as lacking in Harris's course of study. The question of whether children would be interested in such matters or whether the program of studies had the desired effect were things that simply had to be discovered in the setting of the Laboratory School, and modifications would have to be introduced based on the results of that experiment in curriculum.

About a year after it opened, Dewey outlined the general organization of the school and the framework of studies as it had evolved to that point. Insofar as organization was concerned, the nine years of the elementary school had been broken down into three subdivisions: the first included children from four to seven; the second from seven to ten; and the third from ten to thirteen. In the elementary period as a whole, Dewey (1897d) saw the distinguishing aim not as providing technical knowledge or the "possession of a certain amount of information," but as building into the child's consciousness "an orderly sense of the world in which he lives," beginning with that part of the world that touches the child most directly, the family, and moving gradually outward to the school, the neighborhood, and further to the larger society" (p. 74), a general aim strikingly similar to that of Small's. The course of study had three main subdivisions: manual training, history and literature, and science. Dewey saw the purpose of manual training, not in terms of the development of useful motor skills, but in terms of the opportunities it presented "for cultivating the social spirit" and "supplying the child with motives for working in ways positively useful to the community of which he is a member" (p. 72). As basic social activities, furthermore, they could provide the starting point for tracing their evolution to the abstractions represented by the organized bodies of knowledge: "Cooking, for example, is a natural avenue of approach to simple but fundamental chemical facts and principles, and to a study of the plants which furnish articles of food" (p. 72). The introduction of carpentry work was not for the purpose of developing the skills of sawing and hammering, but because it presented an excellent opportunity for introducing calculation within a natural context and for the opportunity it provided of "cultivating a genuine number sense" (p. 72). Dewey was obviously interested in the child gaining a command of chemistry and arithmetic, and he thought this could be best accomplished by introducing these studies to the child in a manner similar to the way they first became matters of urgent necessity to the human race.

From such social occupations as growing food, constructing shelter, and making clothing, conventional subject matter was expected to evolve, but in a more vital and constructive way than in the typical curriculum. Arithmetic, for example, was expected to emerge from cooking activity. In one extant report by the cooking teacher, Miss Scates reported that the fractions 1/3, 2/3, and 3/3 and the ratio of 1:2 had been included in the cooking of flaked rice and flaked wheat, although she noted that the "experiment was not a great success on account of poor scales" ("Scrapbook IX," 1900). Children also were called upon to evaluate their own handiwork on occasion as an apparent culmination of the effort to involve children, not only in the planning stages of their activities, but at their conclusion as well. Dewey's nine-year-old son, Fred, for example reported:

> We made a wigwam. My wigwam is not made well. I could not make a good Indian. Harper's wigwam was very nice. William had a good one too. Yesterday we looked for thread in a sheep's knee. We found it. It was the tendon. ("University Primary School," 1896).

Dewey was concerned as well with the child's mastery of organized subject matter such as science, but he felt that the surest path to that achievement would be by initiating the child into the fundamental social occupations from which science arose. In 1900, for example, Group V tested seeds that would later be used in the garden to determine what percentage would germinate in the spring ("Group V," 1900). In a history class conducted by Miss Camp, children, through some smelting work, discovered the advantages of charcoal over wood in the smelting process ("Group IV," 1900). In another group, children who had been creating a story about a tribe that had left their caves and started down a river expressed a desire to use the clay that the Indians in the story used and began experimenting with the uses of clay.

In developing the activities that were to constitute the curriculum of the Dewey School, Dewey was not reaching for a compromise between the positions of, say, Harris and Hall. Rather, he was trying to reconstruct the issue of the child versus the curriculum in such a way as to make their opposition unnecessary. Dewey (1897c) tried to illustrate his point by reference to certain subject matter. "Geography," he said, "is not only a set of facts and principles, which may be classified and discussed by themselves; it is also a way in which some actual individual feels and thinks the world" (p. 361). To Dewey, the point of education was unquestionably the latter, but the problem lay in the apparent gap between the way the child sees the world and the way a mature adult does. "To the child," he said, "simply because he is a child, geography is not, and cannot be, what it is to the one who writes the scientific treatise on geography. *The latter has had exactly the experience which it is the problem of instruction to induce. . . .* We must discover what there is lying within the child's present sphere of experience (or within the scope of experiences which he can easily get) which deserves to be called geographical" (p. 361). There was, for Dewey, no body of knowledge that had been "eternally set off" and defined as geography or any other subject. If we had a square mile of land, for example, there was no objective reality which would determine that the way of seeing it was geographical, or trigonometric, or botanical, or geological, or, for that matter, historical. The reference point of the individual viewing that territory was the starting point for any kind of logical organization of its features. So far as Dewey was concerned, the first curriculum question was, "how, out of the crude native experience which the child already has, the complete and systematic knowledge of the adult consciousness is gradually and systematically worked out" (p. 364).

As time progressed and the Dewey School grew in terms of both size and recognition, Dewey (1897c) continued to report on the school's activities as well as to refine his theory of the course of study. A matter of increasing concern to him was the apparent opposition that existed in the pedagogical world between the psychological position, insisting on the primacy of the mental operations of the child, on the one hand, and the logical position, insisting on the primacy of the organized bodies of knowledge, on the other. He interpreted the tone of "comparative worthlessness" directed toward the psychological position in Harris's Report of the Committee of Fifteen to the existence of a dualism that unnaturally separated "the subject-matter of experience" from "the mental operations involved in dealing with it" (p. 357). While Dewey recognized that the ordinary teacher did not usually raise such questions but simply followed the curriculum as laid out, he emphasized that those who dealt theoretically with the curriculum as well as those responsible for laying it out could not ignore the question of such an untenable dualism. Regarding Harris's position, one he characterized as "the most philosophic answer which has yet been given to these questions in America," Dewey did not oppose the general proposition that "the standard for selecting and placing a study is the worth which it has in adapting the pupil to the needs of the civilization into which he is born" (p. 359), but he did take issue with the implication in the Committee of Fifteen Report and in other writings of Harris that such a social determination of the curriculum somehow excluded a psychological one. Dewey was thus not taking sides in the continuing battle between the humanists and the developmentalists. He was essentially saying they were fighting over a false issue.

The way history was studied in the Dewey School also illustrates how Dewey was using the school to help him reconstruct the curriculum concepts that were being put forward by the various interest groups of his time. "[T]o study history," he said," is not to amass information, but to use information in constructing a vivid picture of how and why men did thus and so; achieved their successes and came to their failures" (Dewey, 1900, p. 199). The general aim of teaching history was to lead the child to an appreciation of the values of social life and to let the child see the forces that led to effective cooperation among human beings. The record of human history in Dewey's view was a record of how human beings used intelligence to gain command of their environment—"how man learned to think, to think to some effect, to transform the conditions of life so that life itself became a different thing" (p. 200). This applied to the study of how human beings in early times developed tools that helped them overcome adversity. It applied to the study of the American frontier period where people were required "to cope with a raw and often hostile nature, and to regain success by sheer intelligence, energy, and persistence of character" (p. 201). Thinking of history as social history rather than a rendering of events also "prevents any tendency to swamp history in myth, fairy story, and merely literary renderings" (p. 201), a reference to what the Herbartians preached and practiced. "I cannot avoid the feeling," Dewey said, "that much as the Herbartian school has done to enrich the elementary curriculum in the direction of history, it has often inverted the true relationship existing between history and literature" (p. 201). While he had no objection in principle to using *Robinson Crusoe* as a kind of idealization of how a human being can gain intelligent control over an adverse situation, it would be far better, he thought, to carry that theme through American colonial history. The same would be true of *Hiawatha* as a vehicle for the study of so-called savage life. Why not study the accomplishments of the American Indian firsthand and how their social life emerged from the conditions they had to face and overcome rather than through an idealized literary representation? Although Dewey clearly saw much value in the study of history, he questioned the need to follow a strict chronological rendering as implied in Herbartian culture-epochs. In determining the appropriateness of various periods, remoteness in time was not a guiding consideration. What was important was nearness "in spirit" to the child's own psychological outlook. Thus, prehistoric life is much closer to the child than, say, the Babylonian period or the Egyptian period, because, in Dewey's words, either of these periods "does not simplify enough and it does not generalize enough; or, at least, it does not do so in the right way" (p. 202).

In the Laboratory School, therefore, there was nothing of what we would call today a survey of history. Instead, there was an attempt to introduce at appropriate periods in a child's development those aspects of history that provided insight into the social life of people with a particular emphasis on their typical occupations, occupations that served to shape that social life. For the first group, the six-year-olds, there was an initial period of studying the occupations of people who lived in urban and rural areas; seven-year-olds looked at inventions and how they grew out of the need to overcome certain obstacles; and the eight-year-olds studied explorers and discoverers as a transition from the child's immediate surroundings to things that are further removed in time. Chicago and the United States generally provided the main focus for the second group, with the third year of that group's work devoted to a transition by examining connections between European and American life. Finally, in the third group, chronological order was introduced beginning with the ancient world and leading to a more conventional study of European and American history. The order of study, Dewey (1900) was careful to point out, was "the outcome not of thought but of considerable experimenting and shifting of subjects from year to year" (p. 203).

Perhaps the most dramatic and, in the long run, most controversial departure from the conventional curriculum of the day was the manner in which the so-called three R's were treated, and, in particular, reading, which for many people, then as now, was the touchstone of a successful elementary school curriculum. In general, Dewey believed that reading, writing, and arithmetic could be most effectively taught within the context of use and especially in connection with the basic occupations around which the curriculum revolved. Part of this belief was rooted in his overall curriculum theory and partly in his conception of changing American life. In an era when reading and writing meant the difference between being educated and uneducated, "all the meaning that belongs to these ends naturally transferred itself to the means through which alone they could be realized" (Dewey, 1898, p. 316). With the breakdown of the isolation that once existed, the immediate importance of reading and writing as a gateway to a "richer and wider mental life" (p. 316) had been diminished and the advent of the telephone and the telegraph, the great growth in newspapers and magazines, and various forms of amusement, at least in cities, had lessened the motive power that was associated with "those banks termed books" (p. 317). Instead of facing up to the fact of this change in how reading was regarded and then adapting our curriculum accordingly, Dewey felt that we had continued reading "as the centre and core of our course of study, and dressed it out with a variety of pretty pictures, objects, and games, and a smattering of science" (p. 318).

Dewey was obviously concerned that reading be taught successfully, but as long as reading was being taken out of its natural context, it appeared inevitable to him that the child would regard reading merely as a task to be accomplished without any sense of what a book was for. In characterizing the isolation of reading as a subject, Dewey (1898) deplored the fact that a book had become a "reading-lesson" (p. 322), and reading itself was nothing but uttering sounds and recognizing words. "When the bare process of reading is thus made an end in itself," he said, "it is a psychological impossibility for reading to be other than lifeless" (p. 322). The reading books themselves exemplified the "fatal divorce between the substance and the form of expression" in the utter triviality of their content. "Take up the first half-dozen or dozen such books you meet with," Dewey implored, "and ask yourself how much there is in the ideas presented worthy of respect from any intelligent child of six years" (p. 322).

The teaching of reading was so much an outgrowth of the basic activities of the Dewey School that one distinguished former student, a man of remarkable memory, could not ever recall being taught to read (H. K. Tenney, personal communication, October 18, 1976). Reading, writing, and arithmetic were things that occurred naturally in the course of building a clubhouse, or cooking, or raising a pair of sheep. In this way, Dewey was trying to avoid two common effects of the prevailing methods of teaching reading. The first was "exhibited in the paradox of the combination of slavish dependence upon books with real inability to use them effectively" (Dewey, 1898, p. 324), and the other was that "the regimen of the three R's" (p. 325) simply crowded out very important educative activities that children between four and eight or nine could be engaging in. Art, for example, in its various forms—music, drawing, modeling, and so forth—was much more fitted to what the child needed at that age than a concentration on written symbols. Even literature and history suffered because reading material was not chosen for its intrinsic value, but because it presumably matched the child's ability to recognize verbal symbols. What Dewey did not anticipate at this point was that the rise of standardized achievement tests in the twentieth century would sharply accelerate the tendencies in the teaching of the three R's that he so much deplored and would help make his own emphasis on the relationship between reading and human purposes the object of scorn and caricature.

iv

At the same time that Dewey was establishing the order of studies in his school and the manner in which the subjects should be treated, he was also seeking to articulate the theoretical conceptions that guided that work. In April 1899, Dewey delivered three lectures to an audience of parents and others in which he tried to express the basic rationale for the school, and these lectures formed the heart of *School and Society*, which, when it was published that year, added immeasurably to the fame of the school and spread Dewey's ideas to a worldwide audience. In "The School and Social Progress," the first of the lectures, he attempted to link the basic core of his curriculum, the occupations, to the mighty changes that had been wrought in American society, particularly the arrival of what Dewey called the factory system. Dewey (1899b) was not so much expressing nostalgia for the days when "the whole process of getting illumination stood revealed in its toilsome length, from the killing of the animal and the trying of fat to the making of wicks and dipping of candles" (p. 19), as he was trying to point out that such a process, toilsome as it was, was an educative activity in a way that flicking a switch and filling a house with electric illumination could never be. Those activities of an earlier day, furthermore, provided opportunities for cooperative action toward a common goal and for a sense of accomplishment that was not as readily available in a modern technological society. For the "city-bred child of today" (p. 21), such opportunities were no longer present, and the educational problem then became one of recreating in the school something of the occupations that in former times not only provided a sense of real purpose, but linked intelligence and cooperative action to what the work of the world required.

The way to accomplish this, according to Dewey, was to create in the school "a miniature community, an embryonic society," (p. 28) and as various forms of social occupations were introduced, "the entire spirit of the school is renewed" (p. 27) and the school becomes a place to live rather than "only a place to learn lessons" (p. 28). Dewey was again careful to emphasize the social side of these occupations rather than their utilitarian value in what ultimately turned out to be a mostly futile effort to deflect the idea that he was mainly interested in teaching practical skills. "There is nothing which strikes the average intelligent visitor as stranger," he said, "than to see boys as well as girls of ten, twelve, and thirteen years of age engaged in sewing and weaving. If we look at this from the standpoint of preparation of the boys for sewing on buttons and making patches, we get a narrow and utilitarian conception—a basis that hardly justifies giving prominence to this sort of work in the school" (pp. 29–30). The children in the school sheared sheep, made the cards used to card the wool, and then spun the wool on a spinning wheel, hardly practical activities in a modern industrial society. Here, they were following through in something that they designed and created from its most elementary form to a finished product. Dewey once recalled that Plato defined a slave as one who had none of his own ideas but was always expressing those of someone else. How much more urgent it must be in a modern industrial society than it was in Plato's time, Dewey mused, that somewhere people learn to develop and bring to execution their own ideas. "When occupations in the school are conceived in this broad and generous way," he felt, "I can only stand lost in wonder at the objections so often heard, that such occupations are out of place in the school because they are materialistic, utilitarian, or even menial in their tendency" (p. 34). The miniature community that Dewey envisioned was designed to initiate the child into effective social membership and, by "providing him with the instruments of effective self-direction," in the words of one of Dewey's most oft-quoted statements, "we shall have the deepest and best guarantee of a larger society which is worthy, lovely, and harmonious" (p. 40).

In his two subsequent lectures, Dewey tried to indicate how the activities that characterized the school not only had the social value he expressed in the first lecture, but followed the instincts that children brought with them to school. In "The School and the Life of the Child," he amplified on the four instincts or impulses that he believed characterized children's behavior: the social or communicative instinct, the constructive instinct—the desire to make things, the expressive impulse, which grows out of the first two and, finally, the artistic impulse. These impulses, Dewey (1899b) felt, were in fact connected somehow with primitive life as culture-epochs theory implied and that because "there is a sort of natural recurrence of the child mind to the typical activities of primitive peoples," (p. 58) one could use that correspondence in constructing a course of study. Despite his reservations about Herbartian theory, certain aspects of the ideas of its proponents seemed to have made a lasting impression on him. When Dewey turned to the theme of "Waste in Education" in his third lecture, he was careful to delineate his version of waste from the typical emphasis on efficiency, then only in its incipient stages but destined to become a dominant theme in American education in the twentieth century. Dewey declared that he was not so much interested in "waste of money or the waste of things," (p. 75) but the waste in human life that is created by the isolation of the school from social life and, because "all waste is due to isolation," also to the waste created by the isolation of one subject from another as well as "to the lack of coherence in . . . studies and methods" (p. 74).

Increasingly, Dewey was associating the work of the Laboratory School with his epistemological ideas, and, in fact, with his overall philosophy. "The underlying theory of knowledge," he said of the Laboratory School, "emphasized the part of problems, which originated in active situations, in the development of thought and also the necessity of testing thought by action if thought was to pass over into knowledge. The only place in which a comprehensive theory of knowledge can receive an active test is in the process of education" (Dewey, 1936, p. 464). It was for this reason that Dewey tried to see the school as embodying a form of social life, one where cooperative social living in miniature could provide the setting for the development of thought. Dewey specifically denied that there was any desire to "'adjust' individuals to social institutions, if by adjustment is meant preparation to fit into present social arrangements and conditions" (p. 466). It was rather that mental development was essentially a social process and required a congenial social setting in which to develop effectively. In the long run, it was intellectual development that Dewey sought to effect through the curriculum, not only because it gave the individual command of his or her environment, but because intelligent social action held out the most promise for a better society. Dewey's rejection of the traditional course of study was not because it emphasized intellectual content; it was precisely because it lacked it. "Custom and convention," Dewey asserted, "conceal from most of us the extreme intellectual poverty of the traditional course of study, as well as its lack of intellectual organization" (p. 468).

In designing a course of study for his school, Dewey, as usual, rejected both of the alternatives that were presented. One was "to follow the traditional arrangement of studies and lessons"; the other was "to permit a free flow of experiences and acts which are immediately and sensationally appealing, but which lead to nothing in particular" (Dewey, 1936, p. 469). The solution that he sought in the curriculum of the Laboratory School was to find those things within the child's life and interests that offered the best opportunity to lead gradually to a command of the abstract subject matter we associate with logically organized bodies of knowledge. Because Dewey's school, throughout its existence was essentially an elementary school, and because Dewey left the University of Chicago before any attempt was made to develop a program of secondary education, we tend to get a truncated version of what Dewey envisioned as an appropriate course of study, emphasizing primarily children's interests and active occupations and slighting the importance that he attached to a command of the intellectual resources of one's culture.

Written two years before he left the University of Chicago, Dewey's *The Child and the Curriculum* is unquestionably the best known and, in most respects, the clearest exposition of his theory of curriculum. As usual, Dewey (1902a) was trying to dispel what he regarded as an untenable dualism. On the one hand, we had "certain social aims, meanings, values incarnate in the matured experience of the adult" and on the other, "an immature, undeveloped being" (p. 4). The differences between those two "fundamental factors" were obvious. The world of the adult was logically arranged with reference to general principles; it was classified and abstracted from the real world. The child, on the other hand, lived in a world of immediate and direct experiences, and Dewey elaborated on what these basic factors implied when the course of study was considered. Conventionally, subjects are divided into topics and topics into studies and each study into lessons, and finally each lesson into specific facts or skills to be learned. "The road which looks so long when viewed in its entirety," he said, "is easily traveled, considered as a series of particular steps" (p. 8). On the other side, the child and the facts of child development are taken as the starting point. The standard for what is taught lies in the child not with bodies of subject matter.

Dewey saw the solution in reconstructing the problem in such a way as to make that apparent opposition disappear. He believed that he had found the key to that dilemma in the concept of *experience*. One had "to get rid of the prejudicial notion that there is some gap in kind (as distinct from degree) between the child's experience and the various forms of subject-matter that make up the course of study." Once that was accomplished, the child and the curriculum (the course of study) became "simply two limits which define a single process" (p. 11). What Dewey was constructing, essentially, was a continuum of experience, and it was the function of the course of study to move along that line from one defining point, the immediate, chaotic, but integral experience of the child, to the other defining point, the logically organized, abstract, and classified experience of the mature adult. What were being reconstructed in the curriculum, therefore, were not the stages in the development of human history as the Herbartians advocated, but stages in the way human beings gained control of their world through the use of intelligence—stages in the development of knowledge.

But that reconstruction could not be strictly a logical one; it had to be psychologized. Dewey pointed out that while there was no direct opposition between the viewpoint of the scientist and the science teacher, neither were they "immediately identical" (p. 22). The scientist was primarily interested in advancing knowledge, developing new hypotheses, and trying to verify them. While the teacher was also interested in the subject matter of science, his or her primary interest was in how that knowledge became part of the child's experience. It is not so much with knowledge itself that the teacher was concerned but with the effect that knowledge had on the child. As the child progressed in the educational process, the child's experience would begin to take on the form of the logically organized bodies of experiences that we call knowledge and that have evolved over many centuries. Dewey was thus hoping at one and the same time to put children in command of the intellectual resources of their culture and to break down the barriers that life in a technological society had erected between knowledge and human affairs. By reconstructing the evolution of knowledge in the curriculum, Dewey was hoping not only to educate children but to restore the role that he believed knowledge had once played in a preindustrial society.

v

Dewey left the University of Chicago in 1904 after an unfortunate, almost tragic, dispute with President Harper. The Laboratory School continued to exist, but gradually lost some of the particular character that Dewey gave it. His appointment at Columbia University was in its philosophy department, and, although he maintained some connection with Teachers College, his work in his long career at Columbia reflected, in the main, general philosophical interests. Although his magnum opus in education, *Democracy and Education*, was not published until 1916, it is largely a comprehensive synthesis of the ideas that Dewey developed during his Chicago period. Dewey, having established himself as an educational statesman, continued to interest himself in educational questions throughout his lifetime, and his pronouncements often attracted national attention. But, although all sorts of changes in educational policy and programs were attributed to Dewey's influence during his long career at Columbia, and although his work attracted devoted disciples, nowhere do we find a coherent and lasting attempt to implement his course of study. While it would be an obvious exaggeration to say that Dewey's influence on the curriculum of America's schools was nil, other reformers with quite different conceptions of what should be taught were far more successful, or to put it more accurately, their ideas were more congenial to the forces that in fact influenced the course of study in the twentieth century than were Dewey's.

What was there about Dewey's ideas that caused them at best to be translated into slogans and at worst to be distorted altogether? He himself may have had the most significant insights into that question. In a paper given during the period of the Dewey School, he (1901) considered the general question of education reform and why it fails. He tried to draw a picture of how innovations are introduced into the curriculum. First, he said, someone feels that a school system is behind the times, that there are new and exciting things going on elsewhere. Public sentiment is aroused and, after letters are written, editorials appear, and lobby groups do their work, the change is instituted: "The victory is won, and everybody—unless it be some already overburdened and distracted teacher—congratulates everybody else that such advanced steps are being taken" (p. 334). Within a short time, however, complaints are heard that children do not read as well as they used to or that their handwriting is bad; there develops a public outcry to rescind the reform, and there is a return to the status quo ante.

One reason, Dewey (1901) felt, that these cycles occur is that there is "no conscious educational standard by which to test and place each aspiring claimant" (p. 335). Every movement for change, whether it be a new way of teaching arithmetic or a new subject such as manual training, is seen as isolated and independent from the rest of the curriculum; what we have is a multiplicity of standards for judging the worth of each reform, and these standards can easily work at cross-purposes. Second, Dewey called attention to what he called "the mechanics of school organization and administration" (p. 337). Although such things are usually seen as peripheral to the main business of the course of study, in fact, the organizational features of the school are often controlling factors in what gets taught. As long as the grouping of students, the selection of teachers, and the system of rewards remain the same, the reform is doomed. "We forget," Dewey said, "that it is precisely such things as these that really control the whole system, even on its distinctively educational side" (p. 338). The changes that Dewey sought in the curriculum were so sweeping and so revolutionary that they had to be accompanied by an equally great transformation in the way schools were run. And the key organizational features of any school are far more permanent affairs than any branch of study in the curriculum.

Moreover, the things that Dewey sought to promote through his curriculum were difficult to measure and therefore difficult to fit into a system that depended on "that kind of external inspection which goes by the name of examination." "Technical proficiency," he said, "acquisition of skill and information, present much less difficulty" (p. 340). Dewey also called attention to the minimal role that the teacher normally had in designing a course of study. It is, after all, the teacher "who alone can make that course of study a living reality," and "as long as the teacher, who is, after all, the only real educator in the school system, has no definite and authoritative position in shaping the course of study, that is likely to remain an external thing to be externally applied to the child" (p. 341). What Dewey called the question of democracy was also involved, but the practical question was derived from the fact that the teacher was the most important figure insofar as the curriculum was concerned. There was simply no point in attempting a reform of the course of study without the active participation of the teacher and without taking into account the teacher's abilities, interests, and desires. Curriculum change, therefore, required not simply a new conception of the course of study, but a complex process of interaction involving both the organizational structure of the school and those people who were to be instrumental in bringing it to the classroom. From all accounts, such interaction did exist in the Laboratory School, where Dewey had assembled a superb corps of teachers, but accomplishing that same dedication and commitment in the typical public school was another matter. With remarkable prescience, Dewey predicted that, without considered attention to the processes of change itself, "we shall be forever oscillating between extremes: now lending ourselves with enthusiasm to the introduction of art and music and manual training because they give vitality to the school work and relief to the child; now querulously complaining of the evil results reached, and insisting with all positiveness upon the return of good old days when reading, writing, spelling, and arithmetic were adequately taught" (p. 346).

Bandwagonism and pendulum swings from reform to conservatism in educational affairs did, in fact, become a persistent and almost mysterious phenomenon in the twentieth century. But beyond the shifts themselves, there remained a fundamental resistance to the sorts of changes that Dewey sought to introduce. In a larger sense, it is likely that what Dewey saw as the basic function of education, the development of the kind of intelligence that would lead to a command of the conditions of one's life and ultimately to social progress, was not what most people saw as the major requirement of a modern industrial society. The appeal of a stable social order, with each person efficiently fulfilling his or her appointed tasks, was far more compelling. John Dewey, the quintessential American philosopher, may, paradoxically, have been out of step, in at least some significant respects, with dominant American values, and while, personally, he was much revered in his own lifetime, his educational reforms remained confined largely to the world of ideas rather than the world of practice. The question of why certain proposed reforms do not become translated into practice, however, may be, in the long run, of equal importance to the question of why others do.

4 | SCIENTIFIC CURRICULUM-MAKING AND THE RISE OF SOCIAL EFFICIENCY AS AN EDUCATIONAL IDEAL

i

OF THE VARIED AND SOMETIMES FRENETIC RESPONSES TO INDUSTRIALISM and to the consequent transformation of American social institutions, there was one that emerged clearly dominant both as a social ideal and as an educational doctrine. It was social efficiency that, for most people, held out the promise of social stability in the face of cries for massive social change, and that doctrine claimed the now-potent backing of science in order to insure it. This was a vastly different science, however, from either Hall's natural order of development in the child or Dewey's idealization of scientific inquiry as a general model of reflective thinking. It was a science of exact measurement and precise standards in the interest of maintaining a predictable and orderly world. In a period when the influence of certain social institutions such as family and church were believed to be in a state of dangerous decline, the functions of schooling had to be restructured radically in order to take up the slack. The scope of the curriculum needed to be broadened beyond the development of intelligence or mastery of the subjects of study to nothing less than the full scope of life activities, and the content of the curriculum had to be changed so that a taut connection could be maintained between what was taught in school and the adult activities that one would later be called upon to perform. Efficiency became more than a byword in the educational world; it became an urgent mission. That mission took the form of enjoining curriculum-makers to devise programs of study that prepared individuals specifically and directly for the role they would play as adult members of the social order. To go beyond what someone had to know in order to perform that role successfully was simply wasteful. Social utility became the supreme criterion against which the value of school studies was measured.

In a general sense, the advocates of social efficiency were educational reformers. The fact that their brand of reform differed dramatically from that of Hall's and was the virtual antithesis of Dewey's should not obscure the fact that the basic intention of social efficiency's proponents was to overthrow the established order in education as represented by the traditional humanist curriculum. Nor should one assume that the humanitarian impulse usually associated with reform was completely absent. That humanitarian impulse, reflected earlier in the work of Joseph Mayer Rice, expressed itself largely in a concern that the existing curriculum was of no interest and of no value to the new population then entering school, particularly secondary school. Beyond their interest in social stability, many leaders of the social efficiency movement indicated a genuine concern for the dissatisfaction that many children expressed about school and for the high rate of dropouts. In a curriculum tied to direct utility and to tangible, albeit remote, rewards lay the answer.

ii

The social theory that guided the development of social efficiency educators is probably best represented by the work of the renowned American sociologist Edward A. Ross. Ross was not a sociologist of education, but his social ideas, especially as expressed in the most famous of his many books, *Social Control* (1901), strongly influenced the work of such educational sociologists as David Snedden, Ross Finney, Charles Ellwood, and Charles C. Peters and they, in turn, devoted themselves to developing curricula consistent with Ross's ideas. By modern standards, Ross was more of a social philosopher than a sociologist, but in his own day, Ross's work had the full support of science. Ross himself had, early in his life, experienced disillusionment with speculative philosophy, particularly that of Hegel, and he thought of his own work as an effective counterpoint to the vagueness and imprecision of philosophical thinking.

Social Control had its inception in a series of twenty-seven articles that Ross wrote for the *American Journal of Sociology* in the 1890s. By the turn of the century, he had completed his editing of that work, and in 1901 it was published in book form. The book reveals Ross (1901) to be beset by a kind of intellectual schizophrenia. On the one hand, he could scarcely conceal his admiration for "the restless, striving, doing Aryan, with his personal ambition, his lust for power, his longing to wreak himself, his willingness to turn the world upside down to get the fame, or the fortune, or the woman he wants," especially when compared to "the docile Slav or the quiescent Hindoo" (p. 3). In many respects, Ross identified personally and intensely with "the dolichocephalic blonds of the West" (p. 3) and admired the rugged individualism he believed they personified.

On the other hand, he saw civilized society teetering on the edge of a precipice. Modern industrial society, which he generally equated with capitalism, had corrupted those instincts that had once been appropriate in the Teutonic forests, and so American individualism, "the product of the last, most Westerly decanting of the Germanic race" had to be curbed (p. 17). Ross generally rejected the idea of a natural law insuring progress, so prevalent in the work of Spencer, and urged massive intervention in the interest of preserving society. "*Society*," Ross fervently believed, "*is always in the presence of the enemy*," (p. 190), and *Social Control* is, in a significant sense, a compilation of the weapons of self-protection in the arsenal of society. So powerful were these weapons in his view that he was impelled to issue a warning at the end of his book:

> I confess that no light responsibility is laid upon the investigator who explores the mysterious processes that take place in the soul of a people, and dissects in public the ideals and affirmations elaborated in the social mind. The fact of control is, in good sooth, no gospel to be preached abroad with allegory and parable, with bold type and scare headlines. The secret of order is not to be bawled from every housetop. The wise sociologist will show religion a consideration it has rarely met with from the naturalist. He will venerate a moral system too much to uncover its nakedness. He will speak to men, not to youth. He will not tell the 'recruity,' the street Arab, or the Elmira inmate how he is managed. He will address himself to those who administer the moral capital of society— to teachers, clergymen, editors, law-makers, and judges, who wield the instruments of control; to poets artists, thinkers, and educators, who guide the human caravan across the waste. In this way he will make himself an accomplice of all good men for the undoing of all bad men. (p. 441)

The weapons of social control that Ross had amassed in his book were so powerful as to be dangerous in the hands of anyone but the most upright.

Education was one of the most effective of those weapons in society's arsenal, particularly in the light of the decline of other modes of social control. "Underneath the medley of systems," Ross observed," we find *an almost world-wide drift from religion toward education* as the method of indirect social restraint" (p. 176). Unfortunately, according to Ross, American schools had been infused with "an intellectual bias" and, while the development of the intellect was not "without a moral value," that bias had led American schools to "become less an instrument of social control than an aid to individual success" (p. 176). The crisis represented by modern capitalism, he felt, required that the schools adopt a much more direct and more pronounced social purpose.

The decline in the influence of the family was another factor to be taken into account in the design of a proper educational system, but Ross's interpretation of that phenomenon was not entirely consistent with that of other reformers of his time. For Dewey, for example, the fading of the influence of the family meant that the school should build a closer tie between home and school and that the teacher should assume something of the role of an ideal parent by introducing into the course of study those household occupations now lost in an industrial society, social occupations that had once had such great educational value. The diminishing of a beneficent and educative family influence was, for Dewey, a loss that the school somehow had to retrieve. Ross, on the other hand, happily welcomed the same phenomenon. The school in his view was actually in a better position than the family to instill "the habit of obedience to an external law" (p. 164). Anyone can be a parent, but the certification of teachers is a matter of state control. As a result, Ross explained:

> Another gain lies in the partial substitution of the teacher for the parent as the model upon which the child forms itself. Copy the child will, and the advantage of giving him his teacher instead of his father to imitate, is that the former is a picked person, while the latter is not. Childhood is, in fact, the heyday of personal influence. The position of the teacher gives him prestige, and the lad will take from him suggestions that the adult will accept only from rare and splendid personalities. The committing of education to superior persons lessens our dependence on magnetic men. (pp. 164–165)

Rather than decrying the loss of family influence, Ross obviously welcomed the opportunity to put the child in the hands of "picked" persons as one more way of curbing antisocial tendencies. Ross, of course, was not the first to think of schools as an instrument of social control. The general idea of shaping individuals through a system of schooling is at least as ancient as Plato. For Ross, however, the social control function was overwhelming and urgent. Although both Dewey and Ross drew implications for schooling from the same perceived social change, one saw the need to restore in a different setting certain valuable experiences, while the other saw an opportunity to exercise a direct and desirable form of social control. The contrast between these two interpretations is one indication that the relationship between social change and educational doctrine is not so much a direct consequence of the change itself as it is social change as filtered through the perceptions of powerful individuals and groups.

iii

Besides the direct and explicit social control that Ross envisioned, the other key ingredient in social efficiency as a curriculum movement was efficiency itself. Here the principal figure was Frederick Winslow Taylor, the so-called father of scientific management. Like Ross, Taylor did not concern himself directly with education, although, through his disciples in the educational world, his indirect influence was enormous. In fact, the field of curriculum as a distinct area of specialization within the educational world was born in what may be described as a veritable orgy of efficiency, and the aftereffects of that orgy have been felt throughout the twentieth century. The bureaucratization of the American educational enterprise would likely have occurred anyway, as it had already been under way for some time (Tyack, 1974). But it was aided immensely by the metaphors, procedures, and standards of excellence that were drawn from the scientific management movement.

The immediate aim of Taylor's system of scientific management of factories was increased production at lower costs, but beyond that economic purpose lay a penchant for order and regulation that was at least the equal of Ross's. Nor was a moral dimension lacking. In his first paper before the American Society of Mechanical Engineers, Taylor (1895), in making the case for a "piece-rate system," expressed concern for loafing on the job (what was then called "soldiering") and for the techniques that would ensure an honest day's work (p. 856). "If a man won't do what is right," he once said, "*make* him" (Copley, 1923, p. 183). Like Ross, Taylor

(1903) believed that certain natural tendencies in human beings, such as laziness, had to be curbed, but there was promise in the fact that the output of a "first-class man" was considerably greater, "two to four times," that of the average worker (p. 1365). The work of the first-class man, then, could be used as a standard for how quickly and how well a particular job was to be done (p. 1365). Once the standardization of the techniques of production had been achieved, the task of bringing the average worker up to the required level of work could be accomplished. In wage incentives, Taylor thought he had found the means that would, at one and the same time, be in the best interests of the worker and raise the production level of the average man to that of a first-class man. There were limits, of course, to the amount to be paid. "If over-paid," he warned, "many will work irregularly and tend to become more or less shiftless, extravagant, and dissipated" (p. 1346), but a carefully developed economic incentive could eliminate "systematic soldiering" (p. 1351) and bring higher production at lower cost.

By the time Taylor published his classic *Principles of Scientific Management* (1911), he was already widely recognized as the prophet of a new order in industrial society. The heart of scientific management lay in the careful specification of the task to be performed and the ordering of the elements of that task in the most efficient sequence. Taylor summarized the series of steps in this way :

> *First.* Find, say, 10 or 15 different men (preferably in as many separate establishments and different parts of the country) who are especially skilful in doing the particular work to be analyzed.
>
> *Second.* Study the exact series of elementary operations or motions which each of these men uses in doing the work which is being investigated, as well as the implements each man uses.
>
> *Third.* Study with a stop-watch the time required to make each of these elementary movements and then select the quickest way of doing each element of the work.
>
> *Fourth.* Eliminate all false movements, slow movements, and useless movements.
>
> *Fifth.* After doing away with all unnecessary movements, collect into one series the quickest and best movements as well as the best implements. (pp. 117–118)

The technique is probably best illustrated in Taylor's account of how his colleague, Frank B. Gilbreth, analyzed the "art of bricklaying" (p. 77). Every movement of expert bricklayers was analyzed, and, through the elimination of waste, a standard and carefully laid out sequence of movements toward the accomplishment of that standard was established. The key, really, to performing any complex task was to break it down into its most elementary components, each part so simple that it would not tax the ability of the worker, and, thereby, error would be reduced and production increased.

But apart from the mere increase in production, Taylor foresaw that once his system was adopted, a new era in labor relations would emerge. It was in this way that his humanitarian impulse was expressed. In testimony before a Special House of Representatives committee charged with investigating the Taylor system, Taylor argued that scientific management would bring about "the substitution of peace for war; the substitution of hearty brotherly cooperation for contention and strife; of both pulling hard in the same direction instead of pulling apart; of replacing suspicious watchfulness with mutual confidence; of becoming friends instead of enemies" (Taylor, 1912, p. 30). Here was the reformist's zeal that prompted Taylor in carrying through his mission to reconstruct American industry. His watchword was efficiency, but through efficiency, he was trying to achieve the higher purpose of a more orderly and less contentious society. It was a reform that political conservatives could easily embrace.

With the rage for efficiency in full swing by the second decade of the twentieth century, it was inevitable that criticism of the inefficiency of American schools, criticism initiated by Rice's muckraking journalism, should soon be heard. The application of Taylor's system of managing factories to the management of schools was the most immediate and most natural step. In time, however, the use of scientific management techniques went far beyond the application of Taylor's ideas to the administration of schools; it ultimately provided the language, and hence the conceptual apparatus, by which a new and powerful approach to curriculum development would be wrought. The route by which scientific management became the basis for an education doctrine is actually no mystery. Those educational leaders who forged the new doctrine made no secret of the source of their ideas, self-consciously and conspicuously following the principles of Taylorism in an effort to make the curriculum a direct and potent force in the lives of future citizens and, ultimately, an instrument for creating a stable and smoothly functioning society.

iv

No one epitomized the new breed of efficiency-minded educators more than John Franklin Bobbitt. In fact, his work represents in microcosm the development of a field of specialization within education, the field of curriculum. It is probably this identification of social efficiency with the emergence of the field itself that is a significant factor in the persistence of many of its most central ideas today in only a slightly modified form. Bobbitt was brought to the University of Chicago in 1909 by Charles H. Judd, a psychologist who had just been recruited from Yale to head the Department of Education. Judd himself was a major exponent of the scientific study of education, and he probably saw in the young Bobbitt a kindred spirit. In the following year, Bobbitt, now promoted from lecturer to instructor of school administration, introduced a course entitled, simply, Curriculum. In his third year, that course, apparently a great success, was expanded to include both the autumn and the winter quarters. By 1912, Bobbitt published his first significant article on curriculum, "The Elimination of Waste in Education," and his career as a curriculum leader was launched.

A major portion of Bobbitt's (1912) article was devoted to extolling the virtues of the school system that had been developed by Superintendent Willard Wirt in Gary, Indiana, a "city having been practically created by the United States Steel Corporation" (p. 259). Wirt had devised a system, popularly called the "platoon system," that was designed to increase efficiency in the use of space within a school building by shifting students from classrooms to other indoor space, such as the auditorium, and to the playground in a systematic fashion. Bobbitt was impressed by the fact that "the usual plant, if it is fully equipped is operated during school hours at about 50 per cent of efficiency," but that "the educational engineer at Gary was to formulate a plan of operating his plant during school hours at 100 per cent efficiency" (pp. 260–261). While the platoon system was clearly more managerial than curricular as an educational innovation, Bobbitt's use of such terms as "educational engineer" to refer to the superintendent of schools and "plant" to refer to the school was no mere decorative use of language; it had implications far broader than the pedestrian question of space utilization. Bobbitt provided the emerging curriculum field with the root metaphor on which a new and powerful theory of curriculum could be based.

In enumerating the four principles on which an efficient school would be based, Bobbitt's first three, such as optimal use of the school plant, were basically administrative. But in enunciating his fourth principle of scientific management applied to education, he extended the factory metaphor to the question of how a curriculum should be constructed:

> Work up the raw material into that finished product for which it is best adapted. Applied to education this means: Educate the individual according to his capabilities. This requires that the materials of the curriculum be sufficiently various to meet the needs of every class of individuals in the community; and that the course of training and study be sufficiently flexible that the individual can be given just the things that he needs. (Bobbitt, 1912, p. 269)

Individual variation in ability had, of course, been recognized well before Bobbitt's time, but Bobbitt was now asserting that the curriculum be carefully adapted to each "class of individuals" as part of the drive for the elimination of inefficiency in education. People, after all, should not be taught what they would never use. That would be a waste. In order to reduce waste, educators had to institute a process of scientific measurement leading to a prediction as to one's future role in life. That prediction would then become the basis of a differentiated curriculum. Within the framework of the new theory, "education according to need" was simply another way of saying "education according to predicted social and vocational role." Boys, for example, whose "needs" were different from girls in terms of such matters as vocation, recreation, and citizenship were to be given a different course of study from girls in these respects (p. 270). Future men and women were destined to perform different roles in society, and it was simply inefficient to train them in the same way. Bobbitt's concern for the "raw material" in the context of his theory was not so much a concern for individual well-being as it was part of an effort to eliminate waste in the curriculum and, by extension, in the social order generally. The doctrine of social efficiency held out the then very appealing prospect of scientifically attuning the curriculum to the requirements of the new industrial society.

V

One of the most tangible and far-reaching manifestations of the drive to create a more directly utilitarian curriculum had its inception in a resolution passed in 1905 by the Massachusetts Senate and House of Representatives creating what came to be known as the Douglas Commission. That resolution authorized Governor William L. Douglas to appoint the Commission on Industrial and Technical Education in order to investigate the needs of the state in various industries and to determine "how far the needs are met by existing institutions," as well as to "consider what new forms of educational effort may be advisable"(Massachusetts Commission, 1906, pp. 1–2). A social scientist, Dr. Susan M. Kingsbury, was appointed as "expert investigator," and within a year the commission issued its report based on twenty public hearings held in major cities around the state and on the testimony of 143 witnesses including manufacturers, farmers, representatives of labor unions, and school officials. The report indicated general agreement between the "broader-minded students of education" on the one hand and, on the other, those "men and women who have been brought into intimate contact with the harder side of life." The "old-fashioned" curriculum of Massachusetts's schools was perceived to be too far removed from the demands of life created by an industrial society and the answer lay in practical trade training (p. 4). The justifications for this solution were drawn, as would be expected, from the doctrines being so insistently espoused by the emergent reform interest groups of the time. From the developmentalists, there came the expressed concern for the "fullest development of the child" and from the social meliorists the idea that such education could be useful "in the reformation of wayward and vicious children at reform and truant schools" in much that same way "that it is being used to elevate the colored race in the south" (p. 4).

Most pervasive was the insistence that the schools undertake the task of preparation for earning a livelihood. The report indicated that at almost every hearing the commissioners were told that "the processes of manufacture and construction are made more difficult and more expensive by a lack of skilled workmen" (p. 4). In that regard, the commission chided the advocates of manual training for taking too narrow a view emphasizing its value as a "cultural subject a sort of mustard relish, an appetizer— to be conducted without reference to any industrial end" (p. 14). By contrast, the commission cited with approval the establishment of textile schools in Lowell in 1897, in New Bedford in 1899, and in Fall River in 1904 as affording the kind of education that would serve best both the citizens and the Commonwealth of Massachusetts. While the commission recognized that direct trade training was regarded with "suspicion and hostility of many of the labor unions of the State," on the grounds that the labor market was being expanded in order to lower wages, they felt those suspicions to be largely unwarranted (p. 6). Although the commission did not engage in the open and often vitriolic attacks on the academic curriculum that became common in the educational world in later years, their sympathies clearly lay with a new system of education tied to the "callings in life . . . professional, commercial, productive and domestic" (p. 14). In fact, as they viewed it, the decline of the apprenticeship system made such a change a social necessity. Whereas at one time, the report argued, the system of schooling and the institution of apprenticeship were kept in a kind of balance in terms of their influence on youth, that balance had now been destroyed to the point where a dangerous bias had been created with children and youth devoting their time almost exclusively to academic studies in school. That balance could be rectified by restructuring the curriculum in schools to include the functions once performed by the apprenticeship system. This was exactly the kind of argument that appealed to those leaders in American life who sought a restructuring of social institutions in line with what they saw as a major social transformation.

An important addendum to the main report was Kingsbury's "Report of the Sub-Committee on the Relation of Children to Industries," that focused on the 25,000 children between 14 and 16 who were not in school. After a detailed and considered attempt to survey a sample of these adolescents, Kingsbury found that five-sixths of them had not completed an eighth-grade education and that virtually none had ever attended high school. As Helen Todd, the factory inspector, was to find seven years later, it was not economic deprivation that was the principal cause of leaving school to work in factories. The chief blame for the unfortunate state of affairs that Kingsbury found lay in the "dissatisfaction" that children felt with their schoolwork and the fact that "the parent does not know where to find an occupation for his child" other than the unskilled labor available at the textile mills and other factories (Massachusetts Commission, 1906, p. 44). Moreover, with proper training, she argued, "our cloths can compete with the foreign market," and the state would prosper (p. 46). The chief obstacle to that prosperity as well as to the well-being of the child was a curriculum removed from any prospect of reward in occupational terms. Under those circumstances, neither the child nor the parent could see any point to continuing school much after the sixth grade.

Kingsbury's was a powerful and timely case. The issue of school leavers brought into focus elements from several reform streams and promised to become one of the most debated questions in twentieth-century education. But Kingsbury's temperate and balanced treatment of the issue left open the terms that would define that debate. The most powerful of these reform streams—social efficiency—soon moved to reconstruct the issue in its own terms. Three years after the Douglas Commission Report, Leonard Ayres (1909) published his enormously influential *Laggards in Our Schools*, one of the first avowedly "scientific" treatises in education. Ayres, who had once been superintendent of schools in Puerto Rico, had received a grant from the Russell Sage Foundation in 1907 to study the effects of retardation in schools. The term "retardation" did not have the psychological connotations it has today but was used simply to refer to the problem of children not making normal progress in schools. Ayres opened his report by alluding to the 1904 report of Superintendent William H. Maxwell of New York City indicating that 39 percent of the students in the elementary grades were too old for the grade they were in (pp. 1–3). The problem, as he saw it, was to discover why this situation existed and to suggest remedies that might correct it.

Ayres's study was conducted through the careful examination of school records, not through the observation of schools themselves as Rice's had been. The key to the problem, he believed, was that retardation represented a great loss in efficiency. Students who were supposed to be making their way smoothly through the grades were, in an alarming number of cases, taking twice as long to complete a grade as they should. The problem lay, of course, with the curriculum. *"These conditions,"* Ayres asserted with finality, *"mean that our courses of study as at present constituted are fitted not to the slow child or to the average child but to the unusually bright one"* (p. 5). In defining the problem in this way, he was sounding a theme that social efficiency reformers were to echo through most of the twentieth century: the "college-preparatory" curriculum that had held sway for so long needed to be replaced by a curriculum attuned to the needs of a new population and a new industrial order. As a result of an inefficient curriculum, Ayres pointed out, "in the country as a whole about one-sixth of all of the children are repeating and we are annually spending about $27,000,000 in this wasteful process of repetition in our cities alone" (p. 5). No well-run manufacturing establishment would tolerate such waste.

To correct this scandalous situation, Ayres developed his famous Index of Efficiency, which he applied to fifty-eight urban school systems. Given that index, the production metaphor applied to the curriculum could be used with ruthless precision. Ayres wanted to know, for example, the number of students who began each school year so that "the relation of the finished product to the raw material" could be computed. He sought to calculate the "conditions of maximum theoretical efficiency" in each grade so that the "relation of the actual plant in size to the theoretic requirements" could be determined. "Suppose," he argued, "we had a factory which instead of utilizing all its raw material (100 per cent) embodied only 50 per cent in its finished product" (p. 176). That factory would be even less than 50 percent efficient if it were also found that the "theoretical product" of the plant were higher. Using the Index of Efficiency, it was evident that the schools of the nation were even more inefficient than the raw data indicated (pp. 176–177). More importantly, the genuine issue of the appropriateness of the curriculum to the school population that the Douglas Commission raised had been reduced to a problem of simple efficiency and cost-effectiveness. The power and appeal of the factory metaphor applied to curriculum issues was all too painfully evident in the way Ayres reconstructed the problem, a power and an appeal that was to put the social efficiency interest group in a commanding political position in the decades ahead.

In the next few years, the notion that the problem of "retardation" was primarily a problem of curriculum inefficiency became a constantly recurring theme. It was so persistent, in fact, that one of the leaders of the social-efficiency movement, Charles A. Ellwood, a professor of sociology at the University of Missouri, complained, just six years after Ayres's report, that nearly everyone now seems "to think that the only way to remedy this evil is to make the curriculum of our public schools more 'attractive', so as to hold the child's interests longer." While "not opposed to the making of curricula attractive," Ellwood (1914) was more concerned with the loss of social control that the problem of "elimination" presented (p. 572). He was worried about the fact that children, under existing compulsory education laws, could simply "soldier" until they were fourteen and then leave school before their "efficiency as citizens" had been established. Since it was clear to Ellwood that "a *definite* sentence is the greatest of all impediments" in reforming delinquent children, why not impose on all the children of the nation an indefinite sentence of schooling? "If the indefinite period of detention in an industrial or reform school is good for the delinquent child," he insisted, "why is not an indefinite period of instruction and training in our public schools good for the normal child?" (pp. 574–575). In this way, schools would perform the "social service" for which they were intended, fitting the child to the demands of modern society. Even further, the schools, given enough time, could identify the feebleminded that the psychologist H. H. Goddard's investigations had dramatically brought to the fore, and appropriate action could be taken before they "are allowed to go out into life, [and] by the laws of heredity . . . inevitably pass on to future generations their defects and even diffuse them in the population as a whole" (p. 576). In this way, consistent with Ross's ideal of the school as a weapon of social control, the school could serve the social function it so long failed to perform. While Ellwood's recommendations never were implemented in the form he proposed, they illustrate that along with simple efficiency the other key element in the powerful social efficiency equation was social control. It was principally in terms of efficiency and control that the complex and critical issue of "retardation" and "elimination" and their relationship to curriculum were defined for at least a half century.

vi

Two closely interrelated movements in psychology lent vital support to the way proponents of social efficiency defined the key curriculum issues that were to emerge in the twentieth century. One was the development of a psychological theory to replace the moribund faculty psychology, one which fit in neatly with the basic presuppositions of social efficiency; and the other was the mental measurement movement that provided the technology necessary for the kind of assessment and prediction that a curriculum based on social efficiency doctrine required. These two movements, both flowering in the first quarter of the twentieth century, in effect, created a new psychology, one so widely accepted that it inevitably placed the social efficiency interest group in a dominant, though not supreme, position vis-à-vis the others.

One of the most critical points in the development of a new psychology consistent with the emerging ideas of the scientific curriculum makers centered on the psychological concept that is conventionally called "transfer of training." It is universally assumed that what one learns in school somehow carries over to situations different from that particular time and that particular setting, but the process by which that transfer takes place was and remains a subject of great debate. It is, in a sense, part and parcel of what we call learning, and without a plausible account of how we learn, no curriculum theory could really gain widespread acceptance. James had in 1890 fired one of the first salvos at the mental-disciplinarian notion of transfer when he reported that his experiments on memory had failed to show any improvement in what mental disciplinarians had imagined to be a discrete faculty of memory. If memory could not be improved by memorizing, then it could hardly be justified as a pervasive school activity, since much of what was being memorized was hardly worth committing to memory in the first place and would most likely be forgotten in any event.

By the early twentieth century, experimentation to discredit the mental disciplinarian concept of transfer became almost a cottage industry (Rugg, 1916), and leading the way was James's brilliant and illustrious student, Edward Lee Thorndike. (After studying at Harvard, Thorndike pursued graduate work in psychology at Columbia University.) Thorndike had been brought to Teachers College, Columbia University, by Dean James Earl Russell as part of what turned out to be a successful effort to build the pre-eminent institution for the study of education. Thorndike's first major foray into the intricacies of the problem of transfer was a series of experiments he conducted with his student R. S. Woodworth that were published under the general heading, "The Influence of Improvement in One Mental Function Upon the Efficiency of Other Functions" (Thorndike and Woodworth, 1901). In a variety of mental operations, such as estimating the areas of rectangles, subjects were given intensive training until they achieved a high degree of proficiency. Then they were given a similar task, such as estimating the areas of figures of the same size but of different shapes, and the amount of transfer from one learning task to the other was calculated. This was repeated with such other tasks as estimating the lengths of lines or the weights of objects. The effectiveness of the special training in the learned task was not at issue, but only the extent to which learning that task carried over to a similar one. Thorndike's conclusion based on these experiments was devastating to commonly held beliefs about transfer: "Improvement in any single mental function need not improve the ability in functions commonly called by the same name. It may injure it" (p. 250). In a major book published a dozen years later, Thorndike (1913) extended that conclusion to cast doubt on even the existence of such mental operations as memory, perception, reasoning, and observation. They were, in effect, fictions and should be discarded along with a lot of other conceptual baggage left around by faculty psychologists (pp. 363–365). But without those concepts the whole value of general education was cast into doubt.

In place of a concept of mind comprising a limited number of discrete faculties, Thorndike and other psychologists in the early twentieth century sought to construct something more consistent with their experimental evidence. The mind that Thorndike envisioned was a machine in which there were thousands—millions—of individual connections, each one bearing a message having little in common with the next. The mind in his view consisted not of large capacities such as memory and reasoning waiting there to be developed, but of "multitudinous separate individual functions" (Thorndike and Woodworth, 1901, p. 249), a kind of switchboard with innumerable wires (bonds) connecting discrete points.

As if this were not enough, Thorndike conducted an experiment two decades later that was even more unsettling to traditional curriculum beliefs. This time it was the value of particular school subjects that was called into question. Between 1922 and 1923, Thorndike administered two forms of the same intelligence test to 8,564 high school students. To the extent possible, he then divided that population according to groupings of subjects they had studied over the course of that year. Once he had corrected for such factors as initial ability and special training, the value of these courses of study in raising intelligence levels could then be computed. We would then know how much better Latin or mathematics was in raising general intelligence than, say, domestic science. Thorndike's (1924) conclusion in this study amounted to another bombshell: "We find notable differences in gain in ability to think as measured by these tests, but they do not seem to be due to what one studies. . . . Those who have the most to begin with gain the most during the year. Whatever studies they take will seem to produce large gains in intellect" (pp. 94–95). There may be some question as to whether Thorndike was warranted in drawing such sweeping conclusions on the basis of this study as well as his 1901 experiments, but the ready inference that curriculum makers drew was that improving intelligence—in effect, teaching students to think through a course of study designed for that purpose—was a pipe dream. What really mattered was native intelligence.

By 1924, Thorndike's attacks on mental-disciplinarian concepts already had a sympathetic audience. Not only was mental discipline dead as a formal theory, but the new scientific curriculum makers, such as Bobbitt and Charters, were developing a theory of curriculum entirely consistent with the concept of mind inherent in the new psychology. If transfer from one task to another was much less than had been commonly believed, then the curriculum had to be so designed as to teach people specifically and directly those exact skills required for the tasks that lay before them in life. Gilbreth's atomization of the "art of bricklaying," Thorndike's image of the mind as consisting of innumerable tiny functions, and Bobbitt's scientific curriculum drawn from a laborious analysis of the multitudinous tasks that comprise human life were all of one conceptual piece.

So was the companion movement in psychology that was to affect the curriculum of American schools profoundly, the calibration of intelligence into minute units—IQ points. The sources of mental testing lie in the efforts of Francis Galton in England to trace the components of genius as well as the experimental laboratories established in Germany by Wilhelm Wundt, but most directly to the work of Alfred Binet, who was charged by the French Ministry of Education to find a way of identifying those French schoolchildren who needed special education. The simple scale of tasks he developed in that regard underwent a kind of sea change once they were transported to American shores. In the hands of psychologists such as H. H. Goodard, Lewis H. Terman, R. M. Yerkes, and Edward L. Thorndike, that scale became not just a diagnostic device, but a powerful tool by which society could be regulated (Gould, 1981).

As Ross had foreseen, a vital force in the creation of such a stable and orderly society was a system of schools dedicated to that purpose, including, most specifically, a curriculum tied to the destined roles that future citizens were to perform. Since future citizens were to perform different and complementary tasks, a differentiated curriculum was needed in line with the determination of native capacities that a scientific system of mental measurement would provide. In particular, secondary education would be that period when the differentiation should be the sharpest. In fact, the creation of a new educational institution, the junior high school, was given special impetus by the perceived need to "explore" children's needs and capacities before entering upon the high school period.

Thorndike (1906) himself was unequivocal on the need for differentiation in the high school curriculum. "The problem before the high school," he declared, "is to give the boys and girls from fourteen on who most deserve education beyond a common school course such a training as will make them contribute most to the true happiness of the world" (p. 180). That task required exactly the kind of "prognostication" that Hall had earlier proposed and that Eliot, in his defense of the Committee of Ten Report, had so vehemently opposed. Thorndike was in absolute agreement with his fellow psychologist, Hall, that "no high school is successful which does not have in mind definitely the work in life its students will have to perform, and try to fit them for it" (p. 180). The majority of students entering high school, he felt, were not "efficient at dealing with *ideas*, but whose talent is for the manipulation of *things*" (p. 181), making them more suited for cooking than for writing compositions or performing experiments. Moreover, in a modern industrial society, schools had to supply the knowledge that once was the province of other institutions. "The time has passed," Thorndike affirmed, "when the rule of thumb was enough for the building trades; when science was a luxury to the farmer, when old wives' lore passed on from mother to daughter was the best available education for housewifery and motherhood" (p. 181). He went on to estimate that not more than a third of the secondary student population should study algebra and geometry since, in the first place, they were not suited for those subjects and, in the second, they could occupy their time much more efficiently by studying those subjects that would fit them more directly for what their lives had in store. The curriculum for the new education needed to be expanded far beyond the traditional subjects that the Committee of Ten had recommended just a few years before, and curriculum differentiation became a necessary concomitant to that expansion. In the drive to implement such a reform, the mental-measurement movement performed a vital legitimating function.

At the same time that psychologists were shaping a new psychology consistent with the emerging field of curriculum, those sociologists of education who had embraced the social efficiency ideal were not only endorsing the scientific work of their colleagues in psychology, but elaborating the social theory that was to guide the curriculum changes they sought. Ross Finney, for example, an influential professor of sociology at the University of Minnesota, saw clear implications for how the curriculum should be organized from the experience gained from the Army Alpha mass testing. What angered Finney (1928) was the persistence of the "rise-out-of-your-class" philosophy of society that continued to dominate educational policy in the face of conclusive evidence that "the great majority are *predestined* never to rise at all" (p. 180). From Plato to Charles Horton Cooley, Finney felt, social theorists were continuing to make the mistake of assuming that people actually can be taught to recognize or somehow to "discern the one man in the right" when establishing a good society (p. 385). Fortunately that question had been unequivocally settled. "And now come forward the psychologists," Finney announced, "with scientific data for headlining what we all knew before, namely, that half the people have brains of just average quality or less, of whom a very considerable percentage have very poor brains indeed" (p. 386). In spite of that evidence, the mistaken notion persisted that the school's function was to teach people to think, a position he attributed (correctly) to James Harvey Robinson and "Doctor" John Dewey. "But this solution," Finney pointed out, "will hardly bear inspection. In the first place, the barber's IQ is only .78, according to the army tests. IQs below .99+ are not likely to secrete cogitations of any great social fruitfulness" (p. 388). His solution was to teach that half of the population without the power to "secrete cogitations" to follow dutifully what those who have that power tell them to do. In fact, in curriculum terms, he envisioned one curriculum for leadership and another for "followership" designed for that purpose. Finney's is one case in point among many of how the concept of IQ and mental measurement generally fit perfectly into the idea of a curriculum tied to the particular qualities of the "raw material," rather than assuming anything like the ability to think across the entire student population.

Probably the most prolific of the new breed of educational sociologists was David Snedden. Snedden first came under Ross's influence while an undergraduate at Stanford University beginning in 1895. After completing a doctorate at Teachers College, Columbia University, he became an adjunct professor of education there. Later as commissioner of education in Massachusetts, he was in a position to help guide the course of American education, especially in his efforts to enlarge the scope of vocational education and to create a socially efficient curriculum generally. It was in his period as commissioner that he appointed two men who were to put their own marks on the future course of the curriculum in the United States.

Snedden chose his former student Charles Prosser as deputy commissioner for vocational education. Prosser, over his long career, became the pivotal figure in the development of vocational education in the United States and emerged after World War II as instrumental in the ill-fated life-adjustment movement. His second appointment, in 1912, was Clarence Kingsley, a high school teacher from Brooklyn, New York, as his assistant in secondary education. Six years later, Kingsley was to engineer, almost single-handedly, the Cardinal Principles Report, a major landmark in secondary education in the United States. In 1916, Snedden returned to Teachers College to accept a professorship in educational sociology and thus was able to point that fledgling discipline in the direction of his master, Ross. For the next two decades, Snedden was a central figure in a group of educational sociologists that included Ross Finney, C. C. Peters, and Charles Ellwood.

In terms of his ideas on the curriculum, Snedden was in agreement on almost every detail with the preeminent scientific curriculum makers such as Bobbitt and W. W. Charters, but he had a much grander and more explicit social vision. Writing in 1921, Snedden (1921) predicted that "by 1925, it can confidently be hoped, the minds which direct education will have detached from the entanglements of our contemporary civilization a thousand definite educational objectives, the realization of which will have demonstrable worth to our society" (p. 79). Snedden (1923) recognized, however, that it was not necessary nor was it even desirable for all persons to achieve all the objectives that had been so determined. Objectives had to be set in relation to what he called "case groups," defined as "any considerable groups of persons who in large degree resemble each other in common possession of qualities significant to their school education" (p. 290). Like his contemporaries, Snedden felt that the junior high school period was where "differences of abilities, of extra-school conditions and of prospects will acutely manifest themselves, forcing us to differentiate curricula in more ways, probably, than are as yet suspected" (Snedden, 1924, p. 740), and thus the creation of case groups was particularly germane to that institution.

The curriculum itself would be built of "peths," tiny units of which a single spelling word would be an example (Snedden, 1925, p. 262). Persisting in his penchant for neologisms, Snedden then proposed that peths be organized into "strands," built around "adult life performance practices," such as "health conservation through habitual safeguarding practices," for which something like 50 to 100 peths would serve. A strand for anything as simple as becoming a streetcar motorman would require only 10 to 20 peths, but to produce a good farmer or a good homemaker, anywhere from 200 to 500 peths would have to be assembled (pp. 288–289). Snedden (1924) also created the " 'lotment' . . . the amount of work that can be accomplished, or the ground considered, by learners of modal characteristics (as related to the activity covered) in 60 clock hours" (p. 741). Snedden's vision of a school and its curriculum was almost a caricature of Taylor's vision of a factory and the manufacturing process, virtually replete with the stopwatch that had become a symbol of industrial efficiency.

But Snedden's penchant for quaint terminology should not obscure the fact that he was representing what amounted to the dominant curriculum ideology of his day. When in 1923–1924, for example, George S. Counts (1926) conducted his study of high school curricula, the wide acceptance of different curricula for different segments of the high school population was clearly evident. He reported eighteen different curricula in Los Angeles secondary schools and fifteen in Newton, Massachusetts (p. 13). In the same year, Robert and Helen Lynd's (1929) Middletown High School offered no fewer than twelve different courses of study (p. 192).

Snedden's protégé, Clarence Kingsley, the mathematics teacher from Brooklyn, was the man who, in 1918, produced the document that proved to be the capstone of the quarter century of furious efforts at curriculum reform that began with the Committee of Ten Report. The Report of the Commission on the Reorganization of Secondary Education or, as it has been popularly called, the Cardinal Principles Report (National Education Association, 1918) met with almost universal approbation when it was issued, and, unlike Eliot's Committee of Ten Report (which had by this time fallen into widespread disfavor) continues to be cited as embodying the highest wisdom in curriculum matters. It was perhaps inevitable, given the intense and largely successful efforts at curriculum reform since 1893, that some form of repudiation of Eliot's report should be forthcoming and that it should reflect the growing belligerence toward academic subjects through the ascendance of social efficiency in the educational world. Given the pervasiveness of that doctrine and the calls for a radical transformation of the curriculum, Kingsley's report was rather moderate. By far, the most prominent portion of the thirty-two page report was the statement of the seven aims that would guide the curriculum: 1. Health, 2. Command of fundamental processes, 3. Worthy home-membership, 4. Vocation, 5. Citizenship, 6. Worthy use of leisure, and 7. Ethical character (pp. 10–11). With the possible exception of the second, these aims each represented an area of life activity, and the curriculum was directed toward efficient performance within that area. Thus would a much closer connection be maintained between education and the actual activities that people are called upon to perform in their daily lives. Unlike the Committee of Ten report, where the four programs of study represented the heart of the recommendations, the Cardinal Principles Report centered on something beyond the curriculum itself. The curriculum became the instrument through which the aims were to be achieved.

Although a significant shift in emphasis, this represented a rather temperate stance, given the pedagogical climate of the times. Social efficiency proponents such as Bobbitt, Charters, and Snedden were calling for the elimination of the conventional subjects in favor of subjects that were themselves areas of living such as citizenship and leisure. Kingsley, however, did not call for the elimination of history and English—only that they reorient themselves toward the achievement of at least one, and preferably several, of the seven aims. Snedden (1919), Kingsley's erstwhile mentor, decrying the fact that vocation appeared lost amid the full list of seven aims, declared the report to be "almost hopelessly academic" (p. 522) and accused the commission of being "chiefly preoccupied with the liberal education of youth" (p. 526).

Neither did the report go as far as Snedden would have liked in the direction of differentiated curricula. Although the report refers to "curriculums," there was more than a passing reference to the need in a democracy for the school to perform a unifying function through common experiences in school, including during the high school period (National Education Association, 1918, pp. 22–23). In that regard, the commission was unequivocal in its support of the comprehensive high school, a position that in 1918 was being widely debated, with social efficiency educators leading the way in calling for different forms of secondary education for different kinds of youth. As a whole, however, the report reflected with reasonable accuracy the winds of change that had swept the educational world in the previous quarter century. So widely accepted were Kingsley's recommendations that 1918 may be regarded as the year when the humanist position reflected in Eliot's Committee of Ten report was forced to go on the defensive, no longer playing the dominant role it once did in the battle for the American curriculum.

v i i

By 1918, social efficiency as a curriculum theory was almost at its zenith, and attention to curriculum reform had reached the point where curriculum was being recognized as a vital subspecialty within the broader spectrum of education. One sign of the new status accorded the curriculum was the publication of the first modern book devoted exclusively to that topic, a book entitled, simply, *The Curriculum*. In it, Bobbitt (1918) summarized the state of the art up to that point. He also provided what was probably the most concise and, at the same time, most explicit definition of the theory that he and his fellow social efficiency educators were advocating:

> The central theory is simple. Human life, however varied, consists in the performance of specific activities. Education that prepares for life is one that prepares definitely and adequately for these specific activities. However numerous and diverse they may be for any social class, they can be discovered. This requires only that one go out into the world of affairs and discover the particulars of which these affairs consist. These will show the abilities, attitudes, habits, appreciations, and forms of knowledge that men need. These will be the objectives of the curriculum. They will be numerous, definite, and particularized. The curriculum will then be that series of experiences children and youth must have by way of attaining those objectives. (p. 42)

Almost every sentence in Bobbitt's summary of the theory marked off a vital facet of what was the ascendant mode of thinking about the curriculum in the twentieth century. There was, first, its simplicity. Compared to Dewey's conceptually complex version of recapitulation or the mystical romanticism of Hall's culture-epochs, simplicity itself must have had a tremendous appeal. That simplicity was expressed largely in a conception of curriculum planning that could be reduced to a series of steps, an idea perfectly consistent with Taylorism and one that has maintained its appeal even to the present. There was also the appeal to specificity, an ideal drawn from scientific management as well as Thorndike's connectionism, and, in the minds of many, from science itself. Imbedded in Bobbitt's description of the essentials of the theory was the mechanism by which the curriculum would actually be constructed, a mechanism that Bobbitt was convinced was "a scientific technique" (p. 42). Activity analysis or, as it was sometimes called, job analysis, consisted of a procedure whereby one first created an inventory of the "particulars" that comprised human life. These were the things that people in fact did, and those things would be converted into curricular objectives. The next step was simply to create that "series of experiences" that would most efficiently achieve each objective. What Bobbitt was proposing was essentially that Gilbreth's technique for analyzing bricklaying be applied, not simply to "vocational labors" as in the case of scientific management, but to all the activities in which human beings engage, to "their civic activities; their health activities; their recreations; their language; their parental, religious, and general social activities." The scope of the curriculum would be nothing less than "the mosaic of full-formed human life" (p. 43).

Bobbitt recognized that the total range of human activity was so vast that no curriculum could encompass it all, but he found a solution to that problem in the idea of "directed and undirected experiences" (p. 43). Some objectives, Bobbitt asserted, may be "attained without conscious effort" and although the "curriculum-discoverer" must be aware of these as well, "he will be content to let as much as possible be taken care of through undirected experiences." Fortunately, the schools did not have to teach everything. Some things are simply learned through a natural process of socialization. "*The curriculum of schools,*" Bobbitt emphasized, "*will aim at those objectives that are not sufficiently attained as a result of the general undirected experience*" (p. 44). Those abilities not so attained Bobbitt called *shortcomings*, that is, the deficits that people exhibited once the full range of activities had been discovered. (*Shortcomings* is the counterpart of the contemporary concept of "needs" in curriculum construction.) He cited approvingly, for example, the research that his like-minded contemporary W. W. Charters had conducted in discovering the errors made by Kansas City children in both oral and written language. Each of the noted errors in grammar, once classified by type, constituted a shortcoming that had to be addressed. "Only as we list the errors and shortcomings of human performance in each of the fields," Bobbitt concluded, "can we know what to include and to emphasize in the directed curriculum of the schools" (p. 52).

Neither Bobbitt nor Charters gave extensive attention to the implications of their conception of curriculum to larger social questions or to the role of the school in relation to social progress. In the main, they saw themselves simply as bringing the light of science to a field that had been governed by drift, tradition, and fruitless speculation. In *The Curriculum*, for example, Bobbitt seems to have seen the relationship between social progress and what is taught in schools almost exclusively in terms of instrumental efficiency. "As agencies of social progress," he maintained, "schools should give efficient service. And efficient service, we are now-a-days coming to know, is service directed, not by guess or whim or special self-interest, but by science" (p. 69). Schools, in other words, were charged with providing society with what it needed as determined by scientific analysis.

Their own perceptions notwithstanding, there was a highly significant social dimension to the work of the scientific curriculum makers. This is perhaps best illustrated in some of the work of Charters. Charters, even more than Bobbitt, devoted himself to the actual task of activity analysis in a variety of fields. Most of his influential research was related to various occupational roles such as librarian and veterinarian, applying Gilbreth's bricklayer analysis to many other fields as a basis for vocational training in those fields. His *Analysis of Secretarial Duties and Traits* (with I. B. Whitley, 1924), for example, became a classic in the area of business education. But it was when he turned to the more general activities that human beings engage in that some of the techniques that seemed so plausible in a vocational context began to exhibit strong social overtones and where some weaknesses were exposed.

Around 1920, Charters was asked by Stephens College in Columbia, Missouri, a private women's college, to devise a new curriculum. It seemed clear to Charters that the job of being a woman was of the same order as any other job, requiring the same techniques of curriculum development that he had employed in relation to other occupational roles. Charters (1921) took the occasion of his first report on that curriculum to reaffirm the urgency with which he viewed the matter of curriculum reform. "The curriculum situation has become acute," he began. "The masses who send their children to school are growing restive under what they consider to be the useless material taught in the grades" (p. 224). One of the main missions that social efficiency reformers set for themselves was that of replacing what was useless and merely symbolic in the curriculum with what was directly useful. According to Charters (1926a), this involved a combination of an analysis of the activities that human beings engage in along with a determination of the ideals that would control those activities. In accordance with one of the most central principles of social efficiency, he believed that "we should define curriculum on the basis of what people are going to do" (p. 327). Just as we would not provide the same education to a prospective doctor as to a prospective engineer, we should not prescribe the same education for women as for men. As Bobbitt had discovered, men and women were destined to do different things. In order to secure a scientific inventory of women's activities, Charters solicited from the women themselves a statement of what they did during the course of one week. In all, an incredible 95,000 replies were received, and the activities were initially broken down into about 7,300 categories. These were then further divided into categories such as food, clothing, and health, and these categories, in effect, became the subjects in the curriculum. Attention was given to those activities that were characteristic of "homemakers" as opposed to "unmarried women," with only those categories shared by both groups destined to become the required subjects. The study of clothing would be required of all women, but an "appreciation of art . . . would be purely elective," even though the study seemed to point to the conclusion that "the aesthetic is sufficiently prominent among women to presume that they may get greater appreciation from these than from other subjects" (p. 329). Unlike someone like Hall, who would consider interest to be a crucial criterion in determining a curriculum, the social efficiency educators were primarily concerned with efficient performance in a future social role, and using that criterion, aesthetics hardly mattered. In considering a curriculum for homemakers in particular, Charters (1926b) decided to present a list of forty-eight traits to a group of 3,440 judges who were asked to rate them as 1) most important, 2) neither unusually important nor unimportant, and 3) least important (p. 680). When these rankings were subjected to statistical treatment, it was discovered that Care of Health (e.g., "She plans her family's diet to meet their physical needs" (p. 676)) ranked first, and Honesty (e.g., "She shows no deceit in handling of the family finances" (p. 678)) and Love (e.g., "She has an ideal of love and expresses this love for her husband, children, and home" (p. 678)) were tied for second. Ranking last was Philanthropy (e.g., "She is engaged in some organized club work that has a philanthropic purpose" (p. 679)). Such a trait study would be used, according to Charters, to build a curriculum, first, by infusing some attention to these traits in "every subject taught" and, second, by directly training women to secure these traits when an individual profile chart "showed them to be weak in some of them" (p. 684).

As Charters's efforts to create a curriculum for women indicate, scientific curriculum making almost inevitably was tied, first of all, to the social status quo, with the activities that people already were engaging in serving as the norm for what people ought to do, even when, as he never tired of saying, those activities would have to be "idealized" before they could serve as legitimate objectives in a course of study. The curriculum lacked any utopian component, social progress being seen in terms of simply performing more efficiently what one would do anyway. Little or no attention was given to the potential for social change having the effect of transforming the nature and scope of those activities. Second, despite the persistent invocation of science in the interest of a curriculum tied to direct utility, the technique of activity analysis almost inevitably resorted in the end to consensus. Whatever may have been the scientific procedure used to create the list of activities or traits originally, they were incapable of standing on their own as elements in the curriculum without the intervention of human judgment.

This was the case, for example, in Bobbitt's celebrated Los Angeles school survey, a study that culminated in his most influential book, *How to Make a Curriculum*. Although Bobbitt (1924) insisted that the method of activity analysis required that "at all stages of the analyses, attention should be fixed up on the *actual activities of mankind*" (p. 9), the list of curricular objectives he presented in the book represented not direct observation of actual activities but "the practically unanimous judgment of some twenty-seven hundred well-trained and experienced adults" and even, in a few cases, "only majority approval" (p. 10). In point of fact, Bobbitt arrived in Los Angeles with a long list of objectives that his graduate students at the University of Chicago had prepared and then presented them for approval by the Los Angeles teachers (Bobbitt, 1922, pp. 4–5).

Whatever may have been the practical difficulties of activity analysis, one persistent legacy of the scientific curriculum makers is the continued insistence upon stating precise and definite curricular objectives in advance of any educational activity. This is, of course, an argument by analogy from the world of manufacture where, at least according to Taylor, precise specifications and standards had to be established in advance in order to achieve the desired product with maximum efficiency. "The first step in curriculum-making," Bobbitt (1924) asserted, "is to decide what specific educational results are to be produced" (p. 32), and the fact that his injunction became a vital ingredient in the predominant approach to curriculum planning in the twentieth century is testimony to the success of the overall position he represented. The idea of stating numerous, precise, and definite objectives, by contrast, never seems to have arisen in the work of Harris, Hall, or Dewey.

Moreover, the scientific curriculum makers' conception of education as preparation for what lies ahead has become thoroughly infused into contemporary educational thought. As Bobbitt pointed out, "Education is primarily for adult life, not for child life. Its fundamental responsibility is to prepare for the fifty years of adulthood, not for the twenty years of childhood and youth" (p. 8). Dewey (1916a), on the other hand, regarded his own position as one that "contrasts sharply" with any doctrine based on education as preparation. He objected to placing children on a "waiting list," a kind of "probation for another life" (p. 63). That kind of education, he insisted, has no motive power and puts "a premium . . . on shillyshallying and procrastination" instead of capitalizing on the natural powers of attention and energy that children bring with them to school (pp. 63–64). In the end, he claimed, "the principle of preparation makes necessary recourse on a large scale to the use of adventitious motives of pleasure and pain" just because a remote future has no power to direct children's energies. It has cut itself off, he claimed, from the "possibilities of the present" (p. 64). Resorting to a system of education based on preparation also, in Dewey's view, subverted the ethical force of education. "Who can reckon up the loss of moral power," Dewey (1909) once said, "that arises from the constant impression that nothing is worth doing in itself, but only as a preparation for something else, which in turn is only a getting ready for some genuinely serious end beyond?" (pp. 25–26).

Profound differences of the sort that existed between the social efficiency educators and Dewey on such a fundamental matter as whether education should be seen as a form of preparation or not signifies not a single reform thrust aimed at dislodging the old order in education, but several. And, insofar as the effect on actual school practice is concerned, the prominence and persistence of the basic ideas of the scientific curriculum-makers indicates that someone like the relatively obscure Bobbitt may have been far more in touch with the true temper of his times than the world-renowned Dewey.

5 | SOME SUBJECT REALIGNMENT AND THE TRIUMPH OF VOCATIONALISM

i

IT WAS PERHAPS BECAUSE HE SENSED THE DANGER OF A MASSIVE TRANS-formation of the traditional school subjects that Eliot (1908), in a startling, almost inexplicable, repudiation of his long-standing position declared that "teachers of the elementary schools ought to sort the pupils and sort them by their evident or probable destinies" (pp. 12–13). There was, he even emphasized, "no function more important" (p. 12). Alluding to the issue of manual training, Eliot agreed that it had been "rightly introduced" and that it was "a very useful element in the curriculum," but he urged that trade schools should be added that were distinctly preparatory for "a life of skilled manual labor" (pp. 10–11). Without equivocation, the architect of the Committee of Ten report was rejecting one of the committee's most critical recommendations and accepting Hall's stand that the curriculum should be tied to the probable destination of students (and even extending it to the elementary school level), a position he had passionately rejected only three years before (Eliot, 1905). If the humanist values he cherished could not be instilled in the entire school population, as Eliot would have undoubtedly preferred, they could at least be preserved in that segment whose "destiny" it was to go on to college. Without that compromise, it must have seemed conceivable, at least in the context of educational reform during the first decade of the twentieth century, that humanist values might be eradicated altogether from the American school curriculum. Curriculum makers and leaders in the professional education community more and more saw the temper of American life in the early twentieth century and, to some extent, mass public education itself as inconsistent with humanist values and traditions, and this perception served to isolate the humanist tradition from the mainstream of American educational policy making. With the tide of educational change running against them, humanists seemed to be reaching an undeclared détente with the social-efficiency educators, whereby the traditional academic curriculum would be preserved, but only in connection with a select portion of the school population, increasingly defined as "college-entrance" students.

As America moved toward the second quarter of the twentieth century, educational leaders became increasingly strident in their denunciations of the schools for their failure to change their curricula in line with the new ideas reformers like David Snedden and Charles Prosser were espousing. Despite the vigorous efforts of extremist social efficiency educators, many traditional subjects somehow managed to survive. Whatever had been the high hopes of those educational reformers who wanted to wipe the curricular slate clean, they were almost bound to fall short simply because the nature of the reforms proposed were often so far-reaching. Snedden's dream of replacing subjects with peths and strands as the building blocks of the curriculum remained unrealized. But sometimes lost in the disappointment over the seemingly slow pace of curricular change was the fact that reformers had in the century's first two decades also achieved a few notable, even astounding, successes in the direction of the social efficiency ideal.

There had, after all, been a whole new institution created, the junior high school, and with the influx of mental testing into the schools on a mass scale after World War I, that institution could devote itself to determining the true nature of the "raw material," leaving the high school free to provide the differentiated curriculum that the social efficiency reformers so insistently demanded. One of the candidates for the honor of being the first junior high school in America, for example, was the school built in 1910 during the superintendency of Frank F. Bunker in Berkeley, California. Bunker (1916) unabashedly drew from Ayres's research on "laggards" and "retardation" as well as from similar studies by other educational leaders such as Thorndike. The curriculum he reported for that school reflected precisely the vocational orientation that the social efficiency leaders argued would eliminate the waste accruing from the failure of many students to proceed expeditiously through the grades. Much of the rationale for the new institution had also been built around putative evidence brought forward by the developmentalists to the effect that preadolescents were best kept separate from older, postpubescent students. The large-scale incorporation of the junior high school into the American educational ladder is one instance where the success of an important innovation benefited by the fact that the ideas of two or more powerful interest groups intersected at that point.

A second indication of some success was that many of the traditional school subjects, although not being cast out of the curriculum as the more extreme social efficiency reformers demanded, were quietly transforming themselves in line with the new utilitarian curricula. History, for example, was being challenged by other social studies, some of which were aimed directly at the development of efficient citizenship (Sivertson, 1972). Even when the name of a subject like history remained intact, the subject itself frequently took on a new character consistent with the demands of the citizenship aim as the Cardinal Principles Report had recommended (Lybarger, 1981). With concern about an undesirable class of immigrants on the rise, it was to the schools generally and to the social studies in particular that American leaders turned as the most efficacious way of introducing American institutions and inculcating American norms and values.

A pivotal figure in the reconstruction of the social studies along directly functional lines was the director of the department of research for the Hampton Institute, Thomas Jesse Jones. Jones installed a new social studies at Hampton that was designed to equip America's underclass with the skills that would bring it to the level of the white middle class. The prevailing rationale at Hampton and many other educational institutions designed specifically for blacks and Native Americans was that while those races were not inherently inferior, they were in an earlier stage of development than the white race. By designing the program of studies so as to introduce the more advanced white social institutions and social practices to the less advanced races, their progress toward a state of civilization could be speeded up. As Jones (1908) put it, "Because the Negro and Indian races have not had time to develop, they are not equal to certain other races; with time to develop, they may become the equals of other races" (p. 5).

The course in economics at Hampton, for example, was a direct attempt to get African Americans and Native Americans to abandon certain undesirable practices in specific areas of practical concern such as the purchase of clothing and the consumption of food. Emphasis was given to the "Negro's preference for ham instead of beef, for fats and sweets instead of the more nutritive foods, for fancy and brilliantly colored garments instead of the more substantially made clothes" (p. 12). In these respects, the "uneducated Indian was said to be even more reckless than the Negro" (p. 13). Efforts were made to inculcate the habit of saving because "saving results in capital which can be used both to increase the income of the individual and to assist in the general welfare of the community" and to introduce students to various forms of savings institutions (p. 14). "The study of economics," Jones reported, "reminds the pupil of social gradations based on wealth, and enlightens him as to some of the individual characteristics and social forces that have brought about these gradations and that will enable him to pass from one grade to another" (p. 40).

When it came to the study of sociology, Jones emphasized that "possibly the most impressive contributions in the sociological course at Hampton is the realization of the truth that beyond differences in physique, in economic possessions, and in literacy, there are other vital differences in the dispositions, in the mental characteristics, and in the social organizations of races" (p. 40). Census reports were studied in order to point up differences among the races in such areas as marriage relations, occupations, and crime. By studying the actual census figures in these matters, the students at Hampton would learn not to be influenced by data that are "exaggerated and distorted by the inflamed imagination of some 'social reform' novelist" (p. 40). Other topics included comparisons of Negro and white birth and death rates with special emphasis on the responsibility to give "careful consideration" to "economic outlook" before undertaking to have children (p. 42). Social studies at Hampton Institute was obviously designed to have a directly beneficial effect on the lives of its students through the development of what were deemed to be socially desirable habits and ideals, and as early as the turn of the century, the program at Hampton was attracting national and largely favorable attention (Shaw, 1900).

It should not be surprising, therefore, that Jones, as the guiding force behind such widely acclaimed reforms, should be appointed by the National Education Association to head the subcommittee on social studies of the Commission on the Reorganization of Secondary Education. When the preliminary reports of the various subject subcommittees were issued, it was clear that the recommendations for the reconstruction of the social studies would follow the lines that Jones had pursued at Hampton. "Good citizenship," the report declared, "should be the aim of social studies in the high school," and this meant that "facts, conditions, theories, and activities that do not contribute rather directly to the appreciation of methods of human betterment have no claim" (National Education Association, 1916, pp. 16–17). With a passion rarely seen in government reports, Jones sought to redirect the old academic study of history toward the production of good citizens through such new forms of social studies as community civics, to be "offered to the pupil as early as his powers of appreciation allow" (p. 18). Within a short time, the effort to reshape the social studies in line with the citizenship aim mushroomed in terms of scope and intensity (Sivertson, 1972), with civic virtues being defined largely in terms of "obedience, helpfulness, courtesy, punctuality and the like" (National Education Association, 1915, p. 36). When the report of the commission's Committee on Social Studies was issued, it included a direct endorsement of the social studies program at Hampton Institute, declaring that it could find "no better illustration" of its recommendation for the schools of the nation than could be found there (National Education Association, 1916, pp. 53–56). Given the almost obsessive concern with social disintegration and an erosion of traditional American values, it is not surprising that a curriculum originally developed for a social underclass should eventually emerge as a model for the majority of America's schoolchildren.

Other subjects were also undergoing internal transformations. The teaching of reading, for example, the heart of the elementary school curriculum, became increasingly dominated by a torrent of scientific studies of word frequency such as Thorndike's *The Teacher's Word Book* (1921) and by efforts generally to base reading instruction on scientifically determined findings (Gray, 1925). Similar efforts were also carried forward in the area of arithmetic that included systematic testing of persons in various occupations for the purpose of setting curricular standards based on commercial uses (Courtis, 1913). In this way, the scientific curriculum makers' ideal of an array of school subjects keyed to objectively determined demands of modern life was gradually approaching realization.

ii

The most dramatic and, in the long run, the most far-reaching of the successful curricular innovations was vocational education. In 1893, the Committee of Ten had excluded vocational education entirely from its four model programs of study. Given their basic mental-disciplinarian orientation, the members of the committee simply did not deem vocational training a fit subject for a school curriculum, even one, as they saw it, that was designed for "life" as opposed to college entrance. But by 1917, vocational education came to be regarded as such an urgent necessity as to require major federal aid. The significance of the success of vocational education was not simply that a new subject had been added, nor that a major new curricular option had been created, but that many existing subjects, particularly at the secondary level, were becoming infused with criteria drawn from vocational education. This became evident in the increasing popularity of such courses as business mathematics and business English as legitimate substitutes for traditional forms of those subjects. In very visible ways, the whole curriculum for all but the college bound was becoming vocationalized. Superintendent Bunker (1916), for example, pointed with pride to the emphasis being given practical subjects in the new junior high school.

Deliberate efforts to introduce an element of practicality into the traditional humanist curriculum in the United States go back at least as far as the late eighteenth century with the founding of Benjamin Franklin's academy and were even reflected in the controversy leading to the Yale report of 1828. One of the most successful of these efforts was the one by farm and manufacturing groups to enact the Land Grant College (Morrill) Act. When it was finally passed and then signed by President Abraham Lincoln in 1862, this act led, eventually, to the founding of a number of colleges devoted to including the practical arts such as mechanics and agriculture in their curricula. The dominant form of secondary education in the nineteenth century, the academy, had a distinctly practical orientation (Sizer, 1964) and, in general, schools in the nineteenth century were continually preaching the virtues of hard work and the dangers of sloth as part of moral training, reflecting a tradition of some relationship, however ill-defined, between work and school. In addition, as America's industrialization continued into the later nineteenth century, so did the effort to provide an improved professional education especially for engineers, as represented by the creation of Rensselaer Polytechnic Institute, organized around a European model, and the infusion of engineering into the curriculum of the U. S. Military Academy at West Point.

But of all these portents of a drive for a practical curriculum, especially one tied to occupational competence, the most immediate and significant precursor to the emergence of vocational education as a potent force in the American curriculum was the manual-training movement. Manual training, actually, was tied in its very early years to the training of engineers. Under the leadership of John O. Runkle, president of the Massachusetts Institute of Technology and a professor of mathematics, and Calvin M. Woodward, dean of O'Fallon Polytechnic Institute at Washington University in St. Louis, the manual-training movement met with almost unprecedented success. Early in their careers, both Runkle and Woodward had devoted themselves to reforming the professional education of engineers, especially by seeking to infuse into their training a more practical knowledge of tools and basic mechanics than was typical for that period. A turning point in that effort came when Runkle and some of his colleagues attended the Russian exhibit at the Philadelphia Centennial Exposition in 1876. Runkle was enormously impressed with the fact that Victor Della Vos of the Imperial Technical School at St. Petersburg had developed a series of graded exercises designed to teach the very skills that Runkle had thought were so lacking in the education of engineers in the United States. Practical skills, in other words, could be arranged into an orderly sequence, a curriculum that could be taught in schools. Runkle's admiration for that training was such that he soon extended his proposals for the Russian system beyond the professional training of engineers to public education generally. The new programs he envisioned would be as applicable to future mechanics as to engineers.

Woodward's enthusiasm for the new manual training was no less ardent. In 1879, Woodward opened the Manual Training School of Washington University with a three-year program for boys between the ages of fourteen and eighteen. According to Woodward (1885), the curriculum of the school was designed "to foster a higher appreciation of the value and dignity of intelligent labor, and the worth and respectability of intelligent laboring men" (p. 623), not for specific trade training. As his work with the school evolved and as the school gained national visibility, his emphasis tended to waver between the relatively narrow aim of improving preprofessional training for engineers and the much grander vision of reconstructing the curriculum of the public schools in such a way as to redress the imbalance between the essentially literary, humanist curriculum and the handwork that was a mark of modern life. Although he strongly maintained that manual training should be seen in terms of "a wholesome intellectual culture" (Woodward, 1887, p. 245), he also emphasized the "honor and comfort" of work as mechanics, engineers, or manufacturers in contrast to those who "eke out a scanty subsistence as clerks, book-keepers, salesmen, poor lawyers, murderous doctors, whining preachers, penny-a-liners, or hardened 'school-keepers'" (p. 172). For Woodward, manual training was essential not only for proper intellectual and moral education but as a way of restoring the dignity of hand labor, an avenue for youth to a respectable and rewarding occupation, and a way to make the country prosper. In short, manual training was being advertised in terms that all the reform groups of the period could easily embrace.

As a publicist for the new education, Woodward was unsurpassed. Whether by instinct or calculation, he recognized that the power of the humanists was still too strong in the late nineteenth century to be vulnerable to a frontal attack. "It is scarcely necessary," he declared in 1885, "to add that the 'New' education includes the 'Old.' We tear down no essential parts of the old temple" (p. 614). What he proposed instead was that education add two "wings" to the edifice. One was the wing of natural science, which the humanist curriculum had undervalued; the other, of course, was manual training, which completes the old education by introducing "an education through the senses of touch and sight, through the hand and the eye" (p. 614). Unlike Hall's, for example, Woodward's (1890) reforms were represented as a relatively minor adjustment that would painlessly bring traditional education in line with the demands of modern society. He was even able to promote his innovation in mental-disciplinarian terms, arguing that "manual training is particularly strong in furnishing the knowledge and experience, in establishing the major premises essential to logical reasoning" (p. 204). That was an argument of considerable appeal to someone like Nicholas Murray Butler, president of the New York College for the Training of Teachers (later Teachers College). "Manual training is mental training through the hand and eye," said Butler (1888), "just as the study of history is mental training through the memory and other powers" (p. 379).

But with claims of such scope, it was almost inevitable that a few objections should be heard. William Torrey Harris (1889), for example, speaking for the Committee on Pedagogics of the National Education Association found it necessary to "insist that manual training ought not to be begun before the completion of the twelfth year of the pupil, nor before he has had such school instruction in the intellectual branches of school-work, namely, in reading, writing, arithmetic, geography, grammar, and history" (Brown, Hoose, Parr & Harris, 1889, p. 417). Harris was not one to surrender the primacy of his "windows of the soul" without a fight. He claimed that the early imposition of manual training on children could not be accomplished "without dwarfing their human nature, physically, intellectually, and morally, and producing arrested development" (p. 418). Harris (1889) was ready to accept the case for the intellectual value of the study of science but not manual training. "While the student is learning a method of doing something his brain is exercised" he said; "when the process has become a habit it is committed to his hand, and his intellect is not required again except for new combinations" (p. 95). He was thus denying the intellectual value of manual training that its major proponents persistently claimed, but the voice of "the great conservator" was increasingly a lonely one, especially on that subject.

While the nationally known proponents of manual training such as Woodward and Butler preferred to advance their cause in terms of intellectual development, it was the potential for a practical and especially an occupational payoff that school administrators found most appealing. One early debate over manual training's practical value followed in the wake of the founding in 1867 of a manual training school for African Americans and Native Americans in Hampton, Virginia, by Samuel Chapman Armstrong, the superintendent of the Freedmen's Bureau. Like Woodward, Armstrong, the son of missionaries in Hawaii, maintained that the "training of the hand is at the same time a discipline of the mind and will" (Peabody, 1918, p. xv). He exalted labor for African Americans, particularly menial labor, by both men and women. In the dignity of labor and the Puritan ethic, Armstrong saw the salvation of the race from poverty and degradation. Armstrong's disciple, Booker T. Washington (1905), sought to instill a similar ethos in his Tuskegee Normal Institute, founded in Alabama in 1881. Through manual training, the "downtrodden child of ignorance, shiftlessness, and moral weakness" would be converted into a "thoroughly rounded man of prudence, foresight, responsibility, and financial independence" (p. 7).

The practical value of training in menial labor did not go unchallenged. W. E. B. Du Bois, for example, the first black man to be awarded a Ph. D. from Harvard University, argued that the sort of hand labor being promoted at Tuskegee was essentially an anachronism in modern industrial society and that blacks were being denied the intellectual training and professional skills that a twentieth-century economy demanded and therefore being denied a chance at true equality. Moreover, as early as 1902, Du Bois (1902) had pointed out that the range of "callings" was so great that, even if trade schools were to be made much more efficient, they could not serve their intended purpose. "The factory system," he pointed out, "with its minutely developed division of labor . . . renders it absolutely essential that the apprentice should learn his trade in the factory." The second major problem he cited was "the strong opposition of trade unions to Negro labor in all lines save those where the Negro already has a foot-hold." Beyond these questions of the efficacy of manual training, Du Bois raised some broadly philosophical questions:

> Industrial schools must beware placing undue emphasis on the "practical" character of their work. All true learning of the head or hand is practical in the sense of being applicable to life. But the best learning is more than merely practical since it seeks to apply itself, not simply to present modes of living, but to a larger, broader life which lives to-day, perhaps, in theory only, but may come to realization to-morrow by the help of educated and good men. . . . The ideals of education, whether men are taught to teach or to plow, to weave or to write must not be allowed to sink to sordid utilitarianism. Education must keep broad ideals before it, and never forget that it is dealing with Souls and not with Dollars. (p. 81)

Thus, in the context of the education of African Americans, were the practical and moral virtues associated with manual training being questioned, even as that training was being extended to the public schools generally.

But whatever may have been the high-minded justifications for manual training that advocates like Woodward put forward or the principled objections that detractors like Harris and Du Bois raised, its implementation at the school level was largely a combination of trade training and the standard academic curriculum of the day. Some school systems managed to combine these elements for a time, but, for the most part, when local school groups debated proposals for the introduction of manual training in major cities such as Boston and Milwaukee, those debates were framed largely in terms of economic benefits to the boy or girl receiving the training or to the overall economy of the municipality. Although the debates at the local levels were also infused with a concern for the immigrant poor or for the inadequacy of the existing curriculum in terms of holding the children of the masses in school, it was through trade training that this was to be accomplished, not "mental training through the hand," as Butler preferred to define it. Butler's characterization gave it a legitimacy in the councils of the National Education Association and among leaders in education generally, but rarely was manual training so regarded in terms of school practice. One probable side effect of that characterization, however, was to avoid so sharp a differentiation in curriculum as to exclude academic subjects, such as foreign languages, science, and higher-level mathematics, from the early manual training programs. The programs of manual training and industrial education developed in the early years of the manual-training movement, such as those in Fitchburg, Massachusetts, and Milwaukee, Wisconsin, exhibited a rigor and even a high status rarely evident after the vocational education movement was in full swing. In many cases, for example, those early programs were designed to meet college entrance requirements and did not, therefore, represent an educational dead end. The earliest effects on the curriculum of the manual-training movement were primarily in terms of grafting on instruction in areas like drafting and mechanics to what was already in place, rather than transforming the curriculum entirely for a target population (Ringel, 1980; Kean, 1983).

iii

Even in the face of reluctance on the part of educational leaders to accept a definition that equated manual training with direct trade training in the nineteenth century, the movement toward specific vocational education proceeded apace once the new century began. In the long run it was the direct benefits of occupational skills rather than the remote values associated with completing a liberal education by educating through the hand that had the greater appeal. That appeal, in fact, was so great that the major impetus for vocational education began to shift from the relatively obscure journals of education and other professional forums to the larger social and political arena. One turning point was the founding in 1896 of the

National Association of Manufacturers (NAM), which from the outset made school policy a centerpiece of its deliberations. Of particular concern to the association was competition for world markets from Germany. Germany's system of separate and specialized technical schools was held in such high esteem that, one year after its founding, the NAM's annual convention adopted a resolution declaring that since technical education was so critical in the development of industry, its members should support "manual training or other technical schools" ("Resolutions," 1897, p. 92).

In his presidential address of 1898, Theodore C. Search (1898) again emphasized the example of Germany's success in industry and manufacture, attributing that success to its system of technical schools and citing the fact that England was following Germany's example. In the competition for foreign trade, he felt, America's failure to take into account "the obvious demands of industry and commerce" in its educational system put it at an obvious disadvantage. That disadvantage could be redressed by "the establishment of educational institutions which would give us skilled hands and trained minds for the conduct of our industries and our commerce" (p. 22). By 1905, a year before the Douglas Commission report, the NAM's Committee on Industrial Education had picked up the theme of an American school curriculum that was failing the large majority of the schools' students. The report cited alarming statistics on the dropout rate:

> Eighty percent of our public school pupils drop out of the schools before attaining to the high school, and 97 percent of all our public school pupils, from the primary grades to the high schools, drop out before graduation from the high school. Out of 16,225,093 pupils enrolled in the schools of the whole country only 165,000 are students in the colleges or high schools; only one in one hundred has the benefit of a higher training. ("Report," 1905, p. 142)

The report went on to allude to the decline of the apprenticeship system and the failure of manual training to fill the gap in industrial skill development created by that decline. Again, the answer lay in the creation of "trade schools in which the youth of our land may be taught the practical and technical knowledge of a trade," a matter that the report characterized as "the most important issue before the American people to-day" (p. 143).

In subsequent years, the NAM, through its Standing Committee on Industrial Education, never wavered in its continuing effort to redirect

American education toward the system so admired in Germany. The Philadelphia Board of Education, for example, came in for special commendation at the 1907 NAM meeting for being the first to establish a trade school as part of its public school system, as did the State of Wisconsin, which was singled out as the first state to enact a law creating a system of trade schools ("Industrial," 1907, p. 122). Reflecting a now familiar theme, the committee's 1912 report accused the American school system of a distinct literary bias which resulted in a curriculum directed toward "abstract-minded and imaginative children, who learn readily from the printed page" (p. 156) and ignoring the majority who are not so blessed.

Again borrowing from the German system, the association endorsed part-time continuation schools for youth between sixteen and eighteen who were not in school. They recommended a minimum of five hours a week of instruction for such students, as was the case in Wisconsin, and urged employers to pay students their regular salaries for that time. Needless to say, the continuation school should be infused with instruction related to industrial occupations, although continued education for citizenship ought not to be neglected ("Industrial," 1912, pp. 159–160). In general, the curriculum for boys would consist of such courses as mechanical drawing, machine shop, and carpentry and, for girls, dressmaking, millinery, and domestic science.

The response on the part of organized labor to the challenge of vocational skill training in the public schools and to its unqualified support by the NAM was equivocal. The American Federation of Labor (AFL), which was undergoing a period of tremendous growth just after the turn of the century, appointed a committee on education in 1903, but no clear-cut stand emanated from that committee nor from the AFL generally, reflecting uncertainty and conflicting views on educational policy. Dissension emerged as to the extent to which unions should run their own schools as well as to whether the institution of apprenticeship should actually be abandoned. For Samuel Gompers, who by now was the acknowledged leader of organized labor, the ideal solution lay in the creation of schools by the labor unions themselves that would serve in place of the old apprenticeship system. A lack of enthusiasm on the part of the rank and file, however, proved troublesome. The introduction of the Linotype into the printing trade in 1890, for example, represented one opportunity to retrain workers by labor itself, especially in view of the cooperation of one Linotype company. The New York local, however, decided in favor of setting up one more committee to study the matter rather than establishing its own programs for retraining workers. Even when other printing locals developed their own programs and the international union had set up a correspondence course in 1907, there was little support on the part of the workers themselves (Fisher, 1967). Setting up a union-sponsored system was an expensive and risky undertaking. As a result, no concerted opposition emerged from organized labor to the stream of NAM pronouncements on the importance of vocational education.

The course that organized labor was eventually to follow in this matter was foreshadowed by their ready participation in the organization that became the principal lobby group for vocational education, the National Society for the Promotion of Industrial Education. The idea of a national organization to promote industrial education emerged at a meeting called by two prominent educators, James P. Haney, director of manual training at Teachers College, Columbia University, and Charles R. Richards, director of arts and manual training in the New York City public school system. Meeting at the Engineer's Club in New York in 1906, the invited group decided to see whether a new organization could be formed that would represent the combined interests of business, labor, and professional educators. Almost immediately, that organization struck responsive chords in many quarters. On May 24, 1907, for example, President Theodore Roosevelt wrote to the president of the new society, Henry S. Pritchett, that the American school system had been "well-nigh wholly lacking on the side of industrial training, of the training which fits a man for the shop and the farm. . . . We of the United States must develop a system under which each individual citizen shall be trained so as to be effective individually as an economic unit, and fit to be organized with his fellows so that he and they can work in efficient fashion together" (Roosevelt, 1907, p. 6).

Although the prospects seemed exciting, the exact direction that the new organization would follow was not clear from the outset. The early debates reflected some uncertainty as to the respective forms that vocational education should take. Some discussion seemed to indicate a desire to revivify the apprenticeship system with the actual work site becoming the setting where the trade training took place (Deems, 1908) The president of one large Connecticut firm declared his general support for industrial education, but thought on-site training to be indispensable. "We must take the boys that go into our shops and educate them for our particular work," he declared, "The schools cannot do this" (Bullard, 1909, p. 51). On the other hand, one study of the shoe industry indicated that workers were reluctant to lose time teaching apprentices and that learning a new job was unpopular among workers because it frequently meant a reduction in their productive labor and therefore in their earnings (Dean, 1908). Frequently, the German model of continuation schools was represented as an ideal combination of factory- and school-based instruction.

Within a few years of the society's founding, a consensus began to emerge in the organization to the effect that the most appropriate course was direct trade training in the public schools. A word of caution, however, was expressed by Dewey's friend, Jane Addams (1907), head of Hull House in Chicago. Although she had a year earlier idealized the German model of industrial education as one not so much designed to advance industrial development as to promote "human welfare," she now expressed distinct reservations about the emphasis on direct trade training. Industrial education in public schools, Addams (1908) thought, should aim at educating youth "to live intelligently in an industrial community" (p. 95) and not at specific trade training. Alluding to the way modern industry had, through its high degree of specialization, transformed the nature of work, she declared that "it would be a very brave person who would now assert that the worker enjoys such a life" (p. 96). Addams confessed to being "confused" by some proponents of vocational education who were alluding to modern industrial conditions making extensive trade training obsolete, while others pointed to a revival of the apprenticeship system within the factories themselves (pp. 40–42). By this time, however, the momentum in the direction of school-based trade training was far too strong to be denied. Organized labor was suspicious of skill training in factories under the aegis of the manufacturers themselves, yet labor was unable to mobilize its own alternative. Trade training in the public schools seemed to be the most acceptable option. Gompers personally endorsed that policy in 1910.

Another question to be resolved was the role of vocational education for women. Within a year after its formation, the National Society for the Promotion of Industrial Education appointed a subcommittee on industrial education for women, with Jane Addams and Susan Kingsbury among its members. Their report, issued in 1907, was careful to point out that women had always worked, and that, therefore, the working woman should not be taken to be "a peculiar feature of modern times, an interloper as it were, usurping a place which does not rightly belong to her" (Marshall, 1907, p. 6). One major thrust of the report appeared to be an effort to head off any possible attempt to define vocational education for women strictly in terms of domestic science. Another theme, continually being raised by Addams, was related to the changing nature of work brought about by the division of labor. "The tendency to divide and subdivide every operation," the report said," mean[s] that girls can go to work at a very early age, at the same time learning only one minute part of their work and having no chance to see its relation to any other part. Thus they find their progress retarded and growth and development impossible" (pp. 12–13). In this vein the report called for more study, not just in terms of the effect on industry, but on the women themselves, before a suitable form of training be introduced.

Some of the discussions on vocational education for women were tinged with allusions to women's rights. In one address delivered in 1910, a representative of the National Women's Trade Union League indicated that some forms of trade training were depriving women of their "breadwinning capacity":

> There is an agricultural school in one of our Eastern cities, where the girls and boys are taught the possibilities of bread winning as agricultural laborers, agriculturists, gardeners, florists, or whatever you will. When it comes to the boy, he learns the chemistry of the soil, and gets down to the fundamental things in those particulars, but the girl is taught cooking and sewing. I am not saying that cooking and sewing are not necessary, but when we cheat a girl out of the training she ought to have for her bread winning capacity, and substitute something which has nothing to do with the trade she is trying to learn, then we make a great and grave mistake. (Robins, 1910, p. 78)

She concluded her address by underscoring the "need of teaching the girl the value of her labor power" and improving the conditions of laboring women (p. 81). Another speaker at the same meeting in Milwaukee, the president of the Young Women's Christian Association from Hamilton, Ontario, in making the case for a more effective program in homemaking, argued that too much attention was being given to cooking. "I think that is one very clear evidence of man's hand in our educational organization, because he has provided more liberally for cooking lessons than for any other branch of industrial education for girls" (Hoodless, 1910, p. 181). Her address ended with a call to women to participate fully in developing educational programs for women (p. 184).

iv

By the second decade of the century, the main issue before the National Society for the Promotion of Industrial Education was not the form that industrial education should take but how it should be controlled. There were initial efforts in the period around 1910 and 1911 to work with individual states in improving their systems of trade training, but the possibility of developing a unified policy through massive federal intervention soon proved to be an irresistible prospect. By 1911, a bill had been proposed by Senator Carroll S. Page of Vermont to provide federal funds in the area of industrial education, one of a series of such measures going back to the Davis Bill in 1907. Snedden (1912) took the lead in arguing for the efficacy of federal legislation in the area, although he felt that states and local communities should contribute as well (p. 128). He also held out the intriguing prospect that the National Society for the Promotion of Industrial Education could help administer the federal legislation once it was enacted. In fact, Snedden as commissioner of education in Massachusetts and Prosser as his deputy commissioner and new secretary of the society worked closely with Senator Page in framing the legislation (Page, 1912, p. 118). Similar legislation involving agricultural education, the Smith-Lever Bill, was a complicating factor. Both bills were passed and then died when a joint conference committee could not reconcile the two bills, but the Smith-Lever Bill was later reintroduced and signed into law in 1914.

It took more modification to shepherd vocational education through Congress successfully. Alongside the drive for industrial education, a parallel drive among agricultural interests had been emerging since the nineteenth century. Although prompted by almost opposing impulses—one to preserve the virtues of agrarian life and the other to bring the country in line with the new industrial age—the destinies of the two movements were to be eventually intertwined in the Smith-Hughes Act of 1917, as they had been earlier in another major piece of federal legislation involving higher education, the Morrill Act of 1862. One of the most effective campaigns to incorporate agricultural work into elementary and secondary schools had its origins in the work of Liberty Hyde Bailey, who, as a professor in the College of Agriculture at Cornell University, sought to introduce nature study in rural schools. Like the original manual training movement, Bailey's emphasis was not on earning a livelihood, and even the introduction of scientific methods of farming was not for him a paramount concern. Rather, he preached a reverence for the soil and for farm life, a way of life that he saw as in danger of disappearing. Although he favored introducing agriculture into the school curriculum, Bailey (1908) was concerned about the possible detracting effect it would have on the spiritual values that would be derived from nature study.

As early as 1894, Bailey was able to obtain funds from the New York State legislature and soon his work was being disseminated to rural schools throughout the state. Within a decade, some three thousand teachers were receiving instructional material from Bailey. When a Rochester, New York, seed dealer offered seed packets for sale at one cent per packet, schoolchildren purchased eleven thousand of those packets within two weeks (Keppel, 1960, p. 67). Whatever may have been the high romanticism implicit in Bailey's campaign, it struck a responsive chord among those who felt threatened by the intrusion of the new industrial society. Very similar crusades emphasizing the virtues of rural living were undertaken at the same time by "Uncle Henry" Wallace, the editor of *Wallace's Farmer* and William Dempster Hoard, editor of *Hoard's Dairyman*. Hoard, in particular, sought to rally farmers to make rural schools more attuned to the agricultural community.

The National Society for the Promotion of Industrial Education appeared almost oblivious to the popularity these movements enjoyed in the farming community, but Congress was not. Somehow, the increasingly insistent demands for industrial skill training in the public schools had to be balanced against the still potent demands of rural leaders for the preservation of their way of life. Once again Congress found it expedient to link the needs of industry and agriculture under the general aegis of the national interest. The national interest in the case of agriculture was usually expressed in terms of improved methods of farming, such as in the Hatch Act of 1882 when agricultural stations had been set up for the purpose of disseminating the results of agricultural experimentation. When President Woodrow Wilson appointed a commission in 1914 to study the question of federal aid to vocational education, the joining of industrial trade training with farmer's interests was almost a political necessity. Indeed, when the commission reported, the two main recommendations treated the claims of the two groups together. One recommendation called for federal support for the training of teachers in trade and industrial as well as agricultural and home economics subjects, and the other provided funds for paying teachers in those areas. With President Wilson's strong endorsement, the measure finally passed less than two months before America's entry into World War I.

By 1917, the main direction of vocational education was sealed—job skill training in the public schools supported generously by the federal government. The National Society for the Promotion of Industrial Education, now the National Society for Vocational Education, had succeeded in mounting a drive for federal intervention that gave even further impetus to a movement that had already achieved high visibility. When the executive staff was appointed to administer the new law, it was natural for Prosser to be its director, with other members of the organization serving as members. With money, powerful lobbying groups, energetic leadership in high places, and a sympathetic public, vocational education was well on its way to becoming the most successful curricular innovation of the twentieth century. While some compromises were necessary, the appeal of the social efficiency interest group was clearly reaching its peak.

V

Three years before the actual passage of the Smith-Hughes Act, a bitter debate erupted over the direction that the new vocational education was taking. While that dispute had no dramatic effect on pending legislation, it illustrates that beneath the mainstream of social efficiency ideology, there existed a small undercurrent of opposition. Writing in the first volume of *New Republic*, Dewey (1914) took the occasion of the appointment by Congress of a Commission on National Aid to Vocational Education to denounce in uncharacteristically harsh language the nature of the proposals that had been emanating from the supporters of the legislation.

In an apparent reference to the continuing admiration for the German system of education that had flowed from the pronouncements of the NAM, Dewey (1914) cast doubt on its appropriateness as a model for American education. The German educational system, he pointed out, "has been frankly nationalistic." Its actual effect on the well-being of workers had been negligible, Dewey argued. Statistics indicated that skilled workers in Germany received virtually the same salary as unskilled workers. In Germany, he maintained, the "well being of the state as a moral entity is supreme" and the "promotion of commerce against international competitors is one of the chief means of fostering the state." The system of education that had been developed in Germany was openly and directly "a means to this means," which as a model of educational policy he described as "extraordinarily irrelevant to American conditions" (p. 11).

Dewey applauded the efforts in cities like Chicago, Gary, and Cincinnati to adapt instruction in order to keep children in school longer, but this effort, he insisted, should take the form of "making their instruction significant to them" and not "to turn schools into preliminary factories supported at public expense" (p. 12). Throughout his article, Dewey used the term "industrial education" rather than "vocational education." Although these terms were often used interchangeably, Dewey undoubtedly used "industrial education" to indicate that in his view the introduction of such study ought to have a much broader purpose than simply trade training. Consistent with the reservations expressed earlier by Addams, he pointed out that narrow forms of skill training might not even serve the intended purpose since "automatic machinery is constantly invading the province of specially trained skill of hand and eye." Dewey deplored the fact that there were no educators appointed to the new commission since he regarded the issue to be "primarily an educational one and not a business and technical one as in Germany" (p. 12). He took as his example of the "wrong kind" of legislation a new law in Indiana, which, in setting up the continuation schools that the NAM had advocated, provided state funds only if the instruction "deals with the subject matter of the day employment" and where that purpose was extended even to regular schools (Dewey, 1915b, p. 71). Such a narrow interpretation of industrial education he described as "theory run mad" (p. 72).

Snedden (1915), who, along with Prosser, had emerged as one of the twin stalwarts of the trade-training movement, seemed genuinely surprised and dismayed by Dewey's direct attack. Indicating that he had grown accustomed to attacks by educational "reactionaries," he nevertheless found Dewey's criticism to be "discouraging" (p. 40). He found it "incredible" that the cause of vocational education be regarded as "beneficial chiefly to employers" and argued that "greater productive capacity" would ultimately be shared by the laborer (pp. 41–42). He went on to argue that the question of whether vocational education should be part of the general system of education in a state or administered as a separate system, as in the case of Wisconsin, was "merely one of securing the greatest efficiency" (p. 42). Dewey's reply to Snedden did not minimize the extent of their differences.

Dewey (1915a) characterized Snedden's position as "the identification of education with acquisition of specialized skill in the management of machines at the expense of an industrial intelligence based on science and a knowledge of social problems and conditions" (p. 42). He alluded to Snedden's support of the Cooley Bill, which had been introduced in the Illinois legislature in 1913. Drafted by the former superintendent of schools of Chicago, this bill would have provide a dual system of education, one general and the other vocational. That, Dewey felt, would result in a typically "bookish" education for one group and narrow trade training for the other. Dewey concluded his reply by emphasizing that his difference of opinion with Snedden was "not so much narrowly educational as it is profoundly political and social. The kind of vocational education in which I am interested," Dewey insisted, "is not one which will 'adapt' workers to the existing industrial regime; I am not sufficiently in love with the regime for that" (p. 42). In a period when vocational education was going virtually unchallenged, even by organized labor, Dewey had emerged as its most ardent and perhaps even its most vocal opponent.

Dewey's *Democracy and Education* (1916a) appeared while the drive for direct trade training in the schools was already at its height. Alluding to other untenable dualisms—theory and practice, body and mind, mental states and the world—Dewey argued that much of the confusion over vocational education was derived from an unwarranted opposition between labor and leisure. This led, he believed, to singling out the one aspect of a person's life that distinguishes him from others and to ignore those shared with others. In the effort to prepare someone for earning a livelihood, the most significant features of one's education can easily be neglected. Typically, Dewey tried to take terms like "occupation" and "vocation" and redefine them in his own terms:

> The only adequate training *for* occupations is training *through* occupations. The principle . . . that the educative process is its own end, and that the only sufficient preparation for later responsibilities come by

making the most of immediately present life, applies in full force to the vocational phases of education. The dominant vocation of all human beings at all times is living—intellectual and moral growth. In childhood and youth, with their relative freedom from economic stress, this fact is naked and unconcealed. To predetermine some future occupation for which education is to be a strict preparation is to injure the possibilities of present development. (pp. 362–363)

Dewey was thus trying to superimpose his own broad conception of an occupation, "a continuous activity having a purpose" (p. 361), on the common use of the term, a ploy that probably led to further misinterpretation of his position. One thing he was clear on, however, was that current trends in vocational education could easily lead it to become "an instrument in accomplishing the feudal dogma of social predestination" (p. 372). Speaking to a meeting of the Public Education Association on the eve of President Wilson's signing of the Smith-Hughes Act, Dewey (1917) argued that the bill "settles no problem; it merely symbolizes the inauguration of a conflict between irreconcilably opposed educational and industrial ideals" (p. 335). In an apparent allusion to the original manual training position, Dewey held that vocational education conceived as a part of "a liberal education and generous education already supposed to exist" to be "pure romance" (p. 332). The key issue was whose interests would be served by its introduction. He asked rhetorically whether the new vocational education was being directed at an "increase in the industrial intelligence and power of the worker" or whether laborers are to have their skills developed in order to "add to the profits of employers . . . by avoiding waste, getting more out of their machines and materials" in the hope that they will ultimately share in the profits "as an incidental by-product" (p. 333). Whatever may have been Dewey's disillusionment with what passed for a liberal education in his day, he was far from supportive of the alternative that social efficiency doctrine dictated.

vi

In 1924, when Robert and Helen Lynd (1929) undertook their classic study of Muncie, Indiana, in America's heartland, they found that among the twelve courses of study in place was a shorthand course, a bookkeeping course, an applied electricity course, a mechanical drafting course, a printing course, a machine shop course, a manual arts course, and a home economics course (p. 192). Although English was still required for the first two years, it was replaced by commercial English in five of the courses and was an option in the fourth year. "The most pronounced region of movement," they found, "appears in the rush of courses that depart from the traditional dignified conception of what constitutes education and seek to train for specific tool and skill activities in factory, office, and home" (p. 194). Lacking the long and honorable tradition of the academic subjects, the new vocational subjects "frankly adopted the canons of office and machine shop" (p. 194). What is more, these were the courses to which the members of the Rotary Club and the public generally pointed with pride. The head of the school board made his own preferences clear and, at the same time, offered an apt summary of the educational transformation that social efficiency had wrought in little more than a quarter century: "For a long time all boys were trained to be President. Then for a while we trained them all to be professional men. Now we are training boys to get jobs" (p. 194). Insofar as the curriculum for girls was concerned, the home economics program began in the seventh grade with the study of food, household management, and selection of food and clothing. In high school, it included instruction in dressmaking, millinary, hygiene, and home nursing. In the scant three decades since the Committee of Ten recommended its four model "programmes," each with different but distinctly academic, emphases, direct training for one's future occupational role had emerged as a major, if not the predominant, element in the high school curriculum for that segment of the school population whose "probable destination" did not include attendance in college.

Vocational education was the most successful curricular innovation in the twentieth century in the sense that none other approached it in the range of support it received and the extent to which it became implemented into the curriculum of American schools. Although a wide range of studies adduced no persuasive evidence that vocational education, as a substitute for traditional curricular offerings, resulted in a net gain in either employment or salary for students in those programs (Boyer, 1983), the faith in job skill training through the school system continued unabated. Even more important than the particular programs that have evolved has been the effect on the American curriculum as a whole. Preparation for a particular occupational role, including attending college as a form of occupation, has permeated the justifications for virtually all school subjects.

These justifications, in turn, profoundly affect the selection of materials to be studied and the manner in which they are organized for instruction.

On one level, the success of vocational education can be attributed to the fact that it acted as a kind of magic mirror in which the powerful interest groups of the period could see their own reflected ways of reforming what was increasingly regarded as a curriculum out of tune with the times. Virtually the only opponents of any consequence were the humanists like Harris who saw in vocational education a threat to the subjects that developed the intellect and passed on the cultural heritage. Du Bois's arguments that trade training in schools was not as effective as was commonly supposed and that it also served to deprive a segment of the school population of necessary intellectual training were also distinctly humanistic in tone and in general orientation, but they probably reached a very small and unsympathetic audience. Humanist influence in the period was so clearly on the wane that even Eliot, at least temporarily, was forced to come to terms with the prevailing effort to direct the schools' curriculum along the lines of their probable destination. Dewey's opposition, significant though it was, was to the particular direction industrial education was taking and to what it could (and in fact did) become. If anything, Dewey's vague and loosely defined identification as an educational reformer seeking to infuse active occupations into what had become a passive, almost archaic, curriculum, probably served to associate him in the popular mind with the very position he tried to oppose.

That the rise to prominence of vocational education represented a triumph for the forces of social efficiency can hardly be doubted. The key figures in the shaping of the Smith-Hughes legislation and, equally important, in the way it was implemented in later years were people who shared the perspectives of Charles Prosser and David Snedden and not Jane Addams or John Dewey. Vocational education also fit perfectly into the social efficiency ideal of education as preparation for a specific social and occupational role, and, in this sense, it was the most important step in the direction of a policy of curriculum differentiation in order to achieve that ideal. But the existence and the influence of other interest groups meant that it was not a complete victory. Contrary to the distinct preferences of leaders in the vocational education movement like Prosser and Snedden, as well as the National Society for the Promotion of Industrial Education generally, vocational education did not emerge under dual control with separate educational institutions created specifically for a predefined school population. Although separate vocational high schools do exist here and there in the United States, the comprehensive high school established itself as the typical, if not the quintessential, American educational institution, with curricular tracking, both formal and informal, attending to the differentiating function that social efficiency educators considered so critical. While Dewey's appeal to democratic values was not sufficiently persuasive to actually stem the tide of direct trade training, it may have helped to force the compromise that kept a system of schooling where, at least in principle, all children shared a common setting for their education. If nothing else, that compromise preserved the possibility that elements of a common curriculum could reemerge or, at least, that mobility among the various curricular tracks could be facilitated. Moreover, the fact that early manual training programs deliberately avoided some of the most damaging effects of educational predestination often attending curriculum differentiation meant that the course that vocational education took in the twentieth century was by no means inevitable. There were other options.

To be sure, the particular course that vocational education in fact followed was influenced by social conditions existing at the time that the drive was at its height. There was, after all, not only a rising tide of industrialism but a decline of such institutions as apprenticeship, and there is no question that these factors were involved in the campaign for vocational education and its overwhelmingly favorable reception. But these events were filtered through the lenses of particular ideologies that presented not only certain conceptions of the relationship between work and schooling but a vision of a desirable social order. Vocational education did not emerge as a supremely successful curricular innovation because social changes made it so, but because certain ways of interpreting social change made the infusion of vocational education into the public school curriculum the most plausible and politically expedient, although not necessarily the most efficacious, response to those perceived changes.

6 | FROM HOME-PROJECT TO EXPERIENCE CURRICULUM

i

ON THE FACE OF IT, INDUSTRIAL TRAINING IN CITY SCHOOLS AND VOCATIONAL agriculture in rural schools were natural counterparts. Both made the school a bridge to the world of work, one by providing youth with the skills that were required by industry and commerce and the other by attending to the skills needed to run a productive and successful farm. That tie was, if nothing else, a politically expedient one to the framers of the Smith-Hughes legislation, who essentially treated the two as of one piece (along with home economics). In the eyes of Congress, both were also no doubt deemed to be in the national interest. The value of a skilled and abundant industrial labor pool seemed self-evident, and through vocational agriculture, the school could become the center for the dissemination of scientific methods of farming just as experimental stations had been under the Hatch Act. Although both were regarded as forms of vocational training—and in one sense they obviously were—the differences between vocational agriculture and industrial training turned out to be more significant than their similarities. While both can be seen as responses to industrialism and urban growth, one was framed in terms of simply meeting the needs of the new industrial society by training a skilled labor force in schools, while the other had its origins in the effort to preserve certain values associated with rural living in the face of that new society.

Even beyond their differences in origin, the two forms of vocational education, as they actually emerged, exhibited a profound pedagogical difference. The population served by vocational programs tied to manufacturing was preparing youth for a future that was remote both in time and in setting. Students in those programs were being taught skills in the hope that, at some time in the future, those skills would stand them in good stead in the workplace. Unlike the apprenticeship system, which school-based industrial training was intended to replace, it was unlikely that many of those being trained had any direct experience in the real world of manufacturing, much less the particular kind of factory that would one day, presumably, be the source of their employment. The population served by vocational agriculture programs, by contrast, was not only familiar with their workplace, they were, in almost all cases, in daily contact with it. The relationship between school, work, and even home was real and intimate. From the perspective of curriculum, this was potentially a factor of tremendous significance. It bore directly on the question, for example, of whether the curriculum should be seen as a preparation for future living as the social efficiency proponents demanded or tied to issues or problems of immediate interest and value to the learner.

The first known program growing out of the important relationship between home and school that was embedded in vocational agriculture was conceived by Rufus W. Stimson, a teacher at Smith's Agricultural School in Northampton, Massachusetts. In 1908–1909, he implemented what he called a home-project plan in order to help "the boys in applying the teachings of the school in their home farm work" (Stimson, 1914, p. 16). Even in the context of vocational education, there was, in Stimson's view, a danger of "too much reflection, not enough action" (p. 10). Not only could that problem be immediately resolved through the home project, but improved farm procedures could be directly introduced. For example, since it was, in all likelihood, "part of the boy's business to assist in feeding the cows," that boy could be assigned to weighing one cow's rations and calculating the cost to feed her. Samples of the cow's milk could be brought to school for bacteriological tests. The effect of introducing a larger component of clover into the cow's feed could be observed (p. 14). In some cases, students actually earned money in connection with their home projects. By 1911, Stimson's plan had become so successful that the Massachusetts legislature provided additional state aid in order to spread the idea, and two years later, U. S. Commissioner of Education P. P. Claxton asked Stimson to prepare a government publication describing the virtues of agricultural home projects. In short order, the Massachusetts home-project plan, as he called it in the Bureau of Education Bulletin he wrote, was attracting national attention as a way of organizing the curriculum in vocational agriculture.

An educational innovation of such promise did not escape the attention of Charles Prosser, who, in his new position as director of the executive staff for the Federal Board of Vocational Education, asked F. E. Heald, a specialist in agricultural education assigned to the U. S. Department of Agriculture, to prepare a special comprehensive bulletin on the subject. In 1917, Heald had published an article reporting that the project had already "gained a recognized standing in educational and scientific circles" (p. 166). In describing the project, he emphasized the importance of pupil interest "at the outset" and "in which there is some problem more or less new" (p. 167), thus identifying two of the most important characteristics that were to appeal to certain reformers in the educational world in later years.

The report that Heald wrote a year later at Prosser's request, "The Home Project as a Phase of Vocational Agricultural Education" (1918), was far more extensive. It included a historical account of the development of the idea as well as some of the controversies that had developed over the definition of a project. There were also practical suggestions involving how records should be kept and a strong suggestion that a contract be signed by teacher, pupil, and parent setting forth the terms of the project and the level of achievement to be reached. There were also illustrations of projects that could successfully coordinate the work done in school with the farm at home. Although he recognized that financial gain was sometimes a factor in home projects, Heald thought it was "not always the controlling one" (p. 11), arguing that the "main factor" ought to be "the personal interest of the pupil" and even that "the immediacy of motive has a considerable bearing on the final success" (p. 10).

That emphasis contrasted with the position taken by Prosser in the foreword to the bulletin. Prosser reminded the readers that the purpose of the Smith-Hughes legislation was "to fit for useful agricultural employment" (Heald, 1918, p. 5). As would be expected, he urged that "final economic profit should be a definite aim of all such project work, as it is the aim of the farming business as a whole," adding that "economic development should be emphasized as a final goal" (p. 6). Within a decade of its introduction, the home project was beginning to be seen in sharply contrasting terms, depending, of course, on the ideological stance of the observer. From one perspective, the project was a useful vehicle for introducing into the curriculum those habits and skills that would prepare students for their occupational roles in society. From a pedagogical or, more specifically, a developmentalist point of view, the introduction of the project held out the much grander prospect of reconstructing the curriculum around the real and immediate interests of the students.

ii

Paradoxically, it was one of the major leaders of the movement, David Snedden (1916), who, almost casually, may have been the first to make note of the fact that the project could be seen not simply as an addendum to the course of study but as a new unit with potential for replacing the subject as the basic building block of the curriculum. The subject matter that comprises the curriculum, he said, is subdivided into convenient packages we call subjects, and "the primary purpose of making all these divisions and subdivisions is, of course, some form of efficiency—efficiency of organization, of accessibility, of mastery" (p. 419). Just as "cantaloups" are packed in crates, wheat in sacks, and sermons packaged within a certain time frame—all because particular conditions need to be satisfied—so is what we teach packaged for various purposes. The large packages we call subjects are subdivided into lesser units, lectures, exercises, and the smallest of the packages, the question and answer (pp. 419–420). Within the past few years, he noted, a new package, the project, had emerged in the field of vocational agriculture. Snedden acknowledged that a "logical sequence of a series of projects might be hard to find," but he nevertheless noted that since 1912 "the project as a pedagogic unit of organization in practical arts and in vocational education had found a place, if not always a welcome" (p. 422). Perhaps, with the introduction of what he called "modifiers" to describe different types of projects, it would emerge as a useful unit of curriculum organization transcending its original locus, vocational agriculture.

Within a month after Snedden published these observations, a new journal, *General Science Quarterly*, was launched with almost the express purpose of reorganizing the teaching of science around projects. The editors chose as the lead article for the first issue, the transcript of an address that

John Dewey had given to the National Education Association (NEA) three months earlier. Dewey (1916b) proceeded from the assumption that "the end of science teaching is to make us aware [of] what constitutes the most effective use of mind, of intelligence" (p. 3). Since the achievement of such an aim must begin in the elementary school, the curriculum of nature study at that level should be reoriented with a view "to arouse interest in the discovery of causes, dynamic processes, operating forces" rather than its present emphasis—a static, miscellaneous accumulation of "a certain store of information" (p. 4). Dewey urged even those with a sophisticated understanding of science to forget "the conventional divisions of the sciences" and try to see science from "the standpoint of pupil's experience of natural forces together with their ordinary useful applications" (p. 5). He deplored the teaching of science in "definitely segregated areas, concepts and terms which are found in books under the heads of physics, chemistry, etc." and urged instead that the teacher remember "that there is no material in existence which is physical or chemical or botanical, but that a certain ordinary subject-matter becomes physical or chemical or botanical when certain questions are raised, and when it is subjected to certain modes of inquiry" (p. 7). While Dewey's view of the teaching of science was consistent with certain principles associated with the project method, it was not an endorsement of the project as a substitute for a subject. For Dewey, an appropriate organization of the curriculum in science would not be built around "specialized technicalities of a highly matured science" (p. 5), but it would still be science. Beginning with concrete experience, the child's curiosity about the natural world, and daily occupations was simply a surer path to sophisticated and intellectually respectable scientific knowledge. Dewey felt that even many promising future scientists, to say nothing of ordinary students, were "repelled by a premature diet of abstract scientific propositions" (p. 8).

In its first years of existence, *General Science Quarterly* remained dedicated to the promotion of the project as the way to reform the teaching of science. A persistent theme was the one that Dewey had sounded—science, as ordinarily taught in schools, was being presented to the child in a manner inappropriate to the child's level of development and understanding. Just as the home project in vocational agriculture succeeded because it grew out of issues of immediate importance to farming, so projects in science could grow out of the natural interest of students in the world around them. One principal of a high school in Bridgeport, Connecticut, for example, attributed the failure of science in the public schools to the fact that "the subject matter and the method are not vitally connected with the needs and interests of individual students" (Moore, 1916, p. 15). Science projects should arise, he believed, out of spontaneous questions that students raise, such as "Why a crust forms inside the teakettle?" or "Why do boilers explode?" (p. 15). The central thrust of this article as well as the numerous articles and editorials in subsequent volumes of *General Science Quarterly* was not the substitution of practical skills for science in the curriculum. In fact, in his keynote article, Dewey had even urged that science be studied for the full four years of high school. The central point of the campaign was that, through a project organization, science could be made not only more interesting and vital to the student but a more intellectually stimulating subject in the curriculum of elementary and secondary schools.

iii

Without doubt, the single most dramatic event in the evolution of the movement to reform the curriculum through projects was the appearance in the September 1918 issue of *Teachers College Record* of an article with the unpretentious title, "The Project Method" (Kilpatrick, 1918b). Written by a faculty member at Teachers College, William Heard Kilpatrick, the article caused such an immediate sensation that the Teachers College Bureau of Publications was obliged to distribute an astounding 60,000 reprints. Exactly why that particular article aroused such an explosion of interest was not exactly clear at the outset. The extension of the project idea beyond the field of vocational agriculture had, after all, been going on for several years, and educators of the prominence of David Snedden had previously published articles on the subject. Kilpatrick, already in his late forties and having some difficulty in getting promoted to full professor, was probably himself unprepared for such a reception.

Part of the answer, to be sure, lay in Kilpatrick's unusually felicitous style, an inspiring way with words that ultimately helped him become the most popular professor in Teachers College history. But beyond the easy cadence of his writing, Kilpatrick was able to rekindle the diminishing hope that the developmentalists had once ignited—that somewhere in the child lay the key to a revitalized curriculum. G. Stanley Hall, who once epitomized that position, and whose leadership of the child study movement had been so stirring and seemingly full of promise, had met with some sharp reversals as the new century began (Ross, 1972, pp. 341–367). Hall's pseudoscientific approach to the study of the child had been more or less exposed, and his mystical belief in race recapitulation as a basis for an orderly curriculum built on natural law had fallen out of favor. William James's 1899 series of lectures on the relationship between psychology and school practice seemed at times almost a direct attack on the claims that Hall had once boldly set forth for the redirection of the curriculum through the psychological study of the child. In what appears to be a direct reference to Hall, James (1899) said there was "a certain fatality of mystification laid upon the teachers of our day" (p. 6), even going so far as to say that in his "humble opinion there is no 'new psychology' worthy of the name" (p. 7). Emphasizing that teaching is an art and not a science, James was wary of Hall's optimism about turning psychological laws into pedagogical recipes: "I say moreover that you make a great, a very great mistake, if you think that psychology, being the science of the mind's laws, is something from which you can deduce definite programmes and schemes and methods of instruction for immediate schoolroom use" (p. 7).

With someone of the immense stature of James joining other major critics in the psychological world, such as Hugo Munsterberg (1899), Hall's prominence among psychologists and child-centered educators rapidly diminished. E. L. Thorndike, who emerged in the twentieth century as America's leading psychologist of education was openly critical of the assumptions that guided Hall and the child study movement. "What development is can never teach us what it *ought to be*," Thorndike (1901) declared. "No word perhaps is a poorer synonym for 'the good' than 'the natural'" (p. 136). A once promising cause needed a new leader and some new ideas, and "The Project Method" quickly catapulted Kilpatrick, a philosopher, rather than a psychologist, into that role.

Kilpatrick's (1917) first contribution to the growing body of literature in the area of the project method appeared, naturally enough, in *General Science Quarterly*. Actually, it was not an article per se, but a compilation of notes taken by various people who had heard him speak on the subject. While lacking a certain coherence, "Project Teaching" sounded themes that were to stir the imagination of one group of educational reformers for several decades. First, there was the contrast between the logical and the psychological organization of the curriculum. In some sense, this was a rough extrapolation of Dewey's position expressed a year earlier in the same journal where he claimed that adult (logical) versions of science were being inappropriately imposed on children's (psychological) understanding of natural phenomena. As Kilpatrick put it, "we too generally take the child at the beginning stage of experience and try to give him the most complete adult formulation" (p. 68), a theme that Dewey (1897c) had been sounding for at least twenty years. Kilpatrick, an avowed disciple of Dewey's, also incorporated into the project method a definition of thinking that Dewey had set forth in his *How We Think* (1910b). Thinking was basically problem solving. "The primary purpose of thinking," Kilpatrick (1917) said, "is to get out of a difficulty," although he also recognized that a "secondary purpose" of thinking could simply be to satisfy curiosity (p. 69).

When the Committee on Economy of Time reported at the NEA's Atlantic City meeting on February 28, 1918, there appeared, smuggled in among reports on progress in defining minimum essentials for a large number of elementary school subjects, a brief report by Kilpatrick (1918a) from what he described as "a subordinate committee to study the problem of so modifying school practice as to utilize the child and the child's resources more effectively than has been done in our customary practice" (p. 528). As its name implies, the Committee on Economy of Time had been almost exclusively efficiency-oriented, emphasizing, according to one of its principal figures, two major concerns: "the thorogoing acceptance of the point of view of social utility in curriculum making" and "the substitution of scientific method for mere opinion in the actual selection of the content of the course of study" (Horn, 1918, p. 526). Those two "concerns" could easily serve as a most apt and concise explication of the implications of the social-efficiency movement for the curriculum. Minimum essentials were simply the educational counterpart to production standards or quotas where fixed amounts of learning, presumably determined by scientific means such as questionnaires and frequency studies of errors made by children, were presented as the factual and skill requirements in various subjects. Except, perhaps, for an oblique reference to "laws of learning," Kilpatrick's "subordinate" committee report made no allusion to those central concerns. Instead, Kilpatrick expounded on the theme of using children's purposes as the basis for organizing the curriculum, indeed proposing the child's own "purposeful act" as the "typical unit" not only of school life but of the "worthy life" in general (p. 528).

When "The Project Method" (1918b) appeared a few months later, any nominal association with the Committee on Economy of Time was no longer in evidence, and, if anything, what Kilpatrick was proposing was a clear alternative to the reforms being promoted by the social efficiency interest group. He seems to have struck in his proposal a deep wellspring of opposition to the scientific curriculum makers whose hard-line efficiency and scientifically determined standards represented newly dominant ideals in curriculum matters. Although Kilpatrick was usually careful to indicate that the project method of curriculum organization was consistent with what he continued to call the "laws of learning," his primary emphasis was that "education be considered as life itself and not as a mere preparation for later living" (p. 323), a position fundamentally opposed to what scientific curriculum makers like Bobbitt and Charters were espousing. Instead of a curriculum broken into its most minute units and then reassembled into the most efficient arrangement possible, Kilpatrick boldly proposed "the conception of wholehearted purposeful activity proceeding in a social environment," or, in short, "the hearty purposeful act" as the basis around which a curriculum could be built (p. 320). Moreover, since what Kilpatrick called "the worthy life" also consisted of purposeful acts, the life of the school could be made consistent with worthy living. Worthy living, however, was not something you got ready for; it was something you did now. "We of America," Kilpatrick affirmed, "have for years increasingly desired that education be considered as life itself and not as a mere preparation for later living" (p. 323). He was thus taking advantage of the immediacy that the home project had presented as a way of tying education to life and proposing it as the model for all of the curriculum. What he was at least implicitly rejecting was the idea that facts and skills ought to be presented to children and youth in schools in the hope that they would be of practical value in the years ahead.

Kilpatrick (1918b) managed to obfuscate some of the issues by referring to different "types" of projects, including type 4, "where the purpose is to obtain some item or degree of skill or knowledge, as learning to write grade 14 on the Thorndike Scale, learning the irregular verbs in French" (p. 333), a type of project that would make project organization indistinguishable from anything else. The type 1 project, "where the purpose is to embody some idea or plan in external form" (p. 332), however, was clearly where his sympathies lay. It was for that type of project that he proposed four steps as a kind of problem-solving procedure: "purposing, planning, executing, and judging" (p. 333). As to type 4, he simply asserted that "planning had perhaps best come from the psychologist" (p. 334), admitting, along the way, that it was to the "purposeful act with the emphasis on the word purpose that I myself apply the term 'project'" (p. 320).

Kilpatrick's timing was evidently propitious. Within a short time the project method became the major alternative to scientific curriculum making for those reformers who saw the school's traditional curriculum as sadly irrelevant to modern times. Kilpatrick's accomplishment was to take a successful curriculum reform in a restricted area, vocational agriculture, and to recast it so as to make it plausible as a way of reconstructing the entire curriculum. Moreover, his position at Teachers College, which had by the second decade of the twentieth century become the national center of the study of education, put Kilpatrick in a position to spread his ideas to a wide audience. In that galaxy of star faculty that Dean James Earl Russell had assembled, Kilpatrick was the brightest in terms of overall popularity. By the time his career ended, it was estimated that he had taught approximately 35,000 students, many of whom went on to positions of prominence and influence in the educational world. So rapid was the rise in popularity of the project method that Charters (1922) felt compelled to issue a few words of caution. Referring to the fact that the "history of American education is a chronicle of fads" (p. 245), he warned of the project's many limitations. In particular, he felt that the project method simply did not teach future citizens what they needed to know. Without recommending the abolition of projects altogether, Charters urged that projects at least "be accompanied by a systematic study of subjects, by drills, and by exercises" (p. 246).

Despite these criticisms, the project method continued to attract unprecedented loyalty in the educational world. When the National Conference on Educational Method was held in Atlantic City on March 1, 1921, with the express purpose of reforming education along project method lines, the high school auditorium, seating 600, was not only filled to capacity, but many educators had to be turned away. And this was despite the fact that the star attraction, Kilpatrick, could not be present because of illness ("As reported," 1921, p. 37). The rapid growth of the project idea after 1918 was further stimulated by the founding of a journal with what amounted to an avowed intention of spreading and developing the idea. Three years after the appearance of "The Project Method," a devoted disciple of Kilpatrick's, James Fleming Hosic (1921a), founded the *Journal of Educational Method*, with the purpose of presenting the project "as a serious and consistent point of view, likely to have far-reaching effects in bringing about a reorganization of the curriculum" (p. 2). Indicating that no apology was necessary for devoting all that attention to the project method, he pointed out that there were already misconceptions developing as to the real meaning of projects, including one version that considered projects to be simply a new subject of study. Hosic directed the new journal primarily to an audience of practicing school supervisors, hoping thereby to bring the use of the project as a new unit in the curriculum from its newly prominent place in the debates among leaders of various reform groups to the classrooms of elementary and secondary schools across the country. One month after launching the journal, Hosic (1921b) was able to report that every elementary school principal in one large city and the entire faculty "of one of the two best-known state normal schools in the United States" had subscribed to the journal (p. 1).

In the second year of its existence, the *Journal of Educational Method* became the vehicle for an ambitious effort by Kilpatrick to explore the project method in its various ramifications. Central to Kilpatrick's (1922) endeavor was a redefinition of subject matter. Rather than minimum essentials or something set out to be learned, he saw subject matter as a rich reconstruction of the child's experience, one that "results in uplifting insight, inclination, and power" (p. 96). Arguing that the traditional conceptions of subject matter were merely being "reenforced by current conceptions of efficiency" (p. 231), Kilpatrick (1923) tried to make the case for subject matter as functioning "when some activity of the person is held up, hindered, or thwarted, and some new way of behaving is needed in order to get the balked activity going again satisfactorily" (p. 368). He was, in this sense, putting forward a kind of homeostatic view of thinking in which subject matter serves to restore balance in the organism once its purposes are thwarted. Kilpatrick was in this way seeking to reintegrate subject matter into the sphere of human action. Subject matter, under these circumstances, was not simply there to be learned but was to function directly in accomplishing human purposes. It was in that context that Kilpatrick thought it should appear in the school curriculum.

iv

Almost from the time that William Torrey Harris focused national attention to the curriculum, debate had turned largely on the question of curriculum content. The opposition between the traditional humanists and the social efficiency educators had been framed in terms of what knowledge was most appropriate for the curriculum, with the social-efficiency position being that the traditional curriculum consisted largely of deadwood, which had to be summarily lopped off. What they were proposing was the substitution of content that had a much more utilitarian and less academic character. Kilpatrick and his followers were dramatically changing the terms of that debate. They were not merely saying that one kind of content was somehow better than another; they were, in effect, arguing that selection of content was a matter of secondary importance at best. Knowledge was not simply there to be mastered; it was an instrument for accomplishing human purposes. As such, the child's own purposes should provide the basis for the development of the curriculum with subject matter employed instrumentally as it bore on the accomplishment of those purposes. Attacking what he liked to call the "cold storage" view of knowledge, in which facts and skills were stored up for future use, Kilpatrick proposed instead a curriculum that deemphasized the acquisition of knowledge in favor of a curriculum that was synonymous with purposeful activity. As Kilpatrick redefined it, the project was now not simply a way of reorganizing the teaching of, say, science; it became, contrary to Dewey's position, a substitute for science.

Kilpatrick (1924) began one of his major statements on this subject, an address before the Department of Superintendence, with the declaration that "[t]he curriculum question is not so simple as to some it seems" (p. 3). Acknowledging that subject matter and curriculum were "intimately related," he went on to reverse what had been seen as the common relationship between subject matter and life. The curriculum was usually arranged in terms of appropriate subject matter with the expectation that it would have some beneficial effect in later life. Kilpatrick proposed that curriculum planning start with life (or at least what was increasingly being called the problems of living) with subject matter brought in only incidentally as it bore on those problems. "Subject matter," he boldly declared, "is primarily means, not primarily end" (p. 3). Kilpatrick was, in effect, reconstructing what we mean by a curriculum, and an interesting side effect of that redefinition was that the project *method* had become a curriculum. "Read," Kilpatrick urged in his customarily impassioned tone, "[Ellsworth] Collings, *An Experiment with a Project Curriculum*. . . . Read and see. It has worked. It can work" (p. 9).

Collings's (1923) book, described in Kilpatrick's introduction as a "pioneer work" (p. xvii), was a glowing account of how three rural schools in Missouri had successfully implemented the project curriculum. Actually, that book was only one of a spate of books written in the 1920s on the subject. These included not only Kilpatrick's most influential book, *Foundations of Method* (1925), but those of his growing number of disciples and like-minded contemporaries, such as James L. Stockton's *Project Work in Education* (1920), Junius L. Meriam's *Child Life and the Curriculum* (1920), Margaret Wells's *A Project Curriculum* (1921), John A. Stevenson's *The Project Method of Teaching* (1921), E. A. Hotchkiss's *The Project Method in Classroom Work* (1924), James F. Hosic and Sara E. Chase's *Brief Guide to the Project Method* (1926) and Mary H. Lewis's *An Adventure with Children* (1928). With such discipleship, it was inevitable that the impact of the project curriculum should be felt in school practice, albeit not always in its purest form.

Initially, the project organization of the curriculum, as would be expected, attracted the greatest enthusiasm from private and university-associated schools. The Lincoln School of Teachers College, for example, compiled a volume designed to report on the fruits of its experimentation with the project organization of the curriculum (Columbia University, 1927). The school's units, usually referred to as "centers of interest," however, involved rather prolonged activities organized around a central theme presumably reflecting the children's interests. In "A Study of City Life" in the second grade, children began with a study of the city's transportation, one boy making a model of Grand Central Station while others made trains, trucks, buses, taxis, and boats (p. 89). Next they constructed buildings—a wholesale market, a bakery, a post office, a fire station, a bank, and so on (pp. 89–90). Rooms were rented in the buildings and "protests and arguments were numerous between landlords or landladies and tenants over the high cost of rooms or apartments, whether or not the rent should be paid in advance, or whether rental charges should or should not cover the price of electricity and various other details" (pp. 90–91). Eventually, the project led to a six-week study of foods where various foodstuffs were prepared and sold at market prices. "These large units of work," it was reported, "become the core of the elementary-school curriculum" (p. 29). Kilpatrick (1928) himself had some reservations about such large units of work, suggesting that the smaller units employed by Collings were preferable, but he deemed them "far superior to the assignment-in-order-to-cover-specified-subject-matter" (p. 87).

By the 1930s, the movement had grown to such proportions that it outgrew its original identification with the project per se and came to be more grandly advertised as the activity curriculum or the experience curriculum. Like its immediate ancestor, the home project, the experience curriculum was built on the importance of child and adolescent interests, their sense of purpose as a guide to what to study, and on activity, usually overt, replacing what was conventionally seen as the appalling passivity that characterized most school programs. According to its proponents who assembled the 33rd Yearbook of the National Society for the Study of Education (Part II), entitled *The Activity Movement* (Whipple, 1934), the greatest progress had been made in elementary schools. The principal of two elementary schools in Montclair, New Jersey, for example, reported having "changed rather abruptly . . . to an activity-experience type of teaching" (Hartman, 1934, p. 110). In a third-grade class, the activity was a post office unit, which involved the children writing to the postmaster requesting permission to visit the local post office. In a fourth-grade class, children building a feudal castle found "a need to deal with fractions" (p. 111), exhibiting great interest in that most tedious of arithmetic operations. Thus, in the context of the students' purposive activity, were such conventional skills as writing and arithmetic incorporated successfully into an activity organization of the curriculum.

The superintendent of schools in Houston, Texas, reported on a major study designed to test the activity curriculum against a matched control group in the fourth and fifth grades. Responding to the frequent criticism that the activity curriculum would leave young pupils without the basic skills usually taught in elementary schools, he reported that the average gain as measured by the new Stanford Achievement Tests for two experimental groups was 13.3 months, while the control group's average gain was 12.3 months. Teachers in the activity program devoted significantly less time to drill and devoted more to "creative self-expression" (Oberholtzer, 1934, p. 138). Pupils in the two experimental groups, he reported, read an average of 27.9 and 31.9 books per year, while the control group average was only 21.6 (p. 140). Even the quality of teaching was improved in the groups using the activity curriculum, with teachers reporting more enthusiasm in their teaching and planning their work more carefully (p. 141).

One reason for the relative success of the activity or experience curriculum in the elementary school vis-à-vis the high school was undoubtedly the elementary school's greater organizational flexibility. High schools, with virtually immutable class periods and with teachers trained specifically in subject areas, were much more difficult to penetrate.

The most ambitious attempt to bring the experience curriculum to the high school was launched at the annual meeting of the National Council of Teachers of English by John DeBoer in 1935. Sounding a theme long cherished by curriculum reformers, DeBoer (1936) called for a high school curriculum consisting not of isolated compartments, but an integrated curriculum organized around four major divisions: English, science, social studies, and the arts. He challenged teachers of English to make their subject the center of the curriculum and to take the lead in building a curriculum that would "provide the learner with an opportunity to discover significant relation between the facts that come within his experience" (p. 249). Essentially, DeBoer was proposing that the project organization of the curriculum be integrated into the conventional subject divisions that comprise the high school curriculum. The familiar subject labels would be retained, but the curriculum would be built around the life activities of the learners rather than traditional subject matter. In point of fact, the National Council of Teachers of English (1935) already had in preparation a volume entitled, *An Experience Curriculum in English*, which substantially embodied the reforms that DeBoer was advocating. The year *An Experience Curriculum in English* was published, the NEA's department of supervisors and directors of instruction (1936) devoted its 9th yearbook to *The Development of a Modern Program in English*, a volume that largely supported and extended the principles enunciated in *An Experience Curriculum*. For several years thereafter, *The English Journal* continued to publish accounts by high school teachers of successful implementation of the recommendations that the National Council of Teachers of English's report had set forth.

v

In spite of some disappointments in terms of implementation, within a few years, the home project, a promising approach to the teaching of vocational agriculture, had evolved into a messianic curriculum movement replete not only with a high priest but with a successful journal to promote its ideas, an army of followers, a particularly devoted set of energetic disciples, and even some satellite movements. Its influence was felt first and most directly in nonpublic elementary schools of an experimental bent, but extended later to public elementary and even secondary schools. The project curriculum (or, as it came to be called in the 1930s, the activity or experience curriculum), however, was not by any means supreme in the educational world. The developmentalist interest group, once a specific child study movement rooted in genetic psychology but now a more broadly based group of child-centered educators with Kilpatrick at the helm, existed, after all, alongside other powerful interest groups with at least different and often contradictory conceptions of how a curriculum should be wrought. William C. Bagley, for example, Kilpatrick's colleague at Teachers College, was anything but enthusiastic for the idea. Bagley (1921) insisted that many of the assumptions inherent in the project curriculum had "not as yet been established by thoroughgoing experimentation" (p. 289). He was skeptical, for example, of the claim that information mastered in very specific contexts would be successfully retained, indicating that the "transfer potency" inherent in the project organization of the curriculum was probably not as great as the proponents claimed (p. 290). The predominance of the instrumental role of knowledge, so central to Kilpatrick's conception of subject matter, was also a matter of concern:

> The prime function of education on the elementary level, and to a large extent on the secondary level, is to place the child in possession of his spiritual heritage,—the heritage of skill, knowledge, standard, and ideal which represents the gains that the race has made. Only a small fraction of this heritage is instrumental in the narrow meaning of the term. (p. 292)

Bagley also reminded his readers that much of learning is "of a non-purposive sort" and that adult purposes, in contrast to child purposes, should not always be regarded as an evil (p. 296).

Bagley's remarks were presented at a symposium on the project method, and so his criticism (given his position in these matters) was almost demanded by the circumstances. On the whole, however, open debate between proponents of widely different positions in curriculum matters was not as common as would be expected, and this has served to obfuscate the complexity of what passed for curriculum reform efforts in this period. Although there were some notable exceptions, each interest group, by and large, spoke to its own constituency, so that the truly profound differences, say, between the social-efficiency educators and the proponents of child-centered education tended to get blurred in the eyes of an unsophisticated public. With critical cross-exchanges between contending groups held to a minimum, even latter-day commentators continue to see these widely divergent curriculum reform movements as all of one piece.

Easily the most trenchant and most remarkable exception to the absence of criticism of the proposed new reforms in curriculum was Boyd H. Bode's *Modern Educational Theories* (1927). In fact, his book presents not just his own educational ideas but represents a kind of catalog of what went wrong with the rival reform thrusts that reached their zenith in the early 1920s. Like Kilpatrick, Bode drew much of his inspiration from Dewey, but he was not as prone to flamboyance and oversimplification. His approach tended to be more cautious and reasoned, if not more politically sophisticated in its persistent attention to the social implications of the various proposed reforms of the curriculum. Bode never lost sight of the relationship between education and the vision of renewed society, and for him, an improved social order was not synonymous with efficiency or even with the creation of law-abiding citizens. Quoting Emerson, Bode (1927) held that "good men must not obey the laws too well" (p. 12), and that, rather than teaching adjustment to existing social conditions, democracy must be seen as "a progressive humanization of the social order" (p. 14).

As someone who believed that "our national safety lies in the general intelligence of our citizens" (p. 15), a position strongly reminiscent of Lester Frank Ward's, it was natural that Bode should reserve his sharpest criticism for the social-efficiency educators who were skeptical about the ability of the masses to govern themselves and whose social ideas were mainly directed toward achieving social stability. In his book, Bode devoted a whole chapter to the ideas of each of the three major leaders of the movement, Bobbitt, Charters, and Snedden, in each case attacking one major thrust of social-efficiency doctrine. Unlike Dewey, Bode revealed a close familiarity with the work of social-efficiency educators and an acute consciousness of their potency in the educational world.

In his chapter devoted mainly to Bobbitt, Bode expressed some sharp reservations about the claims of scientific curriculum making that were the hallmark of Bobbitt's position. Speaking of "our unbalanced enthusiasm for scientific method" (p. 78), Bode pointed out that those "scientific" methods that Bobbitt so freely espoused ignored "the ideal of a progressively changing social order" (p. 79). Not only did Bode believe that deriving ideals from the collection of facts was a delusion (p. 81), but that using Bobbitt's scientific method for the determination of curricular objectives resulted in "personal bias or preference [being] smuggled in under the guise of an objective, impersonal determination of fact" (p. 85). "When this happens," Bode argued, "educational objectives become once more, as in the past, an excuse for the perpetuation of tradition and the *status quo*" (p. 85).

Bode's chapter on Charters focused primarily on the method of job or activity analysis that had been borrowed from Taylorism in industry. He attacked the bricklayer analogy so prevalent in educational circles of the time, arguing that it was a case of applying what may seem reasonable in one situation to another that is hardly comparable:

Theoretically, at any rate, we can analyze a case of "keen judgment" so as to show just what was done and what sorts of facts and circumstances were taken into account in very much the same way that we can analyze bricklaying. But the analogy does not carry over to the next step. The bricklaying is analyzed in order that the novice may learn to repeat what has been done. The analysis of the case of "keen judgment," on the other hand, is made not to facilitate a simple repetition, but to improve the quality of subsequent judgments that are made under different conditions (pp. 103–104).

Unless our lives follow a fixed pattern in which schooling becomes the setting for the rehearsal of specific responses to anticipated situations (which of course many social efficiency educators believed), the method of activity analysis as a means of discovering curricular objectives is useless or worse.

His chapter attacking Snedden's notion of the sociological determination of educational objectives elaborated on some of Bode's criticism of Bobbitt and Charters. Again, the prevalence of activity analysis as the ultimate first step in curriculum development was treated with contempt. "There is no prospect of getting anywhere with this," Bode declared, "as long as we cling everlastingly to activity analysis 'like a sick kitten to a hot brick'" (p. 119). Instead of a technical formula by which curricula may be scientifically determined, Bode called for a process involving "historical perspective, for theory of mind, for insight into the educational significance of social institutions" (p. 119). In the end, he concluded that the unquenchable hope that Snedden held out for an objective determination of the curriculum through sociological analysis was nothing but a grand delusion (p. 139).

Nor was Kilpatrick's project method immune to Bode's keen critical eye. He was mindful of the numerous definitions of a project, each with its own adherents and appeal. Kilpatrick's definition, "wholehearted purposeful activity," Bode (1927) found to be indistinguishable from simply interest (p. 142). While Bode was sympathetic to some of the criticism of the traditional curriculum that Kilpatrick and his followers had put forward, especially the dehumanizing of knowledge and the wide gap that had been created between school and life activities, he thought that learning limited to the project teaching method was too discontinuous, too random and haphazard, too immediate in its function (p. 150). When the project method is simply "wholeheartedly purposeful activity in a social context," its defining characteristic is not to be found in "the organization of what is learned, but in the attitude of the learner toward his work" (p. 157), he wrote. The emphasis Kilpatrick liked to place on the child constructing his or her own curriculum and on purposive activity without further direction ominously suggested to Bode "a mystic faith in a process of 'inner development' which requires nothing from the environment except to be let alone." He reminded his readers of Dewey's dictum that "There is no spontaneous germination in the mental life" (p. 163). If the child gets no direction from the teacher, he or she will simply get it from someone else. The whole thing smacked more of Rousseau than a constructive approach to curriculum (p. 165). Bode, then, like Dewey, was profoundly skeptical of the fundamental developmentalist assumption that the key to the question of what to teach lay in the unfolding of natural forces within the child.

When Dewey (1931) delivered the Inglis Lecture at Harvard University, that skepticism was clearly evident although, of course, not as bluntly stated. His lecture, entitled *The Way Out of Educational Confusion*, dealt with the two principal ways that had emerged for organizing a curriculum, by subject and by project. As would be expected from Dewey, he clearly endorsed neither. His criticism of the subject organization was similar to the position he had presented in *General Science Quarterly* fifteen years earlier (1916b). Specifically, he asked, "What is the value of the accepted and generally current classification of subjects?" (p. 4). He pointed out that while old subject matter categories and labels tended to break down with the advance of scholarship, the old tags persisted in the school curriculum. The appearance of new fields with hyphenated titles such as astro-physics and bio-chemistry, he said, was apt testimony "to the breaking down of dividing walls between subjects" (p.15), and this breaking down was indicative of the ways in which knowledge was interconnected and interdependent. The persistence of old subject matter labels and the absence of any attempt to integrate knowledge through the curriculum merely insured that students would get a fragmented and artificially isolated conception of what they were studying. The "subjects grow superficial," he said, and "their multiplication brings weariness to the spirit and the flesh" (p. 16). He summed up his objections to the traditionally conceived subject organization of the curriculum, not by rejecting it, but by pointing out that "in a situation where the skills or arts and the subject-matter of knowledge have become interwoven and interdependent," the persistence of a curriculum "on the basis of many isolated and independent subjects is bound to result in precisely the kind of confusion we have at present" (pp. 17–18). It was the traditional and outworn classifications and the absence of correlation among them that Dewey objected to, not the subject organization itself, especially at the secondary and collegiate levels.

When Dewey turned to "the so-called 'project,' 'problem,' or 'situation' method," he warned his listeners immediately that he did not regard this method as the only alternative to the present "confusion" in the curriculum (p. 30). While, like Bode, Dewey admitted that the method "has certain characteristics which are significant for any plan for change" (pp. 30–31), he was anything but enthusiastic about the project as a mode of curriculum organization. For one thing, he felt that projects frequently involved too short a time span and were often casually arrived at. "In short," he said, "they are too trivial to be educative" (p. 31). The knowledge gained in that context, he thought, would commonly be of "a merely technical sort, not a genuine carrying forward of theoretical knowledge" (p. 35). Just in case his point was lost on his listeners, Dewey stated flatly, "I do not urge it [the project method] as the sole way out of educational confusion, not even in the elementary school" (p. 36).

Instead, Dewey took the position that even when traditional titles of subjects were retained, it would be possible to reorganize them so that the interdependence of knowledge and the relationship between knowledge and human purpose would be made clear. Pointing to examples of such programs of study developed by Julian Huxley and H. G. Wells, he indicated it was possible to cut across the traditional specialized divisions in science "yet not at the expense of scientific accuracy but in a way which increases both intellectual curiosity and understanding, while disclosing the world about us as a perennial source of esthetic delight" (Dewey, 1931, p. 37). As he had done fifteen years earlier, Dewey was endorsing science, not projects. What Dewey appeared to be advocating here most closely resembled what has come to be called the "broad fields" organization of the curriculum, a modification of the subject curriculum that attempts to address the problem of the isolation of school subjects from one another by linking together those subjects with some affinity. In this way, the interrelationships within science as a whole would be fostered through the curriculum, not the insulated, specialized subdivisions.

Dewey, perhaps naively, looked to schools of education to lead the way in instituting those practices, but warned that any attempt to refine existing practices "under the protective shield of 'scientific method'" would be "more likely to increase confusion" (pp. 39–40). What he hoped for instead was that the schools of education could "undertake consecutive study of the interrelation of subjects with one another and with social bearing and application" (p. 40). Dewey's "way out of educational confusion" required too much by way of reconstruction of the traditional subjects to appeal to the humanists. It did not lack the romantic appeal of a curriculum nourished by children's natural predilections, but it stopped short of the dramatic rejection of subjects that the advocates of the activity curriculum proposed, and its emphasis on intellectual inquiry and social regeneration at all levels and by all segments of the population made it too vague and imprecise, if not too dangerous, to the scientific curriculum makers and social-efficiency educators. His intellectual stature, his international reputation, and his many honors notwithstanding, Dewey did not have enough of a true following in the world of educational practice to make his impact felt.

7 THE GREAT DEPRESSION AND THE HEYDAY OF SOCIAL MELIORISM

i

ON THE EVE OF THE 1928 PRESIDENTIAL ELECTION, JOHN DEWEY, NOW sixty-nine years old and a regular contributor to the left-wing journal *New Republic*, threw his support squarely behind the Democratic governor of New York, Alfred E. Smith, in what proved to be a futile attempt to stem the landslide for Herbert Hoover, the Republican candidate. Hoover, trained as an engineer and with the reputation as an efficient administrator, was in the minds of most Americans a symbol of the new breed of managers, a man above the hurly-burly of practical politics. While recognizing that Hoover's reputation for efficiency was well deserved, Dewey (1928b) observed that "if he has any human insight, dictated by consciousness of social needs, into the policies called for by the day-to-day life of his fellow human beings, either in domestic or international affairs, I have never seen the signs of it" (p. 321). Lying below the optimism, prosperity, and gaiety that is our abiding image of the "roaring twenties," there seemed to be flowing a strong undercurrent of dissatisfaction ready to surface. Dewey, for example, argued that Hoover's "whole creed of complaisant capitalistic individualism and the right and duty of economic success commits him to the continuation of that hypocritical religion of 'prosperity' which is, in my judgment, the greatest force that exists at present in maintaining the unrealities of our social tone and temper" (p. 321). Dewey along with a substantial number of intellectuals of the time were becoming increasingly vocal about what they perceived as a system riddled by social injustice. When that undercurrent of discord surfaced, it was to affect the course of curriculum reform in the first half of the twentieth century, but in the 1920s, the direction of that curriculum reform was uncertain.

The general notion that the American curriculum needed a drastic overhaul reached new heights in 1926 when both volumes of the National Society for the Study of Education's twenty-sixth yearbook were devoted to curriculum issues. Part I, called *Curriculum-Making: Past and Present*, attempted to catalog the principal trends that had emerged in the field of curriculum and included a rather extensive review of specific experiments in curriculum in a large number of schools, almost all private or university-affiliated, across the country. Part II, *The Foundations of Curriculum-Making*, consisted mainly of statements on major curriculum issues by leaders in the field. Included, of course, were the twin stalwarts of scientific curriculum making, Franklin Bobbitt and W. W. Charters, as well as those who had been arguing the case for the activity curriculum such as William Heard Kilpatrick and Frederick W. Bonser. Representing a different point of view from either the scientific curriculum makers or the child-centered educators were George S. Counts of the University of Chicago and the man chosen to chair the committee that compiled the volumes, Harold O. Rugg of Teachers College, Columbia University. The inclusion of Counts and Rugg among the stars of the curriculum world invited to contribute to the two volumes marked the emergence of yet another force in the drive for curriculum reform, a force reflecting the social concern beginning to gain momentum in the latter part of the 1920s.

The announced purpose of the yearbook was to reach a consensus as to what would comprise the new curriculum. For a quarter century or more, there had been a vigorous drive to replace what was commonly regarded as a curriculum unsuited to the new industrial age and for the new population of students entering both elementary and secondary schools in larger numbers. But the nature of the change was anything but clear, and the yearbook committee, beginning in 1924 under Rugg's direction, made a concerted effort to bring some kind of coherence to the welter of reform that continued to flow from several quarters. The "Composite Statement" that was finally hammered out was not so much a reconstruction or reformulation of the different strains of curriculum reform that had emerged since the 1890s as it was a glossing over of the profound differences as to the direction the curriculum should take. On the question, for example, of whether the curriculum should be directed toward efficient participation in adult life through activity analysis, as the scientific curriculum-makers maintained, or whether the curriculum should derive from the present needs and interests of children, as the experience curriculum advocates proposed, the committee declared that education involved "participation in social life by providing a present life of experiences which increasingly identifies the child with the aims and activities derived from analysis of social life as a whole" (Whipple, 1926b, p. 14). In a similarly noncommittal vein, the committee announced that "[c]urriculum-study should not only be carried on continuously; it should also be comprehensive" (p. 24) and that "The Committee believes that curriculum-makers should seek on every possible occasion to develop sympathetic, broad views of the world" (p. 24).

More interesting than the bland "Composite Statement" are the contributions by curriculum leaders in the pages that follow. Most made a modest gesture of approval of the general statement, but then went on to reaffirm their own signature positions. Charters (1936b), for example, in the briefest of the supplementary statements, barely half a page, expressed his concern that the group might give its stamp of approval to "the position that the curriculum should be based entirely upon a study of the needs and interests of the learners" (p. 71). Apparently satisfied that it did not, he pronounced the conference a success. Kilpatrick (1926), alluding to "extreme divergence" of opinion on the committee, announced that "he may fairly claim the honor—or ignominy—of consistently deviating most from the present practice" (p. 119). In the most elaborate of the supplementary statements, actually more than twice the length of the "Composite Statement," he reiterated much of the position he had heretofore enunciated. By far the most startling of the statements was Bobbitt's (1926). Inexplicably, he repudiated his earlier central position that education represented a preparation for adult living and declared instead, "Education is not primarily to prepare for life at some future time. Quite the reverse; it purposes to hold high the current living. . . . Life can not be 'prepared for.' It can only be lived" (p. 43). One can only speculate that Kilpatrick succeeded in completely mesmerizing him. The avowed intent of the yearbook, to reach a consensus among the broad spectrum of curriculum reformers that had emerged during the first quarter of the twentieth century, was completely unrealized. In fact, a careful reading of the statements by the foremost curriculum leaders of the time leads one to quite the opposite conclusion: Three seemingly irreconcilable reform thrusts were represented. One derived its impetus from the standards of adult living, as Bobbitt had long insisted, and sought to reorient the curriculum in the direction of preparing children and youth for a distinct adult role. A second took the immediate life of the child as the starting point, essentially discarded subject matter whether traditional or directly utilitarian, and conceived of the curriculum as the forum where a child could realize his or her own purposes. And with the emergence of Rugg and Counts on the curriculum scene, we begin to see the beginning of a third curriculum movement, deriving its central thrust from the undercurrent of discontent about the American economic and social system. That last movement, establishing itself under the banner of social reconstructionism by the 1930s, saw the curriculum as the vehicle by which social injustice would be redressed and the evils of capitalism corrected.

Dissatisfaction with what Dewey called "the religion of prosperity" in America had been gathering momentum among a small group of literati for some time and had expressed itself in the novels of Sinclair Lewis and the muckraking of Upton Sinclair. The Russian Revolution had attracted the admiration of a number of American intellectuals unhappy with the direction that capitalism was taking. Some of this dissent had even begun to express itself in the larger electorate, when Eugene Victor Debs, the Socialist candidate running for president for the fifth time in 1920, received 919,000 votes. His vote total was all the more remarkable since he was at the time serving a ten-year sentence in prison, having been arrested under the Espionage Act in 1918 after delivering an antiwar speech. (President Warren G. Harding ordered him released on Christmas Day in 1921 and greeted him in the White House.)

Counts was one of the first among leaders in education to reflect that undercurrent of uneasiness about the American social structure and to direct that malaise to a critical examination of American schools. His (1922) earliest major work sounded the theme that American education, despite its claims, had been serving "the selected few, whether by birth or by talent" (p. 3). He argued that although the tax structure required schools to be supported by all, the American school system was serving a rather narrow and privileged segment of the population. Counts chose four cities—Seattle, Washington; St. Louis, Missouri; Bridgeport, Connecticut; and Mt. Vernon, New York—from which to secure his data. On the basis of his analysis of the social classes represented in the elementary and secondary schools of those cities, he concluded that secondary education differed from elementary education not simply by virtue of the age of their populations but in terms of the selectivity by social class that existed at the secondary level. "Misfortune, as well as fortune," Counts concluded, "passes from generation to generation" (p. 148). The rhetoric of democracy notwithstanding, access to secondary education, he found, was contingent on social and economic standing (p. 149).

Four years later, Counts (1926) published his *The Senior High School Curriculum*, which investigated the secondary school curricula in fifteen American cities. In the 1923–1924 school year, when the data were being collected, he found that "secondary education has been radically altered in the immediate past" and that in "rapid succession new curriculums are appearing, and old curriculums are disappearing" (p. 144). While the pace of change represented some source of satisfaction for Counts, he was disappointed to find that "nowhere has a program been developed in the light of the needs of American civilization" (p. 146). Interestingly, he found that traditional subjects were now being defended in terms of "the great human interests of health, family life, industry, citizenship, and recreation, but the materials of instruction which they are thus defending were not introduced into the program for these purposes" (p. 146), a reflection perhaps of the recommendation of the Cardinal Principles Committee (National Education Association, 1918) that the old subjects reorient themselves in terms of the seven aims they enunciated. In the following year, Counts (1927) returned to the theme of the counterdemocratic tendencies in American schools, this time by analyzing the social composition of boards of education. From the 1,654 school boards in the sample, Counts was able to draw a picture of the typical school board in rural, city, and statewide boards. Although there were differences, with three farmers serving on the typical six-member country board as opposed to business and professional men serving on city boards, Counts concluded that school board members were "drawn from the more favored economic and social classes" (p. 82) and that composition therefore reflected a bias in the control of American educational policy. "Only as the conditioning agencies and forces are won to the support of a liberal and creative type of education," he concluded, "will the school ever be able to make positive contributions toward the regeneration of the individual or the reconstruction of society" (p. 82).

Counts's work in the 1920s called attention to what he saw as an American school system oriented not to a new and better social order, but to preserving and stratifying existing social conditions. And it was to a curriculum directed toward social reconstruction that Counts became identified with once the Great Depression struck.

ii

Whatever may have been the uneasiness expressed during the 1920s about American life in such novels as *Babbitt* and *Main Street* or in earlier exposés like *The Jungle* or even in the evidence being brought forward by dissenting educators like Counts over the course of American education, the business of America, in the words of Hoover's predecessor, Calvin Coolidge, remained business. Although unemployment began to rise markedly in 1926 and certain industries, such as coal mining and textiles as well as farming, seemed to be in trouble, Americans in general remained as optimistic as ever about America's future. Both public and private debt was growing rapidly as stock market investors, continued their buying spree, often buying stocks and bonds with as little as 25 percent in cash. "Black Thursday," October 24, 1929, hit like a thunderbolt, with stocks continuing to drop dramatically. By the following Tuesday, stocks were being sold so fast that the ticker ran two-and-a-half hours behind. By the end of October, some fifteen billion dollars in paper profits on the stock market had disappeared, and by the end of 1929 the loss had reached about forty billion. Within three years, about ninety billion dollars, three-fourths of the total worth of securities on the stock exchange, were wiped out. The vista of endless prosperity had suddenly vanished.

President Hoover, in response, tried to increase federal spending and urged state and local governments to do the same. He pleaded with business leaders not to cut their workers' wages, an appeal they heeded, by and large, until the United States Steel Corporation cut wages by 10 percent in October 1931, an action quickly followed by other leading manufacturers such as General Motors and United States Rubber. Hoover appealed to bankers in 1931 to combine their resources in an effort to save banks that, in increasing numbers, were failing. His advice was ignored. In 1931 the effects of the depression struck Europe, and it was becoming clear that a worldwide crisis existed. By 1932 teachers' salaries had been cut dramatically all across the country, and Chicago teachers had gone unpaid for months. The president of the National Association of Manufacturers attributed the mass unemployment to the laziness of the workers, but leftist American leaders such as Charles A. Beard and Rexford Tugwell were calling for drastic action, including a much larger measure of control over business and more governmental planning.

The seed of social reconstructionism in education that Counts had planted in the mid- and late 1920s flowered. By the early 1930s, his sentiments were being echoed by educational leaders throughout the country. Even some of those who had championed the child-centered movement, like Kilpatrick, were drawn wholeheartedly into the new orbit. Somehow the long unemployment lines and the soup kitchens dampened the spirit of optimism that had earlier prevailed, not only about the future of capitalism, but with respect to romantic ideas about the natural development of the child in the school setting. Both social efficiency—fitting the individual into the right niche in the existing social order—and developmentalism, with its emphasis on freedom and individuality for children and adolescents, gave ground to the feeling that the schools had to address ongoing social and economic problems by raising up a new generation critically attuned to the defects of the social system and prepared to do something about it.

In a book dedicated to John Dewey, Counts (1930) deplored the social conformity, "the standardization of life" as he called it (p. 121), that had taken hold in modern industrial America. At the same time that the individual was being freed "from the coercive influence of the small family or community group (p. 123)," industrial civilization was imposing a new conformity. "The way in which the principle of social conformity finds expression in American Education," he claimed, "is perhaps best illustrated by the methods of curriculum-making which have come into vogue in recent years" (p. 124). In an obvious reference to the technique of activity analysis being promoted by such major leaders in the curriculum field as Bobbitt and Charters, Counts noted that this "interest in curriculum-making happened to be very intimately associated with the movement for the application of the scientific method to the study of education" (p. 124). Reflecting Bode's (1927) earlier criticism, he rejected the idea that a curriculum could be derived from an objective analysis of the activities that people engaged in since "no amount of purely objective study of life activities will produce standards whereby the good may be distinguished from the bad, or the better from the worse" (p. 125). It was obvious to Counts that the critical point in so-called scientific curriculum making was the selection of the judges who were to draw the inferences from the data, and these judges, almost invariably, would reflect dominant interests in American culture. The obvious result would be the preservation of the status quo. As Counts put it, "The inevitable consequence is that the school will become an instrument for the perpetuation of the existing social order rather than a creative force in society" (p. 126).

Counts also attacked the supreme criterion of success to emerge from the social efficiency movement, efficiency itself. Referring to the dominant conception of efficiency, Counts called it "an efficiency without purpose, an efficiency of motion" (p. 137). He was not surprised that "this idolatry of efficiency should impress itself upon the schools" since the entire country had been influenced by the dominant "machine culture" but "an efficiency of management," he declared, "should never be the ideal of education" (p. 138). He deplored the easy classification of students in the name of individualization and the division of the curriculum into "minute units of work" as his colleague, Snedden, so insistently demanded. He included in his criticism of American schools the widely heralded platoon system of Gary, Indiana, as merely a mechanical device to increase efficiency. Even "the accurate measurement of school products" in the name of efficiency was not spared (p. 146). While conceding some scientific value to the "orgy of testing that swept through the entire country," Counts argued that "the feverish and uncritical fashioning of tests in terms of the existing curriculum and in the name of efficiency has undoubtedly served to fasten upon the schools an archaic program of instruction and a false theory of the nature of learning" (pp. 147–148). As long as these approaches to curriculum development remained dominant, Counts maintained, only social drift would result. Counts's unalterable opposition to the social-efficiency interest group and all that it stood for could not have been more evident. Clearly, much of what had passed for curriculum reform in the previous generation only served to perpetuate the very defects he perceived in the American social fabric.

iii

Beginning in the 1930s, there appeared to be a resonance developing between leftist political and social leaders and certain educational reformers. Heretofore, with the exception of a handful of socially progressive leaders, such as

Dewey and Bode, the dominant strains of educational reform had been tied specifically to hard efficiency and the maintenance of the existing social order on one hand and a sentimental belief in the natural unfolding of childrens' natural propensities on the other. The opposition between the social reconstructionists and the social-efficiency educators was becoming clear and well-defined. But a bitter opposition developed between those social meliorists and the developmentalists as well. The arena for that battle turned out to be the Progressive Education Association.

The Progressive Education Association was probably born in the mind of Marietta Johnson whose Organic School in Fairhope, Alabama, represented a model of a school based strictly on developmentalist principles. Founded by Johnson in a Henry George single-tax community in 1907, the school eliminated strict sorting of children by age as well as any kind of evaluation of their work that would produce competition among the children. Activities grew out of the spontaneous interests of the children themselves with strong emphasis on storytelling, singing, and dancing in the early years. Like Hall, Johnson (1926) set great store by fairy tales and folklore and postponed the actual teaching of reading until about the age of eight or nine in line with what she believed to be the natural period for such training. Formal school subjects were postponed until the junior high school years. In the opening lines of her brief contribution to the National Society for the Study of Education's twenty-sixth yearbook (Part I), she proclaimed her creed: "We believe the educational program should aim to meet the needs of the growing child. We believe that childhood is for itself and not a preparation for adult life" (p. 349).

It was with ideas such as these that she approached Stanwood Cobb with a proposal to start a national organization to promote school experimentation. Cobb had himself founded an experimental school, the Chevy Chase Country Day School in Chevy Chase, Maryland. After Cobb finally agreed, the organization was founded in 1919 under the name Association for the Advancement of Experimental Schools, which was changed shortly thereafter to the Association for the Advancement of Progressive Education and then to the Progressive Education Association. The first president was Arthur E. Morgan, himself a headmaster of an experimental school, the Morraine Park School of Dayton, Ohio, but who became president of Antioch College a year after the organization was founded. (President emeritus of Harvard University and architect of the Committee of Ten

Report Charles W. Eliot had been asked to be the first president, but at the age of eighty-five, he declined, serving instead as honorary president (Graham, 1967, p. 2)). With the exception of such an illustrious figure as Eliot, the organization was attractive mainly to a small coterie of teachers and administrators associated with private experimental schools and lay persons interested in school reform along developmental lines.

Whatever its modest beginnings, membership grew rapidly from the eighty-six members in 1919 to its peak of 7,400 in the 1930s. The person who took the lead in developing a platform for the new organization was Eugene Randolph Smith, the headmaster of the Beaver Country Day School in Chestnut Hill, Massachusetts. The Seven Principles of Progressive Education, representing the central creed of the organization, were adopted in 1920. Appearing on the inside cover of every issue of *Progressive Education* for about a five-year period in the 1920s, the prologue stated: "The aim of Progressive Education is the freest and fullest development of the individual, based upon the scientific study of his physical, mental, spiritual, and social characteristics and needs." The Seven Principles that followed provided a clear indication of the child-centered orientation that the organization was trying to promote: I. Freedom to Develop Naturally; II. Interest, the Motive of All Work; III. The Teacher a Guide, Not a Taskmaster; IV. Scientific Study of Pupil Development; V. Greater Attention to All That Affects the Child's Physical Development; VI. Cooperation between School and Home to Meet the Needs of Child-Life; VII. The Progressive School a Leader in Educational Movements. It was a platform that Hall could easily have written.

It was this extreme developmentalist position that became a fierce point of dispute once the Progressive Education Association achieved national recognition. Not coincidently, it was Dewey (1928a) who, in his speech upon accepting the position of honorary president (succeeding Eliot), raised some doubts about the direction the association was taking. He began his address by simply asking the question, "What is Progressive Education?" and attempting "to raise the intellectual, the theoretical problem of the relation of the progressive movement to the art and philosophy of education" (p. 197). Was a school progressive simply because it displayed "a certain atmosphere of informality" or because there was an emphasis on activity? (p. 198). While these characteristics obviously existed, Dewey took them to be merely superficial. The methods and the results obtained in progressive schools marked them off from the traditional ones. The "traditional schools," he said, "set great store by tests and measurements" (p. 199). The use of IQs and of test scores were merely ways of making the traditional schools more efficient. "At all events," Dewey said, "*quality* of activity and of consequence is more important . . . than any quantitative element" (p. 200). Dewey seemed to be deliberately rejecting the reforms introduced by the social-efficiency educators with their emphasis on precise measurement as a way of reforming schools. In an obvious reference to determining curricular objectives through activity analysis, Dewey took the position that "the attempt to determine objectives and select subject-matter of studies by wide collection and accurate measurement of data" would only be appropriate "if we are satisfied upon the whole with the aims and processes of existing society" (p. 200). He urged his listeners not to become complacent about "what already exists" (p. 200). Dewey was thus recommending that the nine-year-old organization not associate itself with reforms that emphasized achievement standards, precise measurement, and the collection of data while ignoring the social impact of education.

He also took the occasion to try to disassociate the position of the organization from the emphasis on individuality and natural development that had been the basis for its founding. He suggested that this emphasis on removing traditional and artificial restrictions on the child in school had served a useful purpose, but, he said, "freedom is no end it itself" (p. 200). "I wonder," he told the membership, "whether this earlier and more negative phase of progressive education has not upon the whole run its course" (p. 201). Although he noted that progressive schools set great store by individuality, he suggested that this was not antagonistic to the orderly organization of subject matter. He even chastised those in the association who felt that the curriculum ought to flow strictly from the individual impulses and predilections of children. "Thus," he said, "much of the energy that sometimes goes to thinking about individual children might better be devoted to discovering some worthwhile activity and to arranging the conditions under which it can be carried forward" (pp. 201–202). He rejected the position taken by many in the child-centered movement that the curriculum ought not to be imposed from without by adults, but designed with the full participation of the children themselves. A mere succession of unrelated activities, he argued, not only failed to present organized subject matter in some coherent form, it also failed to "provide for the development of a coherent and integrated self" (p. 202). He concluded this critique by declaring, that "bare doing, no matter how active, is not enough" (p. 202). He recommended instead that teachers have "not only the right but the duty to suggest lines of activity, and to show that there need not be any fear of adult imposition" (p. 203). Dewey was thus rejecting two of the reform thrusts that had prevailed in the first quarter century. It was obvious that he had little use for the efficiency reformers, particularly their tacit acceptance of the social status quo. He felt that the child study movement had had positive impact through their rejection of traditional and unnecessary restraints on the child, but that the movement was essentially at a dead end through a kind of self-imposed restriction on adult imposition in curriculum matters. Dewey clearly thought that the Progressive Education Association ought to move beyond its developmentalist origins.

i v

If there were a counterpart in the social reconstructionist movement to the stunning impact that Kilpatrick's "The Project Method" had on the educational world, it was the speech that Counts delivered to the twelfth annual meeting of the Progressive Education Association in February 1932. In that address, "Dare Progressive Education Be Progressive?" Counts (1932a) reiterated the theme of an organization lacking direction that Dewey had sounded a few years earlier, but delivered his criticism in much blunter and sterner terms. "The great weakness of Progressive Education," he asserted, "lies in the fact that it has elaborated no theory of social welfare, unless it be that of anarchy or extreme individualism" (p. 258). By "anarchy," Counts was, of course, not implying that the members were allied with political anarchists; he was attacking the long-standing belief of most of its members that any sort of curriculum that did not derive directly from the learners themselves represented an unwarranted intrusion on the child's distinctive individuality. Although he conceded that the members of the association were basically tolerant and liberal-minded, he castigated them as people, who

> have no deep and abiding loyalties, who possess no convictions for which
> they would sacrifice over-much, who would find it hard to live without their
> customary material comforts, who are rather insensitive to the accepted
> forms of social injustice, who are content to play the role of interested

spectator in the drama of human history, who refuse to see reality in its harsher and more disagreeable forms, and who, in the day of severe trial, will follow the lead of the most powerful and respectable forces in society, and, at the same time, find good reasons for so doing. (p. 258)

Such verbal flagellation somehow struck home at a time when the effects of the Great Depression were already openly visible. Counts berated his audience for "at heart feeling themselves members of a superior breed [who] do not want their children to mix too freely with the children of the poor or of the less fortunate races" (pp. 258–259), a reference, no doubt, to the preponderance of private, and usually very exclusive schools, that were represented in the association.

Counts (1932a) challenged the organization to meet the social issues of the day head on, unafraid of "the bogeys of *imposition* and *indoctrination*" (p. 259). He advocated fundamental changes in the economic system alluding to "capitalism, with its deification of the principle of selfishness, its reliance upon the forces of competition, its placing of property above human rights, and its exaltation of the profit motive" (p. 261). Instead he called for a "coordinated, planned, and socialized economy" (p. 261) that would redress the evils rampant in the present system. One of those present on this momentous occasion reported years later that Counts's speech was greeted with a stunned silence that spoke "far more eloquently than applause" (p. 188). The rest of the program for the day was virtually abandoned, and the board of directors felt it necessary to call a special meeting in order to discuss Counts's challenge.

Not a professed Marxist, Counts believed that democratic traditions were consistent with a much stronger measure of control over capitalism gone wild. His message held out the intriguing prospect that the evils so evident in the America of the Great Depression could be corrected not by revolution but by school programs that directed the new generation to changing the fundamental values undergirding the capitalist economy. Counts's call to arms was so enthusiastically received that later that year he issued a new manifesto that included even more radical proposals, *Dare the School Build a New Social Order?* (1932b). He took the view there that the school could act as critic with respect to other social agencies and could undertake new tasks when those social institutions were not functioning successfully. In this respect, he favored an indefinite expansion of the scope of the curriculum much beyond the traditional subjects of study. Moreover, if teachers could mobilize themselves into a militant force, they could serve to correct some of the evils that the society imposed. Counts continued to sound the theme of an extreme individualism as the dominant value in American schooling, a value system that had to be replaced with an educational doctrine that emphasized social justice and reform. After 1932, the Progressive Education Association was never the same. The child-centered position that had held sway in its early years diminished in popularity, and Counts's new radical social policy was in the ascendancy. Well-known professors, drawn largely from Teachers College, began to take over the reins of the organization from the headmasters of private schools and interested lay people who had founded the association, and they succeeded in giving it a different character. In a sense, one interest group wrested control of the organization from the other. Stanwood Cobb, the Progressive Education Association's founder, was once asked why he resigned the presidency in 1930. He replied that, "They took it away from us." "They," he explained, were "the people at Teachers College, Columbia University" (Cremin, 1961, p. 250).

Counts's achievement in stirring the imagination not only of the memberships of the Progressive Education Association but of educational leaders everywhere cannot be underestimated. Just as President Franklin D. Roosevelt's New Deal programs were bringing some hope to the American public, so Counts's message was bringing encouragement to a dispirited educational leadership. A new journal, *Social Frontier*, made its appearance in 1934 and, over the few years of its existence, served as a lively forum for debate on social reconstructionism generally and on the schools' role in creating a new social order in particular. The "Teachers College crowd" was, of course, prominently represented, with the works of John L. Childs, William Heard Kilpatrick, Bruce Raup, Harold Rugg, and Goodwin Watson featured. Dewey remained a regular contributor throughout most of the journal's existence, joined frequently by one of his ablest disciples from Ohio State University, Boyd Bode. A persistent theme running through the articles and editorials was the evils of laissez-faire capitalism and rampant individualism. Although there were differences between "gradualists" and "anti-gradualists" on such issues as the efficacy of the class struggle as a basis for social change or on the merits of indoctrination in schools as a means of bringing about a better society, *Social Frontier* remained a consistent voice for the reconstruction of American life through the intervention of the schools. By 1937, however, the magazine began to falter, and in 1939 it was taken over by the Progressive Education Association in an effort to save it. Renamed *Frontiers of Democracy*, it continued its struggle for existence until 1943 when it died amid severe financial problems and some acrimony among the remaining leadership.

If lively debate and the support of major American intellectuals such as the eminent historian Charles A. Beard were to be the decisive factors in response to Counts's challenge, then certainly social reconstructionism was a resounding success. Beard, for example, was one of the principal figures responsible for the final report of the Commission on the Social Studies in the Schools of the American Historical Association. That report clearly embraced the reconstructionism that Counts (who was himself a member of the commission) had been advocating. The report declared unequivocally that "[c]umulative evidence supports the conclusion that, in the United States as in other countries, the age of individualism and *laissez faire* in economy and government is closing and that a new age of collectivism is emerging" (American Historical Association, 1934, p. 16). Teachers were charged with overcoming their traditional silence in political matters and encouraged to strike out boldly in the interest of a new society, much as Counts had urged. "Today," the commission reported, "because of . . . the timidity and weakness of the profession and the power of vested interests and privileged groups, the teacher seldom dares to introduce his pupils to the truth about American society and the forces that drive it onward" (pp. 75–76). So politically charged was the report that it elicited a number of extremely hostile reviews. As would be expected, Bobbitt (1934) was outraged. He strongly implied that the commission was deliberately vague about the kind of collectivism it was trying to promote. He accused the "integrators" of a desire "to think and to plan for the masses" (p. 205). Sounding an ominous note, Bobbitt suggested that the members of the commission used "the slogans of democracy as a mere protective smoke-screen for a communistic offensive" (p. 205). Alluding to "the revolutionary hysteria that grips all the collectivizing nations" (p. 208), he called upon the American Historical Association either to clarify the ambiguities in the report or to repudiate it. Even Bode, (1934) generally sympathetic to social reconstructionism, wrote a stinging editorial, which declared at the outset, "The cynic who said that teaching is the art of taking advantage of defenseless childhood will find confirmation for his pessimistic view in the recent Report of the Commission on the Teaching of the Social Studies" (p. 1) Reflecting, somewhat, Dewey's position on the issue of social reconstructionism, Bode proceeded to castigate the Commission for appearing to impose a predetermined social ideal on the child while ignoring "the vital importance of freedom in thinking" (p. 1). For both Dewey and Bode, the road to social progress was much more closely tied to the ability of the schools to teach independent thinking and to the ability of students to analyze and to address social problems than it was to an organized effort designed to redress predetermined social evils.

Counts himself continued his rise to preeminence in the curriculum world through his prolific writings and many speeches to professional organizations, sounding the theme that the curriculum should be directed toward correcting social and economic ills. Dissenting voices, however, continued to be heard. Snedden (1935), for example, as would be expected, was anything but enthusiastic about Counts's drive to remake the curriculum along social reconstructionist lines. He did acknowledge that beneath the "romantic nonsense" that had been uttered on the subject of social reconstructionism, there was a genuine problem to be addressed. "The times" he admitted, "are out of joint. America is sick" (p. 48). He was skeptical, however, about the prospect of the million schoolteachers in the nation uniting behind specific social or political programs. Even beyond that, he felt that "dreams of having our schools share directly in the furthering of any plans of social reconstruction are not only visionary, but also subversive of civic decency" (p. 51). What he proposed instead were "really functional civic educations" based on sound sociological principles. He continued to rail against subject matter specialists "including those that had become infected with Utopian radicalism" (p. 53).

More important, however, than the occasional resistance to social meliorism being thrown up by opposing interest groups, like the social-efficiency educators, was the seeming impenetrability of the schools themselves to ideas being put forth by Counts and his allies. There appeared to be more than a superficial disparity in political outlook between the "frontier thinkers" who articulated their views in the pages of *New Republic* and *Social Frontier* and the practical educational administrators who actually ran the schools of the nation. One reporter observed, for example, that when the Department of Superintendence met in Cleveland in 1934, "the Progressive Education Association moved onto the scene

before the superintendents had packed their grips, poked fun at the resolutions the superintendents had adopted, and by voicing 'advanced' ideas
ran off with the headlines" (Boutwell, 1934, p. 297). Apparently, the eastern
establishment was tolerated, but not wholly welcome. Although one reporter
at the Cleveland convention admitted that its tone was "outwardly . . .
distinctly pink" and that the assembled superintendents appeared willing
to undertake some changes in school practice, they remained "averse to
joining the Columbia torch-bearers at the barricades" (p. 297). One superintendent, sympathetic to social reconstructionism and writing in *Progressive
Education*, observed later that, in general, there were just too many
speeches on the subject and not enough grassroots efforts to work with
the teachers themselves. His overall assessment of the movement four years
after Counts's clarion call to the teachers of the nation was pessimistic.
"The stream of words and books about a new social order which has
poured over teachers in the last few years," he observed, "seems very much
like the proverbial water on a duck's back" (Moseley, 1936, p. 337).

v

If there was one major success that the social reconstructionists achieved
at the school level, it was the large-scale adoption by school districts of a
series of social studies textbooks written by Counts's colleague at Teachers
College, Harold Rugg. Rugg came to Teachers College from the University
of Chicago in 1920 as a staff member at the Lincoln School, an experimental school conceived of as a laboratory for testing educational ideas.
The school, founded three years earlier, was created when the General Education Board agreed to sponsor it in part with funds supplied by Mr. and
Mrs. John D. Rockefeller. Following his earlier inclinations and training,
Rugg (1941) embarked almost immediately on a testing program to determine the abilities of the children enrolled in the school, apparently concerned that a school founded on child-centered principles would not give
sufficient attention to achievement in the area of "social needs" (p. 188).

But Rugg's interests turned quickly to the social studies as a particular
area in the curriculum. As an associate professor at Teachers College, he
taught a course called "The Scientific Method in the Reconstruction of Elementary and Secondary School Subjects," and this led him to consider
alternatives to the conventional organization of school studies. In one of
Rugg's (1921b) earliest articles on the subject of reconstructing the social

studies, he seemed to have been pondering the notion that a course could be developed around the "great principles or generalizations in history, economics, politics, industry, geography, etc." (p. 692). In envisioning such a course, he proposed that the conventional subject matter be swept away and that a new curriculum be developed strictly on the criterion of "social worth" (p. 697). For Rugg (1921a), the social studies were a prime example of curriculum fragmentation and unnecessary compartmentalization. What he proposed was a unified social studies built on the laws and generalizations as enunciated by the finest practitioners in the various social disciplines:

> Rather than have teachers attempt the almost impossible task of "correlating" history, geography, civics, economics, and sociology (taught as separate subjects), we postulate that more effective outcomes will be secured by weaving together—lesson by lesson—the facts, movements, conditions, principles, and social, economic, and political "laws" that depend upon one another *and that can be fully comprehended only when they are woven together.* (p. 128)

Rugg saw this approach not only in terms of "social worth" but as a way to encourage independent thinking on the part of the students. From a psychological point of view, he saw a curriculum organized around real social problems as having the potential for replacing the passivity that characterized not only social studies classrooms but schooling generally with an active concern for social justice.

Rugg had been influenced at least to some degree by all the curriculum reform movements of the twentieth century. He had earlier expressed great faith in the power of science to transform what was taught in school; his first book, for example, was considered the experimental evidence on the question of mental discipline (Rugg, 1916), and he later published a statistics textbook for teachers (Rugg, 1925). In the late 1920s, he wrote *The Child-Centered School* (with Ann Shumaker, 1928), generally regarded as a paean to the developing popularity of schools built around the activity principles that Kilpatrick and his followers were promoting. But, throughout the twenties, he also expressed a persistent concern for the social role of the schools. Indeed, he became one of the first in the Progressive Education Association to view with alarm the continued tendency of that organization as late as 1930 to align itself with child-centered experimental schools while neglecting what he regarded as a social crisis. Looking back on that period, Rugg (1947) once recalled the board meetings where few directors took his warnings seriously, some referring to his persistent calls for an organized effort by the Progressive Education Association in the arena of social action as "Harold's annual crisis speech" (p. 576). Once the Great Depression struck, Rugg's allegiance to the social reconstructionists was unequivocal. Increasingly, he saw social regeneration as a worldwide problem. In 1932, for example, Rugg declared dramatically, "The world is on fire, and the youth of the world must be equipped to combat the conflagration" (p. 11). Much of the social unrest he saw in countries like England, France, Germany, Japan, China, and the Philippines he attributed to "the dangerous social effects of a lopsided academic education" or the "phenomenon of hyperintellectual education" (p. 12). Only through a fundamental reconstruction of the educational system could the current drift toward disaster be stemmed. Rugg was in no doubt as to how to proceed: "The first step is the building of a new program of work, a new content for the curriculum, directly out of the problems, issues, and characteristics of our changing society" (p. 13).

Rugg was actually expressing here his hopes for the monumental effort he had undertaken a decade earlier to reconstruct the social studies curriculum through the introduction of an avant-garde series of social studies textbooks. His primary emphasis, of course, was on calling attention to the critical social problems that America faced, but he also wanted his books to embody scientific respectability. Activity analysis, the allegedly scientific approach to curriculum development advocated by the social efficiency educators, was clearly out of the question since Rugg undoubtedly foresaw that using present activities as the basis for a curriculum would only serve to promote the social status quo. Rugg, with an able and dedicated research staff at his command at the Lincoln School, embarked on an effort in 1921–1922 to build the program of studies, not on a catalog of ongoing life activities, but on fundamental problems faced by American society and on generalizations set forth by leading social scientists. In a bold move to get his work into the schools, Rugg (1941) wrote to over three hundred school administrators who had been in his classes at the University of Chicago and Teachers College inviting them to subscribe to the new social science pamphlets "sight unseen" (p. 207), and by June 1922, some four thousand orders for each of the twelve pamphlets had been received. In this way, the experimental edition of *Social Science*

Pamphlets was underwritten in advance. By the end of the summer of 1922, the first seventh-grade pamphlet, *America and Her Immigrants* was shipped. Over the first nine-year period, 750,000 experimental pamphlets were distributed to subscribing school systems.

The program of research that Rugg undertook in connection with his series was enormous. One significant step in the process was the identification by one member of the research team of three thousand important problems facing American society (later reduced to three hundred) which were to be the backbone of the social studies program (Hockett, 1927). Another staff member worked with students from the third through the twelfth grades, determining their ability to deal with the concepts critical to those problems (Meltzer, 1925). Still another key step in the development of the series was the work of Rugg's doctoral student at Teachers College, Neal Billings, in developing a list of generalizations central to the social sciences. The list of generalizations was drawn from a group of books written between 1915 and 1922 by scholars that Rugg called "frontier thinkers." Billings (1929) systematically combed through 61 books written by "frontier thinkers" such as Charles A. Beard, Van Wyck Brooks, John Dewey, Harold J. Laski, W. F. Ogburn, James Harvey Robinson, Thorsten Veblen, Sidney and Beatrice Webb, and Clark Wissler, carefully cataloging and categorizing the social science generalizations he found there. Ultimately, 888 generalizations were compiled (pp. 99–209). Many had a distinct political orientation: "Fortunes sometimes originate in fraud and corruption" (p. 146); "The economic and social advance of women is not favorable to a high birth rate" (p. 151); "Militarism opposes democracy" (p. 161); and "Specialized industry in the factory system has divided society into capitalists and laborers" (p. 180). It would be difficult to establish the extent to which all of these generalizations found their way into the Rugg textbooks, but certainly some of them did. Even the difficult levels of various materials, written and pictorial, were scrupulously studied before they were incorporated into the final version of the *Social Science Pamphlets* (Mathews, 1926; Shaffer, 1930).

Within a few years, the commercial possibilities of the series became apparent, and in 1926, Rugg signed a contract with Ginn and Company to market the series under a new format and the new title, *Man and His Changing Society*. Three months before the stock market crash, in August of 1929, the first volume in the series was ready. By the end of that year alone, 20,000 copies had already been sold. By 1930 that figure reached almost 60,000. Between 1929 and 1939, 1,317,960 copies in the series were sold along with an additional 2,687,000 workbooks (Winters, 1968, p. 91). Especially considering that these sales were achieved in a period of declining school resources as a result of the depression, the sales figures are indeed astounding. But beyond that, Rugg's individual achievement represents the single greatest victory in the attempt by the social reconstructionists to reform the school curriculum in line with their social ideals.

The commercial series was divided into a "First Course" consisting of eight volumes and a "Second Course" consisting of six. Volume One in the junior high school series, to take one example, tackled the question of what is an American. The emphasis was on America as a nation of immigrants, including an effort to break down stereotypes of various nationalities and stressing the contributions of various immigrant groups. Included as well were "African immigrants" brought to the country as slaves. Rugg (1938) presented, particularly in its time, an unusually candid account of the slave trade. The story of James Morley, a gunner on one of the slave ships, for example, was quoted:

> I have seen them under great difficulty of breathing. The women, particularly, often got upon the beams to get air, but they are generally driven down, because they were taking the air from the rest. I have seen rice held to the mouths of sea-sick slaves until they were about strangled. I have seen medicine thrown over them in such a way that not half of it went into their mouths. The poor wretches were wallowing in their blood, hardly having life, and this with blows from a whip, the cat-o'-nine-tails. (p. 117)

In another volume, Rugg (1931) emphasized the disparity between rich and poor. One set of pictures showed two neighborhoods in Washington, D. C. Under one, the heading ran, "This is one of the fine residential neighborhoods in Washington, D.C. Notice the wide, well-kept cement boulevard, the trees, the neat hedges, the large, well-built houses, and the automobile" (p. 53). The heading under the second said, "This is another neighborhood in Washington, D.C. Notice the broken pavement in the alley, the lack of trees, the old tenements, and the carts" (p. 53). The changing role of women in society was also included. One photograph showing a woman wearing a white coat and conducting a scientific experiment had the heading, "Many women find that their housework does not keep them sufficiently occupied, so they enter industry, business, or the professions"

(p. 132). A photograph on the opposite page showed a man and woman at the kitchen sink doing the dishes together. The text appearing below the photograph read, "This was a rare sight in 1890. It is not unusual today" (p. 133). Another unusual facet of the series was the inclusion in the social studies textbooks of one of Rugg's major interests, the arts. Architect Frank Lloyd Wright, poet Carl Sandburg, novelists Sinclair Lewis and Theodore Dreiser, as well as prominent figures in theater and music were included. The central theme of the series, however, was probably best captured by the caption of the last section in the concluding chapter of the volume on problems of American culture: BUT AMERICA IS NOW ENTERING A NEW AGE OF SOCIAL PLANNING (p. 596). Like Counts, Rugg was not calling for revolution, but for a much stronger measure of restraint on the free enterprise system.

It was this anticapitalist theme that eventually was a contributing factor in bringing about the demise of the series. As early as 1934, Rugg's name appeared in a publication by Elizabeth Dilling designed as a "Who's Who and Handbook of Radicalism for Patriots." But it was not until about 1940 that truly organized opposition to the textbooks began to appear. A turning point was the appointment to the Englewood, New Jersey, school board of Bertie C. Forbes, a Hearst newspaper columnist and owner of *Forbes*, a business journal. Using his own journal as a vehicle for his attacks, Forbes (1939) declared, "I plan to insist that this anti-American educator's text books be cast out" (p. 8). Rugg eventually accepted an invitation from the Parent-Teacher Association at Englewood to debate his opponents, but Forbes did not appear at the meeting. Despite further attacks in his magazine, Forbes eventually lost that battle after the mayor did not reappoint him to the board.

Later, similar criticisms of Rugg's series as un-American and subversive began to appear in such cities as Bronxville, New York, Binghamton, New York, Atlanta, Georgia, and Philadelphia, Pennsylvania. In Philadelphia, an official of the Daughters of Colonial Wars attacked the textbooks because they "tried to give the child an unbiased viewpoint instead of teaching him real Americanism" ("Book burnings," 1940, p. 65), although these local attacks were not especially successful. At the national level, the campaign was joined by the National Association of Manufacturers, whose objections received wide publicity through George Sokolsky, the widely read Hearst columnist. Later, the American Legion made the Rugg textbooks a cause célèbre, with the most vigorous attack being launched by Orlen K. Armstrong, long a Rugg opponent, in an article entitled, "Treason in the Textbooks." Armstrong's (1940) analysis of the textbooks led him to conclude that the real purposes of the books were:

1. To present a new interpretation of history in order to "debunk" our heroes and cast doubt upon their motives, their patriotism and their service to mankind.
2. To cast aspersions upon our Constitution and our form of government, and shape opinions favorable to replacing them with socialistic control.
3. To condemn the American system of private ownership and enterprise, and form opinions favorable to collectivism.
4. To mould opinions against traditional religious faiths and ideas of morality, as being parts of an outgrown system. (pp. 51, 70)

A defense on Rugg's behalf was quickly organized. It included some of the "frontier thinkers" whose ideas had been incorporated into his books as well as his colleagues on *Frontiers of Democracy*. Rugg's own *That Men May Understand* (1941) is largely a spirited defense of his work. Some retractions of the most damaging charges were eventually wrested from Rugg's accusers, but the series was never revised and, after 1940, it diminished rapidly in popularity.

Lester Frank Ward, the great anti-social Darwinist sociologist of the 1880s and 1890s has been called by Henry Steele Commager (1967) "the philosophical architect of the welfare state" (p. xxxviii). Indeed, Ward saw the emerging problems of the twentieth century not simply in the maldistribution of real wealth in the society but in the unequal distribution of the cultural capital through the schools. That maldistribution, he felt, could be corrected by intelligent intervention, not by letting raw social and economic forces play themselves out. Insofar as curriculum reform was concerned, those ideas remained largely dormant for years. Roughly half a century after Ward first enunciated these ideas, however, educational leaders like Counts and Rugg managed to reinvigorate them and bring them first to an elite group of mainly eastern intellectuals but, ultimately, in the Rugg textbooks, to hundreds of thousands of schoolchildren. What seems to account for the reemergence of this subterranean stream of American curriculum reform is the interplay of the ideas themselves with social and economic conditions favorable to their survival. Once the prospect of a world conflict loomed on the horizon and criticism of American social conditions was no longer in vogue, social meliorism as a force for curriculum change gave way to curriculum thinking more in tune with the times. The times were no longer right. With the nation's entry into World War II imminent, criticism of American society slipped out of vogue in favor of a wave of patriotism occasioned by an external threat of aggression.

Curriculum fashions, it has long been noted, are subject to wide pendulum swings. While this metaphor conveys something of the shifting positions that are constantly occurring in the educational world, this phenomenon might best be seen as a stream with several currents, one stronger than others. None ever completely dries up. When the weather and other conditions are right, a weak or insignificant current assumes more force and prominence, only to decline when conditions particularly conducive to its newfound strength no longer prevail.

Figure 1. John Dewey (1859–1952), ca. 1902 *(Morris Library, Southern Illinois University at Carbondale)*

Figure 2. Boyd H. Bode (1873–1953), 1926 *(The Ohio State University Photo Archives)*

Figure 3. Children at the Laboratory School, University of Chicago, engaged in the famous clubhouse project, ca. 1900 *(Lander MacClintock Photographs, Morris Library, Southern Illinois University at Carbondale)*

Figures 4 & 5. "Occupations" provided a focal point for the curriculum in Dewey's school. Above, children preparing food. Below, a boy prepares wool for spinning, ca. 1900 *(Lander MacClintock Photographs, Morris Library, Southern Illinois University at Carbondale)*

Figures 6 & 7. Above, "Clothing Laboratory," freshman class, Lower Paxton High School, Harrisburg, Pennsylvania. Below, Woodworking class, same school. The introduction of such courses as home economics, industrial arts, and commercial courses tended to increase gender segregation in schools, 1924–25 *(Collection of the author)*

Figure 8. Many rural schools were ungraded and under the guidance of a single teacher, ca. 1895 *(Collection of the author)*

Figure 9. Particularly in urban schools, moveable desks were considered to be a way of addressing the regimentation of classrooms, but they were frequently arranged in orderly rows just like the fixed desks, ca. 1935 *(Collection of the author)*

8 | THE HYBRIDIZATION OF THE CURRICULUM

i

AT ROUGHLY THE SAME TIME THAT THE SOCIAL RECONSTRUCTIONISTS WERE mounting their offensive in the struggle for the American curriculum, another even more powerful force was affecting the course of curriculum change in the United States. It was not so much a new antagonist emerging as it was a blending of what were once clear-cut ideological positions into new amalgams of curriculum reform. Rather than a distinctive alternative to the existing contenders, it was a sometimes conscious, sometimes unconscious, potpourri of all of them.

By the 1930s, curriculum reform had become a national preoccupation. Change had definitely permeated the curriculum atmosphere, but the direction that the change was taking was uncertain. When the joint committee of the Department of Supervisors and Directors of Instruction of the National Education Association (NEA) and the Society for Curriculum Study (a committee that was the precursor of the NEA's Association for Supervision and Curriculum Development) issued a volume on the state of the curriculum, their opening sentence announced, "Curriculum development is definitely and markedly on the increase, and interest in this movement is nationwide" (Hand & French, 1937, p. 1). The authors went on to point out that well over 70 percent of cities with populations of 25,000 or more, according to their survey, were engaging in organized curriculum development. Not necessarily a particular curriculum doctrine but curriculum change itself was becoming a popular and widespread phenomenon. In the light of that phenomenon, it should not be surprising that some, probably a great many, school districts should undertake programs of curriculum change, not out of any deeply held conviction that the curriculum ought to be revised in a given direction, but so as not to appear out of step with what had become a major national trend. High status and even national recognition were being accorded those school systems that had achieved, or were in the process of engaging in, curriculum revision of whatever sort. It was not in the best interests of school administrators and school boards simply to stand pat. In the minds of more and more Americans, the traditional academic curriculum was becoming increasingly obsolete. Accordingly, many of the curriculum reforms that were emerging in the decade of the thirties represented not so much a victory for one position over the other as a hybridization of what were once distinct and easily recognizable curriculum positions.

Even before the advent of the thirties, some school districts had experimented with curriculum plans that were considered innovative. Of these the Dalton plan of Helen Parkhurst and E. D. Jackman, the Winnetka plan of Carleton Washburne, and the Denver project of Jesse Newlon and A. L. Threlkeld were probably the best known. Each was initiated at the local level and adopted by school systems eager to depart from conventional curricular practices. The direction of the departure in each of these cases, however, is unclear. Ultimately, these plans achieved wide acclaim although none of these curricular innovations was particularly long-lived. Both the Dalton plan and the Winnetka plan seemed to be prompted by an effort to get away from the recitation as the primary form of classroom instruction. What was substituted (although not exclusively) was a kind of contract plan in which students undertook to accomplish a certain amount of schoolwork on their own. Under the Dalton plan in Dalton, Massachusetts, each student was issued an individual monthly card with the assignments for the month. Students maintained their own records of their progress, and, upon completing the assigned work, could elect to be examined on the subject matter. The subject matter itself, however, departed little from the traditional curriculum. What was most important was that "cut-and-dried recitations were altogether to be dispensed with as being forced and artificial" (Jackman, 1920, p. 691). Recitations, the familiar question-and-answer format of most classrooms, had come to be associated with traditional education, and this lent credence to reforms that promised its abolition even when the subject matter remained relatively unchanged.

The Winnetka plan in Winnetka, Illinois, even more closely resembled what came to be known later as programmed instruction. Although the plan was strongly identified with individualized instruction, it was individualized in the sense of children working individually on assigned material, not of their expressing their own individuality. If anything, the individualization at Winnetka was infused with social-efficiency ideas. Reflecting Bobbitt's position, Superintendent Carleton Washburne (1926) once declared, "It is a comparatively simple matter to determine what knowledges and skills are commonly needed" (p. 219). While the Dalton plan was geared mainly toward the student individually completing a large body of material, often culminating in a report, the Winnetka plan concentrated on specific skill attainment, with promotion being based on individual subject achievement rather than by grade placement (Washburne, 1924). Kilpatrick, understandably, was critical of both the Dalton plan and the Winnetka system declaring that "both assume that education mainly and properly consists of learning certain prearranged subject matter for examination purposes" ("Individualizing Instruction," 1925, p. 177). Of the Winnetka plan in particular, he said that "it carries its mechanized work too far" (p. 177). Washburne (1928), in turn, questioned some of the basic assumptions of the project method arguing that it tended "to give children a random, unscientific training, and to ignore the wide differences which exist among individuals" (p. 187). Terms like individualization and individuality in the curriculum were operating not so much as precise descriptions of a particular way to reorganize instruction as a kind of slogan attracting allegiances but meaning quite different things to different groups. To some in the 1920s, individuality meant building the curriculum around the individual child's spontaneous creative interests; to others, individuality meant adapting the pace of instruction to the differences in individual learning capacities. By the 1930s, the social reconstructionists had converted individuality into "rugged individualism," the enemy of cooperation and restraint on the free enterprise system.

The Denver, Colorado, program was initiated in 1922 with an appropriation of $31,500 from the school board for curriculum revision. Elimination of waste seems to have been one of the main considerations. Superintendent Jesse Newlon's recommendation to the school board, for example, pointed out that, in view of the size of the school budget in Denver, if it turned out that as little as "10 percent of the teacher's time is spent on non-essential and misplaced materials in courses of study," that would represent an "annual waste to the Denver taxpayers of $315,000" (Newlon & Threlkeld, 1926, p. 230). For the most part, the money appropriated was for the purpose of releasing teachers to work on curriculum revision projects with prominent leaders in the curriculum field, such as Thomas Briggs, W. W. Charters, and Harold Rugg brought in from time to time to review their work. Again, there was no clear ideological direction, although some of Newlon's early pronouncements on curriculum were strongly tinged with social efficiency ideas. (Later, as a professor of educational administration at Teachers College, Newlon became more closely associated with social reconstructionism.) The most lasting legacy of the Denver program was the emphasis given to active teacher participation in curriculum reform. In fact, what came to be known as "process" in the curriculum world, the emphasis on active participation by school personnel in curriculum change and the group processes associated with it, became a favorite theme of the Association for Supervision and Curriculum Development. Established as a branch of the NEA in 1943 as a result of a merger between the Society of Curriculum Study and the Department of Supervision and Directors of Instruction, the association, through its journal, *Educational Leadership*, and its yearbooks, lobbied ceaselessly for "democratic" as opposed to "authoritarian" curriculum change.

ii

Emphasis on locally initiated curriculum change continued to gain momentum in the 1930s. Probably the most ambitious of the efforts to stimulate curriculum reform at the local level was undertaken by the Progressive Education Association in what came to be known as the Eight-Year Study. For years, members of the organization had been expressing dismay at the slow pace of curriculum change, particularly at the secondary school level. The source of this problem in the minds of most of the leadership was the imposition of entrance requirements by the colleges, and this, they believed, was the prop that held up the traditional academic subjects. As far back as the Committee of Ten report (National Education Association, 1893), complaints were being voiced about alleged domination of the high school curriculum by the colleges, and by the early 1930s, the conviction became firmly implanted in the minds of curriculum reformers that the colleges were the principal impediment to curriculum reform at the secondary school level. As an initial step to break the log-jam, the Progressive Education Association, on a motion by Harold Rugg, appointed a Committee on the Relation of School and College (although variations in the name of the committee appeared occasionally in official documents), with Wilford M. Aikin, headmaster of the John Burroughs School of St. Louis, Missouri, in charge. Aikin (1931b) was generally sanguine about the revolutionary changes that had been accomplished in the elementary school curriculum, but expressed the view that college domination had created a situation where "there are no truly progressive secondary schools, in spite of many attempts to create them" (p. 275).

Beginning in 1932, grants were secured from the Carnegie Foundation and the General Education Board (eventually amounting to $70,000 and $622,500 respectively—munificent sums for their day), and a plan was developed whereby colleges would accept students from a select group of secondary schools without reference to the particular subjects they had taken and without examination in those subjects. The basic idea was to free the secondary schools in the experimental group from the shackles of college domination and then to demonstrate that the graduates of these "unshackled schools" were at least the equal of students who had completed a traditional program of college-entrance subjects. The key test would be to see how the experimental group of students compared with a matched group in terms of success in college. Eventually thirty high schools (later reduced to twenty-nine by one withdrawal) were selected, and approximately 3,600 students in "matched pairs" were included in the sample.

To be research director of this massive undertaking, the committee brought Ralph Tyler from the Bureau of Educational Research of Ohio State University. Tyler had earned his doctorate in 1934 at the University of Chicago under Charles Hubbard Judd, a highly esteemed educational psychologist, who had earned a reputation for bringing scientific respectability to the study of education. He had had some previous experience with the Extension Division of the University of North Carolina, and while at Ohio State University, his own reputation as a scientific student of education grew rapidly. Early in his long career, Tyler (1930) allied himself with the advocates of activity analysis, defending the study by Charters and Douglas Waples (1929) that attempted to derive a curriculum in teacher training through an exhaustive study of the activities that teachers actually performed. In particular, his expertise in the measurement of educational outcomes attracted the Committee on the Relation of Secondary School and College. In that respect, Tyler (1931) may have been the first to argue that "the first step in improving validity is to define clearly the types of behavior which we are trying to teach" (p. 327), thus providing a portent of what was to become a massive behavioral objectives movement in later years.

One problem that emerged early in the study was the actual drawing of the sample that would comprise the "thirty unshackled schools." Schools had to demonstrate their willingness to experiment with their curricula to be eligible, and this tended to skew the sample strongly toward the prestigious private schools whose headmasters still constituted a significant element in the Progressive Education Association. Of the twenty-nine schools in the final sample, fifteen were private schools, among them the most exclusive and expensive in the United States. Typical of those schools chosen were the Baldwin School of Bryn Mawr, Pennsylvania, the Beaver Country Day School of Chestnut Hill, Massachusetts, the Dalton Schools and the Fieldston School of New York City, and Aikin's own John Burroughs School of Clayton, Missouri. Also included were four university-affiliated high schools such as the Lincoln School of Teachers College, the University School of Ohio State University, and Wisconsin High School of the University of Wisconsin. Of the remaining ten public high schools, four were drawn from wealthy suburban communities such as Bronxville High School of Bronxville, New York, and New Trier Township High School of Winnetka, Illinois. The others could reasonably be described as typical American high schools (Lancelot, 1943).

No particular curriculum pattern was imposed on the experimental schools. In line with the growing emphasis on locally initiated curriculum reform, the schools themselves were given free rein to change the existing curriculum. From 1932 to 1934, the schools with the aid of curriculum consultants developed and implemented the changes. The extent to which the schools chose to depart from traditional curriculum patterns was enormous. With some satisfaction, Aikin (1942) cited one report indicating that the North Shore Country Day School of Winnetka, Illinois, had eliminated from its Latin program "such stupid material as the Catiline Orations" and substituted twenty to twenty-five of Cicero's letters as well as about an equal number from Pliny (p. 47). At the Baldwin School, the five-year Latin program was revised to reduce the amount of Caesar studied in the second year, and in the fifth year, readings from Plautus, Terence, Catullus, and Horace were introduced (Spring, 1936). New Trier Township High School reported that, among other innovations, it had introduced into the senior year in English an eight-week study of the drama working back chronologically from the modern play to Shakespeare and finally to the Greek dramatists. Both comedy and tragedy were studied, concluding first with a modern tragedy, Eugene O'Neill's *Emperor Jones*, and then moving to Shakespeare's *Macbeth* (*Thirty Schools*, 1943, p. 514.)

Wisconsin High School on the University of Wisconsin campus, on the other hand, struck out boldly in removing their "shackles." H. H. Ryan (1933), the principal, had long been an advocate of a supremely functional curriculum. Once commenting on the persistent cries for the elimination of "frills" in the curriculum, he urged that "if the tax payer insists on paring the curriculum down to the essentials, it is the educators who must determine what the essentials are" (p. 143). What are the frills, he asked rhetorically, "Algebra or speech training? Latin or home economics? Ancient history or music?" (p. 142). Given his freedom from college domination under the Eight-Year Study, Ryan developed a special experimental curriculum, instituted in 1933 for a segment of the high school population at Wisconsin. Pointing out that a whole series of prestigious commissions from the Cardinal Principles Committee (National Education Association, 1918) on had "declared that the school's job is to help orient and adjust boys and girls in certain 'areas of living,' such as work, leisure, citizenship, family membership, health, and the like" (*Thirty Schools*, 1943, p. 780), he argued that the school curriculum ought to reflect more directly these vital social functions. Whereas Kingsley, in the Cardinal Principles Report, had stated such areas of living as aims of the curriculum, he stopped short of dispensing with the traditional subjects, recommending instead that the existing subjects reorient themselves toward the accomplishment of those functional aims. By the 1930s, the conviction was growing among certain educators that the aims representing areas of living ought to become the subjects. Accordingly, the experimental Wisconsin curriculum was organized around four "constants": community living, health, vocations, and leisure time. These constants, Ryan (1935) reported, made up approximately two-thirds of the school day. In time, this organization of the curriculum became identified as the core curriculum, or more specifically, as the social functions or life functions core. In a portent of what was to come, Ryan (1937) associated the core curriculum with life adjustment. "This universal problem of adjustment," he declared, "is logically the guiding principle for the development of the core-curriculum" (p. 15).

In Tulsa, Oklahoma, a select group of "accelerated" ninth- and tenth-grade students were required to enroll in a two-hour-a-week "Social Relations" program along with either a physical education program or a "creative activity" to form a three-hour "block," also described as a "core program" (*Thirty Schools*, 1943, pp. 643–645). "The Tulsa teachers believe," said one report, that the core portion of the program "should be based upon functional needs and significant life problems" (Hanna, 1939, p. 350). As always, the announced intention was "to meet the needs and interests" (p. 351) of the students, and this meant giving a less prominent role to the traditional subjects of study and more to such problems as health, safe driving, consumer economics, and personal finance. Another strong emphasis was on teacher-pupil planning of the curriculum, usually assigned to a regularly scheduled "conference hour" (Hanna, 1940, p. 66). In one seventh-grade class, for example, joint planning of the curriculum resulted in a year's study on the question, "How Can the Family Spend Their Leisure Time?" (p. 66).

At the Denver high schools, some modest curricular changes were introduced such as the establishment of a correlated curriculum combining social studies and English, but, after four years of experimentation, a core curriculum was also developed "to provide more effectively for the individual interests and needs of pupils . . . as well as to provide for common concerns of all high school pupils" (*Thirty Schools*, 1943, p. 167). The heart of the program was four "areas of living": "Personal Living, Immediate Personal-Social Relationships, Social-Civic Relationships, and Economic Relationships" (p. 169). Among the problems considered in these areas were "learning how to make the most of ourselves in appearance, poise, and social adequacy, through emphasis upon health, grooming, cleanliness, order, and fitness" (p. 173); "preparation for marriage, eugenics, inheritance, the problem of divorce, and the care of children" (p. 174); "the setting up of criteria for the choosing of friends" (p. 174); and "exploring vocational opportunities in the community and the nation and studying the individual's special abilities and capacities in terms of a vocation"

(p. 176). In a strong expression of social efficiency doctrine, one participant at Denver observed that "the subject matter of the core course will be related to those matters which society expects schools to present to youth. No attempt will be made to classify this subject matter under the usual subject-matter headings" (Rice, 1938, pp. 201–202). In the tenth grade, emphasis was placed on the relationship between school, home, and civic affairs. In the eleventh, special consideration was given to "larger social, political, and economic relationships," and in the twelfth, the problems and issues of modern life were the focal point of the curriculum "with attention to personal adjustment to these problems" (p. 202).

Although some of the "unshackled schools" were clearly making only modest changes in their traditional academic programs, others, now beginning to fall under the general rubric of a core curriculum, were experimenting with directly functional courses that, although they had strong social efficiency overtones, were being justified in terms of the needs and interests of the adolescents involved. What society needed and expected of its youth was becoming indistinguishable from what the youth themselves needed. The so-called core curriculum, one of the most abiding outcomes of the Eight-Year Study, was emerging as a hybrid of the social efficiency concern that the schools prepare directly and specifically for the duties of life and the activity curriculum's overriding emphasis on the needs and interests of the learner as the basis of the curriculum.

For years, social efficiency educators had been making the case for trimming the deadwood off the traditional academic curriculum. To teach history, algebra, and foreign languages to people who would never use them was an inexcusable waste. Their campaign, to a large extent, consisted of the effort to cast off those wasteful and inert subjects and to replace them (for most students) with subjects that bore a direct relationship to life, of which vocational education was a prime example. Under the aegis of the Eight-Year Study, at least some schools were able not only to introduce directly functional subjects like personal development and immediate social-personal relationships to the existing curricula, they made a strong effort to put them at the core of the curriculum. In part, acceptance of that drastic change in curricular practice was made possible not simply by force of the old slogans of efficiency and functionalism, but because they appeared to blend smoothly with the claims of the developmentalists that the curriculum ought to meet the common and individual needs of children and youth. Needs, then, or the needs curriculum, provided a convenient meeting ground where two interest groups could converge. Whatever the outcome of the matched-pair race between the students in the experimental "unshackled" schools and their counterparts from the traditional ones, the popularization of the core curriculum as a resilient hybrid was to emerge as one of the long-term outcomes of the Eight-Year Study.

A second development to which the Eight-Year Study gave strong impetus was the infusion of behaviorism in curriculum thinking. Volume Three of the report on the study was concerned with evaluation and declared flatly, "it was assumed that education is a process which seeks to change the behavior patterns of human beings" (Smith & Tyler, 1942, p. 11). From that assumption, it was only a small step to link these behaviorist principles to stating objectives as the crucial first step in the development of a curriculum, a position that Tyler had been advocating for some years. "The kinds of changes in behavior patterns in human beings which the school seeks to bring about," according to Tyler (in the part of the book that he wrote), "are its educational objectives" (p. 11). Objectives, in other words, should not be stated in vague terms such as knowing, appreciating, and understanding, but in terms that described in rather precise terms how the student would behave after a period of study. Moreover, the success of the program would be determined by the extent to which the behaviors embodied in the objectives would be achieved. "An educational program," Tyler asserted, "is appraised by finding out how far the objectives of the program are actually being realized" (p. 12). These objectives, furthermore, had to be stated as a preamble to other curriculum development activities for the "unshackled schools." "As the first step," he declared, "each school faculty was asked to formulate a statement of its educational objectives" (p. 15). In a portent of what later became widely celebrated as "the Tyler Rationale" (Tyler, 1950), Tyler said the objectives would represent "a compromise" based on evidence derived from "the demands of society, the characteristics of students, the potential contributions that various fields of learning may make, the social and educational philosophy of the school or college, and what we know from the psychology of learning as to the attainability of various types of objectives" (Smith & Tyler, 1942, p. 16). Since the framers of the Eight-Year Study specifically declined to promote any particular curriculum ideology, except perhaps change itself, they wound up at least partially supporting all of them. Putting their imprimatur, however, on stating objectives in behavioral terms as a first step in the curriculum-planning process was to have a lasting and profound effect on the future course of curriculum development. It is one indication that in the stew that became the American curriculum in the twentieth century, social efficiency emerged as the principal ingredient. The idea that, in curriculum development, exact specifications ought to be drawn up in advance and that success would be measured in terms of the extent to which those blueprints were followed is derived from the root metaphor of social efficiency, production, by which educational products are manufactured by the school-factory according to the particulars demanded by a modern industrial society.

Early results of the experiment began to trickle through in the 1939–1940 academic year; final reports were published in 1942 and 1943 in a five-volume series under the general rubric of "Adventure in American Education." The actual result was something of an anticlimax. Of the graduates of the "thirty unshackled schools," 1,475 who had been admitted to college under the agreed-upon relaxed entrance requirements were selected for the final study. Given the wide diversity of programs in the experimental schools, the final report indicated that some in that sample were "fairly close to the orthodox program, but many of them almost wildly heterodox" (Chamberlain, Chamberlain, Drought & Scott, 1942, p. xx). Using common criteria of success in college such as grade-point average, the graduates of the experimental schools neither "set the colleges on fire" (p. xx) nor did they compare unfavorably with their counterparts from traditional secondary school programs. Some consolation was derived from the fact that the experimental group came out "*a little ahead*" (p. xxi). Put in its best light, the Progressive Education Association could claim that the traditional college-entrance curriculum was no surer road to success in college than any other one. "Is the traditional program the only safe and sane plan?" they asked. "The answer is, NO—with no more if's and but's about it" (p. xxi). When student grade averages were compared in English, humanities, foreign languages, social studies, physical science, mathematics, and other subjects, there appeared, if anything, a very slight advantage accruing to the experimental group (pp. 27–28). The experimental group, in other words, had acquitted themselves creditably but not spectacularly. In a secondary analysis, the graduates of the six schools judged to be most experimental were compared to their counterparts in traditional programs, and their success in college was said to be greater than the graduates of the six schools judged to be least experimental. Although some of the leaders of the Progressive Education Association appeared jubilant by their apparent success in breaking the back of college domination on the secondary school curriculum, the overall reaction of the educational world and of the general public was strangely muted. What amounted to a tie between the experimental and the control group was not exactly charged with high drama, and the fact that the experimental variable was no particular curriculum pattern, but experimentation itself, made the results difficult to interpret. Much was also made of the fact that the final reports were published shortly after America's entry into World War II, a time when the niceties of curriculum reform were far from the public consciousness.

iii

Throughout the 1930s, eclecticism in curriculum development continued as a major force alongside social reconstructionism. On their side, the social reconstructionists had the stars of the educational world and the more dramatic message, but it was the eclecticists who attracted a strong following among practicing school administrators. The school rank and file were a mixed lot politically and only sporadically responded to the vision of a new social order that the social reconstructionists were advancing. Eclecticism, on the other hand, was not nearly as politically sensitive, and the public appeal of a curriculum tied directly to the needs of children as well as the duties of life made it a much safer course for school administrators to follow. Americans had always been suspicious of elitism in schooling, and a curriculum that proposed to replace what they perceived to be an elitist curriculum, good only as an admissions ticket to college, with one that was directly functional in terms of actual life activities seemed to be a definite step in the right direction. Moreover, although "meeting the needs and interests of children and youth" became an almost universal commonplace when curriculum affairs were being discussed, the long-standing social efficiency appeal of a curriculum tied to the needs of a modern industrial society and a population that was being fitted neatly and efficiently into a stable social order never seemed to lose its efficacy.

One of the mechanisms of change emerging in the 1930s was curriculum revision as a statewide enterprise. For about two decades, educational luminaries such as Ellwood P. Cubberley, Judd, Franklin Bobbitt, and

George Strayer had been hired by school systems to conduct what came to be known as school surveys in which the condition of a particular school system was assessed and recommendations made, usually along social effi- ciency lines, to improve the system (Sears, 1925). In some cases, such as in Mississippi, such surveys were conducted on a statewide basis (O'Shea, 1927). By the 1930s, influenced by the increasingly popular notion that curriculum revision should be undertaken by the participants who would be called upon to implement the innovations, some states initiated major programs of change built substantially on the Denver model.

By far the most famous of these was the Virginia Curriculum Program initiated in 1931. To head this mammoth enterprise, Hollis P. Caswell, fresh from similar projects in Florida and Alabama, was brought in as curricu- lum advisor by State Superintendent Sidney B. Hall from his post at George Peabody University. It was Caswell who was most instrumental in the effort to direct the creation of a new and radically different statewide course of study in elementary schools. Initially, all 17,000 teachers in the state were invited to join in a statewide study program, and according to Superinten- dent Hall's account, an incredible 15,000 joined the study committees that were formed and held in 1931–1932. Hall (1933) claimed that "there was no compulsion; it was entirely voluntary" (p. 341). In systematic fashion, the program proceeded through what became a familiar series of steps in curriculum making, beginning, of course, with stating objectives.

In the second year of the program, the various committees undertook the second step in the process, preparing materials to carry out the objectives. Then the programs were introduced on a trial basis, and after appropriate modifications were made, the curriculum was ready. In substance, it closely resembled what was becoming familiar as the core curriculum. In fact, under Caswell's direction, a new curriculum device, the scope-and-sequence chart, a kind of deliberate cross-hatching of two approaches to organizing the cur- riculum, was developed. One approach, the "major functions of social life" curriculum, was drawn from long-standing social efficiency ideas and pro- vided the scope, the actual subject matter of study; the second, centers of interest, provided the sequence of these activities by attending to the inter- ests that children presumably exhibited as they proceeded from early child- hood to later maturity. The social functions in the elementary school cur- riculum, listed vertically on the scope-and-sequence chart, consisted of such social functions as consumption of goods and services, communication and transportation of goods and people, and recreation. Listed horizontally across the chart were the centers of interest according to sequential grade level. In Grade I, for example, the center of interest was home and school life, in Grade II, community life, and in Grade III, adaptation of life to environmental forces of nature. The vertically listed social functions and the horizontally listed centers of interest formed cells in the body of the scope-and-sequence chart, which would be filled with appropriate subject matter. Thus, where recreation (a social function) met home and school life (a center of interest), the appropriate subject matter would become "How can we have an enjoyable time at home and school?" (Virginia State Board of Education, 1934, p. 16). Whether the centers of interest ranging from Effects of machine production upon our living in Grade VI to Social provision for cooperative living in Grade VII actually represented interests of children in anything like the sense that Kilpatrick and the activity curriculum exponents meant is open to question, but the social functions that formed the scope of the Virginia curriculum, in the main, did in fact closely resemble the areas of living that the social efficiency interest group felt ought to replace the traditional academic subjects.

The same technique was used in extending the curriculum to the secondary level, although the subject designations in English, social studies, science, and mathematics were maintained whereas, in the elementary school curriculum, an attempt was made to integrate all subject areas. The thirteen major functions of social life chosen for the social studies at the high school level were: Protection and conservation of life, property, and natural resources; Production of goods and services; Distribution of the returns of production; Consumption of goods and services; Transportation of goods and people; Communication; Exploration; Recreation; Education; Extension of freedom; Expression of aesthetic impulses; Expression of religious impulses; and Integration of the individual (Alexander, 1934, p. 76). The centers of interest for the four years were: first year—adaptation of our living through nature, social and mechanical discoveries, and inventions; second year—industrialism and agrarianism and their effects upon our living; third year—effects of changing culture and changing social institutions upon our living; and fourth year—effects of a continuously planning democratic social order upon our living (p. 77).

Although it might be stretching a point to think of these as centers of adolescent interest, the latter two indicate that at least some social meliorism made its way into the Virginia curriculum along with developmentalism and social efficiency; for example, where production and distribution of goods and services as a social function intersected with the center of interest on the effects of changing culture (third year), the central theme of the content became, "How can we improve production, establish an economic balance between production and consumption, and provide for a more equitable distribution of the returns of production?" (p. 79). Where the social function, extension of freedom, crossed with the fourth-year center of interest, Effects of a continuously planning democratic social order upon our living, the central topic became, "How can a planning society extend political, economic, intellectual, and social freedom to all people?" (p. 79).

In attempting to evaluate the success of the Virginia state curriculum, particular attention was given to the extent of teacher participation, since, like the Denver program, one of the main outcomes was perceived to be wider participation by the teachers themselves in the process of curriculum development. One questionnaire study, reported on the basis of 4,356 replies, that 85 percent of Virginia elementary school teachers were actually using the course. Some 55 percent were helping develop units of work, and 49 percent were adding to the course of study. Six percent of the teachers were reported to be using the textbook only and 9 percent were described as "disinterested and unwilling to change teaching" (Leonard, 1937, p. 69). While no data had been gathered on the children or children's achievement, the wide acceptance of the program and the extensive participation of the teachers in curriculum development activities were sources of great satisfaction to the Virginia curriculum's promoters. It also was widely discussed on a national level not only as an ideal case of "process" but as a prime example of the core curriculum. Like Tyler and the Eight-Year Study, Caswell's work on the Virginia curriculum put him in the forefront of the second generation of curriculum leaders succeeding the Bobbitts, Charters's and Sneddens of an earlier era. In fact, Caswell was brought to Teachers College in 1937 by Dean Russell to direct a reorganization of its departmental structure and, a year later, became head of the first department of curriculum and teaching.

iv

The word "progressive" had been applied to some practices in education as early as Joseph Mayer Rice's series of articles on American schools in the 1890s. For the most part, it was used synonymously with adjectives like "modern" and "new" to designate something other than traditional practice or, in some cases, simply as a positive term. But with the Progressive Education Association growing in size and visibility in the 1930s, more and more concern was expressed as to what progressive education actually was. For years, the inside track had been held by the developmentalists and epitomized by the activity curriculum, but as reconstructionists bolted into the limelight and attracted adherents like Newlon and Caswell, the picture became positively perplexing. Those sympathetic to reform of the curriculum strove mightily to bring some coherence to the medley of doctrines that had begun to claim some affinity to progressivism as articles, and books began to appear addressing the question, What is progressive education? What emerged from these efforts was sometimes a hodge-podge of incompatible practices laid side by side or an attempt to reconstruct the concept of progressive education along particular lines. In fact, what was known as progressive education became analogous to a chemical mixture in which different elements were thrown together but still retained their own characteristics. The tenuous common cause that held them together was their disillusionment and, in some cases, outright antagonism to the traditional course of study. The source of the opposition, however, varied. By some, the traditional curriculum was seen as ignoring the natural course of development in children and youth as well as their interests and penchant for activity; by others, it was regarded as supremely nonfunctional, dangerously ignoring the actual activities that adults are called upon to play in our society, leaving society bereft of the trained individuals who would make it work; and by still others, it was clearly lacking in social direction, particularly irrelevant to issues of social justice and social renewal.

The chaos that surrounded what was called progressive education increasingly made it an easy target for criticism. Here and there, cries of alarm were heard from academicians such as the youthful president of the University of Chicago, Robert Maynard Hutchins, who sought to revive the humanistic ideal of a liberal education at least at the higher education level (Hutchins, 1936). Other humanist scholars, such as Irving Babbitt, speaking from his perch at Harvard University, consistently deplored the state of decay into which American scholarship had fallen. But apart from the eternal complaint that students were arriving at the great centers of learning with ever-weaker preparation for the rigors of scholarly endeavor, academicians in the 1930s rarely bothered to intervene in the internal affairs of elementary and secondary schools.

Ultimately, a movement began to evolve within the professional education establishment as a counterbore to the curricular practices that were being promoted under the hazy rubric of progressive education. For the most part, these attacks were directed at the activity movement, which in the minds of many of the critics was considered identical with progressive education. The pivotal figure in this growing opposition was William Chandler Bagley of Teachers College. Bagley's (1905) overall position is not easily characterized. He was one of the first to hold up social efficiency as the supreme educational ideal and was a longtime admirer of Ross L. Finney, one of the major figures in the social efficiency movement. As early as the *Twenty-Sixth Yearbook*, Bagley (1926) suggested the "unwisdom" of adjusting the elementary curriculum to the needs of the local community (pp. 31–32), arguing that there ought to be a "reasonable degree of uniformity" (p. 33) in certain crucial subjects in the elementary school curriculum. The most common charge among its detractors was that the activity program lacked rigor, and, as a result, the children of America were simply not learning what they needed to know. Bagley (1929b) was critical, for example, of what he called the "freedom-theory," reminded his listeners, "I told you sixteen years ago that we could not build our democratic structure on the shifting sands of soft pedagogy," proposing instead his own motto, *"Through discipline to freedom"* (p. 146). Bagley (1929a), like Hall before him, consistently deplored what he thought of as the progressive feminization of the schools, linking it to weakness, and he looked to the day when "a more virile and less elusive educational theory" would replace the currently popular effeminate one, at the same time praising the "rugged masculinity" of Henry C. Morrison's work, especially his concept of "mastery" (p. 573). Although Bagley (1930) deplored the flaccidity of the activity curriculum, he also endorsed much of what social reconstructionism stood for, arguing that if a proper investment in education were made, there would flow a "significant amelioration of social ills" as well as a "diminution of corruption in public office . . . [and] a diminution of religious and racial intolerance" (p. 224). Although almost every educational leader in the postdepression period felt impelled to pay at least lip service to the idea that education could respond to social ills, in Bagley's case, the commitment to a fully realized democracy through education seemed genuine. He had, after all, been one of the very few leaders in education to see significant antidemocratic tendencies in the mental measurement movement that swept the country following World War I (Bagley, 1925). Bagley's quarrel was not so much with the political progressives who saw education as a potent instrument of social regeneration, but with the weak and effeminate project curriculum that robbed American children of their common cultural heritage.

By 1933, Bagley was joined in his criticism by a powerful ally, a young émigré from Russia, Michael John Demiashkevich, who helped sharpen the attack on the child-centered school. Demiashkevich received a classical education at the Imperial Historico-Philological Archaeological Institute in Petrograd before coming to Teachers College for his doctorate, which he was awarded in 1926. As against a project method deriving from children's natural impulses, he proposed, much like Harris, a "directed and controlled mastery of systematic, consecutive, and continuous curricula" (Demiashkevich, 1933, p. 170). It was in Demiashkevich's book, *An Introduction to the Philosophy of Education* (1935), that the term "essentialism" was first used as a direct contrast to progressive education. The "first meaning of the term education," he argued, "implies systematic, that is, sequential curricula (adequately covering the subject) and definite, distinctly shaped procedures or methods of study" (p. 5). It was also Demiashkevich who along with Fred Alden Shaw, the headmaster of the Detroit Country Day School, first conceived of building a national organization around the idea of essentialism as a counterpoint to the doctrines that were issuing forth under the name of progressive education. Ultimately, however, Bagley became by far the most prominent member in the group and emerged as its acknowledged leader.

Their manifesto was issued at the annual meeting of the American Association of School Administrators in Atlantic City, New Jersey, on February 26, 1938. Almost from the outset, Bagley (1938a) sounded the theme of American education being "appallingly weak and ineffective" (p. 241), especially when compared with the levels of achievement in other countries. The most direct attack on the new education in America appeared in Section II of the manifesto, "THE CAUSES: B. EDUCATIONAL THEORIES THAT ARE ESSENTIALLY ENFEEBLING" (pp. 244–250), and it was almost exclusively against the activity curriculum that the attack was directed. The history of education, Bagley claimed, could be summed up by pairs of opposites: freedom versus discipline, interest versus effort, individual versus society, play versus work, and in more recent times, immediate needs versus remote goals and psychological organization versus subject organization. (These were dualisms, of course, that Dewey spent a lifetime trying to dispel.) Under the press of mass education, Bagley argued, there was a "loosening of standards . . . [and] the theories which emphasized interest, freedom, immediate needs, personal experience, psychological organization, and pupil initiative . . . naturally made a powerful appeal" (p. 245). Rigorous attention to academic achievement was abandoned, systematic and organized learning was discredited, and the activity movement came into vogue.

Bagley claimed that many of the subjects that required the most exacting study had been virtually abandoned because of the decline of mental discipline under the influence of the psychological experiments, such as those conducted by Thorndike and Woodworth (1901), where the evidence, he claimed, was generalized more than the experiments warranted. A concomitant of the discrediting of mathematics and other exacting studies was the rise of social studies, "the primrose path of least resistance," essentially nothing but "an educational pablum" (Bagley, 1938a, p. 248). It was unfortunate, according to Bagley, that all this should be happening when the situation at home and abroad was so critical. The ideals of democracy, he declared, "are among the first essentials in the platform of the Essentialist" (p. 250). With democracy on trial, however, it became all the more important that in relation to totalitarian states there be developed "a democratic discipline that will give strength and solidarity to the democratic purpose and ideal" (p. 251). "An effective democracy," he insisted, "demands a community of culture" (p. 252), emphasizing that for democracy to survive, it was necessary that a common core be developed in the curriculum that would help create that community. He was bemused by the fact, for example, that in 1933 he found more than 30,000 courses of study in the Teachers College curriculum library. To Bagley, the elements of this common culture, and therefore the essentials in the curriculum, were really self-evident: reading, arithmetic, "at least a speaking acquaintance with man's past," art, "health instruction and the inculcation of health practices," along with basic instruction in the natural sciences (p. 253). He concluded by sounding one of his favorite themes—that American educational enterprise needed a theory that was "strong, virile, and positive not feeble, effeminate, and vague," declaring that the theories that had dominated American education had been "distinctly of the latter type" (p. 256).

The Essentialist Committee for the Advancement of American Education was from the beginning an isolated group, and, apart from Bagley himself, Demiashkevich, Isaac Kandel, and one or two others, never elicited the sympathies of major figures of the educational world. Bagley's was increasingly a lonely voice. Demiashkevich, a young and extremely promising scholar, fell severely ill in April of 1938 and, unable to continue his teaching in the spring quarter at Peabody College, took his own life in August at the age of forty-seven. Bagley (1938b) found some solace in his isolation. He said once, "It will not be a new experience" (p. 565), recalling that in his criticism of the determinism of the IQ tests he basically stood alone. "I had no companions then," he said. "As regards my anti-determinism, I seem now to be traveling with real quality folks. . . . It is better to be right than respectable" (p. 565).

Essentialism is sometimes seen as the intellectual alternative to the naive sentimentalism of the activity curriculum, but its own claims notwithstanding, it never quite asserted the primacy of the intellect that the early humanists made their linchpin. More often than not, essentialism took the form of insisting that there are certain things that future citizens need to know and these elements ought to be the heart of the curriculum. One defender of essentialism, for example, argued that "the true Essentialist believes that only those things that are vitally important should be taught" and took the position that public money should not be spent on courses "unless they can be justified on the grounds of essentiality" (Tonne, 1941, p. 312). That position was much more consistent with social efficiency than with traditional humanism. Bagley himself implied that mass education was inconsistent with quality education. The upward expansion of education, he felt, was "not guarding itself against the most fatal pitfall of democracy," leveling down rather than leveling up (Bagley, 1939a, p. 248). Unlike humanists such as Eliot, Bagley (1939b) regarded this lowering of standards as inevitable. "Rigorous requirements," he said, "simply had to be relaxed, and they have been progressively relaxed over a period now of more than thirty years" (p. 330). It was, Bagley claimed, almost as if educationists had actually welcomed and supported the softening of the American curriculum. But hard, "masculine," rigorous education should not be taken as synonymous with a classical liberal education or an education designed for intellectual mastery of the modern world. It could merely mean including in the curriculum the everyday things that people needed to function in their society and making absolutely sure that every child mastered them. There was much said by the essentialists about the importance of a common cultural heritage, but there were also easily recognizable elements of social-efficiency doctrine. The 1930s was an era where previously clear-cut ideological distinctions were obfuscated, and essentialism may have been a case where the established lines between traditional humanism and social efficiency became hard to delineate.

v

In the same year that the Essentialist Committee for the Advancement of American Education issued its platform, two short books appeared, each written by a highly respected leader in what had become known as progressive education. Both Boyd H. Bode's *Progressive Education at the Crossroads* (1938) and John Dewey's last book on education, *Experience and Education* (1938), attempted to give definition and direction to what had become a loose collection of reform ideas beset by drift, internal dissension, and external threat. Both books, although written by sympathetic critics, painted a somber picture about the then state of affairs in educational reform and sounded an ominous note about the survival of the miscellany of reforms that had become associated with progressive education.

Bode (1938) reemphasized the absence of social direction that had bedeviled the Progressive Education Association since its founding. Pointing to the "grim events" (p. 4) that were occupying the world stage, he felt that, without a guiding social philosophy, the movement was facing a major crisis. In much the same manner that Dewey took his cue from the nature of democracy as a way of life, Bode insisted that, to survive, progressive education had to evolve a democratic education as a way of life, not as a sentimental concern for children. "Progressive education," he said, "must either become a challenge to all the basic beliefs and attitudes which have been dominant for so long in every important domain of human interest, or else retreat to the nursery" (p. 5). He pointed especially to the fact that a so-called progressive school had no real defining characteristics. To be sure, there might be more of an atmosphere of freedom than in a traditional school and perhaps more active participation by the children, but a progressive school was also full of contradictions that made it impossible to define precisely. There was freedom, but there was also guidance and direction. Individualism was emphasized, yet the competitive nature of contemporary society was constantly being criticized. The colleges were regarded as the "citadel of the enemy," yet the private schools that constituted an important part of the movement and "are generally the more prosperous element in society" make preparation for college their "chief business" (p. 10). Bode urged that progressive education, rather than engaging in such shilly-shallying, become "an avowed exponent of democracy" (p. 26), arguing that if democracy is to prevail, it must evolve its own distinctive educational system.

In Bode's terms, the enemy was absolutism. That kind of aristocratic education he attributed to Hutchins, who, according to Bode, would base his educational system on "basic principles, which are valid at all times and in all places for every manner and condition of men" (p. 31). As against that conception, he presented the ideal of modern science where "our tests and standards are not derived from elsewhere but are constructed as we go along" (p. 35). It was out of this rejection of absolutism that Bode believed a democratic system of education could be based. Laws and truths in a democratic society were not handed over to us as they are in totalitarian societies, but constructed and discovered as we went along. The problem was, however, that progressivism was in danger of becoming its own absolutism, with Rousseau's doctrines being the most notable example. "Over and against the absolutes of the social order," Bode said, Rousseau "placed the alleged absolute of human nature" (p. 38). The education that had once been directed by so-called immutable truths was now being controlled by immutable laws of child development. "This," claimed Bode, "is absolutism all over again" (p. 39).

Bode's critique was a last-ditch effort to expunge what had been the child-centered origins of the Progressive Education Association, and, before that, the developmentalist notion that the curriculum ought to spring spontaneously from the interests of children. The immediate interests of children may have their place, Bode felt, but they must spring from a larger social interest and from continuity in trying to achieve it. "To interpret the doctrine of interest as meaning that all activity must be motivated by immediate and spontaneous interest," he claimed, "is to misrepresent it" (p. 53). The answer that Bode proposed was to center an educational system not on submission to authority, but on the cultivation of intelligence. Democracy, Bode insisted, is a system that relies on intelligence, for when interests collide, they are not resolved by an appeal to some final truth but by social adjustments arrived at in relation to some common end.

Bode also reiterated his earlier skepticism about the power of science to determine the curriculum, particularly in this case. He attacked the notion that a curriculum could be derived from an objective study of needs, especially what had come to be called "felt needs," as definitive expressions of the objectives of the curriculum "since a need may be a real need without being felt at all" (pp. 65–66). His contention, however, was that the problem of finding the key to determining the difference between real and spurious needs was something like the problem of finding the key to the difference between good and bad desires. Bode did not object to studies of child and adolescent development, but said, "it is misleading to call them studies of needs, because the needs still remain to be determined after the investigation is completed" (p. 67). To try to discover needs through scientific investigation was not science, but "academic bootlegging" (p. 67). The answer to the dilemma of creating a curriculum, he argued, "will not be revealed by any educational microscope" (p. 68). Bode even claimed that the extraordinary attention that was being lavished on the "needs" of childhood and adolescence had "bred a spirit of anti-intellectualism" and "indiscriminate tirades against 'subjects' in the absurdities of pupil planning, and in the lack of continuity in the educational program" (p. 70).

Bode, one of the great exponents of what had come to be called progressive education, was thus rejecting the two ingredients most commonly associated with it. In the effort to make education a direct and supremely functional preparation for life, some reformers dreamed of a scientifically determined catalog of human activity as the basis for the curriculum. In the effort to champion the child's freedom and to bring the curriculum in line with the child's true nature, other reformers turned to the laws of child growth and development. Each approach in its own way rejected the logical organization of subject matter and attempted to substitute something more scientifically valid. But, said Bode (1938), "if we may assume that the purpose of teaching is to liberate the intelligence of the pupil, it appears that we must go into 'logical organization' and beyond it" (p. 94). He even added a dictum that did not gain currency until about a quarter of a century later: "The pupil must acquire some capacity for thinking as the specialist thinks" (p. 94). The traditional subjects, Bode continued, are something "we neglect at our own peril" (p. 96). The problem with organized subject matter is not that it is organized subject matter but that it has become trivialized. "Tinkering in a laboratory," he argued, "becomes training in the scientific attitude, just as any splotching of colors and any flub-dub in written composition can pass as creative self-expression" (p. 97). If the freedom that progressives seek is ever to be achieved, Bode concluded, it is to be achieved through intelligence, not the other way around. For Bode, then, it was not the promise of a scientific curriculum or a course of study attuned to the real interests of children that constituted progressive education, but the freeing of intelligence as a way to make democracy work.

When Dewey's *Experience and Education* (1938) appeared the same year, it was taken by many to be a repudiation of the things he had stood for since the turn of the century. Actually, however, it can be more accurately described as simply a summing up of what he had been saying all along. Like Bode, Dewey was dismayed by the apparent rejection by the new education of organized subject matter. Just because "external authority is rejected, it does not follow that all authority should be rejected, but rather that there is need to search for a more effective source of authority" (p. 8). One should not assume, said Dewey, that "the knowledge and skill of the mature person has no directive value for the experience of the immature" (p. 8). One of the major problems of the "newer schools," as Dewey called them, is that they "tend to make little or nothing of organized subject-matter of study" (p. 9). What was needed was not a rejection of organized subject matter but a reconstruction of it.

Chapter VII of *Experience and Education* gave a name to the curriculum theory that Dewey had been expounding since the days of the Dewey School—Progressive Organization of Subject-Matter (p. 86). A central principle, enunciated as early as *The Child and the Curriculum* (1902a), was that the disciplines of knowledge, whatever their current lofty status, had their origins in basic human activity. "Anything which can be called a study," Dewey (1938) said, "whether arithmetic, history, geography, or one of the natural sciences, must be derived from materials which at the outset fall within the scope of ordinary life experience" (pp. 86–87). The problem of the traditional curriculum was that these basic origins in human experience were ignored, and hence knowledge was merely being heaped indiscriminately upon unwilling and uninterested children and youth. Dewey's concept of "occupations" was, he hoped, a way of restoring organized knowledge to its human origins. "But," he said, "finding the material for learning within experience is only the first step" (p. 87). That is the step that many of the newer schools had accomplished. But the curriculum remained meaningless without the next step. "The next step is the progressive development of what is already experienced into a fuller and richer and also more organized form, a form that gradually approximates that in which subject-matter is presented to the skilled, mature person" (p. 87). As with Bode, the direction the curriculum should be taking was one in which the learner progressively approximates the intellectual processes exhibited by the mature scholar. "It is a ground for legitimate criticism," said Dewey, "when the ongoing movement of progressive education fails to recognize that the problem of selection and organization of subject-matter for study and learning is fundamental" (pp. 95–96). Moreover, subject matter in its organized and logical form cannot simply be picked up in a cursory manner. While logically organized subject matter cannot provide the starting point of the curriculum, it must be the deliberate direction in which the curriculum must move.

The 1930s were ending in chaos as far as the curriculum and, as it turned out, the whole world, was concerned. Essentialists had mounted a highly visible but somewhat confused attack on the trend that American education had been taking since the 1890s. The Progressive Education Association was becoming moribund. Bode, one of the major stalwarts of what came to be known as the progressive movement, and Dewey, its living symbol, had rejected in unequivocal terms doctrines that many had assumed to be part and parcel of the new education. Curriculum revision was unquestionably in vogue, but local school districts and, in some cases, statewide systems of education were adopting curricula of uncertain pedigree and direction. Even the common front that curriculum reformers had once made against their old enemy, academic subject matter, had developed some cracks. What would be salvaged from a half century of struggle to remake the American curriculum was very much an open question.

9 | THE MOUNTING CHALLENGE TO THE SUBJECT CURRICULUM

i

WHEN THE UNITED STATES OFFICIALLY BECAME AN ACTIVE BELLIGERENT IN World War II on December 8, 1941, the course that the American curriculum had been taking over the previous half century was not so much significantly altered as accelerated. As would be expected, leaders in education insisted that American schools would not stand idly by in a time of crisis. Although, as it turned out, United States soil was not the site of active battle nor was the country subject to massive bombardment, American schools would play their part on the home front. When the Conference on War Problems and Responsibilities of Illinois Schools and Teacher Colleges was held on December 17, 1941, on the University of Illinois campus, a comprehensive outline of the schools' role in the war ahead was outlined. First there was their role in "helping to create and maintain a democratic moral" (Smith, 1942, p. 113). The contrast between the democratic way of life and the regimes of our totalitarian enemies must be made clear. Youth should receive training in first aid and must participate in scrap-metal and paper-collection drives and Red Cross work. Schools must also do what they can to counteract wartime propaganda directed against people of German, Italian, and Japanese descent, and the contributions of different ethnic and cultural groups should be emphasized. Additionally, in times of shortages, consumer education must be strengthened. Vocational training and the subject matter of such courses as physics and mathematics should be reoriented so as to place "greater stress upon aeromechanics, aeronautics, auto mechanics, navigation, gunnery, and other aspects of modern warfare" (p. 115). Subjects like biology and home economics should be redirected toward training in nursing and first aid. With the noble exception of undertaking to preach tolerance toward the descendants of the enemies of the United States, these are the kinds of measures that one might expect schools to take as a country entered into a major war. Later publications recommended similar efforts (Educational Policies Commission, 1943; National Education Association, 1943).

The course that the curriculum took was generally in the direction of those recommendations. Aviation and navigation were given special attention in the context of several subjects, and social studies emphasized war aims. Industrial arts courses were revised to take into account armament needs. Consumer economics and home management also received increased attention in order to help adjust the citizenry to life under wartime conditions (Kliebard, 1999, pp. 200–209). In Detroit, historian Jeffrey Mirel (1993) reports, the school curriculum was reorganized so as to make the maximum contribution to the war effort by tying it to potential service in the military and toward employment in war industries (pp. 156–157). Across the country, some teachers whose subjects were seen as not contributing to the war effort were shifted to teaching subjects of more immediately practical value. One source of pride to educators was that whereas only 20 percent of the armed forces in World War I had completed an eighth-grade education, that figure was close to 70 percent in World War II.

As the hostilities wore on, more and more attention was given not so much to the schools' contribution to the war effort, but to what changes should be wrought in the postwar period. In wartime, when criticism of the American social structure, such as that advanced by the social reconstructionists, could be construed as unpatriotic, and with child-centered education increasingly being attacked on all sides as soft and lacking in social commitment, it was once again social efficiency that moved to center stage. It was, after all, the curriculum doctrine that promised the most direct return from schooling, and with the country fighting a war for democracy, the reordering of the curriculum to accommodate the mass of students was equated with a democratization of the curriculum. As the trend toward the mixing of curriculum ideas persisted, the ideologies of the interest groups that had shaped the American curriculum for half a century became increasingly more difficult to recognize, at least in their pure form.

There is no question, however, that social efficiency was the curriculum's most potent ingredient in the war years and in planning for the postwar period. With concern mounting about the reintegration of millions of returning service men and women into the economy—and even some anxiety about their ability to adapt to peacetime conditions—it was social efficiency that promised the most concrete adjustment to a drastic change in the economy and a measure of stability in what might become a society beset by uncertainty and discontent. The origins of social efficiency as a curriculum ideal went back, of course, to the period shortly after the turn of the century when leaders such as David Snedden, Charles C. Peters, and Ross Finney began to articulate its major premises, but its powerful reemergence in the 1940s had more immediate antecedents. Probably the most significant by-product of the war insofar as school leaders were concerned was the dramatic decline in high school enrollments. From a high of 6.7 million in 1940–1941, enrollments fell to 5.5 million in 1943–1944. Such a steep decline after a half century of astounding growth sounded alarm bells among professional educators. Some of the drop in high school enrollments was undoubtedly due to a declining birth rate during the depression, but early enlistments in the military service and the lure of lucrative work in defense industries were also contributing factors. Increasingly, the holding power of the high school emerged as an overriding issue among school leaders. In large measure, the blame for declining enrollments tended to fall, not on demographic factors or wartime conditions, but on the continued prominence of academic school subjects in the secondary school curriculum, and this led to ever more persistent calls by curriculum reformers for a complete reordering of the high school programs in the direction of a much more functional and work-oriented course of study.

One portent of the renewed urgency was a report of a Special Committee on the Secondary School Curriculum prepared for the American Council on Education's American Youth Commission (1940), *What High Schools Ought to Teach*. The superintendent of schools of Pittsburgh, Pennsylvania, Ben G. Graham, headed the special committee that included three Teachers College professors—Thomas Briggs in secondary education and Will French and George D. Strayer in educational administration—as well as

Charles A. Prosser, the major force behind the Smith-Hughes Act twenty-three years earlier, and Ralph W. Tyler, the research director of the Eight-Year Study and now chairman of the Department of Education at the University of Chicago. *What the High Schools Ought to Teach* began with a historical account of the growth of American schools, tracing the appearance of useful subjects in what, according to the committee, had been a system patterned after the elite schools of Europe. In this regard, the committee touched on the Douglas Commission Report and how it led to the establishment of trade schools in Massachusetts and finally to the creation by Congress of the Board for Vocational Education in 1917. This, they acknowledged, was an important advance, but vocational education tended "to cultivate highly specialized skills," and much of it "fails to meet the needs of pupils because it is quite as specialized as were the traditional preprofessional courses." (Academic subjects from this perspective were considered vocational; their purpose was vocational preparation for the professions.) It was also unfortunate in the eyes of the committee that so much of vocational education consisted actually in the "preparation for so-called 'white collar' jobs," and that, given the state of the economy as they saw it, many students "are sure to be disappointed" (p. 10). This was despite the fact that white-collar jobs had been skyrocketing for about four decades and that by far the most successful vocational courses initiated during the first part of the twentieth century were the commercial and business programs catering principally to girls, not the preparation for industrial jobs that most proponents of vocational education had been endorsing for years. While, according to the commission, what were called "preprofessional" courses were appropriate to one small segment of the school population and vocational courses to another, the majority of students were left with a curriculum that was deficient "in preparing young people to take their place in adult society" (p. 10). The answer, according to the committee, did not lie in adding a new course here and another there. "[The] complete curriculum must be described as inappropriate," they declared, "because of its emphasis on items that do not accord with the ability or the outlook on the future of the majority of pupils" (p. 11).

Almost inevitably, there was a recommendation that reading instruction be improved, but the most persistent theme in the report was the emphasis on the schools' role in the world of work. "Labor is the lot of man," the report announced in no uncertain terms, "and it has not been recognized as it should have been in arranging an educational institution" (p. 15). Reading, by contrast, is easy to institutionalize. It can be taught to a class. "Productive manual work," on the other hand, cannot easily be carried forward in the classroom, and this has led American schools to neglect one of the major features of life. "Manual work," the report noted with regret, "is now no longer a part of the education of a great number of people" (p. 16). The strong emphasis on work, particularly industrial labor, may have been prompted by certain of President Franklin D. Roosevelt's New Deal programs in the 1930s, such as the National Youth Administration and the Civilian Conservation Corps, programs which were designed to provide useful employment to youth in a period of economic crisis. In time, these job programs began to incorporate important educational components. These federal initiatives in the training of youth, once the nearly exclusive domain of schools, were a serious source of concern to many educational leaders, and the prospect of federal intervention into what were once state or local prerogatives haunted many school officials (Kliebard, 1999, pp. 175–209). The report specifically mentioned the federal work projects, implying that the schools could better perform their functions of these federal agencies. While vocational education had long been advocated, and even accepted, as a function of schooling and the drive for federal aid to vocational education had been notably successful in attracting federal support, the role of the school in the development of worthwhile work habits along with occupational skills had rarely been given such an overriding emphasis. Criticisms were also presented of what were called the "conventional subjects" (American Council on Education, p. 27), principally because their role was so ambiguous in what, in their view, should be the main purpose of schooling—preparation for one's adult social and occupational role.

As part of its emphasis on the inadequacy of academic subject matter, the report singled out for particular censure the "vicious aspects of the ninth grade" where an array of courses of no use were presented to adolescents, most of whom were not "academically-minded" (p. 31). "The ninth grade," the committee announced with an unusual degree of finality, "puts an end to all general studies" (p. 31). With appropriate "exploratory" studies in the junior high school years, ninth-graders should be ready for specific training. The report concluded with the general recommendation that schools take the same interest in their products that a good manufacturing company does in its "output" (p. 32). To do this, the schools needed to know "in perfectly explicit terms what a young person is capable of doing" and then be prepared to see to it that those potentialities were realized. Throughout the report, the implications were clear that, insofar as the high school curriculum was concerned, academic subjects were appropriate only for a narrow segment of the school population, and even then, the value of these subjects lay primarily in the role they played in preparing for college.

In 1944 and 1945, two more major reports were issued, attempting to delineate the future course of education in the United States—reports that pointed in quite different directions. The first of these was issued by the Educational Policies Commission, a standing body of the National Education Association, formed in 1935 to serve as a kind of unofficial school board for the nation. The commission periodically issued pronouncements on the state of American education, making recommendations on what they considered matters of import. Of these reports, *Education for ALL American Youth* (Educational Policies Commission, 1944) dealt most directly with the curriculum conflict then being raged. In a rambling and far-fetched attempt at literary novelty, the commission contrasted "The History That Should Not Happen" (p. 2) with two utopian conceptions of American education in postwar America, one a rural school system they called Farmville and one urban, called American City. In "The History That Should Not Happen," the frightening picture of a National Bureau of Youth Service was conjured up as an outgrowth of federal experiments with youth programs in the decade preceding. By 1954, the commission warned, there would even be nationally prescribed courses in secondary schools, junior colleges, and adult classes (p. 9). These radical measures, according to the fictitious history, were made necessary by the shortsightedness of educators, once again, in failing to meet the common and individual needs of the youth of the nation. In the end, the few remaining local high schools had no recourse but to return "to their original function of preparing a selected minority of our youth for strictly cultural pursuits" (p. 9). The nightmare of federal control of the educational system and of a curriculum dominated by academic subjects presumably could be avoided if only the schools could demonstrate their capacity to realign the curriculum in line with the real and urgent needs of their students.

In the ideal postwar school, according to the commission, the needs of youth would be met first of all by vocational preparation. In the tenth grade, only one sixth of the typical student's program would be vocational, but in the eleventh and twelfth grades it would reach a full one third. The common core of subjects, rather than consisting of the traditional academic subjects, would be designed "to help students grow in competence as citizens of the community and the nation; in understanding of economic processes and of their roles as producers and consumers; in cooperative living in family, school, and community; in appreciation of literature and the arts; and in use of the English language" (p. 244). But beyond these common areas of learning there would be special attention paid to the differences of circumstance and ability that exist within the school population with "the curriculum of Grades X through XIV . . . differentiated to suit the needs of individuals" (p. 36). The commission listed ten Imperative Educational Needs of Youth as the basis for formulating the curriculum, the first of which was the need "to develop salable skills" (pp. 225–226), with the abilities of each student dictating a differentiated course of study in relation to those needs. As in the case of *What the High Schools Ought to Teach, Education for ALL American Youth*, academic subjects were portrayed as surviving in the high school curriculum mainly to serve the needs of a chosen few. By the mid-1940s, this was becoming the established position among professional educators, particularly those associated with the design of the curriculum.

As would be expected, the Harvard faculty committee that produced *General Education in a Free Society* (Committee on the Objectives of General Education in a Free Society, 1945), popularly known as the Redbook, was far more generous to academic subject matter. The committee did go out of its way, however, to strike a tone of moderation. American society had indeed changed since the late nineteenth century, as had the nature of the secondary school population, leading the committee finally to endorse a differentiated curriculum. But even for those with "lower facility with ideas," the committee recommended a general education that included "the world, man's social life, the realm of imagination and ideal" (p. 95). Careful not to exclude the now ubiquitous concern with the school's role in developing occupational skills, they tried to couple that function with the school's role in general education. "The aim of education," the committee declared "should be to prepare an individual to become an expert both in some particular vocation or art and in the general art of the free man and the citizen" (p. 54). The special education part of the curriculum would address itself to the former task and the general education part to the latter. And clearly, the sympathies of committee members lay with the general education portion of the curriculum. The core of the curriculum they recommended was expressed in terms of year-long course units: "three in English, three in science and mathematics, and two in the social studies," constituting half of the high school curriculum, a fraction they considered to be the "barest minimum" (p. 100). Although the Harvard Committee report was a far cry from the report of Harvard's former illustrious president Charles W. Eliot (National Education Association, 1893) in terms of its academic recommendations, it did represent a cautious, almost timid, restatement of the traditional humanist ideal.

William Bagley (1945) thought the Harvard report was "one of the most important educational documents of recent years" (p. 69) and interpreted it as a repudiation of Eliot's elective system, citing Eliot as "the pioneer advocate in the higher institutions of what are now known as the 'Progressive' educational theories" (p. 70). Bagley had long championed the idea that, when constructing the curriculum, the essential elements of the cultural heritage ought to be clearly identified and taught to all, and in this regard, he surely thought that the Harvard Committee was on the side of the angels.

Franklin Bobbitt (1946), on the other hand, was appalled by the recommendations. Alluding to the distinction that the Harvard report had made between general and special education, he argued that "placing the strong emphasis on the training of specialists has not been a mistake. Quite the reverse, except for literacy, it is the finest thing that educational institutions have yet done" (p. 327). But he was particularly dissatisfied with the way the Harvard faculty had defined general education. The general portion of the curriculum, he argued, was actually composed of very specific skills in all "ten areas that make up the layman's daily living" (p. 327). These ten areas "call for as many different series of specific competencies" (p. 328). General education, in other words, was quite as specific as specialized education. Rather than defining general education in terms of a set of academic subjects as the Harvard Committee had done, he felt the ten areas of living that he had identified as early as 1918 ought to be scientifically investigated in order to determine their precise components and what was necessary in order to teach them efficiently. Generally, he saw the Harvard report as being built on obviously outmoded academic foundations "that have been patently and conclusively proved unsound" (p. 332). Evidently, he feared that humanist traditions, once enunciated by the likes of Eliot and Harris, were in danger of reasserting themselves. What was needed for American education, according to Bobbitt, was a curriculum guided "not by medieval misconceptions, but by *educational* science" (p. 332). Bobbitt, now a senior statesman in the curriculum world, was obviously alarmed at the possible strengthening of academic requirements in what ought to be a predominately functional education, especially insofar as the general curriculum was concerned. It was in this sense that the nature and function of school subjects became the focus of an increasingly acerbic debate over the course that the American curriculum should follow. The Educational Policies Commission report of 1944 and the Redbook produced by the Harvard faculty were emblematic of the ever-widening split over the course that the curriculum should take.

ii

By the late 1930s, reaching a crescendo in the 1940s, and continuing into the 1950s, the curriculum debate focused on the role of particular school subjects and the subject organization of the curriculum generally. At the elementary school level, the issue continued to be framed largely in terms of an opposition between the interests of the child as the source of the curriculum on one hand, as developmentalists had long advocated, and, on the other, organized subject matter, the established position of the humanist interest group. For the most part, social efficiency educators also questioned the value of traditional subjects, but rather than emphasizing children's interests as the basis for constructing the curriculum, they promoted functional categories, such as preparing for work, family life, and wise use of leisure, that presumably would ensure efficient performance in adult living. Like the developmentalists, social efficiency educators voiced deep reservations about the persistence of traditional school subjects in the curriculum, but for them, it was the failure of such subjects to prepare properly for what presumably lay ahead that was the principal source of their concern and not the immediate interests of children. Social meliorists, on the other hand, although sometimes also impatient with the continued persistence of the traditional subjects as the basis for curriculum organization, were wary of both developmentalism and social efficiency. Given their commitment to social reform, social meliorists were especially critical of the developmentalists' insistence that adult imposition in deciding what to teach was to be avoided, since adult guidance was necessary in directing the child's studies in the direction of social issues. To be sure, children's interests had to be respected, but social meliorists like Harold Rugg and George Counts continued to be frustrated by the reluctance of child-centered educators to take seriously enough the grave problems that society faced. At the same time, they were just as critical of the doctrine of social efficiency for, at least implicitly if not directly, promoting the social status quo.

Although the idea of substituting another unit of study for the conventional academic subject was not a new one, the escalating attention being given to *needs* as the basis for what was now being called the core curriculum gave the efforts to diminish the role of subjects, or even to replace them, new impetus. In a needs-based curriculum, dissimilar positions seemingly began to find common ground as part of the trend toward hybridization. From the beginning, however, core proponents faced a problem of definition, largely because diverse curricular practices often adopted core terminology. By and large, the efforts in behalf of core were directed at secondary schools, because, in the minds of these proponents, the high school had been much more resistant to change than the elementary school. In the late 1930s, for example, reports began to trickle in from secondary schools that were experimenting with the core concept but, by and large, these programs of study found their home within a subject framework and were clearly intended to integrate two or more subjects rather than to replace them; others, few in number, took the more radical approach of actually declaring independence from the conventional subject organization of the curriculum by creating a new basis for its organization. As an example of the former, the Canton, Mississippi Junior High School instituted a program in 1935–1936 that sought to integrate social studies, English, and mathematics around the theme of "Ethiopia, Her Friends and Enemies." (Ethiopia was then under attack by Italian armies.) In social studies, newspaper and magazine articles, newsreels, and pictures relating to Ethiopia formed the basis of class discussions. Oral themes and exercises in letter writing in the English class were keyed to this topic. In the arithmetic class, graphs illustrating Ethiopian imports and exports were shown, distances calculated, and problems based on currency exchange were presented (Lawler, 1937, pp. 310–312). In the Canton program of studies, however, social studies remained social studies, English was still English, and arithmetic was recognizably arithmetic. A common theme was employed to tie them together, but the subjects nevertheless remained intact. On the other hand, the same issue of *Curriculum Journal* carried a "news note" indicating that Calumet High School in Chicago "had embarked on a curricular experiment in which all subject divisions had been abandoned" and where "the school day is divided into interest periods rather than subject periods" ("Curriculum Experiment in a Chicago High School," 1937, p. 287), and it was this conception of core that began to gain favor among leaders in the field of curriculum. Although the term *core* continued to be used in a variety of ways, it became increasingly identified with a form of curriculum organization that rejected the traditional pattern of subjects and sought to employ child and adolescent needs as a viable curricular alternative.

By the 1940s, criticism of the subject organization of the curriculum began to gain momentum. Although interest in the core curriculum waned a bit during the war years, as midcentury approached, it reached its peak of popularity among professional educators associated with curriculum study. In fact, the vast majority of books on curriculum in the late 1940s and early 1950s made the case in one way or another for *core*. Typical of these works, and one of the most prominent, was Ronald C. Faunce and Nelson L. Bossing's (1958) *Developing the Core Curriculum*. As the authors note, the use of the term *core* was initially used to refer to required subjects as distinct from electives (as it still is today), but the distinctive characteristic of the core curriculum that they underscored was *"its freedom from subject-matter patterns. . . .* In the core courses, pupils *use* subject matter as one of several means of solving their common problems of group living, instead of deriving those problems from an already organized pattern of subject matter" (pp. 6–7, original emphasis). In this way the usual relationship between knowledge and use was reversed. Instead of beginning with an organized body of knowledge such as mathematics and then demonstrating its use, the core curriculum started with a problematic situation, such as might be entailed in becoming a wise consumer, and then brought mathematical skills into play instrumentally as they bore on the problem under study. It was not mathematics as a logically organized discipline; it was mathematics as a tool for accomplishing defined tasks.

As examples of the kinds of problems that could form the basis of what were usually called "resource units," Faunce and Bossing cited a list drawn up by fifty-eight Michigan teachers in 1945 for the ninth and tenth grades:

1. Entering a new school
2. Understanding and respecting other members of our democratic society
3. Conserving natural resources
4. Choosing an occupation
6. Getting along better with people (p. 242)

Presumably, these problems would be the direct focus of the curriculum with knowledge and skills learned in the context of addressing them. The ostensible purpose of such a drastic change in the curriculum's center of gravity was to present knowledge in a useful form and thereby not only to attend to student interest, but to create a taut connection between what was studied in school and the lives of the students.

Probably the best-known work in support of the core curriculum specifically at the secondary school level was Harold Alberty's (1953) *Reorganizing the High-School Curriculum*, which first appeared in 1947 and then in a revised edition in 1953. As the title of his book suggests, Alberty was committed not to tinkering with the subjects of study but to a total reorganization of the secondary school curriculum. In line with the prevailing sentiment of curriculum leaders at the time, he pointed earnestly and enthusiastically in the direction of the core curriculum. Whatever may be the differences within the school population with respect to "intelligence level, socioeconomic status, race, nationality, or creed," he said, it was the job of the schools "to meet their needs, solve their problems, and extend their interests in such a way as to promote their fullest personal development as responsible citizens of our democracy" (p. 45). As one example, Alberty (1953) provided a list of areas of study that the Ohio State University School approved for the seventh, eighth, and ninth grades. It was considerably more extensive than Faunce and Bossing's but very similar in tone and substance:

1. Understanding My Body
2. Beliefs and Superstitions
3. Hobbies

4. Managing My Personal Affairs
5. Sports and Recreation
6. Living in the University School
7. Living in the Home
8. Living in the Neighborhood
9. Personality and Appearance
10. Earning a Living
11. Housing
12. Natural Resources
13. Community Agencies and Services
    Recreation
    Protection
    Government
    Education
    Welfare
14. Communications
15. Living in Columbus
16. Living in Ohio
17. Living in Another Country or Other Countries

Although there was no suggestion that all these core areas be covered in just those three grades, the list nevertheless includes a formidable array of nonacademic responsibilities that schools should undertake.

The most difficult problem faced by the proponents of the core curriculum was quite simply implementation. Not only was there an entrenched tradition of building a curriculum around subjects, many relatively impermeable school structures, particularly at the secondary school level, revolved around the very subjects that were being so roundly criticized. The organization of departments, the class schedules that students followed, methods of evaluation, and the very identity of teachers were based on long-established subject matter categories. In addition, teacher education, even at the elementary level, was based largely around the teaching of subjects such as reading, social studies, and science. Installing a curriculum based on child or adolescent needs rather than subjects was not just a question of making the case conceptually (or, for that matter, historically), but in radically reshaping the structures on which schooling and teacher education had rested for a great many years.

There was also another kind of concern that would occasionally creep into debates over whether to base the curriculum around needs. By undertaking to organize the curriculum around the needs of children and adolescents directly, critics would claim, matters of serious consequence in terms of intellectual development may simply be crowded out. As Boyd Bode (1940), for example, once said in the context of an extended critique of a 1940 book on needs, "If we start with needs and insist of following their lead, things of central importance never get into the picture and youth is robbed of its birthright" (p. 536). Bode was arguing, of course, that by attempting to address the myriad needs of youth (even assuming they can be identified and cataloged) schools may, in the end, fail to take seriously enough the crucial role of cognitive development, including initiating children and youth into the organized intellectual resources of the culture, and in neglecting that crucial task, deprive the next generation of the opportunity to share in their rightful legacy. Despite enormous difficulties in terms of implementation and opposition here and there from an occasional critic and a wary public, however, core proponents began to meet with some success in installing its programs in secondary schools.

iii

Among the most vexing problems in trying to assess the actual impact of the core curriculum is the fact that the term *core* continued to be used in diverse ways, which makes any examination of the extent to which it was being translated from advocacy to practice complex and confusing. Not all versions, as already noted, could legitimately be represented as rejecting the subject organization of the curriculum. Faunce and Bossing (1951), for example, cite "a block of time considerably longer that the traditional class period" as justifying the name of "core program" (p. 6), and Alberty's (1953) "Type Four Core" is defined as "the Fusion of Two or More Required Subjects" (p. 174). Leading core advocates, in other words, used their signature term in a variety of ways. As a result, reforms using core terminology may or may not have represented an unequivocal rejection of the subject organization. In many instances, almost certainly a majority, these reforms entailed the integration of two or more existing school subjects, much as was the case with the Canton, Mississippi school that attempted an integration of English, social studies, and mathematics around a common theme of Ethiopia. Although, in some cases, these reforms required considerable effort and ingenuity, they were principally experiments designed to overcome a systemic problem *within* the traditional subject curriculum—the isolation of one subject from another. To this day, high school students typically move from one 50-minute period to another with no sense that one subject could somehow be connected to another. Tying two or more subjects together is an attempt to address this problem by introducing common themes, more often than not in a combined time block. At its most primitive level, this type of *core* is an effort to bridge the gap between one subject and another by prescribing a theme to draw them together. To the extent that such reforms succeeded, they served to strengthen the subject organization of the curriculum by creating relationships (albeit sometimes superficially) that served to connect one subject to another. (Rather than *core*, more appropriate terms for such efforts would be *correlated curriculum* or *fused curriculum*—terms that were actually used to describe such experiments from time to time. Conceptually, they are actually variants on the subject curriculum.)

It was this conception of *core* that seemed to have been most successful in terms of implementation. In a survey undertaken by Grace S. Wright (1949), 11.3 percent of the 11,069 public secondary schools returning the inventory reported having instituted a core program. Almost all of these, insofar as can be determined from the data, however, were combinations of existing school subjects; for example, of the 1,019 schools reporting core programs, 813 were combinations of English and social studies (p. 13). In the vast majority of cases, *core* was taken to mean that there was a block of time set aside that was longer than the traditional class period. Here and there, a needs-based core was reported such as the one in Garrett County, Maryland, grade 10, where the studies were listed as intercultural relations, living in one world, leisure and recreation, and communicating ideas (p. 20).

At the time, the U. S. Office of Education was keenly interested in advancing the cause of core, and Wright (1952) published a second survey, less extensive than the earlier one in scope, but one in which types of core were distinguished. According to the evidence presented, the dedicated efforts on the part of professional educators to shift the emphasis from a subject organization of the curriculum to something reflecting core ideology proved fruitful here and there, but generally alongside a curriculum based on subjects. Wright notes that, "In the early years of the

Eight-Year Study, breaking down subject barriers consisted simply of the correlation of two subjects," but that later "some schools went still further in eliminating subject-matter lines" (pp. 4–5). Drawing on Alberty's classifications of different kinds of core programs, Wright bracketed those programs that were combinations of subjects, referring to them as "core type—but not true core" and reported separately on those where "certain problems are persistent to the lives of all youth" and ones that allow "free choice of problem selection" (p. 7). Of these more radical types of core, 42.8 percent (222 out of 545 schools) reported at least one. Approximately 14 percent of the principals who had recorded some type of core program in 1949, however, reported no core program in 1952, indicating that core had been tried, but, for one reason or another, had been discontinued. The Denver and Minneapolis school systems, for example, found it necessary either to drop core programs entirely or to relegate them to an elective basis "because of serious public relations problems" (pp. 10–11). Overall, Wright's two surveys indicate that although core programs had met with a few successes in terms of implementation, adoption was far more meager than the advocates had hoped for in terms of both the number of secondary schools who had experimented with core and the extent to which such programs displaced the academic subjects that made up the general education portion of the curriculum. To the extent that core was adopted in schools, it was a limited program existing alongside a curriculum that consisted of subjects. Although proponents of a needs curriculum had apparently won the rhetorical battle in the world of professional education, the vast majority of secondary schools remained resistant to the allure of core.

iv

Although U. S. Office of Education data provide important clues as to the extent to which the core curriculum and related practices were implemented at the secondary school level, the paucity of such data on the elementary curriculum makes it much more difficult to get a sense of the extent to which elementary classrooms adopted the array of reforms that the twentieth century produced. For a picture of what urban elementary schools were like at the turn of the century, the best source is Joseph Mayer Rice's series of observations of elementary classrooms (see Chapter 1). For nineteenth-century schools, particularly rural schools, Barbara

Finkelstein's *Governing the Young: Teacher Behavior in Popular Primary Schools in Nineteenth-Century United States* (1989) is an invaluable compendium of memoirs and other reports by former teachers and others. For the twentieth century, two studies stand out in terms of elementary schools: Arthur Zilversmit's (1993) *Changing Schools: Progressive Education Theory and Practice, 1930–1960* and Larry Cuban's (1993) *How Teachers Taught: Constancy and Change in American Classrooms, 1880–1990*.

Zilversmit undertook to assess "the ways in which John Dewey's philosophy affected individual schools" (p. 11), although the school practices he focuses on tend to be generalized reforms drawn mainly from developmentalist thinking rather than what Dewey specifically endorsed. The sites for Zilversmit's research are four suburban or suburban-like Illinois schools systems: Winnetka, Lake Forest, Waukegan, and Mundelein. Winnetka's reputation as an innovative school system goes back to the work of its well-known superintendent Carleton Washburne (see Chapter 8), whose curriculum plan was to set up individual programs of study in key areas of study for each child along with specific goals to be accomplished. Children were to seek to accomplish these goals individually. Once the predetermined goals were successfully reached, the child would be permitted to go on to the next set of tasks. Zilversmit astutely points out in this regard that this highly individualized practice "was antithetical to Dewey's progressive classroom as a community" and that such a focus on so-called essentials "was in harmony with the efficiency movement in education" (pp. 41–42). What were called "group and creative activities," however, made up about half the school day, and by the late 1920s and 1930s, Skokie, in particular, had experimented with student government and activities that at least in part were student-initiated. By the 1940s and 1950s, children in the Crow Island School were engaged in such activities as building a teepee in the classroom and the creation of a "pioneer room" where they could recreate early American pioneer life. The idea of a pioneer room actually does resonate with the kinds of things that Dewey introduced in his Laboratory School, but it is difficult, based on the available accounts, to determine whether anything like a Deweyan curriculum was indeed being pursued in the school. Much would depend in this case on whether, in the course of recreating pioneer life, the children were led in the direction of a deeper understanding of the economic, aesthetic, social, scientific, and moral life of those pioneers. Despite some evidence of innovative practices here and there, Zilversmit concludes from his study of these school systems, that "measured by the high and lofty ideals of progressive education, American schools had failed" (p. 168). Progressivism, however, is such a diffuse and slippery concept that it is difficult to pinpoint what exactly was found wanting. If Zilversmit means that Dewey's ideas, in particular, had little impact on the curriculum of elementary schools in Illinois or anywhere else, then he is on solid ground. Even if the measures of success are criteria that address the extent to which there was some attention paid to student interests in organizing the curriculum or to overcoming the passivity that characterizes many traditional classrooms, the results would still be disappointing to developmentalist-oriented reformers.

Larry Cuban's (1993) important work focuses predominantly on the extent to which American classrooms changed from being teacher-centered to pupil-centered over the course of a century. This is at once a more limited and more manageable focus than whether schools were "progressive" or not. Cuban alludes, for example, to the observations of a journalist, Agnes DeLima (1925), in New York City classrooms that were regarded as "progressive," but who reported nebulous results. Cuban implies, in this regard, that to pose the question as to whether classroom practices were indeed "progressive" would be difficult, if not impossible, to answer. "The ideas nested in 'progressivism,'" he says, "were diverse and ambiguous, appealing strongly to dissimilar reformers in the decades bracketing World War I" (p. 49). Drawing on transcripts and other New York City data for the period 1920–1940, Cuban concludes that about one in four New York City elementary teachers adopted some sort of pupil-centered instruction during that period, although not, by any means, exclusively.

At the same time in Denver, a school system strongly influenced by the Eight-Year Study, Cuban found that the superintendent, Jesse Newlon, was much more committed to installing such reforms, resulting in greater success in terms of implementation. Nevertheless, by criteria such as the amount of teacher-centered instruction as opposed to student-centered instruction, a mixed pattern tended to emerge, and insofar as the amount of talk by teachers, as distinct from that of elementary pupils, is concerned, a combination of both predominated. In Washington, D.C., during the same two decades, the pattern was closer to that of New York City than of Denver, indicting that, in all likelihood, the dedication of key administrators, like Newlon, affected the outcome of the reforms. In general, the effort to shift from teacher-centered to pupil-centered instruction was far more successful at the elementary than at the secondary level (pp. 86–87).

In terms of creating a more child-centered classroom, extant evidence seems to indicate that, despite some shifts here and there, the results were still decidedly mixed. Cuban's estimate that, overall, not more than one fourth of teachers adopted some sort of pupil-centered practices is as good as any (p. 273). Probably most noteworthy is the evidence that indicates a hybrid emerging as a consequence of the dedicated efforts of a range of reformers. Although leading reformers tended to be purists in what they advocated, the exigencies of school life and public expectations virtually dictated that, at best, some kind of composite in terms of classroom practice would materialize.

v

Seven years before the onset of the twentieth century, the Committee of Ten unabashedly set forth its vision of a revised secondary school curriculum framed in terms of academic subjects. Within a couple of decades, curriculum reformers of various stripes undertook to challenge that fundamental assumption. Projects, functional categories such as leisure and family living, social problems, and, of course, needs were at one time or another proposed as replacements for—or more often as supplements to—conventional subjects. Representatives of interest groups supporting such changes could point to a success here and there, but, by and large, dethroning school subjects turned out to be a much more formidable task than the proponents of such change ever imagined. Their inability to dislodge the subject as the basic unit out of which a curriculum would be constructed did not mean, however, that their efforts were completely fruitless. Some schools adopted core practices while retaining standard subject labels, and, understandably, some subjects were more vulnerable to the allure of core than others. The fact that changes by curriculum reformers were both limited and subtle, however, makes their successes all the more difficult to assess. (The ways in which some subjects adopted core or needs terminology and practices while still retaining the subject label is discussed in Chapter 10.)

At the secondary level, the call for a rejection of school subjects in favor of a core curriculum organized around needs was justified in large measure by the contention that the persistence of subjects like algebra, history, and the natural sciences was the result of the malevolent influence of the colleges on secondary education. College domination of the secondary school curriculum, after all, had been the war cry of the Eight-Year Study back in the 1930s, and that massive undertaking was undertaken to show that so-called college-preparatory subjects were not especially successful even in terms of students' success in college. Since the study of academic subjects was not even warranted in that regard, so the criticism went, what good was it?

Commentators on this phenomenon often cited the mistaken conviction that as many as two-thirds of the high school population around 1900 were on their way to college (viz. American Association of School Administrators, 1968, pp. 156, 166). In one expression of this widespread belief in the primacy of college preparation, Galen Jones (1949), the director of the Division of Elementary and Secondary Schools of the U.S. Office of Education, declared in 1949, "When the primary purpose of secondary education was preparation for college, higher education institutions very largely determined the content, form, and standard of instruction of the preparatory schools." Jones then went on to argue that "as the numbers of youth seeking a high school education increased, secondary schools found it necessary to provide curriculums which were not primarily intended to meet college entrance requirements since most of the youth would not go to college" (p. iii). In general, the argument was that, whereas the so-called college-preparatory curriculum may have made some sense in an era when most high school students were college bound, a new and different secondary school population required a drastic reordering of that outmoded course of study. The subject organization of the curriculum, it was argued, was simply a relic of that bygone era.

In 1889–1890, however, the percentage of public high school students preparing for college was reported to be only 14.4, and in 1908–1909, when high school enrollments were already beginning to burgeon, that percentage fell to below 7 percent, according to one early estimate (Kelsey, 1911, pp. 4–5). After a careful review of the data on college preparation at the turn of the century, historian Edward A. Krug's (1962) estimates were relatively modest. He concluded that not more than one third of the graduates of public high schools around the turn of the century actually went on to college. Moreover, as Krug (1964) also pointed out, admission to college around that time was based largely on individual examinations administered by the colleges themselves, not by requiring specific credits in certain subjects, and preparation for these examinations was mainly accomplished through private study. Sometimes, such preparation was provided by the colleges themselves.

Data on college attendance by high school graduates in the early part of the twentieth century are consistent with Krug's (1962) estimate. In 1921, 31.4 percent went on to higher education; in 1933, it was 21.3 percent, and in 1937, it was 24.0 percent (Latimer, 1958, p. 162). The declines in 1933 and 1937 are probably due in large measure to the effects of the Great Depression. Even insofar as Latin, often regarded as the quintessential "college-entrance" subject, is concerned, it is likely that enrollments remained so robust early in the twentieth century (with around half of the total public secondary school population enrolled) not because Latin was required by colleges but simply because it was perceived as a mark of a learned person, and many high school students with no intention of going to college had such aspirations. After all, the high school at that time was frequently looked upon as the "people's college." In any case, beginning around 1900, colleges were increasingly dropping Latin as a requirement for admission. To the extent that Latin survives today as a high school subject, it is still seen largely as conferring academic status on students who choose that option.

Even the notion that high schools came into being for the purpose of college preparation has little or no basis in the historical record. In the definitive history of the nineteenth-century American high school, William J. Reese (1995), for example, referring to "the myth of the early college-dominated high school" concluded that "from their inception in the 1820s, high schools had emphasized the practical side of life, represented by the English studies, and in both theory and practice had already moved far away from the traditions of the old-time Latin grammar school"(p. 260). Whatever may have been the reasons that academic subjects remained a staple of the high school curriculum, it was not because high schools functioned at some imagined point in the remote past primarily as college preparatory institutions. That assumption becomes more credible, however, after midcentury. Whereas, in 1939, the number of high school graduates stayed at about a third of the secondary school population, that figure reached more than half—1,225,000—by the 1960s. Additionally, by that time, many colleges did, in fact, specify certain academic requirements for college admission. This reinforced the long-standing article of faith among some curriculum reformers that the main purpose of studying an academic subject was to provide an admission ticket for college. To this day, academic subjects like algebra, chemistry, and foreign languages are referred to as college-entrance subjects as if that is all they are good for, and students who take them carry the label of college-entrance students. Whatever role subjects such as these may play in the intellectual develop-ment of students or in simply contributing to their education as human beings was, by midcentury, largely submerged.

The romantic notion that high schools were at one time citadels of aca-demic learning also has little historical basis. Although their curricula were clearly built around traditional schools subjects, early high schools were, by and large, not havens for rigorous intellectual activity and lofty ideals of scholarship. Rather than nurturing "inquiring minds," nineteenth-century high schools concentrated on seeing to it that the students were "punctual, deferential, and obedient" (Reese, 1995, p. 261). For good or ill, the presumption that academic subjects existed principally in earlier times for furthering the careers of a predominantly college-entrance population is not historically accurate. Neither is the belief that there was at one time a blissful era when public schools were sites for the developing reason, gaining power and subtlety in the use of language, engaging in scientific inquiry, learning to respond to music and the fine arts, or effectively addressing social and human problems. It certainly may be the case that the subject curriculum had the potential for promoting such intellectual ideals, but the first half of the twentieth century was not a time when those considerations took center stage.

10 | THE STATE OF SCHOOL SUBJECTS AT MIDCENTURY

i

ALTHOUGH IT IS OBVIOUS THAT SCHOOL SUBJECTS WERE FAR FROM vanquished by core proponents, data on enrollments and internal changes in the main subject areas serve to illustrate the extent to which school subjects were affected by the immense increase in secondary school registrations in the first half of the twentieth century. Undoubtedly, the determined efforts by some school reformers to break the grip of traditional academic subjects on the secondary school curriculum played its part as well. Just below the surface of the argument that college-entrance requirements were controlling the high school curriculum was a widespread conviction among many school reformers that traditional academic subjects were not only of no interest and no real use to the new population of students but simply beyond their reach. Even the subjects that continued to appear on official records over the years were, in some cases at least, being quietly transformed. In the aftermath of the Cardinal Principles report (National Education Association, 1918), a tacit accord had been reached whereby those students identified as college bound would continue to enroll in academic courses, but other options would be developed, either modified forms of the standard subjects or new ones relating to future occupational roles or to some aspect of personality development and life functions. These would become the fare for those students who presumably had no inclination for academic study or, for that matter, no aptitude for it.

Although many secondary schools, especially the larger ones, accepted that compromise and introduced forms of tracking, proponents of core persisted in their effort to break the grip of academic subjects on the high school curriculum by installing a curriculum organized around child and adolescent needs. Almost from its inception, the U. S. Office of Education has published enrollment data on secondary school subjects, and something of the fate of these school subjects can be ascertained by examining these data on the major areas of study in the first half of the twentieth century. On the whole, they indicate some stability, of course, but there are also some radical shifts in course-taking patterns by secondary school students and even some indications of the way the subjects were being transformed internally. Unfortunately, comparable data on elementary school course taking are virtually nonexistent. Curriculum reformers around midcentury were not exactly gratified by the pace of change in elementary schools, but secondary schools were increasingly being seen as the new battleground. The meager record of adoption of reforms at the elementary level was a source of concern, but social efficiency educators, in particular, regarded secondary schools as better positioned to prepare the school population for its adult place in society.

For the most part, Office of Education reports indicate declining enrollments in academic school subjects over the first half of the twentieth century when calculated as a percentage of total enrollment in grades 9 through 12. These data were unquestionably influenced by burgeoning high school enrollments, beginning around 1890; in some cases, therefore, greater *numbers* of students were actually taking a subject such as algebra as the twentieth century progressed, even as the percentages declined. There were some notable exceptions, however, and a composite picture of the fate of school subjects over the course of the first half of the twentieth century may emerge from a capsule review of how the major secondary school subjects fared.

ii

Classical languages were frequently cited by latter-day reformers as benefiting from a secondary school population geared to college entrance at the turn of the twentieth century. Ancient Greek, however, was never studied to any appreciable extent in American secondary schools, having achieved an enrollment of only 3.1 percent of the secondary school population in

1890, three years before the Committee of Ten report was issued. By 1922, registrations in Greek had dropped to less than 1 percent, and enrollments after that were too small even to mention. Latin, a very much more popular subject at the turn of the century, suffered a similar fate. About a third of the public high school population was enrolled in Latin in 1890 with 100,144 students registered. In both the 1900 and 1910 reports, Latin enrollment reached its apogee of around 50 percent, with 362,548 public high school students (147,598 boys and 214,950 girls) enrolled in 1910; by 1922, however, Latin enrollments had already dropped precipitously to 27.5 percent. An Office of Education survey issued in 1938 reporting registrations as of the 1933–1934 school year, noted that "the mortality in registration [in Latin] was especially heavy between the second and third years" and continues into the fourth year, but approximately 16 percent of all students in grades 9 through 12 were still enrolled in Latin in 1934, and more than 63 percent of American high schools were still offering that subject (U.S. Department of the Interior, 1938 p. 10). By 1949, however, Latin registrations had dropped to 7.8 percent (Latimer, 1958, p. 26).

Exact causes for these declines in percentages may never be established definitively, but the data are certainly consistent with the messages promulgated by social efficiency reformers, especially in the 1920s, when subjects like classical languages—and, to a somewhat lesser extent, modern foreign languages—were deemed next to useless in terms of adult living. In that earlier era, reformers like Bobbitt and Snedden demanded to know whether all that language study, among other things, would actually be reflected in the lives of students when they became adults. Once that criterion was established, it was difficult for defenders of classical languages to make their case. By the 1940s and early to mid-1950s, such messages were, if anything, being delivered with even greater force by a new generation of curriculum leaders. To be sure, massive social changes impelled by the industrial revolution were also implicated in the decline in Latin's popularity. Moreover, the popular explanation, entailing, as it did, not just the increase in the size of the secondary school population but a major shift in terms of students' interests, aspirations, and aptitudes, unquestionably played its part as well.

Interestingly, modern foreign languages did not benefit materially from the virtual disappearance of Greek from the high school curriculum and from the precipitous decline in Latin enrollments. The study of German, for example, peaked in 1910 at 23.7 percent of enrollments in grades 9 through 12. In 1934, only one high school in fifteen offered German, and by 1949 registration in German had declined to 7.8. French fared no better. The high point for French was 15.5 in 1922. About 35 percent of high schools were offering French in 1934, and enrollments stood at only 11 percent. Spanish enrollments were virtually nonexistent in the first three decades of the twentieth century. As late as 1934, only one in six high schools offered Spanish, and only 2.5 percent of high school students were taking it, but by 1949, enrollments had climbed to 8.2 percent. Overall, in 1934, a bit more than half of high school students were registered for any foreign language in ninth grade, slightly less than half in the tenth, and by the eleventh grade fewer than one eighth of high school students were enrolled in any foreign language. Some in the latter group were actually beginning a foreign language as juniors, so that figure should not be interpreted as representing a third year of a single foreign language (U.S. Department of the Interior, 1938, p. 11). For all foreign language enrollments, classical and modern, the highest percentage, 84.1, was reached in 1922.

iii

Mathematics, a cornerstone of scholarly study since the days of ancient Greece, retained its lofty status for a time around the turn of the century but ultimately began to lose some ground. Mathematics, of course, continued to be a mainstay of the curriculum, but enrollment percentages in subjects like algebra and geometry declined. In 1890, 45.4 percent of the 203,000 students in public secondary schools were enrolled in algebra. When secondary school enrollments climbed dramatically to 519,000 in 1900, the percentage of students taking algebra actually *rose* significantly to 56.3 percent, and even in 1910 when public high school enrollments reached 739,000, algebra registrations as a percentage did not suffer. Slightly more than half of the students taking algebra in 1910 were girls, but course taking by girls in algebra (and geometry as well) began to decline thereafter (Latimer, 1958, p. 145). It is certainly possible that as commercial courses began to assume new prominence in the curriculum of American secondary schools, girls, who were flocking to these programs in anticipation of office work, did not see academic mathematics as contributing materially to their career choices (Kliebard, 1999, pp. 221–223).

Beginning in 1922, when high school registrations reached 2,155,000, algebra began to slip, falling to 40.2 percent. Twelve years later, when enrollments in grades 9 through 12 more than doubled once again, reaching 4,437,000, algebra enrollments fell again to 30.4 percent and then to 26.8 percent in 1949 (Latimer, 1958, p. 23). Enrollments in geometry followed a similar pattern. Trigonometry enrollments were always reported as insignificant in this period. General mathematics did not make its first appearance in official reports until 1934 with an enrollment of 3.0 percent, which rose to 13.1 percent by 1949. After collating a number of reports on patterns of mathematics enrollments, Angus and Mirel (2003) point out that although gross enrollments in mathematics rose steadily in the first part of the twentieth century, this was due largely to the phenomenal increase in overall enrollments in grades 9 to 12. As a percentage, however, student enrollments in all high school mathematics courses declined from a high of 76.9 percent in 1914 to 55 percent in 1948 (p. 451). Although algebra and geometry percentage enrollments were falling rather sharply between 1921 and 1933, this loss was not exactly the result of new nonacademic options then beginning to make their appearance on official reports. Data on these courses are rather spotty, but Angus and Mirel (2003) estimate that even when arithmetic and commercial arithmetic are taken together in grades 9 through 12, their combined enrollment percentages actually dropped from 12 to 9 percent during that period (p. 454). Rather than embracing these alternatives to academic mathematics, many students apparently chose to omit mathematics altogether.

The prevailing high school graduation requirement in mathematics at midcentury was one Carnegie unit (an academic year of study). To meet this requirement, according to one survey, approximately 60 percent of students took algebra, and the other 40 percent elected general mathematics. In that period, algebra below ninth grade was rarely taught. About 80 percent of students in grades 7 and 8 were enrolled in arithmetic and the remaining 20 percent in general mathematics (Cummings, 1949). Other high school mathematics courses were not exactly flourishing. A survey conducted in 1952–1953 indicated that only one third of tenth graders were taking geometry, and about one fourth of eleventh graders were enrolled in intermediate algebra. By the twelfth grade, only one tenth of students were registered in mathematics (Brown, 1953).

The study of academic mathematics was subject to the same kind of criticism by many curriculum reformers that was directed at foreign languages. Practical mathematics was one thing, but higher mathematics was quite another. When, for example, the Progressive Education Association's *Mathematics in General Education* (1940) appeared, it reflected an extension of the skepticism that had been emerging earlier in the century in relation to academic subjects for the general student. Understandably, the book emphasized the vast expansion of the high school population—from roughly 700,000 in 1900 to 6,500,000 in 1939—and therefore the urgent need to re-create the curriculum for these new students. As would be expected, the authors expressed a profound pessimism about the ability of this new population to cope with the rigors of academic mathematics. "[T]he complete curriculum must be described as inappropriate," they said, "because of its emphasis on items that do not accord with the ability or the outlook on the future of the majority of pupils" (p. 11). Like other volumes in the Progressive Education Association's series on general education, the recommendations for change centered around a fourfold classification of what were being called needs, although they bear a close resemblance to the classifications of human activity reflected in the aims of the Cardinal Principles report in 1918 and to subsequent efforts to organize the curriculum directly around categories of life activity. The four main categories of needs—personal living, immediate personal-social relationships, social-civic relationships, and economic relationships—were conceptually very similar (p. 20), for example, to what core curriculum advocates had been promoting all along, in part at least, as a substitute for the subject curriculum. The main difference in this instance was that these "needs" were being proposed as the basis of a curriculum specifically in mathematics. The authors of *Mathematics in General Education* were unequivocal on this point: "The Committee advocates planning curricular sequences primarily on the basis of concrete problems encountered in meeting educational needs in these four areas, rather than on the basis of logical sequences of the familiar sort, or separate subjects like algebra, plane geometry, solid geometry and so on" (p. 72).

America's official entry into World War II brought with it new calls for rigor in teaching mathematics because of its relevance to the kind of technical expertise that military and defense needs required (Kliebard and Franklin, 2003, pp. 430–433), but, not surprisingly, these new calls for mathematics literacy were strongly tinged with the long-standing social efficiency emphasis on direct utility. The study of mathematics was not, for the most part, being promoted because of its standing as a vital cultural and intellectual resource or, as it had been in an earlier era, as a way of developing reasoning power. Its advocates saw it as a tool for achieving a defined and urgent task. In the years immediately following the end of hostilities, curriculum reformers sympathetic to the main tenets of social efficiency redoubled their efforts to install a mathematics curriculum based on the specific tasks that adult living required, such as balancing a checkbook and preparing a tax return. Referring to the postwar period, Alan W. Garrett and O. L. Davis Jr. (2003) conclude that "this period of curriculum planning was constrained by adherence to the concept of social efficiency and its limiting precept that students need only study what they likely would apply in a straightforward manner later in life. For most students, this ultimately implied a diminution of the role of mathematics in the curriculum" (p. 509). By the late 1940s, social efficiency, in other words, was reasserting its commanding position among the various strains of curriculum reform in terms of mathematics as well as in the curriculum generally.

iv

Although the traditional sequence in high school mathematics—elementary algebra, plane geometry, intermediate algebra and trigonometry, advanced algebra—saw little change over the course of the first half of the twentieth century, science in schools underwent remarkable transformations both in terms of the sequence and in terms of subject-matter content. Because these reconstructions occurred within the familiar subject framework, however, they tend to be overlooked. The most dramatic and enduring of these changes was the emergence of biology as a school subject. At the turn of the twentieth century, the highest enrolled science subjects were physiology at 27.4 percent, geology at 23.4 percent, and physics at 19.0 percent (Latimer, 1958, p. 28). Physiology was the science subject that was thought to bring the most direct health benefits, and it was for this reason that physiology was endorsed by many physicians, the editor of *Popular Science Monthly*, William J. Youmans, and the Woman's Christian Temperance Union (Pauly, 1991, pp. 662–668). In the physical sciences, 22.8 percent of high school students were registered in physics in 1890, with 10.1 percent taking chemistry. Between 1890 and 1915, physics enrollments were twice that of chemistry. Thereafter, percentages show a steady decline in these subjects, with physics falling to 6.67 percent in 1934 and chemistry to 7.56 (U.S. Department of the Interior, 1938, p. 29). Biology did not make an appearance in Office of Education data until 1910 when a mere 1.1 percent of the then 2,155,000 public secondary school students were registered in the subject. By 1922, that percentage was still a low 8.8, but it began to flourish thereafter. The data seem to indicate that various individual subjects in what came to be known as the "life sciences" were successfully fused into a single school subject called biology, and, as a result, certain once-popular specialized sciences lost ground. Subjects like physiology and botany, for example, virtually disappeared from the high school curriculum by midcentury. According to one survey (Brown, 1956), a full 75.5 percent of tenth graders were taking biology as compared to 34.6 percent of eleventh graders in chemistry and 24.3 percent of twelfth graders in physics (p. 9). The same survey indicated that while 18.2 percent of American high schools offered neither physics nor chemistry, only 9.7 percent were not offering biology (p. 6).

The remarkable rise of biology as a school subject, however, was only incidentally the result of a deliberate national effort to reorganize the science curriculum, although articles on biology as a school subject began to appear early in the century (viz. Linville, 1907; Gallaway, Caldwell, and Norris, 1909). Probably the biggest impetus to its adoption in the curriculum of secondary schools was the publication of biology textbooks such as Francis Lloyd and Maurice A. Bigelow's (1904) *The Teaching of Biology in Secondary Schools* and George W. Hunter's (1907) *Elements of Biology*. Much of the work in developing and promoting biology as a school subject was done at DeWitt Clinton High School, then located in Hell's Kitchen in New York City, one of the most notorious slums in the United States. Harry R. Linville, who was closely allied with John Dewey and chair of the Department of Biology, and George W. Hunter were both biology teachers there, as was Benjamin C. Gruenberg, who was also managing editor of the journal, *American Teacher* (Pauly, 1991, pp. 667–673). Their remarkably successful school-based efforts were reinforced in the world of science outside of schools where there was an interest increasingly being expressed in linking natural sciences together. The emergence of novel combinations in science such as astrophysics and biochemistry were related phenomena.

Another new science subject, general science, which emerged in the 1920s, was an even more ambitious effort in the direction of a unified science. Like biology, general science seems to have been a by-product of a concerted effort by leading scientists like Albert Einstein to bring a new unity to science, although in the case of general science as a subject, it was also the product of a deliberate national drive to install it in the school curriculum. A journal, *General Science Quarterly*, was founded in 1915, and when general science made its first appearance in Office of Education reports in 1922, 18.3 percent of student in grades 9 through 12 were already enrolled (Latimer, 1958, p. 28). Conceptually, however, general science was a much more ambitious undertaking at unification than was biology. Although subjects like anatomy, botany, physiology, and zoology could plausibly be fused together under the aegis of life sciences, accomplishing the same task with all (or nearly all) of the natural sciences was not nearly as successful. To this day, general science has high enrollments, but, for most of its existence, it has taken the form of a few weeks of one science followed by a few weeks of another. To use a chemical analogy, the elements that made up biology were, by and large, fused into a compound, a distinct substance, whereas the constituent elements that made up general science formed a mixture retaining their original properties.

Another notable and still controversial phenomenon in the evolution of science as a school subject, also related to the dream of a unified science, was the emphasis increasingly being given to what came to be called the scientific method. To a considerable extent, the notion of a distinct scientific method was also tied to the emergence of laboratory science in schools, something the Committee of Ten (National Education Association, 1893) had strongly endorsed in 1893. Four years earlier, in 1889, a young physicist at Harvard, Edwin H. Hall, undertook to develop a series of forty laboratory exercises in physics which were eventually published in 1886 and then again as a pamphlet in 1889. When supply companies began producing the equipment in Hall's laboratory exercises for school use, they referred to Hall's design for school experiments as components of a "National Course in Physics," thereby conferring on it a special prominence (Rudolph, in press, pp. 1–9).

It should not be surprising that John Dewey was attracted to this new emphasis on laboratory work, since he had become convinced that too much emphasis in the science curriculum was being given to conveying the findings of scientific research, with little or no attention being given to the process of inquiry that bought these scientific results into being. In an article in *Science*, Dewey (1910a) pointed out that "science teaching has suffered because science has been so frequently presented just as so much ready-made knowledge, so much subject-matter of fact and law, rather than as the effective method of inquiry into any subject matter" (p. 124). With respect to scientific inquiry, Dewey said, "such knowledge never can be learned by itself; it is not information, but a mode of intelligent prac-tise an habitual disposition of mind. Only by taking a hand in the mak-ing of knowledge by transferring guess and opinion into belief authorized by inquiry, does one ever get a knowledge of the method of knowing" (p. 125). Laboratory work, in other words, did not represent for Dewey an opportunity to prepare future scientists for a career but a vehicle for intro-ducing children and youth to one way in which warranted knowledge could be created.

In 1910, as well, Dewey (1910b) published one of his most important works, *How We Think*, which was specifically addressed to teachers. Prob-ably the best known discussion in the book was Dewey's depiction of the process of thinking. He summarized the complete act of thought as entail-ing "(i) a felt difficulty; (ii) its location and definition; (iii) suggestion of possible solution; (iv) development by reasoning of the bearings of the suggestion; (v) further observation and experiment leading to its accept-ance or rejection" (p. 78). Although Dewey was articulating a version of how thinking in general takes place, the act of thought he formulated ulti-mately became transformed into a series of five more or less invariant steps constituting *the* scientific method for high school students. John L. Rudolph (in press) attributed this misconception to the desire on the part of educators to appeal to student interest as well as to the growing trend toward utilitarianism. "Dewey's method," he says, "presented a universal means of approaching any situation from a scientific point of view with-out having to bother with formal rules of psychology, articulating a description of method that would harmonize well with the movement toward social utility and student interest" (pp. 23–24). In the revised edi-tion of *How We Think*, published more than twenty years later, Dewey (1933) included among other changes a reference to the new edition as "a restatement" in the subtitle, the word "phases" instead of "steps," and a new section under the title, "The Sequence of the Five Phases Is Not Fixed." His efforts at reconstructing his version of reflective thinking and correcting some confusion was, as seemed to be Dewey's fate by and large, ignored. The controversial belief that there existed a series of sequential steps comprising *the* scientific method has persisted to the present as a staple of the teaching of science.

V

The development of the subject of English in the twentieth century followed a pattern that in certain limited respects was similar to science, especially biology. What was once a collection of separate subjects became fused together, although imperfectly. Rhetoric, for example, had a robust enrollment of 38.5 percent in 1900 and reached 57.1 percent in 1910, but, thereafter, Office of Education reports simply combined those enrollments into English. Similarly, English literature around the turn of the century enrolled 42.1 percent of high school students and 57.1 percent in 1910 (Latimer, 1958, p. 33), but by midcentury, rhetoric and English literature had about the same curricular status as physiology and botany in science. New specialized subjects such as public speaking, journalism, and dramatics show up in the 1933–1934 report but with no significant enrollments. As in the case of general science, however, it is not clear that various elements of English such as literature, English usage, written expression, and grammar had actually been unified. To a large extent, they still existed as separate and distinct studies loosely combined under one subject label.

Unlike science (and mathematics for that matter), the porous subject matter boundaries of English made the subject much more vulnerable to the popular pedagogical trends of the times and particularly to demands that the curriculum attend to the needs of children and adolescents directly. Beginning around the time of the Eight-Year Study, English increasingly was correlated with social studies, although in practice, social studies was the dominant partner in these arrangements. Those combinations, however, were often regarded by leading core proponents as merely tinkering with the subject curriculum. The use of the term "experience" became particularly prevalent after a commission of the National Council of Teachers of English (1935) published its *An Experience Curriculum in English*. Rather than prescribing a preferred curriculum in English, the commission organized its recommendations around what they called "experience units," which they recommended for use as a starting point for school districts to follow in creating their own content. In literature, an array of "experience strands" was presented where, for example, the "Primary Objective" would be "to observe man's industrial expansion" and "Enabling Objectives" would include "to compare industry as it was before our time with our own industrial age" and "to participate vicariously with men and women who worked and who are working under conditions both good and bad." Then, "Typical Materials" in line with these objectives would be suggested such as *Silas Marner* and *David Copperfield* (p. 49). With the possible exception of the now-established convention of preceding each unit of study with an obligatory statement of objectives, the approach was quite traditional.

Early reports emanating from the Eight-Year Study are replete with instances of the correlation of English and social studies. In an apparent effort to publicize and encourage such experiments, the National Council of Teachers of English (1935) issued a new report under the title *A Correlated Curriculum*. The report makes the case that the "failure to correlate the various subjects of instruction leaves the student unaware of their connection as related parts of the scheme of life. The burden of pulling together what they called the "pieces in a great picture," the report said, "should not be left for students to accomplish unaided" (p. 1). Connections among school subjects would be demonstrated by tying them together in a manner visible to students. That modest reform, however, was simply too tame for someone like L. Thomas Hopkins (1937), now a rising star in the curriculum firmament. He observed that "throughout the volume the starting-point is subject matter in English set out to be learned with correlation accepted as a device to aid pupils in the learning of that subject." "The English program" he added with obvious distaste, "is determined by the teacher" (p. 418). Franklin Bobbitt's criticism (1937) was even a bit harsher, although, as would be expected, he was not so much concerned with the way students "experienced" the curriculum as he was with breaking the grip of the subject curriculum in a more radical way. He urged that "English must take of matters more fundamental than correlation before it can be ready to prepare anything more fundamental than a merely descriptive account" (p. 420). For many curriculum reformers of different orientations, as Hopkins and Bobbitt were, correlation of two or more subjects was simply too timid a way to address the problems inherent in the subject curriculum. Nothing less than a direct attack on the subject itself as the basic unit of the curriculum would do. As was true from the turn of the century on, curriculum reformers were as reproving of one another as they were of their common enemy.

In 1933–1934, English was reported to be offered in all high schools, and almost every student from the seventh through the twelfth grades was enrolled, the only exceptions being those who substituted electives in the twelfth year. Public speaking was the most prominent of these, with spelling, dramatic art, and journalism also being mentioned (U.S. Department of the Interior, 1938 pp. 9–10). Because English was so widely designated a required subject, enrollment data in English followed the trends in high schools generally, with registrations in English increasing tenfold between 1900 and 1949 (Applebee, p. 280). Unlike Latin, for example, English enrollment did not decline in terms of numbers; the significant changes insofar as English was concerned occurred within the subject itself as its enrollments soared.

By the 1940s, English was increasingly identified with realizing one's potential or developing one's distinctive personality (viz. Roody, 1947). In a 1943 compilation of activities in English classes, one teacher reported that there was no "standing before the class and talking as Hamlet or Little Eva might if they were to meet in the Globe Theater. It means discussing real experiences, and getting real advice, sympathy and understanding" (Murphy, 1943, pp. 193–94). This was consistent with the stated purpose of English as expressed by the editors of the volume: "It is the pervading purpose of language to help all people grow and develop so that their whole lives are better, freer, richer, happier, and more effective for themselves, and for all their fellows of every race, nationality, economic position, and political and religious belief " (Roberts, Kaulfers, & Grayson, p. 17). In some respects, the subject of English began to resemble a needs-based core, while at the same time retaining its traditional subject label.

Increasingly, the choice of reading matter to be assigned in high school English classes reflected what were identified as the needs of adolescents or their defined interests. In some instances, books of genuine literary distinction published during the 1950s became staples of the English curriculum, such as *Diary of Anne Frank* and *Catcher in the Rye*, but others were formulaic depictions of problems that adolescents presumably faced. The National Council of Teachers of English's Commission on the English

Curriculum, formed in 1945, issued a number of reports reflecting the new emphases on needs. Under the direction of Dora V. Smith, the first of these reports was published in 1952. Rather than emphasizing certain content and approaches in teaching language and literature, the report stressed the processes by which local school districts and curriculum committees could undertake that determination. For example, the commission listed a series a steps for deciding on the content of the English curriculum beginning with "Describing the Characteristics of Young People at Each Level of the System" and "Determining Experiences Needed by Each Group" (National Council of Teachers of English, 1952, p. 59). Suggested activities at each grade level would then be developed in line with the defined characteristics and needs of the students. In this respect, the commission was following a major trend in curriculum work at midcentury that emphasized *process*, the way in which a curriculum comes into being as distinct from proposing a particular set of learning activities. Rather than taking on the traditional curriculum question—What should we teach?—the new approach proposed to address the question, How should we go about deciding on what to teach?

A second volume issued by the commission continued to stress a curriculum in line with how students at various ages were defined. For example, the first characteristic of 12–15 year olds was described as follows: "Go through a period of rapid growth and development, making many new adjustments necessary (many girls are approximately a year ahead of boys in physical and metal maturity)." The language characteristics associated with this stage of development were then described as: "Desire to have fun, a fact which manifests itself in language expression related to sports, amusements and humorous situations; develop increased maturity in interests through clubs and teamwork; show interest in language activities related to animals, adventure, mystery, collections, and explorations, but resist tasks requiring lengthy application; girls show interest in sentiment and romance" (National Council of Teachers of English, 1956, p. 16).

In drawing such prominent attention to the characteristics of children and youth as the source of the curriculum, at the expense of other relevant factors, the commission was adopting the position that developmentalists had been promoting since the turn of the twentieth century, particularly as advanced by their most revered leader, G. Stanley Hall. Regrettably, the latter-day version suffers from the same defects. Whether the "desire to have fun," for example, is any more salient a characteristic among early adolescents as a group than it is with thirty-somethings or, for that matter, seventy-somethings, is not supported by either science (as Hall would have claimed) or ordinary experience. In providing advice to local curriculum groups as to how the English curriculum should be developed, the same report reminded them that "[l]anguage arts teachers throughout the nation accept personal, social and occupational competence as the goal of education." The commission went on to suggest an array of possible language arts experiences under the headings of "Cultivation of Wholesome Personal Living," "Development of Social Sensitivity and Effective Participation in Group Life," and "Linguistic Competence Necessary for Vocational Efficiency" (pp. 44–45).

Toward the late 1950s, four professional organizations, the American Studies Association, the College English Association, the Modern Language Association, and the National Council of Teachers of English, launched a series of conferences on the state of English as a school subject. The pamphlet they issued to summarize their findings, *Basic Issues in the Teaching of English* (1958), listed thirty-five issues they believed to be of utmost significance. The first and most basic was "What Is English?" "Has the discipline of English been replaced," they asked, "by *ad hoc* training in how to write a letter, how to give a radio speech, manners, dating, telephoning, vocational guidance?" (p. 7). Apparently, fundamental internal changes that had taken place in English over the course of nearly half a century had not gone entirely unnoticed.

v i

Even more than English, history and social studies have been the site of fierce culture wars. Inevitably, the social studies curriculum becomes the arena where emotionally charged issues like the meaning of democracy, civic virtue, and national identity are defined and debated. Beginning in the early years of the twentieth century, questions arose as to whether the study of history per se was up to that task, or whether there should exist a broader category of social studies that would undertake to perform those vital functions. Something of the development of the subject, therefore, can be traced through the internal struggle that was waged between the defenders of history and proponents of a broad and directly functional social studies. That conflict went far beyond a quibble about terminology.

Accounts of the modern development of school subjects in the United States often begin with the Committee of Ten report (National Education Association, 1893), and history is no exception. As with other major subjects, a subcommittee was appointed to address issues particular to that subject. The Conference on History, Civil Government, and Political Economy was a distinguished one. Headed by Charles Kendall Adams, president of the University of Wisconsin, it included among its members James Harvey Robinson, who was later to publish his influential *Mind in the Making* (1921), in which the role of critical thinking was extolled as a cornerstone in the development of modern civilization. Another notable conference member was a young faculty member in jurisprudence and political economy at Princeton University, Woodrow Wilson. Included among the values attributed to the study of history and related disciplines such as political economy was its potential "to broaden and cultivate the mind," thus counteracting "a narrow and provincial spirit." The ability to "prepare the pupil in eminent degree for enlightenment and intellectual enjoyment in after years" as well as, of course, exercising "a salutary influence upon the affairs of the country" (National Education Association, 1893, pp. 166–167) was also cited. "Enlightenment and intellectual enjoyment," as a purpose lying behind the study of any subject, quickly suffered an untimely fate, never to be resuscitated in any twentieth-century document on the value of schooling. In the end, the conference recommended a sequence of courses whereby history would be studied every year from the seventh to the twelfth grades: American history and elements of civil government in the seventh, Greek and Roman history in the eighth, French history in the ninth, English history in the tenth, American history again in the eleventh, and finally "a special period, studied in an intensive manner" in the twelfth.

The issue of college-entrance requirements had been hotly debated ever since the Committee of Ten recommended that no curricular distinction be made between secondary students preparing for college and those who were not. To deal with that still simmering controversy, the National Education Association appointed a new committee instructed to report its findings to the American Historical Association. The Committee of Seven (1899), as that new committee was called, went well beyond that narrow charge. On the college-entrance question, *The Study of History in Schools* was unequivocal: "[I]t is certainly wrong to shape secondary courses primarily with a view to college needs. In the great majority of schools the curriculum must be prepared with the purpose of developing boys and girls into young men and women, not with the purpose of fitting them to meet college entrance requirements or of filling them with information which some faculty thinks desirable as a forerunner of college work" (p. 120). As to the particular value of history, the Committee of Seven felt that along with a knowledge of the physical world "the habits of ants and bees," "the laws of floral growth," and chemical reactions, "it is even more desirable that [the student] should be led to see the steps in the development of the human race" (pp. 16–17). History's particular contribution to intellectual development was that it "cultivates the judgment by leading the pupil to see the relation between cause and effect, as cause and effect appear in human affairs" (p. 21). The actual recommendations of the Committee of Seven somewhat shortened the sequence in history for secondary schools, limiting it to ancient history in the ninth grade, European history, medieval to modern in the tenth, English history in the eleventh, and American history and civil government in the twelfth. Hazel Whitman Hertzberg (1981) calls the Committee of Seven report "probably the most influential in the history of the social studies, if influence is measured by adoption" (p. 16). Rolla M. Tryon (1935), for example, cites a 1914–1915 survey of 7,197 high schools in which approximately 85 percent offered ancient history, 80 percent mediaeval and modern history, 64 percent English history, and 86 percent American history (p. 26). For a time at least, history was firmly entrenched in the American school curriculum.

A symbolic turning point in the struggle between history and social studies was the 1916 subcommittee report on the social studies of Cardinal Principles (National Education Association, Committee on the Social Studies, 1916). Although the significance of that social studies committee can be overemphasized in terms of the extent to which it actually shaped the course of the subject in ensuing years, it remains, as O. L. Davis, Jr. (1981) says "useful as a marker" (p. 27), signaling, in this case, a recognition of the growing conflict between the upholders of history on one hand and the array of reformers who sought a more socially oriented and more inclusive set of disciplines organized under the banner of social studies on the other. With Arthur W. Dunn, author of *The Community and the Citizen* (1907) as well as other works on citizenship education at the helm, something of the direction of the subcommittee report was preordained, although James Harvey Robinson was again appointed to the new committee. In contradistinction to the Committee of Seven report, the 1916 committee, at least implicitly, subscribed to a different purpose not only for social studies education but indeed all subjects in the curriculum. "The keynote of modern education is 'social efficiency,'" the main report declared, and instruction in all subjects should contribute to this end" (National Education Association, 1918, p. 9).

In fact, however, the social studies recommendations of the *Cardinal Principles* subcommittee did not differ greatly from those of the Committee of Seven. The six-year course of study was divided into two "cycles," one covering grades seven through nine and the second for grades ten through twelve, although a number of alternatives were included. Social studies in the first cycle consisted of European history, American history, and civics, while the second cycle consisted of European history (again), American history (again), and an interesting addition, Problems of Democracy, was recommended for the twelfth grade. Given Dunn's professional predilections, however, it is not surprising that the role played by community civics in terms of its role in training for citizenship was singled out for special recognition. In particular, it was portrayed as "organized with reference to the pupils' immediate needs, rich in its historical, economic, and political relations, and affording a logical and pedagogically sound avenue of approach to later social studies" (p. 34). The report as a whole, however, was an eclectic affair. Robinson's commitment to the "new history" received considerable attention, and, in the end, the main casualty insofar as history was concerned was ancient history. The report of the Cardinal Principles subcommittee on social studies was more of an incipient sign of revolt than an open one. Differences with the Committee of Seven turned out to be more a matter of tone than of substance.

Shortly thereafter, however, signs began to appear of a serious challenge. Surely, one of the earliest shots across the bow of history as a staple of the secondary school curriculum was the one fired by David Snedden (1917). Taking a sample of examination questions in history from the College Entrance Examination Board (e.g., "What was the policy of the Jacobin party during the French Revolution? Were its members high-minded patriots or bloodthirsty ruffians? Give reasons for your answer."), Snedden was quick to point out that the questions "indicate the concrete objectives controlling history-teaching today . . . memorization of highly concentrated facts and generalizations of almost encyclopedic extent and variety" (pp. 272–273). For Snedden, it proved difficult to imagine how facts and generalizations in history would function in the future lives of the students.

As his solution to this state of affairs, Snedden declared that, as an indispensable first step, objectives ought to be made clear, and the source of these objectives was self-evident: "[It] must be obvious to any careful student of current educational theory, [that] the demonstrated needs of society and of individuals must determine these objectives" (p. 276). The values of history, in other words, were not to be found within the discipline itself or from the intellectual satisfaction that the study of history might bring, but in defined purposes derived from the projected social functioning of adults. Snedden outlined a simple plan for accomplishing this. He would randomly choose 100 men between thirty and forty years of age, and "competent judges" would rank these men in terms of whether each one of them was a cultivated man and a good citizen. Once the 100 men had been categorized, with the first 20 in group A, the next 30 in group B, the next 30 in group C, and the remaining 20 men in group D, a complete survey would then be conducted "to cover all our classes of [male] adults." From this survey the basis for determining the educational objectives for history would emerge. For example, it would be desirable to know "to what extent and in what ways are their various forms of civic behavior and moral conduct based on their knowledge and appreciation of events in the history of their country prior to 1790?" beginning with the "above average" class B men. Deficiencies in the group would be revealed as "we, looking in from the outside and with presumably sharpened social insight" discover them, and such technical questions as time allows could then be addressed (pp. 276–278). (The "we," equipped with their "sharpened social insight," would presumably be Snedden and his comrades in arms.) Apparently, a sea change in thinking about the values of history as a school subject had been emerging in the short period between the Committee of Seven report (1899) and the newly minted "scientific" approach to curriculum construction. Although Snedden did not actually call for the elimination of history from the curriculum, the criterion of direct social utility he proposed, if rigorously applied, would at best relegate the subject to the outer fringes of the curriculum.

By the 1920s, historians, possibly recognizing an ominous threat to their discipline, moved to deal with it. The American Historical Association (AHA), long active in the affairs of elementary and secondary schools, undertook a major effort to redefine what history and social studies should be taught in schools, particularly as it related to citizenship. Evidently, they accepted social studies as the appropriate name for the subject, and among the many scholars invited to design the project and write the volumes in the AHA series were political scientists, geographers, and educators, as well as historians. To head its Commission on the Social Studies, the AHA appointed A. C. Krey, a well-known historian at the University of Minnesota, who had shown considerable interest in the teaching of social studies at the elementary and secondary levels. The Carnegie Commission lent its financial support with a grant of $50,000. For its response, the AHA moved some of its heavy artillery into place including Charles Beard, Avery O. Craven, and Merle Curti, but the participation of educators with such diverse views as Harold Rugg, Boyd Bode, Franklin Bobbitt, Ernest Horn, Jesse Newlon, and George Counts virtually insured a disjointed outcome.

One sure sign of trouble was the declaration that "the supreme purpose in civic instruction" was "the creation of rich and many-sided personalities" (p. 93) in the first of the volumes to appear, *A Charter for the Social Sciences in the Schools* (Beard, 1932). Edward A. Krug (1972) has fittingly characterized that statement of purpose as having "anticipated the rhetoric of life adjustment education" (p. 243). David Snedden's (1932) reactions to the *Charter* at the time of its publication were by now predictable. Although he praised the work for holding up civic education as "the supreme purpose" of social studies (p. 358), he was scornful of what he saw as the implication that the "social studies . . . are still conceived of ends in themselves" instead of being geared directly "to produce desirable civic behaviors" (p. 358). The AHA had made some concessions in this regard, but for Snedden, they had not gone nearly far enough. He was, however, not singling history out for special condemnation. As the quintessential social efficiency educator, he was determined to root out waste wherever he found it. "Can any serious observer doubt that during the last century," he asked, "'wastes' in our school teachings of grammar and geography, algebra and ancient history, Latin and physics, French and classical English literature have not been several times greater than the wastes found in cotton spinning or steel making?" (p. 359).

Once what was intended to be the culminating volume in the series, *Conclusions and Recommendations* (American Historical Association, 1934), appeared, the whole enterprise became mired in political controversy. The ensuing debate focused on the commitment to collectivism that was evident in that volume, and any identification with the teaching of history, or for that matter social studies, became secondary (see Chapter 7). The most enduring legacy of this massive AHA undertaking was the publication of Merle Curti's (1935) *Social Ideas of American Educators*, a classic in the history of education.

The internal conflict between history per se and a more inclusive social studies was never formally reconciled, although an implicit compromise seems to have emerged. *Social studies* overwhelmingly became the preferred term for the subject, but the actual content remained predominantly historical. Much depended on the predilections of the teacher and, as in the case of English, the pedagogical fashions of the day. The percentage of students enrolled in history actually doubled between 1890 and 1910 (U.S. Department of the Interior, 1938, p. 5), but, by 1949, American history registrations stood at only one third of the high school population (Latimer, 1958, p. 30). By 1956, two units of social studies continued to be required for high school graduation, largely because of its alleged contribution to good citizenship, but what exactly was being required remains uncertain because there were no less than thirty-two courses commonly being offered as well as sixty-six infrequently offered courses (Hovet, 1956, pp. 79–80).

Apart from the internal struggle to define social studies, there was a still larger conflict over *whose* social studies should prevail. For better or worse, one of the principal battlegrounds for that culture war has been the history textbook. Prize-winning author Frances FitzGerald (1979) explains why:

> History textbooks for elementary and secondary schools are not like other kinds of histories. They serve a different function, and they have their own traditions, which continue independent of academic history writing. In the first place, they are essentially nationalistic histories. . . . In the second place, they are written not to explore but to instruct—to tell children what their elders want them to know about their country. This information is not necessarily what anyone considers the truth of things. Like time capsules, the texts contain truths selected for posterity.
>
> The surprise is how quickly and how thoroughly these truths for posterity have changed. (p. 47)

Under these circumstances, what receives quasi-official sanction in the form of a history or social studies textbook adoption assumes enormous symbolic significance. What gets included becomes a matter of which values are being celebrated and which disparaged; and, perhaps more importantly, who gets included becomes a matter of whose identity is being honored and whose is being disrespected.

A true phenomenon in the history of textbook publishing is the astounding success of David Saville Muzzey's (1911) *An American History*. Following its original publication in 1911, the text survived in print for no less than sixty-five years. What is also remarkable about Muzzey by today's standards is his outspokenness. His text is hardly the fuddy-duddy history that it is sometimes portrayed to be, and, although it includes its share of attitudes and pronouncements that could not, under any circumstances, pass muster today, it is quite progressive for its time in its interpretations of the American heritage. Muzzey, after all, was a student of James Harvey Robinson's at Columbia University, and he clearly absorbed his mentor's teaching as to the "new history." In his introduction to the first edition, Robinson proclaimed the book to be representative of "the new tendencies in historical writing," while at the same time praising Muzzey for his narrative skill (p. iii). Although some of Muzzey's characterizations of Native Americans, for example, reflect popular stereotypes, he nevertheless concluded that "it was chiefly the fault of the white man's cruelty and treachery that the friendly curiosity of the red man was turned so often into malignant hatred instead of firm alliance" (p. 25). Even the revered founding fathers were not spared when Muzzey turned to the issue of slavery. "That our colonial forefathers, " he says, "could have been so jealous for the protection of their own rights and freedom and for the proper forms of the worship of God, and still hold human beings in bondage, seems to us utterly inconsistent" (p. 305). His depiction of the brutal slave trade and particularly "the horrors of the middle passage" is unalloyed and, in some passages, actually moving.

Muzzey's final chapter, "Entering the Twentieth Century," is, as its title implies, a kind of projection of what lies in store for the American people. "Socialism," he suggests, "cannot be explained in a paragraph," but he seeks to separate it from anarchism and communism, and as "individualism was the watchword of the nineteenth century; cooperation will be the motto of the twentieth" (pp. 617–618). In so doing, he anticipated a theme that permeated the Rugg social studies texts years later. Insofar as race was concerned, Muzzey reflected the then common notion that although "negroes . . . have made considerable progress . . . , still they are as a race, far, perhaps centuries, behind whites in civilization," but, he concludes that "the prolongation of race hatred can bring only detriment and sorrow" (pp. 619–620). To be sure, Muzzey did not transcend his time in terms of prevailing attitudes. Women, for example, were virtually nonexistent in his version of American history; there was no discussion of the women's suffrage movement, for example, which by the time of the publication of Muzzey's first edition had achieved some notable success at the state level. Nevertheless, the fact that Muzzey's was able to express his social views so freely, apparently without fear that his textbook would be relegated to oblivion, says something about the times in which he lived as compared to later periods. As Diane Ravitch has persuasively argued (2003), much of what appears in modern textbooks and related ventures, such as testing, is not so much a matter of governmental control, but a result of intensive vigilance on the part of pressure groups and a relentless cleansing through self-censorship by publishers.

By the 1920s, history and social studies texts were already becoming a political flash point. Even later editions of Muzzey's history textbook came under fire during this time. In the 1920s, a textbook called *Modern History* was attacked by Chicago mayor "Big Bill" Thompson for its alleged pro-English bias. In addition, there were notable instances where African American and Jewish spokespersons were critical of the fact that their ethnic identities were being underrepresented in texts; Catholics, particularly the Knights of Columbus, also began to complain about the way they were being portrayed. At the same time, other critics were calling for texts to be 100 percent American (Zimmerman, pp. 17–25). The fierce battle over the Rugg textbooks (see Chapter 7) was hardly an isolated case. In the thirties, the distinguished historian Carl L. Becker's text was condemned for its alleged socialist leanings, and with the coming of the New Deal, as Zimmerman points out, "'Americanism' became defined less by ethnicity than by an economic system: capitalism" (p. 60). By 1949, even an edition of Frank Abbott Magruder's (1917) venerable, *American Government*, by far the leading civics text, was being charged with endorsing a welfare state (Zimmerman, pp. 83–84). Whether women as well as various religious, ethnic, and racial groups are indeed underrepresented in social studies textbooks and the extent to which such texts present a valid historical interpretation of the country's political and social identity are deserving of serious and sustained debate. Such matters raise serious questions about historical scholarship; but, when rigid criteria are applied to what actually is to be included in social studies textbooks, the result is not entirely salutary.

Without question, history and social studies have survived the isolated attacks to their existence in the first half of the twentieth century. What has emerged, however, is a vapid and barren rendering of the American heritage that contains little or nothing of the intense drama, arresting political conflict, and serious social inquiry that social studies as a school subject should embody. Coverage and a ritualistic all-inclusiveness have come to occupy a central role as it relates to the social studies curriculum and the textbooks that are supposed to embody it. As a result, "don't know much about history" is becoming a source of pride rather than an abject admission of ignorance.

vii

Above and beyond the fate of individual schools subjects is the question of whether the subject, any subject, should remain the fundamental building block of the curriculum. Whatever the reasons being adduced for the subject organization's durability, and despite the dedicated efforts of many curriculum reformers to unseat it, its persistence cannot be attributed merely to college domination of the high-school curriculum. More persuasive reasons can readily be advanced. For one thing, organizational structures of schooling are much more critical in shaping the program of studies than is sometimes acknowledged. Those managerial aspects of schooling, in other words, that may seem at first glance to be peripheral to what is actually taught in schools may actually control the classroom situation. The way schools are organized, how children are grouped in classrooms, and the time periods allocated for teaching this or that ultimately and profoundly affect what is being taught.

In these respects, the structure of secondary schools is less amenable to reforms that reject subject categories than are elementary schools. The secondary school faculty has long been divided into subject area departments, teachers are licensed to teach certain subjects, and graduation requirements are defined in terms of subject distributions. David Tyack and Larry Cuban (1995) metaphorically refer to such fundamental structures as "the grammar of schooling" and document how impervious that grammar has been to the determined efforts of many school reformers to reshape school studies over the course of the last century (pp. 85–109).

As a case in point, Tyack and Cuban cite the creation around 1906 of the now familiar Carnegie unit, originally established as a basis for awarding pensions for retired college faculty. The idea was born out of the need to find a way to distinguish between college faculty and those in lower schools. (Many secondary schools referred to themselves as colleges.) In order to make the distinction clear, the trustees of the Carnegie Foundation used as one standard that authentic colleges require at least fourteen units of study at the secondary school level for admission. Thus was born the idea of a Carnegie unit, which over the years has become not only a unit of measure for college admission but for high school graduation and requirements in individual subject areas (pp. 91–94). It is not true, as is sometimes alleged, that the Carnegie unit was responsible for the idea that subjects should be taught five periods a week, since the report specifically allowed for fractions of a unit to be counted in the case of subjects taught for fewer than five days (Pritchett, 1906, pp. 38–39), but the notion that requirements of various kinds should be stipulated in terms of units of subject matter has become an integral part of the "grammar of schooling."

Calling attention to structures such as these should serve to remind reformers that winning the rhetorical battle is not even half a victory. For success to be achieved in terms of implementation, along with at least the prospect of durability, reformers need to contend with the relatively impervious structures of schooling that stand in the way of successful curriculum reform. Reforms like the project method hardly stand a chance in terms of widespread success and longevity when, for example, the tests by which students' and, in effect, teachers' and administrators' success are measured are not attuned to the attributes that presumably favor project teaching. This and similar reforms, therefore, have no role in the way success is defined and determined.

The fact that the subject organization of the curriculum is supported by many of these structures, particularly at the secondary school level, however, does not fully account for its resiliency in the face of the long-standing and determined efforts to depose it. There is also a long-buried conceptual argument to be made. Actually, the basis of a case for the subject curriculum can be found as early as Dewey's (1902a) *The Child and the Curriculum* and in sections of *Democracy and Education* (1916a), as well as in Boyd Bode's

(1927) *Modern Educational Theories*. By the time Dewey's (1938) *Experience and Education* appeared, his own position on this matter should have been clear, but it was, as usual, clouded by popular misconceptions.

In the world of professional education, a subdued recognition of some of the virtues of the subject curriculum began to take shape around 1950 when much of the creative energy that had fueled the core phenomenon started to dissipate. One visible sign of such a trend appeared in William B. Featherstone's (1950) *A Functional Curriculum for Youth*, although, as the title implies, the book is primarily a brief for a curriculum that attends directly to the needs of the adolescent population. When Featherstone undertakes to examine the subject organization of the curriculum, however, his approach is less than damning. He examines the commonly expressed objections to that organization, but then indicates how those objections could be met without entirely abandoning it. One objection he notes, for example, is that "a subject is a limited body of knowledge organized in terms of an inherent and internal logic which is and can be meaningful only to scholars—never to learners or novices." But he then goes on to argue that "subjects are made and remade all the time" (p. 5) and that the objections that subjects are by nature "abstract and meaningless to youth . . . can be met in large part by paying adequate attention to the kind of concrete material used in developing that subject-matter" (p. 97). Featherstone also alludes to what he regards as the most frequently heard objection that subjects are by their very nature rarefied and fragmented abstractions that do not conform to the unity of one's life. He points, however, to recent efforts to unify or integrate the school subjects and argues that "there is no apparent reason why a subject cannot be unified and made meaningful in terms of a logic of learning" (p. 102).

Remarkably, for someone with his professional commitments, Featherstone devotes considerable attention to an effort to bring a greater sense of unity to the subject curriculum. He does this in part by addressing the prospect of a *broad fields* curriculum. At least since the Eight-Year Study in the 1930s, efforts had been made to correlate subjects that have traditionally been taught independently, but some of these, such as the plan to correlate social studies, English, and mathematics around the theme of Ethiopia, were forced and artificial (Lawler, 1937). At the same time, developments within certain subject areas have moved in the direction of unifying subject specializations into a broader and more cohesive entity, with the emergence of biology as a school subject being a prime example. A similar pattern is illustrated by the trend toward social studies, where, as Featherstone (1950) puts it, "in place of approximately a dozen different conventional subjects, each concerned with some limited aspect of the social environment, the social studies appear" (p. 114). Although he voices some pessimism about the ability to create a broad field around the arts or to fuse the language arts successfully and eventually turns to functional approaches to curriculum organization, Featherstone nevertheless sees broad fields as having some value in alleviating "the impasse produced by too many fields and too little time" (p. 128).

A more potent and unequivocal expression of values inherent in the subject organization of the curriculum is reflected in the essay in the 1956 yearbook of the Association for Supervision and Curriculum Development by Arno A. Bellack. From the outset, Bellack (1956) characterizes the reform tradition as "in large measure a reaction against a conception of schooling that placed major stress on 'logically organized subject matter set out to be learned'" (pp. 97–98). Drawing liberally from Dewey's philosophy, he goes on to analyze the reform tradition that seeks to select and organize the curriculum "on the basis of life functions or youth needs" (p. 106). Bellack recognizes certain advantages to this approach, but at the same time, he alludes to considerable difficulties. In the end, he points out that serious students of education such as James B. Conant (1948) and the philosopher Harry Broudy (1954) have tended to organize their understanding of modern knowledge in terms of a limited set of categories, reflective of the broad fields approach to curriculum organization. Conant and Broudy, Bellack (1956) points out, "call attention first of all to the fact that the systematized fields of study represent significant aspects of the culture which the school is uniquely equipped to introduce to youth in meaningful ways. . . . No other agency or institution in our society has the personnel and other essential resources to perform this function successfully" (p. 11).

Although the scholarly disciplines may not address directly the immediate needs of children and adolescents, Bellack says, "[e]ach major field contributes a unique set of intellectual tools which are of inestimable help in dealing with the varied problems of modern living" (p. 114). The point, of course, is that logically ordered knowledge is not simply a convenient basis for organizing a curriculum; such structure also increases its potential for use. Bellack's defense of structured knowledge as the basis of the curriculum at the secondary school level, however, was considered rank heresy given the reigning orthodoxy of the time and earned him considerable criticism.

By the 1940s and 1950s, Dewey's long-standing quest to reconcile children's immediate and personal knowledge with the logically organized knowledge that characterizes the scholarly disciplines had been almost completely ignored not only in terms of school practice but in the proposals put forth by leading curriculum reformers. Admittedly, in many instances, the reasons advanced for abandoning the subject curriculum in favor of something more directly useful were seemingly persuasive. The teaching of subjects has frequently led to rote teaching, passive learning, and the sense that knowledge is a possession rather than an instrument for coming to an ordered understanding of one's world and thereby gaining some control over one's destiny. Nonetheless, the early to mid-1950s brought a limited reconsideration of the long-standing reform tradition that many years earlier had been enunciated by the likes of Charles W. Eliot and William Torrey Harris.

The question remains, however, as to whether the acknowledged difficulties associated with subjects are inherent, or whether, with the necessary ingenuity and dedication, these problems could be overcome, or at least minimized, while preserving the virtue of gaining something of the command of knowledge that foremost scholars in their fields possess. This was, after all, the direction that Dewey had sought to impose on the education of children and youth ever since his work with the Laboratory School. When he (1938) later used the term "progressive organization of subject matter" to refer to his theory of the curriculum, he was not, of course, referring in any sense to "progressive education" but to proceeding in progressive stages from the interest that children find in "occupations" to a logically organized understanding of the subjects of study (pp. 86–112). Dewey knew that without arranged and systematic knowledge at one's command, it would be difficult to function successfully in the modern world. Knowledge can, of course, be picked up indiscriminately, but the potential for that knowledge to be translated into action is enhanced to a crucial extent by the ability to give such knowledge an order. It is what distinguishes it from "tricks of the trade." In this regard, Boyd Bode (1927), as usual, went straight to the heart of the matter. "Even the humblest ragpicker," he said, "organizes his knowledge" (p. 49).

11 | LIFE ADJUSTMENT EDUCATION AND THE END OF AN ERA

i

ALONGSIDE THE CONCERTED EFFORT TO INSTALL A CORE CURRICULUM AND TO reduce the prominence of academic subjects, there was a closely allied movement that, while it shared many of the basic assumptions underlying core, expressed itself in terms of a more explicit social message—the short-lived and ill-fated ideology that emerged under the banner of life adjustment education. Although promoted as new and especially suited to postwar conditions, life adjustment's roots are clearly traceable to the beliefs that were being enunciated by social efficiency educators like Snedden and Bobbitt early in the twentieth century. The social message being conveyed, of course, was that each new generation needed to internalize the social status quo, and it was the job of the schools to promote that end, not just through an informal process of socialization, but explicitly and resolutely. At midcentury, those ideas were receiving unprecedented public attention and even a kind of official sanction by the U.S. Office of Education.

Life adjustment education actually has a semiofficial birthday: June 1, 1945. The gestation period began in January of 1944 when the United States Office of Education commissioned a study called *Vocational Education in the Years Ahead*. Even with over 150 people working on the project, the report took about a year and a half to complete. Finally, the results of the study were presented at a conference in Washington, D.C., on May 31 and June 1, 1945. There was agreement that the youth of the nation were not being adequately served by the high school, but the direction that reform should take was not exactly clear. Finally, the participants turned to Charles A. Prosser, director of the Dunwoody Institute of Minneapolis, Minnesota, and veteran of the battle over the Smith-Hughes legislation, to summarize the proceedings. Responding to the challenge, Prosser delivered what has come to be known as the Prosser resolution, the opening salvo in the campaign for life adjustment education:

> It is the belief of this conference that, with the aid of this report in final form, the vocational school of a community will be able better to prepare 20 percent of its youth of secondary school age for entrance upon desirable skilled occupations; and that the high school will continue to prepare 20 percent of its students for entrance to college. We do not believe that the remaining 60 percent of our youth of secondary school age will receive the life adjustment training they need and to which they are entitled as American citizens—unless and until the administrators of public education with the assistance of the vocational education leaders formulate a comparable program for this group.
>
> We, therefore, request the U. S. Commissioner of Education and the Assistant Commissioner for Vocational Education to call at some early date a conference or a series of regional conferences between an equal number of representatives of general and of vocational education—to consider this problem and to take such initial steps as may be found advisable for its solution. (U. S. Office of Education, 1951, p. 29)

Without dissent, the consulting committee of the conference adopted the resolution. What is more, the idea of life adjustment education received the Office of Education's enthusiastic endorsement of the resolution, especially through its official organ, *School Life*.

According to plan, the series of regional conferences seeking to implement the resolutions began in New York City on April 11 and 12, 1946 (Broder, p. 12). The ever-present Prosser, a forceful and dynamic advocate, declared that:

> Social and economic facts point to the failure of our total educational system to meet the real need of an efficient life adjustment training for America's young people. The vocational educational forces of the country have a potential service to the high schools of the Nation involved in the adjustment of these youth. The . . . sad tales of the social and economic maladjustment of millions of America's citizens is evidence enough of the failure of the education forces to render the service they

should. They also indicate unmistakably a failure on the part of the general high school itself. Thus the tale constitutes a general indictment of both services. All the evidence shows that both of us are just poor sinners. (p. 13)

In the four regional conferences that followed the one in New York City, Prosser preached essentially the same message. The traditional humanist curriculum in secondary education had failed the 60 percent that he had identified in his original resolution. What was needed was a curriculum attuned to the actual life functions of youth as a preparation for adulthood. Actually, in time, the original percentages that Prosser had enunciated (20 percent college-entrance, 20 percent vocational, 60 percent life adjustment) had become something of an embarrassment since they implied that the curriculum had to be reorganized for only a majority of the school population. Life adjustment education, in line with its most immediate ancestor, social efficiency education, needed to be applied to the total school curriculum.

Almost from the outset, life adjustment education faced a problem of definition. Although support from a large segment of the professional educational community was enthusiastic from the beginning, there was some question as to what precisely it sought to accomplish. Kandel (1947) felt with some justification that "It implies that all the contingencies which human beings are likely to encounter in their lives must be anticipated and education must be adjusted to them. Among these contingencies are dating, marriage, mating, rearing of children, work experience, vocations, and all the social issues which make up the day's headlines in the newspapers" (p. 372). Harl R. Douglass (1949), one of life adjustment's stalwart supporters, associated life adjustment education with education in a democracy, arguing that the 40 percent dropout rate across the country indicated that American schools were failing to serve a significant proportion of the school population. He rejected what he regarded as the unsound theories that preceded life adjustment, the "decorative" theory, the "disciplinary" theory, and the "college preparation" theory as inappropriate to a democratic social order (pp. 110–111). Like Bobbitt's criticism of the Harvard Report, Douglass identified general education, not with a core of basic disciplines, but with adequate preparation for various categories of life activities. "Reduced to its simplest terms, he said, life adjustment education "stands for *an adequate program of secondary education for fairly complete preparation for all the areas of living in which life adjustment must be made, particularly home living, vocational life, civic life, leisure life, and physical and mental health*" (p. 114). In line with the definitions of life adjustment education advanced by both its detractors and its proponents, the guide to its implementation produced by the Illinois Secondary School Curriculum Program proceeded from a compilation of the needs of youth: "Tools of communication; Strong body, sound attitude toward it; Satisfactory social relationships; Competence in and appreciation of improved family living; Knowledge of, practice in, and zeal for democratic processes; Sensitiveness to importance of group action; Effectiveness as consumers; Adjustment to occupation; and Development of meaning for life" (Houston, Sanford & Trump, 1948, p. 23). These, rather than mathematics, history, English, science, and so on constituted the general education of youth, a position that bore some obvious indebtedness to the *Cardinal Principles of Secondary Education* (National Education Association, 1918). In its early years of existence, life adjustment education enjoyed unprecedented political support. U. S. Commissioner of Education John W. Studebaker was an enthusiastic advocate and quickly helped set in motion the two national conferences on life adjustment designed to spread its message.

The first Life Adjustment Conference was held in 1947 with Benjamin Willis, the superintendent of schools of Yonkers, New York, acting as chair. Although no new dramatic pronouncements were issued, the conference served to maintain the momentum initiated by the Prosser resolution. It did, for example, recommend that "there be established a National Commission on Life Adjustment Education for Youth," with members of various national education organizations serving as members (Basler, 1947, p. 6). Prosser, with his usual sense for high drama, concluded the meeting with a call to arms:

> Never was there such a meeting where people were so sincere in their belief that this was the golden opportunity to do something that would give to all American youth their education heritage so long denied. What you have planned is worth fighting for—it is worth dying for. (United States Office of Education, 1948, p. 20)

Enthusiasm for the program was so strong that Studebaker's successor, Commissioner of Education Earl James McGrath, was moved to remark: "Terms such as 'flapdoodle' have been ruinous to certain educational projects, but I am confident that no incident of name calling can similarly endanger Life Adjustment Education. It is too well established in the public confidence" ("Life Adjustment," 1949, p. 40). By the time the Second National Commission met in 1951, however, some of the original zeal was lacking, and much of the proceeding became bogged down in discussions of monetary problems (Broder, 1977).

One unfailing bastion of support was the National Association of Secondary School Principals. Over the course of the twentieth century, the self-perception of school administrators had been evolving from that of educators to hard-headed business managers (Callahan, 1962), and an education attuned to the real business of life, as opposed to the remote values of the academic curriculum, must have had an enormous appeal. Besides, the threat of federal intrusion into the world of schools remained a source of concern, and the answer seemed to lie in demonstrating that school administrators were ready to transform secondary schools into a potent force in American social and economic life, not simply as preparatory institutions for the colleges. The association sponsored several "discussion groups" on life adjustment education, and its *Bulletin* frequently ran articles extolling its virtues. At one of these discussion groups, the superintendent of public instruction of the State of Illinois identified life adjustment education with the schools' concern for "real-life problems." Accordingly, he could enunciate a test for schools: "If the products of our schools turn out to be healthy and patriotic citizens who are good husbands, good wives, good fathers, good mothers, good neighbors, good workers, good employers, wise spenders of income, wholesome users of leisure time and so forth, we know that our schools are good" (Nickell, 1949, p. 154).

One major feature of life adjustment education was its emphasis on the indefinite expansion of the scope of the curriculum. That position was echoed at the meeting of the association a year later. One speaker from the state department of education in Connecticut also emphasized the theme of "real problems" and presented a similar conception of what the real problems were: "preparation for post-secondary education, preparation for work, doing an effective day's work in school, getting along well with other boys and girls, understanding parents, driving a motor car, using the English language, engaging in recreational activities, and so on are representative areas encompassing real problems faced by youth" (Collier, p. 125). It was this attention to "real life" problems that was of such attraction to school administrators, particularly the promise that a curriculum drawn along those lines would have a dramatic effect on reducing the dropout rate.

Catholic educators were included in many of the regional life adjustment conferences, and the impact of the new movement was beginning to be felt in that quarter as well. One Catholic educator saw in life adjustment education the opportunity to stem "a steady and disastrous lowering of purely academic standards which has made a joke of college education" (Townsend, p. 363). He interpreted the Prosser resolution as proposing to create "a vast network of terminal high schools" (p. 364). Since few Catholic high schools could justify their "prep school" status, he thought, the obvious implication was that a similar pattern should be followed in Catholic education. The superintendent of schools of the Archdiocese of Milwaukee was particularly sympathetic to the idea of preparation for living, rather than simply a classical education. He felt that through "life situations we effect an intimate relationship between the curriculum and life experiences, between principles of Christian living and the 'profane' materials embodied in the curriculum" (Goebel, 1948, p. 377). Sister Mary Janet (1952), one of life adjustment education's most vigorous supporters, saw in the movement a positive concern for "home and family living" and a much healthier attitude toward shop courses and vocational education (p. 344). In general, the rhetoric of life adjustment education was infused with a seemingly genuine concern for the mass of students not being served by contemporary secondary education, and this gave it a humanitarian appeal that reached into a variety of different quarters.

ii

Although life adjustment was receiving unprecedented support in professional educational journals and among highly placed school officials, the extent to which the "areas of living" curriculum it was promoting was actually replacing the traditional curriculum built around subjects is difficult to establish. As early as December of 1947, *Time* reported that schools in thirty-five of the forty-eight states were trying to implement at least some aspects of life adjustment education ("Get Adjusted," p. 64), but it would be easy to imagine reluctance on the part of the various state departments of education to report no initiatives in the direction of such a widely popular reform. On the same day that the *Time* article appeared, *Newsweek* made note of the alarming dropout rate in many areas of the country (Passaic, New Jersey, 45 percent; New York, 42 percent; Minneapolis, Minnesota, 31 percent) and commented favorably on the attempts by the U. S. Office of Education to implement the Prosser resolution as a response. *Newsweek* reported Commissioner Studebaker as feeling that "old standbys like Milton's 'Il Penseroso' and George Eliot's 'Silas Marner' would probably disappear from the schools" ("High school overhaul," p. 86) as a result of the reforms.

Of the actual attempts to put life adjustment education into action, two of the most prominent were the Illinois Secondary School Curriculum Program and Battle Creek High School of Battle Creek, Michigan (Broder, 1977). Illinois was clearly the hotbed of life adjustment education, enjoying not only the strong support of State Superintendent of Public Instruction Vernon L. Nickell but some of the most prominent faculty in the College of Education at the University of Illinois, such as Harold Hand and Charles W. Sanford. In line with the pattern set in Denver by Newlon and the support given to it by the Association for Supervision and Curriculum Development, teacher participation in curriculum development was central to the Illinois program. The program in Canton High School was built around a core of common learnings that included personality, etiquette, family living, and vocations (p. 184). A high school in Peoria developed a program for high-ability seniors including a course in "senior problems" (p. 185). Other life adjustment programs were developed in Crystal Lake, Decatur, and Gillespie high schools.

A model of its kind was the life adjustment curriculum developed in Battle Creek, Michigan, organized around the central theme of "basic living" ("Cooperative Research," p. 408). Arising out of a 1944 study of dropouts, the program developed links with the Horace Mann–Lincoln Institute of Teachers College and with faculty there such as Hubert Evans, Stephen M. Corey, and Arthur Jersild. In line with the now widely accepted idea that the teachers themselves should participate in curriculum planning, teachers were organized into committees dealing with various aspects of the basic living theme. The health committee, for example, investigated health hazards in the school such as "no soap" and "dirty erasers" (p. 413). Further investigation revealed that tenth graders were dropping out of school in disproportionate numbers and were responsible for the most discipline problems. In response, the health committee organized a yearlong course around units such as "the food we eat" and "understanding ourselves and getting along with others" (p. 416). The heart of the basic living curriculum was described as "the problem-centered group" (p. 438). The problems investigated were so-called personal-social problems such as "Basic Urges, Wants and Needs, [and] Making Friends and Keeping Them" (p. 443). As in the case of other life adjustment programs, the basic living curriculum developed at Battle Creek was considered to be components of the new general education. The intent, of course, was to dispense with the traditional subjects of study that the Harvard Committee (1945) had defined as general education and replace them with areas of living that were directly relevant to the needs of youth.

The extent to which the principles of life adjustment education that were enunciated at regional and national conferences, as well as in a growing body of professional literature on the subject, depended to a large degree on the commitment and energy of local school officials. Even what passed for life adjustment education varied considerably from the model established in Battle Creek. In Billings High School in Billings, Montana, for example, four years of English, one in American history, a half year of civics, and one half year of another social science were retained as minimum requirements (*Life Adjustment Curriculum*, 1949, p. 2). Students were also expected to contribute, however, to the good of the community, and this was monitored through a system of "activity points" (pp. 3–12), with each student expected to amass at least 200. Losses of points were imposed for antisocial behavior, including violation of school regulations. Earning points in some areas such as "School and Life Planning" and "Growth toward Maturity" (p. 5) were required, while others, such as "Learning to Work" (pp. 6–7), "Boy-Girl Relationship" (p. 10), and "Preparation for Marriage" (p. 10) were elective. Two to ten points could be earned by "participation in initiation of sophomores" (p. 11). An alternative to the life adjustment curriculum called "The Scholarship Plan for Graduation" was available, but stringent requirements such as 97 percent attendance were instituted. A severe warning was attached to the page in the student handbook describing the Scholarship Plan:

> The Scholarship Plan was a misnomer. It might be better named a plan for recalcitrants and was merely a protective device:
>
> Students and parents who have not accepted the Life Adjustment plan may graduate under the conditions of our old plan with the more stringent requirements to offset failure to do the work, develop the habits,

and improve the attitudes inherent in the present program. Our reasoning is as follows: If students and their parents believe that the only
value of the high school is in learning subject matter then the school
will insist that they do more than a minimum standard. Our counsel-
ing is definitely pointed to Life Adjustment method of graduation for
all students. (n.p.)

Clearly, the percentages that Prosser had originally stated in his resolution
were gradually being ignored in Billings High School.

The successes that life adjustment education achieved cannot be measured by formal adoptions alone. Documents of the sort that the Battle
Creek and Billings school systems produced are relatively few. As was the
case with the efforts to install a core curriculum, however, many of the
achievements can be seen in the partial measures that schools took to align
themselves with the main thrust of life adjustment education. Although
core curriculum proponents were far from successful in actually replacing
academic subjects, they did succeed to some extent in transforming subjects internally—some more than others. In the postwar period, English
was hardly the subject it was early in the twentieth century. Life adjustment education met with similar limited successes.

Something of these achievements can be illustrated in the extraordinary
popularity of so-called mental hygiene films that were produced for school
use. In the period from 1946 to 1950 alone, films with such names as *Are
You Popular? A Date with Your Family, Dating Do's and Don'ts, Junior Prom,
Shy Guy,* and *You and Your Family* were produced. Between 1951 and 1955,
more films continued to be made available for school use with names like
Habit Patterns, How to Say No, Molly Grows Up, More Dates for Kay, and
Skipper Learns a Lesson (Smith, 1999, p. 26). In 1953 alone approximately
5,000 16mm films were released by an array of studios, and about 10 percent were devoted to "mental hygiene" themes (p. 25). (Driving safety was
also an extremely popular subject.) Much of the popularity of these films
derived from fears that, without the proper guidance, the rebelliousness of
youth would ultimately threaten the foundations of society, and schools
were seen as the place where that menace could be minimized. The director of research for the Portland, Oregon, Public Schools was quoted as saying in 1947, "All education is indoctrination. The real question is whether
indoctrination shall be confined merely to the mores and taboos of the
past, or whether it shall be directed toward solving the problems of the

future. In time, parents will recognize that the hope of the future lies in such a new curriculum" (quoted in Smith, p. 25).

The subject matter of these films is consistent with what their titles indicate. Probably the first social guidance film *Are Your Popular?*, produced in 1947, contrasts the popular Caroline Ames "the kind of girl you'd like to know," and about whom "there is no whisper of scandal," with Ginny "a crude-looking and acting girl." To make sure the message was clear, the narrator warned the viewers, "Girls who park in cars are *not* really popular." Wally Johnson, of course, chooses to date Caroline (p. 118). The 1953 film *As Others See Us* concentrates on avoiding "the embarrassment of doing the wrong thing." Rules of behavior in meeting people, eating in restaurants, and at dances are made abundantly clear (p. 120). The number of films made to advance "mental hygiene" among America's youth is not exactly known, but Smith estimates it to be around 3,000 (p. 31). No figures are available as to how often such films were actually shown in schools, but their sheer number indicates that making them must have been a profitable enterprise.

The fact that these films reached the peak of their popularity during the life adjustment era is, of course, no coincidence. They can probably be described as an adjunct to the curriculum or part of the informal curriculum rather than *the* curriculum in any formal sense, but that does not mean that their influence was not felt. They conveyed precisely the messages that life adjustment advocates thought to be the most salient. One matter of paramount importance to life adjusters was the estrangement of youth from schools and the school curriculum, and, by addressing directly what they perceived to be the real interests of youth, they hoped to ameliorate that problem. At the same time, however, they were promoting a conventional adjustment to existing social mores. Whatever may have been the intellectual shortcomings of the life adjustment movement, this appeal to fitting youth into the existing social order was a great source of its popularity.

Again and again, proponents of life adjustment education expressed their concern for the high dropout rate in particular and for the alienation of youth from school in general. The clear source of the problem as they saw it was a curriculum rooted in a discredited ideal of scholarship remote from the interests of the vast majority of the school population. This was a theme that had been heard at least since the Douglas Commission Report (1906), but by the early 1950s, it was no longer an isolated concern; it had become conventional wisdom in the educational world. In earlier periods, the problem had been addressed by providing special programs such as vocational education for those few not suited to scholarly endeavor, but as the momentum for change accelerated, the segment of the school population not inclined to such pursuits seemed to grow ever greater and greater. In fact, the group for whom the conventional curriculum was deemed appropriate had decreased to such insignificant proportions that it constituted a kind of "college-preparatory" aberration within the schools. If there was a single defining characteristic in the array of practices that defined life adjustment education, it was, like its core curriculum counterpart, the desire to transform general education from subjects representing common elements of the cultural heritage, as Harris had advocated since before the turn of the century, to functional areas of living. In general, however, subjects proved to be more resilient than had been thought, and areas of living were more likely to be incorporated within certain subjects rather than replace them, although, admittedly, *Silas Marner* and *How to Make Friends and Keep Them* must have been strange bedfellows.

iii

Life adjustment education turned out to be the prod that awoke a slumbering giant. For about a half a century, ever since the major figures of traditional humanism like Charles W. Eliot and William Torrey Harris had retired from the scene, leaders in the academic world had given only sporadic attention to what was being taught in elementary and secondary schools. Robert Maynard Hutchins (1936) was perhaps the most notable exception, but his seemingly elitist proposals and his association with a rather far-fetched great books program attracted only a small coterie of followers. Jacques Maritain (1943) proposed similar platforms but, like Hutchins, his following was restricted on the whole to the elite of higher education institutions. As the proponents of life adjustment education increasingly promoted programs like basic living, not merely as an addendum to the traditional curriculum, but as a substitute for it, however, the wrath of academicians was aroused. After a period of neglect almost amounting to disdain, an intense interest began to develop among leading scholars in a variety of disciplines as to the state of the curriculum in the lower schools.

Some of the attacks on the state of schooling in America at midcentury were concentrated on Satan and alleged political radicalism in the public schools, and these campaigns achieved some success. Willard Goslin, for example, the superintendent of schools in Pasadena, California, was induced to resign his position by pressure groups inspired by Allen A. Zoll's National Council for American Education (Hulburd, 1951). Beleaguered educators sometimes failed to distinguish, however, that another sort of challenge was rapidly emerging as the more potent of the two. It was a frontal attack on the intellectual respectability of what passed for public education in America. Two books published in 1949 were portents of the floodtide of criticism to follow. Bernard Iddings Bell's *Crisis in Education* (1949) dwelt on the theme of godlessness and ethical relativism in the schools, but Mortimer Smith's *And Madly Teach* (1949) raised the issue of an anti-intellectual strain in the leadership of American education. He questioned the sheer scope of what was being included in the curriculum, ranging down to the most trivial, and argued that modern educators were unduly pessimistic about the ability of American youth to grapple with the higher reaches of scholarship.

But the most vitriolic of the criticisms were yet to follow. Harry J. Fuller, a professor of botany at the University of Illinois and retiring president of the local chapter of Phi Beta Kappa, delivered a scathing attack at the society's annual banquet on not just the state of education in America but on professors of education. Alluding to "the foe and his tactics," Fuller (1951) sounded four basic themes:

I. The falsity of the basic assumptions from which education professors commonly proceed in their anti-intellectual activities

II. The deterioration in the contemporary training of students, particularly in the high schools

III. The substitution of "societally significant" subjects for sound education in the humanities, the arts, and the sciences

IV. The confusions and inconsistencies that dominate the thinking (perhaps my use of this word is inexcusably charitable), the utterances, and the activities of many education professors (p. 33)

He also cited some recent statements by "the foe" and then pronounced them to be "rubbish . . . consistent and colossal rubbish" (p. 34). That Fuller should sprinkle his address with anecdotes about deterioration in the use of English or high school graduates "who could not name the lake against which Chicago nestles" (p. 36) should not have been surprising. What was most striking was the sheer ferocity that his address exuded. Apparently, however, such resentment had been seething just below the surface in the academic world. *Scientific Monthly*, the journal that published the address, received 248 responses to Fuller's article, 226 of them favorable.

Almost without warning, the decade of the 1950s became a period of criticism of American education unequaled in modern times. Although some of the criticism was an offshoot of the campaign of Senator Joseph McCarthy of Wisconsin to root out communists and subversives from a wide range of influential positions, the enduring assault was made by academics speaking from their platforms on university campuses. Probably the most persistent and effective of these critics was Arthur E. Bestor, Jr., a professor of history at the University of Illinois. Like Fuller, Bestor (1952b) saw professors of education as largely responsible for the mess, but his most pervasive theme was that schools had been diverted from their central function, the development of the intellect. Bestor ridiculed the ten so-called imperative educational needs of youth that had been included in *Education for ALL American Youth* and had then become semiofficial dogma in the National Association of Secondary-School Principals. He objected to the "vague inclusiveness" of any statement that attempted to define education in terms of the needs of youth. "It is *not* the job of the school," he insisted, "to meet the common and the specific individual needs of youth" (p. 415). Instead, he argued that the school was a particular kind of institution with a distinctive function to perform. It was not, as many professional educators claimed, the heir to functions not performed successfully by other social institutions. "Much of the cant about education for 'home and family living,'" he argued, "is a disguised way of saying that the school must take responsibility for things that the family today is supposedly failing to do" (p. 416). What was missing from statements by the supporters of life adjustment education was the central role of the school in intellectual training even for the "masses." Citing the 60 percent figure in the Prosser resolution, Bestor (1953a) interpreted it to be blatantly antidemocratic in that it assumed that a majority of people "are incapable of being benefitted by intellectual training" (p. 12). Reminiscent of Eliot's (1905) defense of the Committee of Ten report, Bestor argued that such a division of the school population "enthrones once again the ancient doctrine that the

majority of people are destined from birth to be hewers of wood and draw-
ers of water to a select few who, by right of superior fitness, are to occupy
the privileged places in society" (pp. 12–13). A first-rate polemicist, Bestor
was reaching an ever-larger portion of the intellectual community and even
attracting some attention in the mass media.

Bestor (1953b) capped his attacks in periodicals with a book, *Educational
Wastelands*, that set forth the striking contrast between his own ideal of education and that of the proponents of life adjustment education. Bestor was
reluctant to associate life adjustment education with progressive education
because progressive education was such a "vague and ambiguous" term that
it tended to be applied to such a wide variety of programs, toward many of
which he felt "hearty sympathy" (p. 44). "I consider myself fortunate," he
said, "to have received my high school training, from 1922 to 1926, in one
of the most progressive schools in the country, the Lincoln School of Teachers College, Columbia University" (p. 45). Bestor seemed to realize what
other critics did not—that life adjustment education was not a descendant
of reforms that Dewey had advocated. In fact, he quoted a lengthy passage
from Dewey's *Experience and Education* (1938) as illustrative of "the points
I have been making" (p. 51). As a student of the life adjustment literature,
he was able to provide prime examples of the anti-intellectualism he perceived in the movement. Perhaps his favorite example, cited on several occasions, was from an article that had appeared in the *Bulletin* of the National
Association of Secondary-School Principals:

> When we come to the realization that not every child has to read, figure,
> write and spell . . . that many of them either cannot or will not master
> these chores . . . then we shall be on the road to improving the junior
> high curriculum.

> Between this day and that a lot of selling must take place. But it's coming.
> We shall some day accept the thought that it is just as illogical to assume
> that every boy must be able to read as it is that each one must be able to
> perform on a violin, that it is no more reasonable to require that each girl
> shall spell well than it is that each one shall bake a good cherry pie.

> When adults finally realize that fact, everyone will be happier . . . and
> schools will be nicer places in which to live. (Lauchner, 1951, p. 299)

An expert marksman like Bestor had little trouble hitting such a grossly
inflated target.

Like other academic critics of American education in the 1950s, Bestor was prone to hyperbole, and his passion on the subject sometimes got in his way. Nevertheless, he was able to expose a serious problem that had been festering since life adjustment education and, before that, social efficiency education had captured the imagination of certain educational reformers. In their effort to reach out to a new population of students and to attune the curriculum directly to the many activities that children and youth would need to perform as members of the society, these reformers had relegated the school's role in intellectual development to an inferior status or, in many instances, saw it as worth preserving only for a small college-going contingent.

Whether by design or default, Harold C. Hand, a professor of education at the University of Illinois, became the knight-errant in the cause of life adjustment education. Early in the controversy, he and Harold W. Sanford, the associate dean of the College of Education of the University of Illinois (in collaboration with the executive committee of the National Association of Secondary-School Principals, the curriculum planning and development committee of that organization, the executive committee of the Illinois Curriculum Program, and the National Commission on Life Adjustment Education for Youth), undertook a lengthy analysis of some of Bestor's initial attacks (Hand & Sanford, 1953). One response was that Bestor, while recognizing that public education had expanded, had failed to take into account significant differences in the learning ability of the new school population, and, therefore, his charges as to the decline in scholarly achievement over the course of the century could be attributed to that change, not to the innovations being implemented in the name of life adjustment. "The level of a pupil's innate intelligence," they insisted, "is a very real determinant of how much intellectual training he is capable of acquiring" as is "the pupil's family situation" (p. 464). Referring frequently to the report of the Harvard Committee (1945) for support, Hand and Sanford interpreted its recommendations as endorsing the tripartite division of the school population embodied in the Prosser resolution. Much of their argument revolved around Bestor's alleged propensity for taking quotations out of context as a way of dramatizing his charges. Bestor, for example, had used *The Schools and National Security* as one of his prime examples of life adjustment (Sanford, Hand, & Spalding, 1951). In particular, he cited a reference to a proposed study of dating patterns. Hand and

Sanford meticulously reviewed the entire context for this reference, arguing that it was but one of 66 suggestions for classroom practice and not necessarily indicative of the tone of the document as a whole. Hand, a dynamic, even inspiring, speaker, somehow seemed overly cautious, relying on small detail to undermine the charges. Unable to mount a counterattack in sufficient force to overwhelm the enemy, life adjustment education quickly began to lose credibility first with the intellectual community and, ultimately, with the general public as well.

For one thing, the vision of life adjustment education was simply too grandiose. Instead of reconstructing the existing curriculum for general education, social efficiency reformers worked to replace it. Not satisfied with the new prominence given to vocational education or a subject realignment that gave greater attention to utilitarian outcomes, life adjustment proponents ultimately sought to score a victory over competing interest groups in the struggle for the American curriculum. Life adjustment education was a dramatic and highly publicized attempt to demonstrate the direct social value of a secondary education in part by demonstrating the uselessness of conventional subject matter. That effort proved ill timed. The sheer magnitude of the proposed changes was so great as to arouse the intellectual community into a spirited defense of academic subject matter. While there were attempts to dismiss their effort as representing the biases of the academic world as against the majority of schoolchildren, academicians stuck to their charge that intellectual development as the basic function of schooling was being undermined by the effort to install a new and supremely functional general education.

Surprisingly, the counterattack by the academic community reached a sympathetic public. The stature of the intellectual had been rising since the days of President Franklin D. Roosevelt's "brain trust," and, although there was some backtracking, the success of scientists in creating the atomic bomb and the context of a technological race with the Soviet Union had created a new respect for the intellectual. An "egghead" candidate, Adlai Stevenson, ran for the presidency in 1952 and 1956, and although he lost to a national hero, Dwight Eisenhower, a new admiration for intellectual prowess was emerging. This gave the critics of life adjustment education a fertile ground for denouncing the work of educational reformers who assumed that an academic curriculum was clearly unacceptable to the mass of American students. The road to prosperity, social reform, and even national security, it seemed, was tied not to adjustment to existing conditions but to intelligent action.

iv

Life adjustment education was already in steep decline when on October 5, 1957, *Sputnik*, the world's first earth-orbiting satellite, was launched by the Soviet Union. Within a matter of days, American mass media had settled on a reason for the Soviet technological success. Just as Prussian schools were widely believed to be the basis for the victory of the Prussians over the Austrians in the Battle of Königgrätz in 1866, so, implausibly, did the Soviet technological feat become a victory of the Soviet educational system over the American. Quickly, life adjustment education was seen as the prime example of America's "soft" education in contrast to the rigorous Soviet system. While American schoolchildren were learning how to get along with their peers or how to bake a cherry pie, so the explanation went, Soviet children were being steeped in the hard sciences and mathematics needed to win the technological race that had become the centerpiece of the Cold War.

Some of the seeds for this interpretation of the Soviet success had been planted in a series of speeches delivered by Vice Admiral Hyman G. Rickover (1959), beginning around 1956, which were eventually published in book form. Rickover, who was usually credited with the development of the atomic submarine, had acquired a reputation as an intellectual and carried considerable influence with many members of Congress. In his criticisms of American education, he consistently called attention to Soviet technological advances, emphasizing that "the greatest mistake a nation can make is to underestimate a potential enemy. Russian engineering and scientific development constitute a threat to our military power" (p. 50). As the core of this problem, he singled out the superiority of the Soviet system of education over that in the United States. As would be expected, life adjustment education was a favorite target, but he also indicated John Dewey as one whose ideas had led to an educational system gone soft. Rickover liked to compare the American curriculum not simply with that of the Soviet Union, but of European countries, generally arguing that a misconceived notion of equality had led American schools to degenerate.

One of Rickover's major themes was that the gifted and talented of the country were neglected as part of the effort to increase the holding power of schools. He pointed out that 60 to 70 percent of the scientists who had been instrumental in developing the atomic bomb were foreign-born and educated (Rickover, 1959, p. 153). After making a count of Nobel Prize winners in physics and chemistry through 1955, Rickover concluded that the combined "brain power" of Germany, England, France, Denmark and Italy was precisely "eleven times as rich as we" in those scientific fields (pp. 152–153). Reflecting a position that the academic critics had taken, Rickover argued that "*the school's concern is with the intellect alone*" (p. 154). He was, like the others, a champion of the liberal arts, but his interest in developing the intellect was infused with his intense desire to outstrip the Soviet Union in scientific and technical areas. He decried "piecemeal attempts to toughen the schools," contending that these would be insufficient to "put our educational system in the forefront—at least ahead of the Russians" (p. 154). As such, there was, oddly enough, a distinct element of social efficiency thinking in Rickover's criticism. The development of the intellect was not so much a good in itself or for the purpose of giving the individual a way of mastering the modern world but a direct avenue to victory in the Cold War. That, more than the standard humanist arguments, had strong popular appeal and helped convert what had been a rather limited battle between academicians and professional educators over control of the curriculum into a matter of urgent national concern.

Within a year after *Sputnik*, Congress reacted to the national clamor by passing the National Defense Education Act on September 2, 1958. The first paragraph in the act made the intent clear:

> The Congress hereby finds and declares that the security of the Nation requires the fullest development of the mental resources and technical skills of its young men and women. The present emergency demands that additional and more adequate educational opportunities be made available. The defense of this Nation depends upon the mastery of modern techniques developed from complex scientific principles. (National Defense Education Act of 1958)

The main body of the act was concerned with curriculum revision in mathematics, science, and foreign languages, with additional attention given to strengthening guidance services, an outgrowth of the increasing concern about identifying talented students. As in the case of the Smith-Hughes Act of 1917, Congress felt impelled to pass a specific measure designed to meet a national emergency. Unlike the Smith-Hughes Act, however, administrative control of the massive amount of money involved did not fall to professional educators. Their credibility impaired by the excesses of life adjustment education, professional educators were no longer to be given free rein in curriculum matters. Congress had clearly accepted the verdict of the academic critics that educators had foisted a soft and intellectually puerile curriculum on American schools.

Much of the money for curriculum revision was funneled through the National Science Foundation, which had been established in 1950 as an agency of the executive branch of government for the support of science. Of the principal beneficiaries of Congress's largess were curriculum reform programs in science and mathematics that had been under way prior to the passage of the 1958 act. The physical sciences study committee, for example, headed by Jerrold R. Zacharias, a professor of physics at the Massachusetts Institute of Technology, began work in 1956 and subsequently received strong support in its effort to restructure the teaching of physical sciences. Over its first five years of existence, the committee expended approximately six million dollars for that project including the production of teaching materials and another six million for the retraining of teachers in the use of those materials. The University of Illinois committee on school mathematics had been working on new mathematics curricula since 1952, but others such as the School Mathematics Study Group, the Chemical Education Material Study, and the Biological Sciences Curriculum Study were not undertaken until after the passage of the National Defense Education Act. Unlike the Smith-Hughes Act of 1917, when the nation saw skilled workers as the key to prosperity and security, the mood had swung to the intellectual, particularly to scientists, mathematicians, and engineers, as the key to world preeminence.

V

The burgeoning of these curriculum projects represented the end of an era in several respects. First, almost without exception, the directors of these major projects were drawn from academic departments in major universities. Control of curriculum change in other words had reverted from its traditional locus in the professional education community to specialists in the academic disciplines. Second, as would be expected, the effort to replace the academic subjects as the basic building block of the curriculum, going back about half a century, was brought to an abrupt end. No longer would projects or areas of living be actively promoted as substitutes for the subject. Third, the long-standing emphasis on local efforts at curriculum change was replaced by a trend toward centrally controlled curriculum revision. Although the major revision projects of the National Science Foundation and related programs did not have the legal power to mandate the changes they were recommending, they did transform the process of curriculum change to one in which the curriculum would be developed first by experts at a center set up for that purpose, with the local school systems perceived as consumers of external initiatives. The extent to which these highly significant changes would survive the immediate social and political climate in which they were born or their efficacy as ways of addressing curriculum issues remains to be determined.

The entry on a massive scale of the federal government in the battle for the curriculum of American schools dramatically altered the relative strength of the various interest groups. With huge sums of money available for changing the way school subjects were taught, a version of the humanist position became dominant almost overnight. Efforts were directed not at replacing the academic subjects or reconstructing them to make them more functional, but to bringing them in line with the frontiers of scholarly endeavor. There remained, here and there, the feeling that the intellectual riches being purveyed should be available only for a select few, but by and large, there was an effort to raise the intellectual level for all—ultimately extending to the social sciences and the humanities as well as the natural sciences and mathematics. The other interest groups, however, were not exactly vanquished. For better or worse, the changes accruing from the new federal involvement in the curriculum did not obliterate the victories that had been achieved over the previous sixty-five years of curriculum reform. Developmentalists had partially succeeded in drawing attention to the nature of child life as a key element in curriculum thinking. Social efficiency educators had reinforced an instinctive belief on the part of Americans that education ought to be tied to tangible rewards. Social meliorists brought to the fore the issue of schooling in relation to social progress. The school, for example, more than any other social institution, became the focus of the civil rights struggle.

The one fortress that proved virtually impregnable was the school subject. The subject as the basic unit in the curriculum successfully resisted the more ambitious efforts to replace it with anything like functional areas of living or projects arising from student interest. If the success of the 65-year effort to reform the American curriculum is to be judged by the extent to which English, mathematics, science, history, geography, and the like simply survived the assault against them, then the effort must be counted a failure. But subject labels alone may be misleading. Some of the reforms advanced by the various interest groups were accomplished within the overall context of the subject organization of the curriculum, with the subjects, in varying degrees, incorporating certain of the reforms. To be sure, not all the changes may be regarded as signs of progress, but modest successes were achieved in restructuring, integrating, and modernizing the subjects that comprise the curriculum. The subjects survived, but in an altered form.

As the struggle proceeded, distinct indications of the efforts of all the various interest groups became evident in terms of what was taught under the subject labels. English, for example, had been affected by the experience curriculum movement, and social studies had absorbed significant elements of both social efficiency and social reconstruction. In that sense, the outcome of the struggle for the American curriculum was an undeclared, almost unconscious, détente. At one and the same time, the curriculum in the twentieth century had come to represent a reasonably faithful reflection of the intellectual resources of our culture and its anti-intellectual tendencies as well; it served to liberate the human spirit and also to confine it; it was attuned to the well-being of children and youth and also contributed to their disaffection and alienation from the mainstream of social life; and it represented a vehicle for social and political reform as well as a force for perpetuating existing class structures and for the reproduction of social inequality.

AFTERWORD
THE SEARCH FOR MEANING IN PROGRESSIVE EDUCATION: CURRICULUM CONFLICT IN THE CONTEXT OF STATUS POLITICS

THE EFFORT TO DEPICT THE MELANGE OF REFORMS WE HAVE COME TO lump together as progressive education has itself developed something of a history; that is to say, apart from the history of the reforms themselves, the way historians have defined progressive education has acquired a kind of story of its own. The rendition of reform efforts between 1893 and 1958 that constitutes *Struggle for the American Curriculum* is particularly indebted to a spirited debate that erupted in the 1960s as to how the history of education should be written. To a large extent, that controversy took the form of a challenge to an established tradition in writing history of education. Under the form of historiography of education that has come to be called celebratory history or "house history" (Tyack, 1974, pp. 8–9) or sometimes, Whig history, new developments in education were generally treated as evidence of progress; educational reformers were the heroes, and various opponents of change were the villains. In effect, the history of education was represented as a march of progress. Progressive education, for example, was a movement that challenged the benighted educational practices that had dominated schooling in the nineteenth century and earlier and then ultimately triumphed some time around the middle of the twentieth century. According to most of those accounts, it was a victory of democracy and enlightenment over the forces of elitism and hidebound tradition.

For many years, that approach to the history of education was particularly appealing to those historians affiliated with schools of education who saw their task as using history in order to instill a sense of pride in future teachers and other education professionals. The study of history was, and to a large extent still is, considered to be a part of professional socialization of teachers. History was considered to be one instrument for instilling pride in becoming a member of a noble profession, comparable to the use of history as a way of promoting patriotism or good citizenship. It was also linked to the idea that history could provide direct solutions of sorts to present-day problems. At the least, it could keep us from repeating old mistakes. How else could the study of history of education by future teachers be justified?

A major challenge to that form of historiography was issued by Bernard Bailyn in the introductory essay to his *Education in the Forming of American Society* (1960), and the publication date of that book is as good a date as any to mark a turning point in historiography of education. Bailyn notes with some sympathy the attempt to use history of education as part of a process of initiation for teachers, but he concludes that many of the problems in the historiography of education derive from that impulse. History written by "educational missionaries" will inevitably reflect well-meaning, but externally directed, intentions. Much of the social and cultural context becomes lost, and schools get depicted as "self-contained entities." More importantly, professional biases, such as the desire to instill professional pride into novitiates, profoundly affect how history of education is interpreted. "To these writers," Bailyn concludes, "the past was simply the present writ small" (p. 9). In other words, it serves to explain how present institutional arrangements and practices got that way and, in effect, to justify their existence.

Just about the time that celebratory history was being taken to task by Bailyn, Lawrence A. Cremin published his *Transformation of the School: Progressivism in American Education, 1876–1957* (1961). It is now almost trite to say that the publication of that book was a landmark. In fact, more than any historian, Cremin succeeded in establishing history of education as an integral part of social and cultural history, and the writing of history of education has never really been the same since his book appeared. That he was consciously trying to break new ground is suggested by the carefully worded subtitle of his book. He clearly intended his book not to be a parochial history of progressive education but about a larger social and political progressivism *as it affected education*. As Cremin himself expresses the point in his preface to the book, progressive education was "the educational phase of American Progressivism writ large" (p. viii).

That central theme stated, Cremin then goes on to interpret progressive education in terms of three defining characteristics: (1) the expansion of the function of schooling beyond intellectual development into such areas as health and occupational competence; (2) the application of scientific research to pedagogical practice; and (3) "tailoring instruction" to different types of students variously identified within the school population (pp. xiii–ix). He also cites the desire on the part of progressive reformers, as an overall article of faith, to democratize intellectual culture to the point where it can be made available to all. The identification of these general characteristics notwithstanding, Cremin concludes his preface with a disclaimer: "The reader will search these pages in vain for any capsule definition of progressive education. None exists, and none ever will; for throughout its history progressive education meant different things to different people, and these differences were only compounded by the remarkable diversity of American education" (p. x). Cremin may not actually provide a "capsule" definition in the conventional sense, but "the educational phase of American Progressivism writ large" along with the three characteristics he enumerates come pretty close.

Three years after Cremin posited his interpretation, the first volume of Edward A. Krug's *Shaping of the American High School* (1964) appeared. The subtlety of Krug's style has sometimes tended to obscure the really radical nature of his interpretation of progressive education.[1]

For one thing, Krug is not nearly as sanguine as Cremin about the course that education took in what is usually considered the progressive era. To be sure, neither Cremin nor Krug provides a heavy-handed assessment of the movement. Both let their interpretations emerge, more or less, from their narratives, but Cremin's is clearly positive "on balance" (to use one of his favorite expressions), and his tone of regret at the expiration of the movement is unmistakable. While progressive reformers may not have realized fully their aspirations for American schools, he says, theirs was a high-minded, democratically inspired movement.

By contrast, Krug's assessment is much more mixed, with many of the proposed reforms of the period at least tacitly rejected. Curriculum differentiation in relation to variously identified segments of the school population, for example, means something vastly different to Krug than it does to Cremin. What for Cremin (1961) appears as "tailoring instruction" (p. ix) to meet the needs of a diverse school constituency is seen by Krug (1964) as a policy where it is difficult "to shake loose the implications of caste education" (p. 203). Moreover, although Krug speaks in general terms about the period in general as "an age of criticism directed against established orders" (p. xiii), he does not attempt to list its particular attributes, as Cremin does. In fact, for Krug, progressive education as an identifiable entity is virtually nonexistent. His index, for example, includes one reference to the journal *Progressive Education* and a few references to the Progressive Education Association and none at all to progressive education itself, whereas the listing in Cremin's index for progressive education is a full two columns.

One of Krug's major contributions is his reintroduction of the concept of social efficiency as an ideal identified with the progressive era in education. Although the term was in widespread use in the period itself and had many openly proclaimed adherents, it had somehow fallen out of favor as a way of characterizing a pervasive ideology of the period by historians of education. Almost parenthetically, Cremin (1961) refers to one "stream of curriculum reform during the twenties [that is] more radical in its antiformalism and more conservative in its ultimate social impact" (p. 198). He is also briefly critical at this juncture of Franklin Bobbitt's scientism, but this is a relatively insignificant part of his overall interpretation. By contrast, social efficiency as a potent ideology, including its emphasis on social control, is central in Krug's work. In fact, at one point, he declares emphatically, "In the end, social efficiency conquered all" (p. 276). In his insistence on social efficiency as a crucial ideological refrain of the period, Krug is not simply acknowledging what Cremin (1961) refers to as the "pluralistic, frequently contradictory character" of progressive education (p. x); he is also giving the whole movement a much more negative aspect.

Finally, Krug gives the school curriculum a far more central role in his account than does Cremin. Krug was intensely interested in the efforts to reform the curriculum during this period and especially in the effects of those reforms that sought to replace or drastically reconstruct the traditional school subjects. In fact, Krug concludes his first volume with an examination of the extent to which school subjects were actually affected by the effort to transform them. Cremin, by contrast, concludes *Transformation* with a seven-point exposition of why the progressive education movement collapsed so abruptly. Cremin's index contains no entry at all for curriculum or course of study.[2] His focus is on social forces affecting the progressive education movement; Krug's is on the social implications of proposed reforms on school practice in roughly the same period.

An important early indication that a new history of education was emerging was the appearance of Michael Katz's (1968) *The Irony of Early School Reform*. Although it is more of a historical case study than a broad-scale history and covers a period that antedates what most historians have regarded as the progressive era, Katz's book prefigures many of the themes as well as the interpretations that revisionist historians were to adopt. He takes as his task the eradication of the prevailing "myth" of public education. "For the most part," Katz argues, "historians have helped to perpetuate this essentially noble story, which portrays a rational, enlightened working class, led by idealistic and humanitarian intellectuals, triumphantly wresting free public education from a selfish, wealthy elite and from the bigoted proponents of orthodox religion" (p. 1). In place of that myth, he tells a story of how elite groups prompted by self-interest, middle-class parents concerned with status, and an emerging class of professional educators worked to impose particular educational reforms in line with their own interests on the schools of Beverly, Massachusetts, in the mid-nineteenth century.

By the 1970s, a new group of younger historians began to convey a criticism of progressive education that was indebted to Krug but much harsher in tone and substance than anything that Krug ever envisioned. These critiques were more closely tied to social class considerations. The radical revisionists, as they came to be called, virtually turned celebratory history on its head. Reforms and reformers, once depicted as advancing the cause of democratic popular education, were now seen as repressive, serving mainly the interests of dominant elites. Joel Spring's *Education and the Rise of the Corporate State* (1972), dedicated to Krug, is as good an example as any. Spring proclaims his thesis at the outset: "The public schools of the twentieth century were organized to meet the needs of the corporate state and consequently to protect the interests of the ruling elite and the technological machine" (pp. 1–2). There follows a devastating attack on the reforms that have come to be associated with the progressive era. Relentlessly, Spring points to one innovation after another that served only to further the interests of what he calls the corporate state. Even Kilpatrick's project method is not spared. It is interpreted as insisting on "social conformity" by seeing to it that "the individual was conditioned to respond at all times to the desires of the group" (pp. 59–60). In the end, Spring holds out no hope for reform of the system because the organizational features of schooling inevitably inhibit freedom and individuality and demand social adaptation. "Any talk about changing the goals of socialization without considering these factors," he concludes, "is meaningless. The only possible solution is ending the power of the school" (p. 172).[3]

The radical revisionists had launched what was certainly a visible and largely successful attack on what celebratory historians had called progressive education. They had taken the broad movement for reform that had been the subject of so much adulation and reinterpreted it as an instrument of social and political elites; but what was this entity called progressive education that the two sides were debating? Whichever position one took in this matter, there was still a progressive education out there that remained to be defined and interpreted.

A second way to address the problem of defining progressive education is to narrow the range of phenomena that the term progressive education is supposed to encompass. The most notable and successful of these efforts is David Tyack's (1974) *The One Best System: A History of American Urban Education.* Tyack chooses as his subject the "*organizational* revolution that took place in American education" (p. 3, emphasis added). His is the "success story" (pp. 182–198) of how an elite group of reformers ("administrative progressives") undertook a program of reform to centralize the control of schools along the model of corporate boards of directors, with certain responsibilities delegated to professionally trained superintendents and their staff of "experts." The other progressives, the "pedagogical progressives," who are further subdivided into "libertarians and radicals" (pp. 196–197), are discussed more or less only in passing, and theirs is anything but a "success story." "Administrative progressives" earn a place in Tyack's index, but "pedagogical progressives" do not.

Tyack's approach has certain obvious advantages. For one thing, his emphasis on urban education and, more importantly, on administrative and organizational reform permits him to identify progressive education with the kind of municipal reform that Samuel P. Hays (1964), for example, explored in the context of political progressivism. Within the framework of administrative reform, Cremin's earlier identification of progressive education with political progressivism makes sense. Second, by restricting his focus to "administrative progressives," Tyack can not only speak comfortably about progressive education as a movement and attribute to it a reasonably coherent ideology but claim for it a distinct measure of success. Progressive education is, for Tyack, "a movement with identifiable actors and coalitions" that "gained substantive power in urban education" (p. 128). There is no compelling reason to take issue with Tyack's characterization of progressive education as a movement so long as it is identified as a very particular kind of organizational reform.[4]

The question of what was progressive education, however, remains very much a puzzle when the pedagogical reforms that many historians have identified with the period are factored in; and it becomes particularly problematic when the politically and socially regressive nature of curricular reforms proposed by the likes of key players in the drama such as Franklin Bobbitt, W. W. Charters, and David Snedden are considered. This is, after all, what much of the criticism by the radical revisionists was about. To be sure, they, as well as others identified in various historical accounts of the period as progressive educators, concerned themselves with the organizational structure of schooling. They were also very closely identified with particular educational practices, such as activity analysis as a scientific method for constructing a curriculum, and with the different kinds of knowledge that schools should purvey to different social groups, variously identified. The triumph of vocationalism early in twentieth-century American education, for example, is only in small measure attributable to organizational change.

A more recent example of narrowing the range of phenomena as a way of defining progressive education is Arthur Zilversmit's, *Changing Schools: Progressive Education Theory and Practice, 1930–1960*. Central to Zilversmit's (1993) interpretation is his belief that "it is important to recognize that progressive education was only one of several contemporary educational reform movements" (p. 2). In other words, he holds that there were progressive reformers acting independently (more or less) from what might be called nonprogressive reformers. As an example of nonprogressive reformers, he cites those who "were primarily concerned with applying principles of efficiency, centralization, and bureaucratic decision making, based on the example of modern business, to the schools" (p. 2). Zilversmit is thereby excluding from his definition of progressive education the very "administrative progressives" that Tyack (1974) made the focal point of his book. (Vocational education and the drive to Americanize immigrants are also excluded.) But, like Tyack, Zilversmit has every right to give his dog a name, and, like Tyack, his narrow definition of progressive education permits him to deal effectively with a restricted body of reform. Progressive education for him is associated with the work of John Dewey, Francis Parker, and William Heard Kilpatrick, reformers he feels were primarily concerned with "meeting the needs of individual children" (p. 2) by creating a "nurturing environment" (p. 3).[5] That restricted focus it should be noted, however, is very much like a stipulative definition. In effect, Zilversmit is putting his readers on notice that the term *progressive education* will mean only certain things and not others insofar as his book is concerned. In so doing, he excludes what some historians of education, at least, regard as the most notable and abiding of the reforms of the time, as well as what some highly regarded general historians of the progressive period, such as Samuel Haber (1964) and Robert Wiebe (1967), think was its dominant refrain.

Restricting the range of reforms that will count as progressive education makes for a much cleaner story, but stipulating the way in which the term progressivism will be used neither reflects common usage the way a dictionary definition would nor does it shed light on the question of why so many inconsistent and contradictory reforms managed to acquire one label. Was John Dewey a progressive or not? Just about Tyack's only mention of Dewey is (quite correctly) to exclude him from the domain of administrative progressivism (1974, pp. 197–198); Zilversmit, on the other hand, identifies progressive education almost entirely with the work of Dewey and his like-minded contemporaries. To take another example, Edward L. Thorndike was probably the most influential of the progressives that Cremin (1961) identifies, and his emphasis on creating a science of education becomes a crucial aspect of what for Cremin progressive education is. In Zilversmit's (1993) account, Thorndike's impact on education of the period is acknowledged, but he does not qualify as a progressive, largely because Zilversmit believes (quite correctly) that his political philosophy differed so sharply from that of Dewey's (pp. 9–11). For Zilversmit, Dewey's philosophy of education becomes the measuring rod against which any claim to progressivism is to be gauged.

A third way of approaching the problem of defining progressive education is to challenge the way the question is formulated.[6] Obviously, the
question, as posed, seems to assume that there was, in fact, something that
could be reasonably characterized as a reform movement and that the task
of the historian is to find a legitimate way of characterizing and interpreting it, even though, as almost everyone seems to agree, there are certain incontrovertible inconsistencies and contradictions in that movement.
The issue is not by any means restricted to whether the term *progressive*
can reasonably be applied to the period in question. The term itself, however,
does go to the heart of the question of whether what we have come to call
progressive education was the educational offshoot of a larger social and
political progressivism, as Cremin claimed. In fact, it is the term *progressive*
that in an odd way became the focal point of the work of the radical revisionists.[7] What they seem to have demonstrated (to their credit) is that
much of what we have insisted on calling progressive education all these
years has had the effect, at least here and there, and perhaps principally,
of restricting educational opportunity, inhibiting social mobility, and
maintaining an unequal and unfair distribution of political power. We are
left with the feeling that much of what went on in the progressive era was
socially and politically, and perhaps even pedagogically, regressive.

But beyond the question of whether progressive education was indeed
progressive in a social and political sense lies the even more fundamental
question of whether there is anything there to be characterized as progressive or anything else. Debating the question of whether progressive
education was truly progressive still assumes that there is something there
to be described and interpreted. Interestingly enough, however, as early as
the 1960s, the concept of American progressivism as a social and political
movement (that is, "writ large") was beginning to be challenged by historians outside the field of education. In 1964, for example, Daniel Levine
concluded that the term had essentially become an empty concept. "The
word 'Progressive'" he argued, "has been used in so many ways that it has
lost all clear meaning except as a designation for a particular time period
or a particular political party. As a description of either an ideology or a
political program, I find it worthless and misleading" (p. xi).

Debate began in earnest after Peter G. Filene's (1970) "An Obituary for
the 'Progressive Movement'" was published. Filene begins his analysis by
carefully reviewing the interpretations that historians of the era have

advanced in order to characterize the movement with some degree of precision. At first, he examines the way in which any movement may reasonably be defined. It is obvious, he observes, that a movement as a form of mass behavior may be diffuse in certain respects, but, as he describes it, a movement is certainly more sustained than a fad, more encompassing than a panic or riot, and broader than a cult. A movement is also to some degree self-conscious rather than a term that can be applied to a category of persons who simply share one or more common characteristics. "The members of a social movement," Filene argues, "combine and act together in a deliberate self-conscious way, as contrasted to a noncollective or 'aggregative' group (such as blonds or lower-income families) which has a common identity in the minds of social scientists or other observers rather than in the minds of members themselves" (p. 21). Persons identified with a movement, in other words, see *themselves as sharing common programs or beliefs*.

Once a movement is understood in this way, one can then go on to determine whether the term *progressive* can legitimately be applied to such a collective, but it is not clear at all that such a collective exists. Filene finds that efforts to define progressivism ("writ large") in terms of ideological convictions and programs (e.g., women's suffrage) seem to founder on the rocks of inconsistency even when geographical differences (e.g., progressives from the South) are factored in. If, for example, the inconsistencies could be explained in terms of regional differences, then some ideological basis for the designation could be sustained, albeit with clearly defined exceptions. But that does not seem to be the case. Similarly, according to Filene's argument, when efforts to define progressivism in terms of the demographic characteristics of its proponents (e.g., urban, middle-class, young, political novices, etc.), the result is similarly unpersuasive. In short, neither in terms of the coherence of the program for reform nor in its membership nor in its overall ideology can a definition of progressivism as a social and political movement be articulated. In the end, Filene concludes that what we call the progressive era can best be portrayed by what he calls "shifting coalitions around different issues" (p. 33). It is not, obviously, that individuals usually identified as "progressives" actually lacked ideological or political convictions; it is that, as a group, their stands on particular issues, rather than being dictated by a consistent ideology, were prompted by what Filene refers to as "opportunism" or "improvisation" (pp. 33–34). The picture that emerges from Filene's analysis is that while old patterns and values were indeed giving way in the period 1890 to 1920, this breakdown did not eventuate in a consistent social vision or political program.

Filene's challenge to the very notion of a progressive movement created considerable stir among historians and even prompted a book (Buenker, Burnham, & Crunden, 1977) in which three historians critically examined his thesis. In that work, John D. Buenker (1977), for example, largely endorses Filene's position. "Loose, shifting coalitions," he argues, "suffer from few of the conceptualizing disabilities associated with a coherent movement" (p. 33). The notion of shifting coalitions does away with the requirement that common ideological threads be found in reforms of the period. The coalition that formed around a reform like workmen's compensation, for example, was hardly the same one that demanded prohibition (p. 49). Despite the controversy it engendered, the Filene thesis went virtually unnoticed in the world of educational historiography, even though some of the most exciting work in history of American education was being done in the 1970s. One exception is Carl Kaestle's (1972) essay review of four books published around this time. Early in his essay, Kaestle suggests that "the bewildering variety of programs and philosophies" that characterized the period from 1890 to the 1920s "leads one to vote with Peter Filene to 'tear off the familiar label' and recognize the ambiguity and variety of the period" (p. 216). Later, in the context of his examination of Marvin Lazerson's (1971) *Origins of Urban Education: Public Education in Massachusetts, 1870–1915*, Kaestle notes that "the word 'Progressive' appears nowhere in the book, although many familiar themes associated with Progressive education occurred in Massachusetts" (p. 227). Where, for example, are the writings of John Dewey or the recommendations of the Cardinal Principles report?

All this raises the question of why Lazerson, obviously a highly competent historian, in a scrupulous examination of such educational reforms as the introduction of the kindergarten and manual training in Massachusetts in what was unquestionably the "progressive era," neglected to acknowledge the movement that presumably provided the context for those reforms. Can it really be the case that the introduction of the kindergarten and manual training was not prompted at least in part by ideological considerations? Hardly. Clearly, the reformers themselves did not lack ideological convictions. The commissioner of education in Massachusetts at the time, David Snedden, for example, was never shy about expressing his vision of the good society. As individuals, the reformers' political and social convictions may have been perfectly consistent. The problem is that, in the aggregate, the reasons for supporting any given reform differed dramatically from one reformer to the next. In other words, consistent with Filene's thesis, reformers with different ideological positions formed coalitions around particular educational reforms. It appears that Lazerson at least implicitly recognized that the reforms he examined were not prompted by a single ideological position and were not part of what may be called a movement.

Manual training as an educational reform is a case in point. Around that particular curriculum innovation there clustered a variety of reformers who saw in manual training quite different virtues. There were those like Calvin Woodward who saw in it a way of preserving the dignity of work in school programs; there were Snedden and Frank Leavitt who despaired of ever accommodating the new school population without a highly differentiated curriculum; and there were those like Dewey who saw in manual training an opportunity to dissolve the artificial barriers that existed between traditional academic studies and the world outside of schools. What we have in manual training, in other words, is very much the kind of "coalition" that Filene was talking about. Here we have spokespersons for clearly defined but obviously different and even opposing ideological positions coming together to support one reform precisely because they see in it different things. Although the term *coalition* sometimes implies conscious choice, it is clear that the coalition in this case, and most likely in others as well, was largely tacit and unacknowledged. That the coalition was also "shifting" is evident by the fact that the very same spokespersons who coalesced around manual training were clearly opposed to one another on different, equally critical matters of school reform. In fact, it is this magic-mirror quality some reforms reflected that may account for the measure of success they achieved.

It is worth repeating that the point is not that there were no identifiable or consistent ideological positions. As I tried to delineate in *Struggle*, at least a few can be identified in the period. It is that behind *any particular reform* one can find diverse and contradictory expressions of support. In a sense, then, Filene's proposition that progressivism consists of a series of "shifting coalitions," while hitting the mark in a very significant respect, is nevertheless somewhat elliptical. Once we accept Filene's construction, the question becomes *shifting coalitions of what?* If the coalition is merely a disparate collection of individuals acting more or less independently, then the whole debate loses much of its significance. Clearly, however, the coalitions are composed of like-minded groups of reformers with identifiable ideological positions and reasonably coherent programs of change. In an educational context, it can hardly be doubted that Bobbitt, Charters, and Snedden would have recognized each other as kindred ideological spirits and endorsed a more or less common reform agenda. Similarly, G. Stanley Hall, Marietta Johnson, and Stanwood Cobb shared certain key ideas and a recognizable weltanschauung. The same would be true of Boyd Bode, George Counts, and Harold Rugg. The point is that while common ideological characteristics of social and political progressivism as a movement, as well as *mutatis mutandis* progressive education, have eluded even the most careful scrutiny, reform subgroups can be defined in terms of their shared ideological characteristics. It is these reform subgroups that the accounts by historians of the progressive era such as Tyack (1974), Zilversmit (1993) and others have at least implicitly recognized and that I consciously tried to depict in my own way as well in *Struggle*.

In some such accounts, the subgroups are identified within particular locales. James W. Fraser (1986), for example, identifies what he calls "three very different progressive movements" (p. 10) in Boston in the period between 1905 and 1925: administrative progressives, militant teachers, and curriculum reformers. In Chicago, Julia Wrigley (1982) finds three interest groups struggling for control of educational reform: business leaders allied for the most part with school administrators, middle-class municipal reformers, and militant teachers tied to the Chicago Federation of Labor. In William J. Reese's (1982) *Power and the Promise of School Reform: Grass-Roots Movements during the Progressive Era*, an even wider array of subgroups are identified in the four cities he studied, including "women's organizations, parent associations, labor unions, Social Gospelers, and Populist and Socialist parties" (pp. xxi–xxii). Whether each subgroup also qualifies as a movement of sorts depends on how a movement is to be defined. To my way of thinking, Filene's analysis suggests that the term *movement* may be used to apply to *a broad category of persons who share certain fundamental beliefs and who, over a sustained period of time, self-consciously act to gain public acceptance for those beliefs.* The women's suffrage movement, the temperance movement, and the civil rights movement of the 1960s would be prime examples. According to that definition, Tyack's "administrative progressives" would qualify as movement but progressive educators would not because no one has been able to identify their shared fundamental beliefs with any degree of precision.

In order to support the claim that reform subgroups (whether they qualify as movements or not) can be identified in terms of their ideological characteristics, one should consider the mechanism by which they can be identified. In other words, it should be possible to explain how the reformers themselves were able to recognize one another as members of the same ideological family, and this, in turn, would give us some clue as to how latter-day historians can identify them as a reasonably coherent subgroup. In the case of political parties, unions, and formal organizations generally, such identification is relatively clear-cut, but, more often than not, membership in subgroups is not a matter of record, and affiliation must be identified in other ways. An especially intriguing point of departure in that regard is suggested by Daniel T. Rodgers (1982) in his review of the debate over the concept of social and political progressivism. After examining the efforts to redefine progressivism and finding them at least to some degree inadequate, he concludes that what has been called progressivism may have been part of the larger phenomenon of "the rise of modern, weak-party, issue-focused politics" (p. 117). It may be, in other words, the very fluidity of progressivism that is its most abiding and defensible feature. It is in this respect that Rodgers claims that "the better organized players—the professional lobbies, the well-disciplined interest groups, and above all the corporations—held massive advantages" (p. 121).

Rodgers appears to accept the general outlines of Filene's argument as to "shifting coalitions," but then carries it a step or two further. Like Filene, he rejects the notion that progressivism can be defined by "extracting a stable list of core progressive values" (p. 122), but he feels nevertheless that they were held together by a common faith in their ability to use particular languages in order to build a constituency. "What ideational glue," Rodgers asks, "allowed some of the coalition builders to recognize each other in the new sea of competing interest groups?" The answer he finds lies in what he calls "three distinct social languages." The first he identifies as antimonopolism, the second as "an emphasis on social bonds and the social nature of human beings" (p. 123), and the third as the language of social efficiency. These three languages, Rodgers emphasizes, do not add up to one coherent entity that may be called progressivism or anything else. Rather, they identify the ideological configuration from which people who called themselves progressives were able to construct political support. As Jeffrey E. Mirel (1990) perceptively points out, "Rodgers's identification of three languages is not the same as defining three wings in a movement. Instead, the notion of social languages—what rhetoricians and sociologists of knowledge call 'communities of discourse'—provides an analytic framework for explaining how diverse groups came together in the many shifting coalitions of the Progressive era" (p. 159).

Almost all of this debate, it should be recalled, exists in the context of social and political progressivism. Even when one acknowledges the validity and usefulness of Rodgers's analysis with respect to progressivism "writ large," it should not be assumed that exact counterparts exist in the realm of progressive education. That would be to take Cremin's (1961) interpretation of progressive education as "the educational phase of American Progressivism" (p. viii) far too literally. As it turns out, however, two of Rodgers's three social languages do have their parallels in education debates of the period. Leaving antimonopolism aside, the emphasis on the social nature of human beings is reflected very prominently in the work of such figures as Jane Addams, Dewey, and Counts and, clearly, they used that language in building their constituency. Similarly, Snedden, Bobbitt, and Charters consistently used the language of social efficiency to gain adherents for their reform platforms.

Other languages particular to educational reform of the period can also be identified. The language of romanticism as a way of characterizing childhood, for example, is one strong candidate. At various times, any number of educational leaders of varying stripes found it appropriate or expedient to express themselves in reverential and sometimes even mystical terms about the nature of childhood. The word *kindergarten* itself reflects that usage. It is also the case that all four interest groups identified in *Struggle* frequently found it advantageous to use the language of democracy in support of their positions. Such seemingly incongruous expressions of doctrine as Eliot's (1905) impassioned defense of the Committee of Ten recommendations and the Cardinal Principles report (1918) were conspicuously framed in terms of democratic rhetoric, as was much of the drive for vocationalism. If, by invoking the language of democracy, the opposing position could be made to seem somehow aristocratic or elitist or, in some cases, even just academic, then its legitimacy could be undermined.

It appears, then, as if what Rodgers calls social languages serves at least two crucial purposes: (1) the consistent use of a particular language permits members of an ideological subgroup to identify one another as committed to the same general configuration of reforms; and (2) any of the languages can be drawn upon to form a temporary coalition of different subgroups behind a particular reform. It would do violence to Rodgers's position to assume that any social language is the exclusive possession of any group, even though certain subgroups may display a distinct propensity to use one social language much more conspicuously than another. Rather, the languages are "out there" as potential political instrumentalities. In fact, it may be useful to think of these social languages as slogan systems (as Rodgers suggests) whose primary function is not so much to communicate as to secure political allegiances both within a particular subgroup and across subgroups in behalf of a specific reform. It is this very fluidity that becomes the constitutive property of progressivism—not a list of stable attributes.

Where does that leave the search for progressive education? The two dominant approaches to interpreting progressive education have been (1) to define progressive education in broad terms, often acknowledging obvious inconsistencies and contradictions (e.g., Cremin); and (2) to single out a particular subgroup or program of reform and to exclude everything that may be inconsistent with it from what may legitimately be defined as progressive education (e.g., Zilversmit). The third approach, suggested here, differs from both of these in certain important respects. First, it requires that one abandon the quest to define progressive education in terms of an inventory of stable attributes; second, it recognizes that reform subgroups (whether or not they are called interest groups, as in the case of *Struggle*) can be defined in terms of rather consistent and recognizable ideological positions and that these positions can be identified to some extent through the social language they characteristically employ; and, third, it accepts the proposition that behind any particular reform a coalition may be formed among these subgroups. In fact, the most successful of the proposed reforms are those around which a powerful alliance of reform subgroups managed to coalesce. Like progressivism "writ large," as interpreted by historians like Filene and Rodgers, then, progressive education becomes a reaction against traditional structures and practices but with multiple ideological positions and programs of reform emerging. Although efforts to define progressive education seem to have reached a dead end, it nevertheless seems possible to identify reasonably coherent subgroups and movements that functioned within what we usually think of as the progressive era. In no sense, however, do they add up to one progressive education movement.

It should be obvious that elements of the preceding discussion as to the meaning of progressive education strongly influenced the way in which educational reform was interpreted in *Struggle*, written during what we commonly think of as the progressive era, even though I confess that not all the elements were clearly in place at the time. I did studiously avoid direct reference to anything called progressive education, for example, except for the discussion of the Progressive Education Association and some references to the doubts expressed by key players in the drama, such as Dewey and Bode, as to what progressive education was all about. In part, this was because I shared the view expressed by Krug, and later of certain radical revisionists, that some of the reforms that had somehow acquired the progressive label were in fact regressive. But, more importantly, I was also sympathetic to the skepticism expressed by Filene and Rodgers as to whether a single movement, whether progressive or not, ever existed.

The framework for *Struggle*, then, is based on the four identified subgroups I chose to call interest groups in order to call attention to the fact that these groups did, in fact, share common interests even though they were not defined by a membership list, charter, or formal set of principles. While I had despaired of ever using a single ideological entity to frame what was commonly thought of as progressive education, the use of interest groups as a framework permitted me not only to identify the key ideological refrains in the period but to emphasize, rather than merely acknowledge, the contrasting agendas for reform that the various interest groups advanced. In fact, the use of the term *struggle* in the title was carefully chosen to convey the idea that the curriculum was (and, for that matter, is) contested terrain. In an important sense, it was the prize for which the various interest groups competed.

The question may then be raised as to why this struggle was so bitterly fought. The most immediate answer is that it was a battle for control over the forms of knowledge as well as the values that an important social institution would pass on to the next generation. As such, much legitimate discussion and debate among historians, sociologists, and others as to whether the reforms proposed by the key players actually made their way into schools and classrooms or whether this was a drama being played out in an arena of its own. In fact, much useful research, such as that reported by Barry Franklin (1982), Larry Cuban (1993), Jeffrey Mirel and David Angus (1986), and Arthur Zilversmit (1993), is directed at the question of the extent to which the reforms being proposed by leaders in education succeeded in any sense of the term. Much of this research must necessarily be in the nature of a case study within particular schools or school districts.

In *Struggle*, there is some discussion of the extent to which certain reforms, such as life adjustment education, actually made their way into schools, but center stage is given to the national rather than local debates over the direction that the curriculum should take, and certain caveats should be kept in mind in this regard. First, it can be taken for granted that what is proposed in national forums by way of curriculum reform will always be transmuted in some way if and when it reaches the schools. On the other hand, it should not be assumed that these national debates go on independently of what takes place in local sites. In fact, what evidence has accumulated supports the idea that the key reforms that were being advanced at the national level did have some impact on what was being studied in school. Franklin's research is a case in point. In examining the way the Common Learnings Program was implemented in the Minneapolis school district, Franklin found that local factors such as state Department of Education regulations and opposition by the parents council diluted the impact of social efficiency. The program that was implemented, however, included unmistakable strains of that doctrine. The issue being raised by Franklin and others in this regard is not simply the extent to which the reforms made an impact, but how and in what ways local actors and circumstances influenced the reforms themselves. There are, then, two scenes of action: the national one in which leaders argue and debate the merits of their proposals and the local one in which the ideas are further debated and, in some instances at least, translated into concrete courses of study. These two arenas, however, are not independent of one another.

There is another kind of answer that may be given as to why the four interest groups struggled so vigorously. That answer has less to do with the extent to which the curriculum reforms they proposed would or would not be implemented and more to do with the symbolic sanction being sought by the contending parties. There can hardly be any doubt that key actors on the national scene like Harris, Bobbitt, Hall, and Counts wanted their proposed reforms to reach into classrooms and thereby realize the social purposes that lay behind them. In many instances, they labored mightily to accomplish just that; but they were also fighting to have their treasured social beliefs and values endorsed through acceptance into the national debate over the American curriculum. In a brilliant insight, Joseph R. Gusfield (1986) observes that, rather than being primarily instrumental in their effect, "curricular changes 'bear witness' to . . . the domination of one cultural group and the subordination of another. As most educators know, schools are run for adults, not for children. There is more than expression of feeling in such demands. There is an effort to dominate the rituals by which status is discerned" (pp. 181–182). In the context of status politics, the debate over vocationalism, for example, was not so much a matter of whether occupational skills could be taught successfully in schools; it was over such questions as whether an effete academic curriculum would continue to represent American values or would be replaced by values reflecting a new rugged industrialism. It became a drama of ritualized dominance and subordination. In this sense, the struggle was over semiofficial status and recognition as well as actual changes in school practice.

Whether or not the ideas and platforms that were being enunciated on the national scene by curriculum leaders were instrumental in accomplishing their announced purposes is unquestionably a significant question and should be addressed. But, seen in terms of status politics, subgroups such as the humanists, developmentalists, social efficiency educators, and social meliorists were also seeking to establish or, in some cases, to preserve the status of their treasured beliefs and moral standing. The political infighting among these interest groups, in other words, was not *just* for the purpose of effecting particular changes in schools. Material interests exist alongside and are sometimes even subordinated to status interests. "Political life," as Richard Hofstadter (1955) points out, "is not simply an arena in which the conflicting interests of various social groups in concrete material gains are fought out; it is also an arena in which status aspirations and frustrations are, as the psychologists would say, projected" (p. 43). In an era when there was a heightened perception of a world in the making, one in which older values were disintegrating and new ones emerging to take their place, those status aspirations and frustrations became all the more acute and urgent.

For the most part, these struggles for status take place in the context of political actions such as the making of laws and in governmental undertakings generally, but they also find expression in debates about the rituals of schooling. While the four interest groups identified in *Struggle* may not have been, in any strict sense, political alliances, they were certainly political in that they were united for the purpose of exercising power. More significantly, in terms of status politics, they were unquestionably projecting their treasured social and moral creeds into the question of what should be taught in schools. Whatever else the curriculum may be in terms of what actually gets taught to children, it is also the arena where ideological armies clash over the status of deeply held convictions. If, for example, the significance of the temperance movement in American political and social life was restricted to the extent to which the prohibition of alcoholic beverages as a specific reform had been implemented, there would have been little to talk about since 1933 when the Twenty-first amendment rescinded the Eighteenth; but, as Joseph Gusfield (1986) ably demonstrates, when interpreted in the context of status politics, there is a lot to talk about besides implementation. "When a society experiences profound changes," he says, "the fortunes and the respect of people undergo a loss or gain. We have always understood the desire to defend fortune. We should also understand the desire to defend respect. It is less clear because it is symbolic in nature but it is not less significant" (p. 11). The question of whose cultural and moral values will emerge as dominant in any society is hardly a trivial matter.

In the context of status politics, then, the curriculum in any time and place becomes the site of a battleground where the fight is over whose values and beliefs will achieve the legitimation and the respect that acceptance into the national discourse provides. Even in this context, the instrumental question of what actually gets taught in schools should not be

ignored; but neither should the symbolic conflict over status and approbation. The leaders of the various interest groups in the struggle for the
American curriculum were in the vanguard of sometimes hidden con-
stituencies who were seeking sanction for their most cherished beliefs in
the face of what they perceived to be a massive social upheaval. Behind the
words and actions of the leaders of the interest groups lay the hopes and
fears of millions of Americans who were troubled by an uncertain world
and who found a certain promise and comfort in ideas about how the curriculum should be redesigned. Neither the hopes nor the fears were fully
actualized, and, to be sure, the curriculum reforms that were being proposed were only imperfectly achieved, but the different platforms for
restructuring the curriculum became part and parcel of a national morality
play in which those hopes and fears were enacted. The articulation of those
platforms thereby precipitated a searing conflict which ultimately was
fought over whose deep-seated convictions would predominate in the
emerging new society.

More than anything, it is that conflict that this book seeks to portray.

NOTES

The literature on the history of progressive education, as well as the history of
social and political progressivism, is vast, and no attempt is being made here to
write a comprehensive bibliographical essay on those subjects. Rather, the purpose
is to trace something of the evolution of interpretations of "progressivism" and
"progressive education" since about 1960 insofar as they relate to a theoretical
framework for this book. The bibliographical notes that appear at the end of
Lawrence A. Cremin's *Transformation of the School* (1961) and the two volumes
of Edward A. Krug's *Shaping of the American High School* (1964, 1972) are models
of their kind and should be consulted by those interested in the available bibliographical sources pertaining to the period we identify with progressive education.

1. Michael Katz (1975) credits Krug's work with being "an indispensable source of
information on the development of the high school curriculum" (p. 199).

2. In a perceptive essay review of the three volumes that comprise Cremin's mag-
isterial *American Education*, Jurgen Herbst (1991) has pointed out that the word
curriculum does not appear in the index of any of the volumes (p. 133).

3. The forward to Spring's book was written by Ivan Illich, whose proposals for
"deschooling" are consistent with Spring's conclusions. Some of Spring's interpretations parallel those in James Weinstein's (1968) *The Corporate Ideal in the Liberal
State*. Other radical revisionists whose criticisms of the educational reforms of the
period are equally harsh include Clarence Karier, Paul Violas, Colin Greer, and
Walter Feinberg.

4. Certain themes relating to organizational issues of schooling are further developed by Tyack in a later book written with Elizabeth Hansot (1982), *Managers of Virtue: Public School Leadership in America, 1820–1980*. There, Tyack and Hansot emphasize even more strongly the diversity that characterizes what has come to be called progressive education. "Thinkers such as John Dewey," they say, "proposed philosophies of education quite different from those advocated by the administrative progressives" (p. 114).

5. As is the case with just about any encapsulated version of Dewey's philosophy of education, Zilversmit's is somewhat misleading. The balance in Dewey's educational philosophy is much more in the direction of the social than the individual, and the "nurturing" is not so much for the purpose of meeting a host of "needs" as to foster intellectual mastery.

6. In its most elemental form, the question may be stated as, What was progressive education?

7. As early as 1970, Spring launched a direct attack on Cremin's (1961) interpretation.

REFERENCES

Adams, C. F. (1879). *The new departure in the common schools of Quincy and other papers on educational topics.* Boston: Estes & Lauriat.

Addams, J. (1907). Address. *Bulletin No. 1 of the National Society for the Promotion of Industrial Education* (pp. 37–44). New York: National Society for the Promotion of Industrial Education.

Addams, J. (1908). Discussion. *Bulletin No. 5 of the National Society for the Promotion of Industrial Education* (pp. 92–97). New York: National Society for the Promotion of Industrial Education.

Aikin, W. M. (1931a). Committee on the relation of school and college. *School and Society*, 33, 274–276.

Aikin, W. M. (1931b). Report of the committee on college entrance and secondary schools. *Progressive Education*, 8, 318–320.

Aikin, W. M. (1942). *The story of the eight-year study, with conclusions and recommendations.* New York: Harper & Brothers.

Alberty, H. (1953). *Reorganizing the high-school curriculum.* (Rev. ed.). New York: Macmillan.

Alexander, F. M. (1934). Social studies in Virginia. *The Clearing House*, 9, 76–81.

American Association of School Administrators (1968). *The high school in a changing world.* Thirty-sixth yearbook. Washington, DC: American Association of School Administrators.

American Council on Education, American Youth Commission. (1940). *What the high schools ought to teach: The report of a special committee on the secondary school curriculum.* Washington, DC: American Council on Education.

American Historical Association. (1934). *Conclusions and recommendations of the Commission on the Social Studies.* New York: Charles Scribner's Sons.

Angus, D. L. & Mirel, J. E. (2003). Mathematics enrollments and the development of the high school in the United States, 1910–1994. In G. M. A. Stanic & J. Kilpatrick J. (Eds.) *A history of school mathematics.* Vol. I. Reston, VA: National Council of Teachers of Mathematics.

Armstrong, O. K. (1940, September). Treason in the textbooks. *The American Legion Magazine*, pp. 8–9, 51, 70–72.

As reported. (1921). *The Journal of Educational Method*, 1 (1), 37–41.

Ayres, L. P. (1909). *Laggards in our schools: A study of retardation and elimination in city school systems*. New York: Charities Publication Committee.

Bagley, W. C. (1905). *The educative process*. New York: Macmillan.

Bagley, W. C. (1921). Projects and purposes in teaching and learning. *Teachers College Record*, 22, 288–297.

Bagley, W. C. (1925). *Determinism in education: A series of papers on the relative influence of inherited and acquired traits in determining intelligence, achievement, and character*. Baltimore: Warwick & York.

Bagley, W. C. (1926). Supplementary statement. In G. M. Whipple (Ed.), *The foundations and technique of curriculum-construction, Part II. The foundations of curriculum-making. The Twenty-Sixth Yearbook of the National Society for the Study of Education* (pp. 29–40). Bloomington, IL: Public School Publishing.

Bagley, W. C. (1929a). Discipline and dogma: A reply to Professor Scholtz. *Educational Administration and Supervision*, 15, 561–573.

Bagley, W. C. (1929b). Some handicaps of character education in the United States. In National Education Association, *Official Report of the Department of Superintendence, February 24–28, 1929* (pp. 140–146). Washington, DC: Department of Superintendence.

Bagley, W. C. (1930). The future of education in America. *Proceedings of the Sixty-Eighth Annual Meeting of the National Education Association*, 68, 218–225.

Bagley, W. C. (1938a). An essentialist's platform for the advancement of American education. *Educational Administration and Supervision*, 24, 241–256.

Bagley, W. C. (1938b). Some relations of education to the status quo. *School and Society*, 47, 562–565.

Bagley, W. C. (1939a). An essentialist looks at the foreign languages. *Educational Administration and Supervision*, 25, 241–250.

Bagley, W. C. (1939b). The significance of the essentialist movement in educational theory. *The Classical Journal*, 34, 326–344.

Bagley, W. C. (1945). The Harvard University report on "General education in a free society." *School and Society*, 62, 69–70.

Bailey, L. H. (1908). *On the training of persons to teach agriculture in the public schools*. Washington, DC: U.S. Government Printing Office.

Bailyn, B. (1960). *Education in the forming of American society*. New York: Vintage.

Basic Issues in the Teaching of English (1958). Being definitions and clarifications presented by members of the American Studies Association, College English

Association, Modern Language Association, and National Council of Teachers of English. No Publisher. Available from the sponsoring societies.

Basler, R. (1947). Life adjustment education for youth: Commission to develop program for universal secondary education. *School Life* 30, 3–6.

Beard, C. A. (1932). *A charter for the social sciences in the schools.* New York: Charles Scribner's Sons.

Bell, B. I. (1949). *Crisis in education: A challenge to American complacency.* New York: Whittlesey House.

Bellack, A. A. (1956). Selection and organization of curriculum content: An analysis. In A. A. Bellack (Ed.), *What shall the high schools teach?* 1956 Yearbook of the National Association for Supervision and Curriculum Development. Washington, DC: National Association for Supervision and Curriculum Development.

Bestor, A. E., Jr. (1952). 'Life-adjustment' education: A critique. *Bulletin of the American Association of University Professors*, 38, 413–441.

Bestor, A. E., Jr. (1953a). Anti-intellectualism in the schools. *New Republic*, 128, 11–13.

Bestor, A. E. (1953b). *Educational wastelands: The retreat from learning in our public schools.* Urbana: University of Illinois Press.

Bigelow, M. A. (1904). *Teaching of biology in secondary school.* New York: Longmans, Green and Co.

Billings, N. (1929). *A determination of generalizations basic to the social studies curriculum.* Baltimore: Warwick & York.

Bobbitt, F. (1912). The elimination of waste in education. *The Elementary School Teacher*, 12, 259–271.

Bobbitt, F. (1918). *The curriculum.* Boston: Houghton Mifflin.

Bobbitt, F. (1922). *Curriculum-making in Los Angeles.* Chicago: University of Chicago Press.

Bobbitt, F. (1924). *How to make a curriculum.* Boston: Houghton Mifflin.

Bobbitt, F. (1926). The orientation of the curriculum-maker. In G. M. Whipple (Ed.), *The foundations and technique of curriculum-construction, Part II. The foundations of curriculum-making. The Twenty-Sixth Yearbook of the National Society for the Study of Education* (pp. 41–55). Bloomington, IL: Public School Publishing.

Bobbitt, F. (1934). Questionable recommendations of the Commission on the Social Studies. *School and Society*, 40, 201–208.

Bobbitt, F. (1937). A correlated curriculum evaluated. *English Journal*, 26, 418–420.

Bobbitt, F. (1946). Harvard reaffirms the academic tradition. *School Review*, 54, 326–333.

Bode, B. H. (1927). *Modern educational theories.* New York: Macmillan.

Bode, B. H. (1934). Editorial comment. *Phi Delta Kappan*, 17, 1, 7.

Bode, B. H. (1938). *Progressive education at the crossroads.* New York: Newson.

Bode, B. H. (1940). Needs and the curriculum. *Progressive Education*, 17, 532–537.

Book burnings. (1940, September 9). *Time*, 64–65.

Boutwell, W. D. (1934). The Cleveland meeting. *School and Society*, 39, 296–305.

Boydston, J. A. (1969). A note on applied psychology. In J. A. Boydston (Ed.), *The early works of John Dewey, 1882–1898: Vol. 3. 1889–1892: Early essays and Outlines of a critical theory of ethics* (pp. xiii–xix). Carbondale: Southern Illinois University Press.

Boyer, E. L. (1983). *High school: A report on secondary education in America.* New York: Harper & Row.

Brickman, W. W., & Lehrer, S. (Eds.). (1961). *John Dewey: Master educator* (2nd ed.). New York: Society for the Advancement of Education.

Broder, D. E. (1977). *Life adjustment education: An historical study of a program of the United States Office of Education, 1945–1954.* Unpublished Ed. D. report, Teachers College, Columbia University.

Broudy, H. (1954). *Building a philosophy of education.* New York: Prentice Hall.

Brown, G. P., Hoose, J. H., Parr, S. S., & Harris, W. T. (1889). The educational value of manual training. *Journal of Proceedings and Addresses of the National Education Association, Session of the Year 1889,* 417–423.

Brown, K. E. (1953). *Mathematics in public high schools.* Office of Education, Federal Security Agency, Bulletin 1953, No. 5. Washington, DC: U.S. Government Printing Office.

Brown, K. E. (1956). *Offerings and enrollments in public high schools.* Office of Education, Pamphlet No. 120, 1956. Washington, DC: U.S. Department of Health, Education and Welfare.

Buenker, J. D. Essay. In Buenker, J. D., Burnham, J. C., & Crunden, R. M. *Progressivism.* Cambridge, MA: Schenkman Publishing Co.

Buenker, J. D., Burnham, J. C., & Crunden, R. M. (1977). *Progressivism.* Cambridge, MA: Schenkman Publishing Co.

Bullard, E. P. (1909). Training through the apprenticeship system. In *Bulletin No. 9 of the National Society for the Promotion of Industrial Education* (pp. 51–63). New York: National Society for the Promotion of Industrial Education.

Bunker, F. F. (1916). *Reorganization of the public school system.* Washington, DC: U.S. Government Printing Office.

Butler, N. M. (1888). *The argument for manual training.* New York: E. L. Kellogg.

Callahan, R. E. (1962). *Education and the cult of efficiency: A study of the social forces that have shaped the administration of the public schools.* Chicago: University of Chicago Press.

Chamberlain, D., Chamberlain, E., Drought, N. E., & Scott, W. E. (1942). *Did they succeed in college? The follow-up study of the graduates of the thirty schools.* New York: Harper & Brothers.

Charters, W. W. (1921). The reorganization of women's education. *Educational Review*, 62, 224–231.

Charters, W. W. (1922). Regulating the project. *Journal of Educational Research*, 5, 245–246.

Charters, W. W. (1926a). Curriculum for women. *Bulletin of the University of Illinois*, 23 (27), 327–330.

Charters, W. W. (1926b). Statement. In G. M. Whipple (Ed.), *The foundations and technique of curriculum-construction, Part II. The foundations of curriculum-making. The Twenty-Sixth Yearbook of the National Society for the Study of Education* (p. 71). Bloomington, IL: Public School Publishing.

Charters, W.W. (1926c). The traits of homemakers. *Journal of Home Economics*, 18, 673–685.

Charters, W. W., & Waples, D. (1929). *Commonwealth teacher-training study*. Chicago: University of Chicago Press.

Charters, W. W., & Whitley, I. B. (1924). *Analysis of secretarial duties and traits*. Baltimore: Williams & Wilkins.

Collier, P. D. (1950). What is education for life adjustment? *Bulletin of the National Association of Secondary-School Principals*, 34, 122–128.

Collings, E. (1923). *An experiment with a project curriculum*. New York: Macmillan.

Columbia University. (1927). *Curriculum making in an elementary school, by the staff of the Elementary Division of the Lincoln School of Teachers College, Columbia University*. Boston: Ginn.

Commager, H. S. (Ed.). (1967). *Lester Ward and the welfare state*. Indianapolis: Bobbs-Merrill.

Committee of Seven. (1899). *The study of history in schools*. New York: Macmillan.

Committee on Correlation of the National Council of Teacher of English. *A correlated curriculum*. Monograph No. 5. New York: D. Appleton-Century.

Conant, J. B. (1948). *Education in a divided world*. Cambridge, MA: Harvard University Press.

Cooperative research and curriculum improvement. (1950). *Teachers College Record*, 51, 407–474.

Copley, F. B. (1923). *Frederick W. Taylor: Father of scientific management*, Vol I. New York: American Society of Mechanical Engineers.

Counts, G. S. (1922). *The selective character of American secondary education*. Chicago: University of Chicago Press.

Counts, G. S. (1926). *The senior high school curriculum*. Chicago: University of Chicago Press.

Counts, G. S. (1927). *The social composition of boards of education: A study in the social control of public education*. Chicago: University of Chicago Press.

Counts, G. S. (1930). *The American road to culture: A social interpretation of education in the United States*. New York: John Day.

Counts, G. S. (1932a). Dare progressive education be progressive? *Progressive Education*, 9, 257–263.

Counts, G. S. (1932b). *Dare the school build a new social order?* New York: John Day.

Courtis, S. A. (1913). The Courtis tests in arithmetic. In *Report on educational aspects of the public school system of the City of New York to the Committee on School Inquiry of the Board of Estimate and Apportionment*, Vol. I (pp. 391–546). New York: City of New York.

Cremin, L. A. (1961). *The transformation of the school: Progressivism in American education, 1876–1957.* New York: Alfred A. Knopf.

The critic at sea. (1894). V. *Education*, 15, 149–157.

The critic at sea. (1895). VII. *Education*, 15, 288–297.

Cuban, L. (1993). *How teachers taught: Constancy and change in American classrooms, 1880–1990* (2nd ed.) New York: Teachers College.

Cummings, H. H. (1959). *Requirements and high-school students' programs*. U.S. Office of Education, Federal Security Agency, Circular No. 300, February 1949. Washington, DC: U.S. Government Printing Office.

Curriculum experiment in a Chicago high school. *Curriculum Journal*, 8, 287.

Curti, M. (1935). *The social ideas of American educators*. New York: Charles Scribner's Sons.

Curti, M. E. (1951). *The growth of American thought* (2nd ed.). New York: Harper.

Davis, O. L. Jr. (1981). Understanding the history of the social studies. In H. D. Mehlinger, & O. L. Davis, Jr. (Eds.) *The social studies*. 80th yearbook of the National Society for the Study of Education, Part II. Chicago: University of Chicago Press.

Dean, A. D. (1908). Education of workers in the shoe industry. In *Bulletin No. 8 of the National Society for the Promotion of Industrial Education* (pp. 7–110). New York: National Society for the Promotion of Industrial Education.

DeBoer, J. J. (1936). Integration—a return to first principles. *School and Society*, 43, 246–253.

Deems, J. F. (1908). Trade instruction in large establishments. In *Bulletin No. 5 of the National Society for the Promotion of Education* (pp. 51–55). New York: National Society for the Promotion of Industrial Education.

DeLima, A. (1925). *Our enemy the child*. New York: New Republic.

Demiashkevich, M. J. (1933). Some doubts about the activity movement. *Harvard Teachers Record*, 3, 170–178.

Demiashkevich, M. J. (1935). *An introduction to the philosophy of education*. New York: American Book.

Dewey, J. (1894). Review of Lester Frank Ward, *The psychic factors of civilization*. *Psychological Review*, 1, 400–401.

Dewey, J. (1895). Plan of organization of the university primary school. In J. A. Boydston (Ed.), *The early works of John Dewey, 1882–1898: Vol. 5 1895–1898: Early essays* (pp. 223–243). Carbondale: Southern Illinois University Press, 1972.

Dewey, J. (1896a). Interest in relation to training of the will. In *Herbart Yearbook for 1895*, 2nd supp. (pp. 209–246). Bloomington, IL: National Herbart Society. [Rev. ed., Chicago: National Herbart Society, 1899, pp. 5–38.]

Dewey, J. (1896b). Interpretation of the culture-epoch theory. *The Public School Journal*, 15, 233–236.

Dewey, J. (1896c). The university school. *University [of Chicago] Record*, 1, 417–419.

Dewey, J. (1897a). Criticisms wise and otherwise on modern child study. *Journal of Proceedings and Addresses of the Thirty-Sixth Annual Meeting of the National Education Association*, 867–868.

Dewey, J. (1897b). The interpretation side of child-study. *Transactions of the Illinois Society for Child-Study*, 2, 17–27.

Dewey, J. (1897c). The psychological aspect of the school curriculum. *Educational Review*, 13, 356–369.

Dewey, J. (1897d). The university elementary school: History and character. *University [of Chicago] Record*, 2, 72–75.

Dewey, J. (1898). The primary-education fetich. *The Forum*, 25, 315–328.

Dewey, J. (1899a). *Lectures in the philosophy of education, 1899*. R. D. Archambault (Ed.). 1966. New York: Random House.

Dewey, J. (1899b). *The school and society*. Chicago: University of Chicago Press.

Dewey, J. (1900). The aim of history in elementary education. *Elementary School Record*, 1, 199–203.

Dewey, J. (1901). The situation as regards the course of study. *Journal of Proceedings and Addresses of the Fortieth Annual Meeting of the National Education Association*, 332–348.

Dewey, J. (1902a). *The child and the curriculum*. Chicago: University of Chicago Press.

Dewey, J. (1902b). Interpretation of savage mind. *Psychological Review*, 9, 217–230.

Dewey, J. (1909). *Moral principles in education*. Boston: Houghton Mifflin.

Dewey, J. 1910a). Science as subject matter and method. *Science*. 28, 121–127.

Dewey, J. (1910b). *How we think*. Boston: D. C. Heath.

Dewey, J. (1914). A policy of industrial education. *New Republic*, 1, 11–12.

Dewey, J. (1915a). Education vs. trade-training—Dr. Dewey's reply. *New Republic*, 3, 42–43.

Dewey, J. (1915b). Industrial education—A wrong kind. *New Republic*, 2, 71–73.

Dewey, J. (1916a). *Democracy and education: An introduction to the philosophy of education*. New York: Macmillan.

Dewey, J. (1916b). Method in science teaching. *General Science Quarterly*, 1, 3–9.

Dewey, J. (1917). Learning to earn: The place of vocational education in a comprehensive scheme of public education. *School and Society*, 5, 331–335.

Dewey, J. (1928a). Progressive education and the science of education. *Progressive Education*, 5, 197–204.

Dewey, J. (1928b). Why I am for Smith. *New Republic*, 56, 320–321.

Dewey, J. (1931). *The way out of educational confusion*. Cambridge, MA: Harvard University Press.

Dewey, J. (1936). The theory of the Chicago experiment. In K. C. Mayhew & A. C. Edwards, *The Dewey School: The laboratory school of the University of Chicago, 1896–1903* (pp. 463–477). New York: D. Appleton-Century.

Dewey, J. (1938). *Experience and education*. New York: Macmillan.

Dewey, J. M. (Ed.). (1939). Biography of John Dewey. In P. A. Schilpp (Ed.), *The philosophy of John Dewey* (pp. 1–45). Evanston: Northwestern University Press.

Dilling, E. (1934). *The red network: A "who's who" and handbook of radicalism for patriots*. Kenilworth, IL: The author.

Discussion of [the] report of Dr. Harris. (1895). *The Journal of Education*, 41, 165–167.

Discussion [on work and play in youth]. (1901). *Journal of Proceedings and Addresses of the Fortieth Annual Meeting of the National Education Association*, 518–523.

Douglass, H. R. (1949). Education of all youth for life adjustment. *Annals of the American Academy of Political and Social Science*, 265, 108–114.

Drost, W. H. (1967). That immortal day in Cleveland—the report of the Committee of Fifteen. *Educational Theory*, 17, 178–191.

Du Bois, W. E. B. (1902). *The Negro artisan*. Atlanta, GA: Atlanta University Press.

Dunkel, H. B. (1970). *Herbart and the Herbartians: An educational ghost story*. Chicago: University of Chicago Press.

Dunn, A. W. (1907). *The community and the citizen*. Indianapolis: Echo Press.

Educational Policies Commission. (1943). *What the schools should teach in wartime*. Washington, DC: Educational Policies Commission, National Education Association and the American Association of School Administrators.

Educational Policies Commission. (1944). *Education for ALL American youth*. Washington, DC: Educational Policies Commission, National Education Association and the American Association of School Administrators.

Eliot, C. W. (1892a). Shortening and enriching the grammar school course. *Journal of Proceedings and Addresses of the National Education Association, Session of the Year 1892*, 617–625.

Eliot, C. W. (1892b). Wherein popular education has failed. *The Forum*, 14, 411–428.

Eliot, C. W. (1905). The fundamental assumptions in the report of the Committee of Ten (1893). *Educational Review,* 30, 325–343.

Eliot, C. W. (1908). Industrial education as an essential factor in our national prosperity. In *Bulletin No. 5 of the National Society for the Promotion of Industrial Education* (pp. 9–14). New York: National Society for the Promotion of Industrial Education.

Ellwood, C. A. (1914). Our compulsory education laws, and retardation and elimination in our public schools. *Education.* 34, 572–576.

Engelhart, M. D., & Thomas, M. (1966). Rice as the inventor of the comparative test. *Journal of Educational Measurement,* 3, 141–145.

Evans, H. R. (1908). A list of the writings of William Torrey Harris, chronologically arranged, with subject index. In Bureau of Education, *Report of the Commissioner of Education for the year ended June 30, 1907, Vol. 1.* Washington, DC: U.S. Government Printing Office.

Faunce, R. C., & Bossing, N. L. (1958). *Developing the core curriculum.* (2nd ed.) Englewood Cliffs, NJ: Prentice Hall.

Featherstone, W. B. (1950). *A functional curriculum for youth.* New York: American Book.

Filene, P. G. (1970). An obituary for the 'Progressive movement.' *American Quarterly,* 22, 20–34.

Finkelstein, B. (1989). *Governing the young: Teacher behavior in popular primary schools in nineteenth-century United States.* New York: Falmer.

Finney, R. S. (1928). *A sociological philosophy of education.* New York: Macmillan.

Fisher, B. M. (1967). *Industrial education: American ideals and institutions.* Madison: University of Wisconsin Press.

FitzGerald, F. (1979). *America revised. History textbooks in the twentieth century.* Boston: Little, Brown.

Forbes, B. C. (1939, August 15). Treacherous teachings. *Forbes,* p. 8.

Franklin, B. M. (1982). "The social efficiency movement reconsidered: Curriculum change in Minneapolis, 1917–1950." *Curriculum Inquiry,* 12, 9–33.

Fraser, J. W. (1988). "Who were the progressive educators anyway? A case study of the progressive education movement in Boston, 1905–1925." *Educational Foundations,* 2, 4–30.

Fuller, H. J. (1951). The emperor's new clothes, or *prius dementat. Scientific Monthly,* 72, 32–41.

Galloway, T. W., Caldwell, O. W., & Norris, H. W. A consideration of the principles that should determine the courses in biology in secondary schools. *School Science and Mathematics,* 9, 241–247.

Garrett, A. W., & Davis, O. L. Jr. (2003). A time of uncertainty and change: School mathematics from World War II until the new math. In G. M. A. Stanic & J. Kilpatrick (Eds.), *A history of school mathematics.* Vol. I. Reston, VA: National Council of Teachers of Mathematics.

Get adjusted. (1947, December 15). *Time*, p. 64.

Goebel, E. J. (1948). The total experience of the school child for life adjustment. *Bulletin of the National Catholic Educational Association*, 45, 376–381.

Gompers, S. (1910). President Gompers' report. *Report of Proceedings of the Thirteenth Annual Convention of the American Federation of Labor*, 14–53.

Gould, S. J. (1981). *The mismeasure of man*. New York: Norton.

Graham, P. A. (1967). *Progressive education, from Arcady to academe: A history of the Progressive Education Association, 1919–1955*. New York: Columbia University Teachers College.

Gray, W. S. (1925). *Summary of investigations relating to reading*. Chicago: University of Chicago Press.

Group IV. (1900). Unpublished material. Columbia University, Teachers College Collection, February 3, 1900.

Group V. (1900). Unpublished material. Columbia University, Teachers College Collection, 4/5–01.

Gusfield, J. R. (1986). *Symbolic crusade: Status politics and the American temperance movement* (2nd ed.). Urbana: University of Illinois Press.

Haber, S. (1964). *Efficiency and uplift: Scientific management in the progressive era 1890–1920*. Chicago: University of Chicago Press.

Hall, G. S. (1883). The contents of children's minds. *Princeton Review*, 2, 249–272.

Hall, G. S. (1888, June). The story of a sand-pile. *Scribner's Magazine*, 690–696.

Hall, G. S. (1892). Editorial. *The Pedagogical Seminary*, 2, 3–8.

Hall, G. S. (1895). Child study. *Journal of Proceedings and Addresses of the National Education Association, Session of the Year 1894*, 173–179.

Hall, G. S. (1901a). How far is the present high-school and early college training adapted to the nature and needs of adolescents? *School Review*, 9, 649–665.

Hall, G. S. (1901b). Ideal school as based on child study. *Journal of Proceedings and Addresses of the Fortieth Annual Meeting of the National Education Association*, 474–488.

Hall, G. S. (1902). The high school as the people's college. *Journal of Proceedings and Addresses of the Forty-First Annual Meeting of the National Education Association*, 260–268.

Hall, G. S. (1903). Coeducation in the high school. *Journal of Proceedings and Addresses of the Forty-Second Annual Meeting of the National Education Association*, 446–451.

Hall, G. S. (1904a). *Adolescence: Its psychology and its relations to physiology, anthropology, sociology, sex, crime, religion and education*, Vol. 1. New York: D. Appleton.

Hall, G. S. (1904b). *Adolescence: Its psychology and its relations to physiology, anthropology, sociology, sex, crime, religion and education*, Vol. 2. New York: D. Appleton.

Hall, G. S. (1904c). The natural activities of children as determining the industries in early education, II. *Journal of Proceedings and Addresses of the Forty-Third Annual Meeting of the National Education Association*, 443–447.

Hall, G. S. (1911). *Educational problems, Vol. 2.* New York: D. Appleton.

Hall, G. S. (1923). *Life and confessions of a psychologist.* New York: D. Appleton.

Hall, S. B. (1933). Cooperation in Virginia. *Educational Record*, 14, 338–345.

Hand, H. C., & French, W. (1937). Analysis of the present status in curriculum thinking. In H. Harap et al., *The changing curriculum* (pp. 1–31). New York: D. Appleton-Century.

Hand, H. C., & Sanford, C. W. (1953). A scholar's documents. *Bulletin of the National Association of Secondary-School Principals*, 37, 460–504.

Hanna, L. (1939). The plan of the core curriculum in Tulsa. *Curriculum Journal*, 10, 350–352.

Hanna, L. (1940). The operation of the core curriculum in Tulsa. *Curriculum Journal*, 11, 66–68.

Harris, W. T. (1880). Equivalents in a liberal course of study: Formal and substantial studies. *Journal of Proceedings and Addresses of the National Education Association, Session of the Year 1880*, 167–175.

Harris, W. T. (1886). Psychological inquiry. *Journal of Proceedings and Addresses of the National Education Association, Session of the Year 1885*, 91–101.

Harris, W. T. (1888). What shall the public schools teach? *The Forum*, 4, 573–581.

Harris, W. T. (1889). The intellectual value of tool-work. *Journal of Proceedings and Addresses of the National Education Association, Session of the Year 1889*, 92–98.

Harris, W. T. (1896a). How the will combines with the intellect in the higher orders of knowing. *Journal of Proceedings and Addresses of the Thirty-Fifth Annual Meeting of the National Education Association*, 440–446.

Harris, W. T. (1896b). Professor John Dewey's doctrine of interest as related to will. *Educational Review*, 11, 486–493.

Harris, W. T. (1898a). The pedagogical creed of William T. Harris, U.S. Commissioner of Education. In O. H. Lang (Ed.), *Educational creeds of the nineteenth century* (pp. 36–46). New York: E. L. Kellogg.

Harris, W. T. (1898b). *Psychologic foundations of education: An attempt to show the genesis of the higher faculties of the mind.* New York: D. Appleton.

Hartman, A. L. (1934). Comments by leaders in the field. In G. M. Whipple (Ed.), *The activity movement. The Thirty-Third Yearbook of the National Society for the Study of Education, Part II* (pp. 110–112). Bloomington, IL: Public School Publishing.

Harvard Committee on the Objectives of General Education in a Free Society. (1945). *General education in a free society: Report of the Harvard Committee.* Cambridge, MA: Harvard University Press.

Hatfield, W. W. (1935). *An experience curriculum in English: A report of the Curriculum Commission of the National Council of Teachers of English.* New York: D. Appleton-Century.

Hays, S. P. (1964). The politics of reform in municipal government in the progressive era. *Pacific Northwest Quarterly,* 55, 157–169.

Heald, F. E. (1917). "The project" in agricultural education. *General Science Quarterly,* 1, 166–169.

Heald, F. E. (1918). *The home project as a phase of vocational agricultural education.* Issued by the Federal Board for Vocational Education. Washington, DC: U.S. Government Printing Office.

Herbst, J. (1991). Cremin's American *Paideia. American Scholar,* 60, 128–140.

Hertzberg, H. W. (1981). *Social studies reform, 1880-1980.* Boulder, CO: Social Science Consortium.

High-school overhaul. (1947, December 15). *Newsweek,* p. 86.

Hockett, J. A. (1927). *A determination of the major social problems of American life.* New York: Teachers College, Columbia University.

Hofstadter, R. (1955). The pseudo-conservative revolt. In D. Bell (Ed.), *The new American right.* New York: Criterion Books.

Hoodless, A. (1910). The education of girls. In *Bulletin No. 10 of the National Society for the Promotion of Industrial Education* (pp. 179–184). New York: National Society for the Promotion of Industrial Education.

Hopkins, L. T. (1937). A correlated curriculum evaluated. *English Journal,* 26, 417–418.

Horn, E. (1918). Economy in learning in relation to economy of time. *Journal of Proceedings and Addresses of the Fifty-Sixth Annual Meeting of the National Education Association,* 526–528.

Hosic, J. F. (1921a). Editorially speaking. *Journal of Educational Method,* 1, 1–2.

Hosic, J. F. (1921b). Editorially speaking. *Journal of Educational Method,* 1, 1.

Hosic, J. F., & Chase, S. E. (1926). *Brief guide to the project method.* Yonkers-on-Hudson, NY: World Book.

Hotchkiss, E. A. (1924). *The project method in classroom work.* Boston: Ginn.

Houston, V. M., Sanford, C. W., & Trump, J. L. (1948). *Guide to the study of the curriculum in the secondary schools of Illinois.* Springfield: Illinois Secondary School Curriculum Program.

Hovet, K. (1956). What are the high schools teaching? In In A. A. Bellack (Ed.), *What shall the high schools teach?,* 1956 Yearbook of the Association for Supervision and Curriculum Development. Washington, DC: Association for Supervision and Curriculum Development.

Hulburd, D. (1951). *This happened in Pasadena.* New York: Macmillan.

Hunter, G. W. (1907). *Elements of biology.* New York: American Book.

Hutchins, R. M. (1936). *The higher learning in America*. New Haven: Yale University Press.

Individualizing instruction. (1925). *School Life*, 10, 177.

Industrial education. (1907). *Proceedings of the Twelfth Annual Convention of the National Association of Manufacturers*, 109–138.

Industrial education. (1912). *Proceedings of the Seventeenth Annual Convention of the National Association of Manufacturers*, 149–177.

Jackman, E. D. (1920). The Dalton plan. *School Review*, 28, 688–696.

James, W. (1890). *The principles of psychology*, Vol. 1. New York: Holt.

James, W. (1899). *Talks to teachers on psychology, and to students on some of life's ideals*. New York: Holt.

Johnson, M. (1926). The educational principles of the school of organic education, Fairhope, Alabama. In G. M. Whipple (Ed.), *The foundations and technique of curriculum-construction, Part I. Curriculum-making: Past and present. The Twenty-Sixth Yearbook of the National Society for the Study of Education* (pp. 349–351). Bloomington, IL: Public School Publishing.

Jones, G. (1949). Foreword. In G. S. Wright, *Core curriculum in public high schools: An inquiry into practice*. Washington, DC: U.S. Office of Education.

Jones, T. J. (1908). *Social studies in the Hampton curriculum*. Hampton, VA: Hampton Institute.

Kaestle, C. F. (1972). Social reform and the urban school. *History of Education Quarterly*, 12, 211–228.

Kaestle, C. F. (Ed.). (1973). *Joseph Lancaster and the monitorial school movement: A documentary history*. New York: Teachers College Press.

Kaestle, C. F. (1984). Class schools. *Chicago History*, 13, 71–72.

Kandel, I. L. (1947). Adjustment to life. *School and Society*, 65, 372.

Katz, M. B. (1968). *The irony of early school reform: Educational innovation in mid-nineteenth century Massachusetts*. Boston: Beacon Press.

Katz, M. B. (1975). *Class, bureaucracy and schools: The illusion of educational change in America*. New York: Praeger.

Kean, C. J. (1983). *The origins of vocational education in the Milwaukee public schools, 1870–1917: A case study in curricular change*. Unpublished Ph. D. dissertation, University of Wisconsin-Madison.

Kelsey, F. W. (1911). *Latin and Greek in American education*. New York: Macmillan.

Keppel, A. M. (1960). *Country schools for country children: Backgrounds of the reform movement in rural elementary education, 1890–1914*. Unpublished Ph.D. dissertation, University of Wisconsin-Madison.

Kilpatrick, W. H. (1917). Project teaching. *General Science Quarterly*, 1, 67–72.

Kilpatrick, W. H. (1918a). The problem-project attack in organization, subject-matter, and teaching. *Journal of Proceedings and Addresses of the Fifty-Sixth Annual Meeting of the National Education Association*, 528–531.

Kilpatrick, W. H. (1918b). The project method. *Teachers College Record*, 19, 319–335.

Kilpatrick, W. H. (1922). Subject matter and the educative process—I. *Journal of Educational Method*, 2, 95–101.

Kilpatrick, W. H. (1923). Subject matter and the educative process—II, III. *Journal of Educational Method*, 2, 230–237, 367–376.

Kilpatrick, W. H. (1924). How shall we select the subject matter of the elementary school curriculum. *Journal of Educational Method*, 4, 3–10.

Kilpatrick, W. H. (1925). *Foundations of method: Informal talks on teaching*. New York: Macmillan.

Kilpatrick, W. H. (1926). Statement of position. In G. M. Whipple (Ed.), *The foundations and technique of curriculum-construction, Part II. The foundations of curriculum-making. The Twenty-Sixth Yearbook of the National Society for the Study of Education* (pp. 119–146). Bloomington, IL: Public School Publishing.

Kilpatrick, W. H. (1928). Curriculum-making in an elementary school [Book review]. *Progressive Education*, 5, 86–88.

Kliebard, H.M. (1999). *Schooled to work: Vocationalism and the American curriculum, 1876–1946*. New York: Teachers College Press.

Kliebard, H. M., & Franklin, B. M. (2003). The ascendance of practical and vocational mathematics, 1893–1945: Academic mathematics under siege. In G. M. A. Stanic & J. Kilpatrick (Eds.), *A history of school mathematics*, Vol. I. Reston, VA: National Council of Teachers of Mathematics.

Krug, E. A. (1962). Graduates of secondary schools in and around 1900: Did most of them go to college? *School Review*, 70, 266–272.

Krug, E. A. (1964). *The shaping of the American high school, 1880–1920*. New York: Harper and Row.

Krug, E. A. (1972). *The shaping of the American high school, 1920–1941*, Vol II. Madison: University of Wisconsin Press.

Lancelot, W. H. (1943). A close-up of the eight-year study. *School and Society*, 58, 449–451.

Latimer, J. F. (1958). *What's happened to our high schools?*. Washington, DC: Public Affairs Press.

Lauchner, A. H. (1951). How can the junior high school curriculum be improved? *Bulletin of the National Association of Secondary-School Principals*, 35, 296–304.

Lawler, N. (1937). Experimenting with a core curriculum. *Curriculum Journal*, 8, 310–312.

Lazerson, M. (1971). *Origins of the urban school. Public education in Massachusetts, 1870–1915*. Cambridge, MA: Harvard University Press.

Leonard, J. P. (1937). Is the Virginia curriculum working? *Harvard Educational Review*, 7, 66–71.

Levine, D. (1964). *Varieties of reform thought*. Madison: State Historical Society of Wisconsin.

Lewis, M. H. (1928). *An adventure with children*. New York: Macmillan.

Life adjustment curriculum. (1949). Billings, MT: Billings Senior High School.

Life adjustment education for youth—"Statesmanship of a very high order . . . in operation." (1949). *School Life*, 32, 40–42.

Linville, H. R. (1909). Biology as method and as a science in secondary schools. *Schools Science and Mathematics*, 7, 264–272.

Lloyd, F., & Bigelow, M. A. (1907). *The teaching of biology in secondary schools*. New York: Longmans, Green.

Lybarger, M. B. (1981). *Origins of the social studies curriculum: 1865–1916*. Unpublished Ph.D. dissertation, University of Wisconsin-Madison.

Lynd, R. S., & Lynd, H. M. (1929). *Middletown: A study in contemporary American culture*. New York: Harcourt, Brace.

Maguder, F. A. (1917). *American government*. Boston: Allyn and Bacon.

Maritain, J. (1943). *Education at the crossroads*. New Haven: Yale University Press.

Marshall, F. M. (1907). Industrial training for women: A preliminary study. *Bulletin No. 4 of the National Society for the Promotion of Industrial Education* (pp. 5–59). New York: National Society for the Promotion of Industrial Education.

Martin, J. (2002). *The education of John Dewey: A biography*. New York: Columbia University.

Mary Joseph, SC. (1952). The Catholic schools and life adjustment education. *Bulletin of the National Catholic Educational Association*, 49, 341–345.

Massachusetts Commission on Industrial and Technical Education. (1906). *Report of the Commission on Industrial and Technical Education*. Boston: Wright & Potter Printing.

Mathews, C. O. (1926). *The grade placement of curriculum materials in the social studies*. New York: Columbia University, Teachers College.

Mayhew, K. C., & Edwards, A. C. (1936). *The Dewey School: The laboratory school of the University of Chicago, 1896–1903*. New York: D. Appleton Century.

McCaul, R. L. (1959). Dewey's Chicago. *School Review*, 67, 258–280.

McLellan, J. A., & Dewey, J. (1889). *Applied psychology: An introduction to the principles and practice of education*. Boston: Educational Publishing.

McMurry, C. A. (1893). *The elements of general method based on the principles of Herbart*. Bloomington, IL: Public School Publishing.

Meltzer, H. (1925). *Children's social concepts: A study of their nature and development*. New York: Columbia University, Teachers College.

Meriam, J. L. (1920). *Child life and the curriculum.* Yonkers-on-Hudson, NY: World Book.

Mirel, J. E. (1990). Progressive school reform in comparative perspective. In D. N. Plank and R. Ginsberg (Eds.), *Southern cities, southern schools: Public education in the urban south.* New York: Greenwood Press.

Mirel, J. E., and Angus, D. (1986). "The rising tide of custodialism: Enrollment increases and curriculum reform in Detroit, 1928–1940." *Issues in Education,* 4, 101–120.

Mirel, J. (1993). *The rise and fall of an urban school system: Detroit, 1907–81.* Ann Arbor: University of Michigan Press.

The model school. (1896, January 16). *University of Chicago Weekly,* p. 707.

Moore, J. C. (1916). Projects. *General Science Quarterly,* 1, 14–16.

Moseley, N. (1936). Content and conduct of teachers' conventions. *Progressive Education,* 13, 337–339.

Mott, F. L. (1941). *American journalism: A history of newspapers in the United States through 250 years, 1690–1940.* New York: Macmillan.

Munsterberg, H. (1899). *Psychology and life.* Boston: Houghton, Mifflin.

Murphy, G. (1943). Classrooms—seedbeds for democracy. In H. D. Roberts, W. V. Kaulfers, & G. N. Kefauver (Eds.), *English for social living.* New York: McGraw-Hall.

Muzzey, D. S. (1911). *An American history.* Boston: Ginn.

National Council of Teachers of English. (1935). *An experience curriculum in English.* New York: D. Appleton-Century.

National Council of Teachers of English, Commission on the English Curriculum. (1952). *The English language arts.* New York: D. Appleton-Century-Crofts.

National Council of Teachers of English, Commission of the English Curriculum (1956). *The English language arts in secondary school.* New York: D. Appleton-Century Crofts.

National Defense Education Act. (1958). Public Law 85-864, 85th Congress, September 2, 1958.

National Education Association. (1893). *Report of the Committee on Secondary School Studies.* Washington, DC: U.S. Government Printing Office.

National Education Association. (1895). *Report of the Committee of Fifteen on Elementary Education, with the reports of the sub-committees: on the training of teachers; on the correlation of studies in elementary education; on the organization of city school systems.* New York: American Book.

National Education Association. (1913). *Preliminary statements by chairmen of committees of the Commission of the National Education Association on the Reorganization of Secondary Education.* Washington, DC: U.S. Government Printing Office.

National Education Association. (1915). *The teaching of community civics, prepared by a special committee of the Commission on the Reorganization of Secondary Education.* Washington, DC: U.S. Government Printing Office.

National Education Association. (1916). *Social studies in secondary education: A six-year program adapted to the 6-3-3 and the 8-4 plans of organization. Report of the Committee on Social Studies of the Commission on the Reorganization of Secondary Education.* Washington, DC: U.S. Government Printing Office.

National Education Association. (1918). *Cardinal principles of secondary education: A report of the Commission on the Reorganization of Secondary Education.* Washington, DC: U.S. Government Printing Office.

National Education Association. (1936). *The development of a modern program in English. Ninth Yearbook of the Department of Supervisors and Directors of Instruction.* Washington, DC: National Education Association.

National Education Association. (1943). *Wartime handbook for education.* Washington, DC: National Education Association.

Newlon, J. H., & Threlkeld, A. L. (1926). The Denver curriculum-revision program. In G. M. Whipple (Ed.), *The foundations and technique of curriculum-construction, Part I. Curriculum-making: Past and present. The Twenty-Sixth Yearbook of the National Society for the Study of Education* (pp. 229–240). Bloomington, IL: Public School Publishing.

Nickell, V. L. (1949). How can we develop an effective program of education for life adjustment? *Bulletin of the National Association of Secondary-School Principals, 33,* 153–156.

Oberholtzer, E. E. (1934). Comments by leaders in the field. In G. M. Whipple (Ed.), *The activity movement. The Thirty-Third Yearbook of the National Society for the Study of Education, Part II* (pp. 136–142). Bloomington, IL: Public School Publishing.

Offerings and registrations in high-school subjects, 1933–34. (1938). Bulletin No. 6, U.S. Department of Interior. Washington, DC: U.S. Government Printing Office.

Original papers in relation to a course of liberal education. (1829). *American Journal of Science and Arts, 15,* 297–351.

O'Shea, M. V. (1927). *A state education system at work. Report of an investigation of the intellectual status and educational progress of pupils in the elementary and high schools and freshmen in the colleges, public and private, of Mississippi, together with recommendations relating to the modifications of educational procedure in the state.* Washington, DC: Bernard B. Jones Fund.

Page, C. S. (1912). Federal aid for vocational education from the standpoint of a United States Senator. In *Bulletin No. 16 of the National Society for the Promotion of Industrial Education* (pp. 116–121). Peoria, IL: Manual Arts Press.

Pauly, P. J. (1991). The development of high school biology, New York City, 1900–1925. *Isis, 82,* 662–688.

Peabody, F. G. (1918). *Education for life: The story of Hampton Institute, told in connection with the fiftieth anniversary of the foundation of the school.* Garden City, NY: Doubleday, Page.

Pritchett, H. S. (1906). Report of the president. *First annual report of the president and treasurer.* New York: Carnegie Foundation of the Advancement of Teaching.

Progressive Education Association. (1940). *Mathematics in general education.* New York: D. Appleton-Century.

Progressive Education Association, Commission on the Relation of School and College. (1942–1943). *Adventure in American education* (Vols. 1–5). New York: Harper & Brothers.

Ravitch, D. (2003). *The language police: How pressure groups restrict what students learn.* New York: Knopf.

Redefer, F. L. (1949). Resolutions, reactions and reminiscences. *Progressive Education, 26,* 187–191.

Reese, W. J. (1982). *Power and the promise of school reform: Grass roots movements during the progressive era.* Boston: Routledge and Kegan Paul.

Reese, W. J. (1995). *The origins of the American high school.* New Haven: Yale University Press.

Reese, W. J. (in press). *America's public schools: Continuity and change since the early nineteenth century.* Baltimore: Johns Hopkins University Press.

Report on industrial education. (1905). *Proceedings of the Tenth Annual Convention of the National Association of Manufacturers,* 141–151.

Resolutions regarding technical education. (1897). *Proceedings of the Second Annual Convention of the National Association of Manufacturers,* 92–93.

Rice, J. M. (1893a). *The public-school system of the United States.* New York: Century.

Rice, J. M. (1893b). The public schools of Chicago and St. Paul. *The Forum,* 15, 200–215.

Rice, J. M. (1912). *Scientific management in education.* New York: Hinds, Noble & Elredge.

Rice, T. D. (1938). A high school core program. *Curriculum Journal,* 9, 201–203.

Rickover, H. G. (1959). *Education and freedom.* New York: E. P. Dutton.

Ringel, P. J. (1980). *The introduction and development of manual training and industrial education in the public schools of Fitchburg, Massachusetts, 1893–1928.* Unpublished Ph.D. dissertation. Teachers College, Columbia University, New York.

Robins, R. (1910). Industrial education for women. In *Bulletin No. 10 of the National Society for the Promotion of Industrial Education* (pp. 77–81). New York: National Society for the Promotion of Industrial Education.

Robinson, J. H. (1921). *Mind in the making: The relation of intelligence to social reform.* New York: Harper.

Rodgers, D. T. (1982). "In search of progressivism," *Reviews in American History,* December, 113–132.

Roody, S. I. (1947). Developing personality through literature. *English Journal*, 36, 299–304.

Roosevelt, T. (1907). [Letter to Henry S. Pritchett.] In *Bulletin No. 3 of the National Society for the Promotion of Industrial Education* (pp. 6–9). New York: National Society for the Promotion of Industrial Education.

Ross, D. (1972). *G. Stanley Hall: The psychologist as prophet.* Chicago: University of Chicago Press.

Ross, E. A. (1901). *Social control: A survey of the foundations of order.* New York: Macmillan.

Rudolph, J. L. (2002). *Scientists in the classroom. The cold war reconstruction of American science education.* New York: Palgrave.

Rudolph, J. L. (In press). Epistemology for the masses: John Dewey and the scientific method in American Schools.

Rudolph, J. L. (In press). The importance of place: Chicago and the origin of general science, 1904–1920.

Rugg, H. O. (1916). *The experimental determination of mental discipline in school studies.* Baltimore: Warwick & York.

Rugg, H. O. (1921a). How shall we reconstruct the social studies curriculum? An open letter to Professor Henry Johnson commenting on committee procedure as illustrated by the report of the joint committee on history and education for citizenship. *Historical Outlook*, 12, 184–189.

Rugg, H. O. (1921b). Needed changes in the committee procedure of reconstructing the social studies. *Elementary School Journal*, 21, 688–702.

Rugg, H. O. (1925). *A primer of graphics and statistics for teachers.* Boston: Houghton Mifflin.

Rugg, H. O. (1929–1932). *Man and his changing society. The Rugg social science series of the elementary school course* (Vols. 1–6). Boston: Ginn.

Rugg, H. O. (1931). *An introduction to problems of American culture.* Boston: Ginn.

Rugg, H. O. (1932). Social reconstruction through education. *Progressive Education*, 9, 11–18.

Rugg, H. O. (1938). *Our country and our people: An introduction to American civilization.* Boston: Ginn.

Rugg, H. O. (1941). *That men may understand: An American in the long armistice.* New York: Doubleday, Doran.

Rugg, H. O. (1947). *Foundations for American education.* Yonkers-on-Hudson, NY: World Book.

Rugg, H. O., & Shumaker, A. (1928). *The child-centered school: An appraisal of the new education.* Yonkers-on-Hudson, NY: World Book.

Ryan, H. H. (1933). The teaching and learning situation in junior high-school classrooms. *Bulletin of the Department of Secondary-School Principals*, 17(45), 139–147.

Ryan, H. H. (1935). Experimental college entrance units: A committee report. I. Introductory statement. *North Central Association Quarterly*, 9, 345–350.

Ryan, H. H. (1937). Some principles behind the core-curriculum. *California Journal of Secondary Education*, 12, 14–16.

Sanford, C. W., Hand, H. C., & Spalding, W. B. (Eds.), (1951). *The schools and national security: Recommendations for elementary and secondary schools.* Springfield, IL: Department of Public Instruction.

Saunders, F. H., & Hall, G. S. (1900). Pity. *American Journal of Psychology*, 11, 534–591.

Schneider, H. G. (1893). Dr. Rice and American public schools. *Education*, 13, 354–357.

Scrapbook IX. (1900). Unpublished material. Columbia University, Teachers College Collection, September 1899–June 1900.

Search, T. C. (1898). [President's annual report.] *Proceedings of the Third Annual Convention of the National Association of Manufacturers*, 3–32.

Sears, J. B. (1925). *The school survey: A textbook on the use of school surveying in the administration of public schools.* Boston: Houghton Mifflin.

Shaffer, L. F. (1930). *Children's interpretations of cartoons: A study of the nature and development of the ability to interpret symbolic drawings.* New York: Teachers College, Columbia University.

Shaw, A. (1900, June). 'Learning by doing' at Hampton. *American Monthly Review of Reviews*, 417–432.

Sivertson, S. C. (1972). *Community civics: Education for social efficiency.* Unpublished Ph.D. dissertation, University of Wisconsin-Madison.

Sizer, T. R. (Ed.). (1964). *The age of the academies.* New York: Teachers College, Columbia University, Bureau of Publications.

Small, A. W. (1896). Demands of sociology upon pedagogy. *Journal of Proceedings and Addresses of the Thirty-Fifth Annual Meeting of the National Education Association*, 174–184.

Smith, B. O. (1942). The war and the educational program. *Curriculum Journal*, 13, 113–116.

Smith, M. B. (1949). *And madly teach: A layman looks at public school education.* Chicago: Henry Regnery.

Smith, E. R., & Tyler, R. W. (1942). *Appraising and recording student progress.* New York: Harper & Brothers.

Smith, K. (1999). *Mental hygiene: Classroom films, 1945–1970.* New York: Blast Books.

Snedden, D. (1912). Report of Committee on National Legislation. In *Bulletin No. 15 of the National Society for the Promotion of Industrial Education* (pp. 126–134). New York: National Society for the Promotion of Industrial Education.

Snedden, D. (1915). Vocational education. *New Republic*, 3, 40–42.

Snedden, D. (1916). The "project" as a teaching unit. *School and Society*, 4, 419–423.

Snedden, D. (1917). History and other social sciences in the education of youths twelve to eighteen years of age. *School and Society*, 5, 271–181.

Snedden, D. (1919). Cardinal principles of secondary education. *School and Society*, 9, 517–527.

Snedden, D. (1921). *Sociological determination of objectives in education.* Philadelphia: J. B. Lippincott.

Snedden, D. (1923). "Case group" methods of determining flexibility of general curricula in high schools. *School and Society*, 17, 287–292.

Snedden, D. (1924). Junior high school offerings. *School and Society*, 20, 740–744.

Snedden, D. (1925). Planning curriculum research. *School and Society*, 22, 259–265, 287–293, 319–328.

Snedden, D. (1932). The social studies—for what? *School and Society*, 36, 358–362.

Snedden, D. (1935, April 3–6). Social reconstruction: A challenge to the secondary school. *Pennsylvania Schoolmen's Week*, 48–54.

Spring, E. (1936, March 25–28). An adventure in Latin teaching. *Pennsylvania Schoolmen's Week*, 503–507.

Spring, J. (1970). Education and progressivism. *History of Education Quarterly*, 10, 53–71.

Spring, J. (1972). *Education and the rise of the corporate state.* Boston: Beacon.

Stevenson, J. A. (1921). *The project method of teaching.* New York: Macmillan.

Stimson, R. W. (1914). *The Massachusetts home-project plan of vocational agricultural education.* Washington, DC: U.S. Government Printing Office.

Stockton, J. L. (1920). *Project work in education.* Boston: Houghton Mifflin.

Taylor, F. W. (1895). A piece-rate system, being a step toward partial solution of the labor problem. *Transactions of the American Society of Mechanical Engineers*, 16, 856–903.

Taylor, F. W. (1903). Shop management. *Transactions of the American Society of Mechanical Engineers*, 24, 1337–1480.

Taylor, F. W. (1911). *The principles of scientific management.* New York: Harper & Brothers.

Taylor, F. W. Testimony before the Special House Committee. (1912). In F. W. Taylor, *Scientific management.* New York: Harper & Row, 1947.

Thirty schools tell their story. (1943). New York: Harper & Brothers.

Thorndike, E. L. (1901). *Notes on child study.* New York: Macmillan.

Thorndike, E. L. (1906, October). The opportunity of the high schools. *The Bookman*, 180–184.

Thorndike, E. L. (1913). *Educational psychology, Vol. 2. The psychology of learning.* New York: Columbia University, Teachers College.

Thorndike, E. L. (1921). *The teacher's word book.* New York: Teachers College, Columbia University.

Thorndike, E. L. (1924). Mental discipline in high school studies. *Journal of Educational Psychology,* 15, 1–22, 83–98.

Thorndike, E. L., & Woodworth, R. S. (1901). The influence of improvement in one mental function upon the efficiency of other functions. *Psychological Review,* 8, 247–261, 384–395, 553–564.

Todd, H. M. (1913, April). Why the children work: The children's answer. *McClure's Magazine,* 68–79.

Tonne, H. A. (1941). Is essentialism synonymous with traditionalism? *School and Society,* 53, 311–312.

Townsend, A. M., OP. (1948). Implications contained in the life adjustment program concerning the tools of learning. *Bulletin of the National Catholic Educational Association,* 45 (1), 363–375.

Troen, S. K. (1976). The discovery of the adolescent by American educational reformers, 1900–1920: An economic perspective. In L. Stone (Ed.), *Schooling and society: Studies in the history of education* (pp. 239–251). Baltimore: Johns Hopkins University Press.

Tryon, R. M. (1935). *The social sciences as school subjects.* New York: Charles Scribner's Sons.

Turbayne, C. M. (1962). *The myth of metaphor.* New Haven: Yale University Press.

Tyack, D. B. (1974). *The one best system: A history of American urban education.* Cambridge, MA: Harvard University Press.

Tyack, D., & Hansot, E. (1982). *Managers of virtue: Public school leadership in America, 1820–1980.* New York: Basic Books.

Tyack, D., & Cuban, L. (1995). *Tinkering toward utopia: A century of public school reform.* Cambridge, MA: Harvard University Press.

Tyler, R. W. (1930). Evaluating the importance of teachers' activities. *Educational Administration and Supervision,* 16, 287–292.

Tyler, R. W. (1931). More valid measurements of college work. *Journal of the National Education Association,* 20, 327–328.

Tyler, R. W. (1950). *Basic principles of curriculum and instruction.* Chicago: University of Chicago Press.

U.S. Office of Education. (1945). *Vocational education in the years ahead: A report of a committee to study postwar problems in vocational education.* Washington, DC: U.S. Government Printing Office.

U.S. Office of Education. (1948). *Life adjustment education for every youth.* Washington, DC: U.S. Government Printing Office.

U.S. Office of Education. (1951). *Vitalizing secondary education: Education for life adjustment*. Washington, DC: U.S. Government Printing Office.

University Primary School. (1896). Unpublished material. Columbia University, Teachers College Collection, March 6, 1896.

Van Liew, C. C. (1895). The educational theory of the culture epochs viewed historically and critically. In *First Year Book of the National Herbart Society for the Scientific Study of Teaching* (pp. 70–121). Bloomington, IL: National Herbart Society.

Virginia State Board of Education. (1934). *Tentative course of study for Virginia elementary schools, Grades I–VII*. Richmond, VA: Division of Purchase and Printing.

Ward, L. F. (1883). *Dynamic sociology, or applied social science as based upon statical sociology and the less complex sciences*, Vol. 2. New York: D. Appleton.

Ward, L. F. (1893). *The psychic factors of civilization*. Boston: Ginn.

Washburne, C. W. (1924). Merits of the individual plan of instruction. *School Life, 9*, 179.

Washburne, C. W. (1926). The philosophy of the Winnetka curriculum. In G. M. Whipple (Ed.), *The foundations and technique of curriculum construction, Part I, Curriculum-making: Past and present. The Twenty-Sixth Yearbook of the National Society for the Study of Education* (pp. 219–228). Bloomington, IL: Public School Publishing.

Washburne, C. W. (1928). The limitations of the project method. In National Education Association, *Official Report of the Department of Superintendence, February 26 to March 1, 1928* (pp. 187–188). Washington, DC: Department of Superintendence.

Washington, B. T. (Ed.). (1905). *Tuskegee and its people: Their ideals and achievements*. New York: D. Appleton.

Weinstein, J. (1968). *The corporate ideal and the liberal state, 1900–1918*. Boston: Beacon Press.

Wells, M. E. (1921). *A project curriculum, dealing with the project as a means of organizing the curriculum of the elementary school*. Philadelphia: J. B. Lippincott.

Wesley, E. B. (1957). *NEA, the first hundred years: The building of the teaching profession*. New York: Harper.

Whipple, G. M. (Ed.). (1926a). *The foundations and technique of curriculum-construction, Part I. Curriculum-making: Past and present. The Twenty-Sixth Yearbook of the National Society for the Study of Education*. Bloomington, IL: Public School Publishing.

Whipple, G. M. (Ed.). (1926b). *The foundations and technique of curriculum-construction, Part II. The foundations of curriculum-making. The Twenty-Sixth Yearbook of the National Society for the Study of Education*, Bloomington, IL: Public School Publishing.

Whipple, G. M. (Ed.). (1934). *The activity movement. The Thirty-Third Yearbook of the National Society for the Study of Education, Part II.* Bloomington, IL: Public School Publishing.

Wiebe, R. H. (1967). *The search for order, 1877–1920.* New York: Hill & Wang.

Williams, B. A. (1998). *Thought and action: John Dewey at the University of Michigan.* Ann Arbor: Bentley Historical Library, University of Michigan.

Winters, E. A. (1968). *Harold Rugg and education for social reconstruction.* Unpublished Ph.D. dissertation, University of Wisconsin, Madison.

Wolff, C. F. (1740). *Psychologia rationalis: methodo scientifica pertractata . . . cognitionem profutura proponuntur.* Frankfurt: Lipsiae.

Woodward, C. M. (1885). Manual training in general education. *Education, 5,* 614–626.

Woodward, C. M. (1887). *The manual training school, comprising a full statement of its aims, methods, and results, with figured drawings of shop exercises in woods and metals.* Boston: D. C. Heath.

Woodward, C. M. (1890). *Manual training in education.* New York: Scribner & Welford.

Wright, G. S. (1949). *Core curriculum in public high schools: An inquiry into practices, 1949.* Washington, DC: U.S. Office of Education.

Wright, G. S. (1952). *Core curriculum development: Problems and practices.* Bulletin 1952, No. 5. Washington, DC: U.S. Office of Education.

Wrigley, J. (1982). *Class politics and the public schools: Chicago, 1900–1950.* New Brunswick, NJ: Rutgers University Press.

Zilversmit, A. (1993). *Changing schools: Progressive education theory and practice, 1930–1960.* Chicago: University of Chicago Press.

Zimmerman, J. (2002). *Whose America? Culture wars in the public schools.* Cambridge, MA: Harvard University Press.

INDEX